W9-CMN-983

Once Upon a Time in the Italian West

For Clara

ONCE UPON A TIME IN THE ITALIAN WEST

The Filmgoers' Guide to Spaghetti Westerns

HOWARD HUGHES

I.B. TAURIS

LONDON · NEW YORK

Published in 2004 by I.B.Tauris & Co Ltd
6 Salem Road, London W2 4BU
175 Fifth Avenue, New York NY 10010
www.ibtauris.com

In the United States and Canada distributed by Palgrave Macmillan,
a division of St. Martin's Press, 175 Fifth Avenue, New York NY 10010

ISBN 1 85043 430 1
EAN 978 1 85043 430 6

A full CIP record for this book is available from the British Library
A full CIP record for this book is available from the Library of Congress
Library of Congress catalog card: available

Typeset in Ehrhardt by Dexter Haven Associates Ltd, London
Printed and bound in Great Britain by TJ International Ltd, Padstow, Cornwall

CONTENTS

Preface   vii

Acknowledgements   ix

Sundowner: An Introduction to European Westerns   xi

Spaghetti Western Top Tens   xxi

1   'Life Can Be so Precious'
— Sergio Leone's *A Fistful of Dollars* (1964)   1

2   'It's a Matter of Principle'
— Duccio Tessari's *A Pistol for Ringo* (1965)   17

3   'A Man Who Hopes, Fears'
— Duccio Tessari's *The Return of Ringo* (1965)   29

4   'Were You Ever Young?'
— Sergio Leone's *For a Few Dollars More* (1965)   40

5   'I Was Away, Too Far Away'
— Sergio Corbucci's *Django* (1966)   57

6   'It's the Reason Why I Live, Why I Breathe'
— Carlo Lizzani's *The Hills Run Red* (1966)   70

7   'Time Was When We'd Pay a Dollar For His Scalp'
— Sergio Corbucci's *Navajo Joe* (1966)   81

8   'In This Life, One Can Die Too'
— Damiano Damiani's *A Bullet for the General* (1966)   94

9   'There Are Two Kinds of People in the World'
— Sergio Leone's *The Good, the Bad and the Ugly* (1966)   106

10   'We Got Problems…Even Up in Heaven'
— Giulio Questi's *Django Kill* (1967)   124

11   'I Don't Even Respect the Living'
— Sergio Corbucci's *The Hellbenders* (1967)   136

12   'The Dogs of Juarez'
— Sergio Sollima's *The Big Gundown* (1967)   146

13   'I See You're a Man of Your Word'
— Giulio Petroni's *Death Rides a Horse* (1967)   158

14   'All Men Must Die in Time'
— Sergio Sollima's *Face to Face* (1967)   170

15   'I'll Kill You Any Way You Want'
— Tonino Valerii's *Day of Anger* (1967)   182

16   'Since When Are Wolves Afraid of Wolves?'
— Sergio Corbucci's *The Big Silence* (1967)   193

17   'You Play By the Rules, You Lose'
— Sergio Corbucci's *A Professional Gun* (1968)   205

18   'A Wise Man Keeps His Distance'
— Gianfranco Parolini's *Sabata* (1969)   217

19   'He Keeps Alive With His Colt .45'
— Enzo Barboni's *They Call Me Trinity* (1970)   229

20   'The Secret of a Long Life is to Try Not to Shorten it'
— Tonino Valerii's *My Name is Nobody* (1973)   240

Bibliography   255

Index   257

PREFACE

When I was a kid, I used to make believe I was Jack Beauregard.[1] Perhaps it was my inherent immunity to bad dubbing, from a childhood spent watching poorly synchronised European adventures like *Michel Strogoff* and *The Flashing Blade* during the school holidays. Or maybe it was watching late-night TV showings of *For a Few Dollars More* and *Sabata*, or even listening to my parents' crackly 45rpm single of Hugo Montenegro's *The Good, the Bad and the Ugly*. Whatever the reason, I've been interested in westerns, and especially Italian 'spaghetti' westerns, for nearly as long as I can remember.

The term 'spaghetti western' was a derisive label applied by American critics to describe westerns made in Italy and Spain between 1963 and 1977. The most famous spaghetti westerns (of the 500-plus made) are Sergio Leone's amoral, trend-setting 'Dollars Trilogy' – *A Fistful of Dollars* (1964), *For a Few Dollars More* (1965) and *The Good, the Bad and the Ugly* (1966) – which made an icon of Clint Eastwood's poncho-clad gunfighter, 'the man with no name', and brought international recognition to composer Ennio Morricone. The spaghetti western is a cinema of contradictions, with abstract cartoon title sequences and black humour contrasting with striking religious imagery, blood-drenched violence and echoing, ethereal music.

The 20 spaghetti westerns I have selected to be the focus of this book were made between 1964 and 1973, and encompass the genre's many differing forms. *A Fistful of Dollars* is the first internationally successful spaghetti western; *The Good, the Bad and the Ugly* is the most successful of all time. Enzo Barboni's *They Call Me Trinity*, Sergio Corbucci's *A Professional Gun* and Leone's *For a Few Dollars More* were hugely popular worldwide. Also discussed are important films by three key directors: Sergio Corbucci (*Django*, *Navajo Joe*, *The Hellbenders* and *The Big Silence*); Sergio Sollima (*The Big Gundown* and *Face to Face*) and Duccio Tessari (*A Pistol for Ringo* and *The Return of Ringo*). More offbeat contributions include Gianfranco Parolini's acrobatic western *Sabata*; Damiano Damiani's political spaghetti *A Bullet for the General*; Carlo Lizzani's Hollywood-inspired *The Hills Run Red*; Giulio Questi's controversial *Django Kill*; two tales of Italian-style revenge (Giulio Petroni's *Death Rides a Horse* and Tonino Valerii's *Day of Anger*); and Valerii's *My Name is Nobody*, a reverential epilogue to the genre. All of these films are worthy contenders for any spaghetti western 'Top Ten'. They are also representative of the scenarios and themes the genre explored, from revenge, companionship and progress, to justice, greed and betrayal.

---

1 Jack Beauregard is the renowned western gunfighter in Tonino Valerii's *My Name is Nobody* (1973), a spaghetti western examining the relationship between cinema heroes and fandom.

Each film is analysed in detail, with biographies and filmographies of the key personnel, accounts of the films' making (including details of sets and locations), their reception at the box office and influence on the genre. There are notes on the historical frontier period, with comparisons between how the Italians depicted the west and how it really was. There are also extensive notes on the musical scores (often composed by the prolific Ennio Morricone), full cast lists and a selection of stills, poster artwork, lobby cards and LP covers, many of which have never before been published.

In examining the films' cinematic sources, I've incorporated many of the finest, and most influential, Hollywood westerns – *High Noon*, *Shane*, *The Man from Laramie*, *The Last Wagon*, *The Searchers*, *Forty Guns*, *Day of the Outlaw*, *Rio Bravo*, *The Magnificent Seven* and *The Wild Bunch*. But spaghetti westerns had a myriad of non-western influences, and many other popular genre films are included here: Japanese samurai movies (*Yojimbo*), European Horrors (*Black Sunday*, *The Awful Dr Orloff*, *Mill of the Stone Women* and *Black Sabbath*) and muscleman epics (*Hercules in the Haunted World* and *Goliath and the Vampires*); even Italian spy capers, swash-bucklers, pirate adventures and German 'cowboy and Indian' movies.

There are also notes on many other European westerns, made by Britain, France, Germany, Spain and, of course, Italy. These include early films like *The Savage Guns*, *Zorro the Avenger*, *Winnetou the Warrior* and *Buffalo Bill, Hero of the Far West*, well-known Italian westerns like *Once Upon a Time in the West*, *A Stranger in Town*, *Sartana* and *Compañeros*, and the inevitable parodies: *For a Few Dollars Less* (1966), *Il Bello, Il Brutto, Il Cretino* (1967, 'The Handsome, the Ugly, the Cretinous') and the unforgettable musical spaghetti western *Rita of the West* (1967). By way of avoiding such surprises, I have also asked Professor Sir Christopher Frayling, Alex Cox and Tom Betts, three genre *aficionados*, to list their own 'Top Ten' spaghetti westerns, in an effort to distinguish the good films from the bad and the ugly.

ACKNOWLEDGEMENTS

I would like to thank the following people, who have helped with the research and production of this book: Philippa Brewster, my editor at I.B. Tauris, for her hard work, enthusiasm and great ideas, which have made the writing of *Once Upon a Time* so enjoyable. I also thank Robert Hastings at Dexter Haven Associates and Deborah Susman, Ben Usher and Nicola Denny at I.B. Tauris for their invaluable contributions and for making this project such a success. I would also like to thank Professor Sir Christopher Frayling, Tom Betts, Donald S. Bruce, Alex Coe (for the hours we've spent watching the best and worst in world cinema), William Connolly, Mike Coppack, Alex Cox, Paul Duncan, Mike Eustace, Andy Hanratty, Rene Hogguer, Belinda Hughes, Professor Mario Marsili and Lionel Woodman.

Many of the illustrations in this book have been provided by Tom Betts, the editor of the US fanzine *Westerns All'Italiana*, from his private archive. I would also like to thank Tom for taking the time to help with my many questions, and for his interview with Spanish actor Aldo Sambrell.

The comparison photographs of Almeria and Mini Hollywood were provided by Donald S. Bruce from his collection *An Archaeological History of the Films of Sergio Leone*. Thank you for allowing me to reproduce them here. Other illustrative material is from my own collection.

I must also thank Andy Hanratty, for his meticulous restoration work on the stills, posters, LP covers and artwork.

Thank you also Professor Sir Christopher Frayling, Alex Cox and Tom Betts for their Italian western 'Top Tens', which demonstrate that Lee Van Cleef and Clint Eastwood remain by far the most popular stars of the genre, and Sergios Leone, Corbucci and Sollima the most gifted directors.

Thanks to Professor Mario Marsili, who allowed me to reprint information from his interviews with director Sergio Sollima (June 2003) and actor Benito Stefanelli (July 1999). Many of the films discussed here were located by Euro film specialist Rene Hogguer of 'Cine City' in Hilversum, Holland. Most soundtracks were obtained from Lionel Woodman (of 'Hillside CD Productions' in Rochester), who also helped with information on composers Ennio Morricone and Bruno Nicolai.

Thanks too to the following: Isabel Coe, Nicki and John Cosgrove, Simon Hawkins, Ann Jones, Gareth Jones, Mike Oak and Tracey Mansell, Sonya-Jayne Stewart and Bob Bell, Nick Rennisson and David Weaver.

Finally, thanks to my parents, Carol (for the hours spent reading and rereading pages of material) and John (to whom I owe my love of westerns). And especially to Clara, without whose help, patience and support this book would never have been written.

SUNDOWNER: AN INTRODUCTION TO EUROPEAN WESTERNS

In the late fifties and early sixties Rome was second only to Hollywood as the international film capital of the world. Many Hollywood productions were filmed there, including *Helen of Troy* (1955) and *Ben Hur* (1959). Others epics, like *El Cid* (1961), *King of Kings* (1961) and *Lawrence of Arabia* (1962), were shot in Spain, because production and labour costs were much cheaper than in Hollywood. Alongside these American-financed epics, the Italians made historical spectaculars in their own inimitable style. Their 'Sword and Sandal' muscleman craze saw pneumatic heroes like Hercules, Maciste and Goliath steamrollering through outlandish mythical adventures. Though occasionally juvenile, these fantastical escapades were big box office, even in the States, where they became popular on drive-in double-bills. Papier-mâché boulders, rickety sets, rubber spears and cardboard acting defined the genre, but there were some notable exceptions: Mario Bava's *Hercules in the Haunted World* (1961), Vittorio Cottafavi's *Goliath and the Dragon* (1960) and *Hercules Conquers Atlantis* (1961), Sergio Corbucci's *Goliath and the Vampires* (1961) and *Romulus and Remus* (1961), Giorgio Ferroni's *Hercules Against Moloch* (1963), Nick Nostro's *Spartacus and the Ten Gladiators* (1964) and Duccio Tessari's *Sons of Thunder* (1962).

Pietro Francisci's *Hercules* (1958) and *Hercules Unchained* (1959), starring Steve Reeves, were the first muscleman films to become successful in the UK and US, largely due to Joseph E. Levine's advertising campaign; they were among the first films to be advertised on TV. But by 1963 this phoney Roman Empire, which had been the cornerstone of the Italian film industry at Rome's Cinecitta Studios, was beginning to crumble. When some of the most expensive productions (in particular Robert Aldrich's biblical epic *The Last Days of Sodom and Gomorrah* and Luchino Visconti's adaptation of Giuseppe Di Lampedusa's *The Leopard*) bombed spectacularly internationally, the American financiers pulled out, the money dried up, and the Italians were left with a selection of vast ancient monuments and a surplus of togas.

In an effort to find the next craze, opportunistic Italian film–makers tried every conceivable genre. They made contemporary thrillers (*The Evil Eye, Blood and Black Lace*); Gothic horrors (*Black Sunday, Castle of Blood, The Terror of Dr Hitchcock, Kill Baby Kill*); science fiction (*Battle of the Worlds*); ancient court intrigues and love stories (*Sign of the Gladiator, The Trojan War*); Tartar adventures (*Ursus and the Tartar Princess*); Viking sagas (*Erik the Conqueror*); swashbucklers (*Seven Seas to Calais, Sandokan the Great*); *El Cid* rip-offs (*The Castillian* and *Son of El Cid*); genie and flying-carpet Arabian adventures (*The Golden Arrow*); Mondo shockumentaries (*Mondo Cane*) and pirate films (*Queen of the Pirates*). To make things more interesting, directors crossed genres to produce some unexpected hybrids. *Knives of the Avenger* was a Viking horror, *Maciste in Hell*, *Night Star: Goddess of Electra* and *Hercules in the Haunted World* were horror muscleman epics, while *Planet of the Vampires* blended sci-fi with horror. Curiosities like *Robin Hood and the Pirates* were self-explanatory, with a Caribbean 'Sherwood Forest', though unfortunately the Italians never staged *Robin Hood – Prince of Thebes*.

While these oddities came and went, two perennially popular subjects were war movies and spy capers. The war cycle had begun with the Jack Palance vehicle *Warriors Five* (released in early 1962), but the genre flourished in the late sixties, with combat set in North Africa (*Commandos*), Europe (*Fall of the Giants*) and the Far East (*A Place in Hell*). Aping the Bond films, the spy movies were also successful in their own right and gave the Italians their very own 'Universal Export'. George Ardisson and Frederick Stafford were typical heroes of these popular adventures: Ardisson played Walter Ross, 'Agent 3S3', while Stafford appeared as Hubert Bonniseur, codename 'OSS 117'.

In the late fifties, high production costs on Hollywood westerns and the popularity of western TV shows like *Gunsmoke* and *Rawhide* effectively killed off the genre at the US box office. But a Hollywood western like *The Magnificent Seven* (1960), which grossed only moderately in the US, made a fortune in Europe. To fill a gap in the home market, several European countries decided to begin making westerns of their own.

In Spain the British western *The Sheriff of Fractured Jaw* (1959, with Kenneth Moore and Jayne Mansfield) was shot on a town set built at Colmenar Viejo ('Old Beehive') and in the colourful surrounding area to the north-east of Madrid. Shortly afterwards, Spanish directors began to make a series of movies based on the Zorro legend, initially with Frank Latimore in the lead. In late 1961, Michael Carreras shot *The Savage Guns*, based on a specially commissioned screenplay: 'The San Siado Killings' by Peter R. Newman. This was one of the first proto-spaghettis filmed in Almeria, southern Spain. 'It started the whole trend of making westerns in Spain,' reckoned Carreras. *Savage Guns* was a UK/Spanish co-production (released by MGM) and featured American leads (Don Taylor, Richard Baseheart and Alex Nicol), with a Spanish supporting cast (including Jose Manuel Martin, Fernando Rey and Jose Niento as the villain Ortega). The film was traditional western fare for the most part, but the Spanish settings (including deserts, palm trees, agaves and decaying whitewashed villages) looked distinctive, and the violence was more graphic than Hollywood westerns (Carreras had been involved with Hammer Studios). The good guy (Baseheart) wore black and the bad guy (Nicol) wore white, a reversal of normal western conventions, while Baseheart had both his hands crushed by wagon wheels, in a bloody precursor of later spaghettis. When Dirk Bogarde appeared in *The Singer Not the Song* (1961), a British western shot in Torremolinos (near Malaga), as a leather-clad homosexual sadist, it was obvious the Europeans were approaching the genre from a new angle.

It was somewhat surprising that the most successful of these early sixties European westerns were made by the West Germans and Yugoslavs, in the 'Wild East' of Yugoslavia. These initial outings were in the mould of other German 'outdoor adventures', which had altered little since Bela Lugosi's *Last of the Mohicans* (1920). Here a stalwart Teutonic trapper teamed up with a virtuous Indian, Uncas (played by Lugosi). But in adapting Cooper's story, the German producers were ignoring one of their own greatest writers. Until his death in 1912, Karl May had written a series of successful books about the Mascalero Apache chief Winnetou and his white blood brother 'Old Shatterhand'. Their exploits were ideal fodder for the German outdoor adventure genre, and in 1962 Harald Reinl directed an adaptation of May's torn-treasure-map story, *The Treasure of Silver Lake*. The film was financed by Rialto Film (of Hamburg) and Jadran Film (based in Zagreb), and was shot in the otherworldly frontier landscape of the former Yugoslavia – with its beautiful white rocks, azure lakes, glistening waterfalls and pine woods. Harald G. Petersson reworked May's story, American ex-Tarzan Lex Barker played 'Old Shatterhand' ('the great bear killer') and Frenchman Pierre Brice played Winnetou. The heroes help Fred Engel (Götz George) to locate the treasure; they have half the location

Cowboys and Indians, European style: Old Shatterhand (Lex Barker) helps to defend the town of Roswell from an Apache attack in *Winnetou the Warrior* (1963).

map, evil Colonel Brinkley (Herbert Lom) and his 'Tramps Gang' have the other half, resulting in a well-paced tug-of-war.

The Treasure of Silver Lake sets the tone for the series, with magnificent scenery, spirited action sequences and stirring music. Martin Böttcher's grand-sounding western compositions (partially recycled in later efforts) are up there with Elmer Bernstein's and Dimitri Tiomkin's western scores, with thumping brass, rousing percussion and expansive, romantic interludes. Ernst W. Kalinke's craning, panning cinematography looks beautiful in Cinemascope and Eastmancolor, and even the phoney European-looking guns and self-conscious comedy moments (with Ralf Wolter as irascible Sam Hawkens and Eddie Arent as the butterfly-collecting Duke of Glockenspiel) don't mar the exciting pace. Several set pieces stand out. The arrival of a driverless stagecoach full of corpses outside the 'Prairie Saloon' in Tulsa; the Tramps' attack on the stockade at Butler's Farm; the Ute Indians' impressive procession into camp; and the gripping finale at the beautiful 'Silver Lake', with its white cliffs and cascading falls.

The Treasure of Silver Lake was one of the most popular releases in Germany in 1962; it won a 'Golden Screen' award for its huge returns. It was also a hit in France and Italy, and a sequel followed in 1963. Slicker than *Treasure*, *Winnetou the Warrior* (also called *Winnetou I* or *Apache Gold*) went back in time and told how a greenhorn surveyor with the Great Western Railroad (GWR) matured into the buckskinned adventurer Old Shatterhand. It also explained how he became a blood brother to Apache chief's son Winnetou ('Friend and protector of all who need help'). The villain was Fredrick Santer (Mario Adorf), who was introduced massacring a herd of buffalo. Santer is menacing the GWR with the help of the Kiowas (the railroad workers are laying tracks across sacred Indian land), while he tries to steal a cache of Apache gold. Shatterhand falls for Winnetou's pretty sister Chochi ('Beautiful Day', played by Marie Versini), but she's killed in the finale, as is Santer, who falls off a cliff onto a bed of spears. Again Böttcher's romanticised, percussive score is atmospheric, Kalinke's photography evocative (especially the scenes at an Apache pueblo) and the set pieces memorable. A powder wagon is blown up during a Kiowa attack on a wagon train; the Kiowas ransack the town of 'Roswell' (the Tulsa town set from *The Treasure of Silver Lake*) and Shatterhand is chased by the Apaches in a canoe down the Pecos River. The best scene in the film is when Santer and his men are trapped in a saloon in Roswell. As they try to tunnel out, railroad workers lay tracks through the night leading to the saloon, and at daybreak they drive a locomotive into the building, completely demolishing it.

As if driving a train through a saloon wasn't exciting enough, the next movie, *Last of the Renegades*, or *Winnetou II* (1964) was even more eventful, with Winnetou saving Assiniboin maid Ribanna in the opening sequence by rugby-tackling a bear. The villain was Joe Forrester (British actor Anthony Steel from *Where No Vultures Fly*, 1951) and his coonskin-hatted henchman Lucas (a brutal performance from Klaus Kinski), who have an oil well at New Venango and want to foment Indian trouble.

Eddie Arent reappeared as Lord Castlepool (formerly redubbed 'The Duke of Glockenspiel', as comic relief for English-speaking audiences). Karin Dor (previously the love interest in *Treasure*) played Ribanna, and young Mario Girotti (later 'Terence Hill') portrayed US Lieutenant Robert Merrill. Though more was made of the romantic element in the story, Reinl wasn't sparing with the action. Lucas and his gang raze a Ponca Indian village to the ground, Forrester massacres a wagon train of peaceful settlers, then attempts to kill Winnetou and Shatterhand with a huge siege catapult which fires powder kegs, and in an epic scene hundreds of Indians arrive for a powwow with the army at Fort Niobara. In the most extravagant sequence, Forrester's oil well catches fire; later the villain ends up full of Assiniboin arrows when Winnetou and the Indians abseil to the rescue in the cave-set *dénouement*.

Several more inferior 'Winnetou' movies followed. *Desperado Trail* (*Winnetou III*, 1965) ended with Winnetou being killed, though he was resurrected soon afterwards. Brice played the chief in all 11 instalments of the series, and was teamed with several different blood brothers. *Thunder at the Border* (1966) saw Rod Cameron playing Davy Crockett lookalike 'Old Firehand'. *Flaming Frontier* (1965), *Rampage*

The Santa Fe Gamblers ride through town; the Santa Fe sequence of Sergio Leone's *The Good, the Bad and the Ugly* (1966) was shot in Mini Hollywood, now a tourist attraction in Almeria, Spain.

at *Apache Wells* (1966) and *Among Vultures* (1964, also released as *Frontier Hellcat*) featured 'Old Surehand'. Only *Among Vultures* equalled the opening three films of the series. Stewart Granger played 'Old Surehand', a buckskinned, wisecracking, mahogany-tanned adventurer in a big white hat, as a parody of Barker's Old Shatterhand. His sidekicks were an inept marksman Old Wobble ('You couldn't hit a house,' comments Surehand, 'A big one!') and sharpshooting Miss Annie (Elke Sommer), who introduced sexy cleavage and a blonde beehive to Winnetou's west. Surehand and Winnetou faced a bandit gang known as the Vultures, led by Preston (Sieghardt Rupp), and it included an exciting battle in the 'Valley of Death', a Shoshoni burial ground. Simultaneously, Barker and Brice continued the Winnetou/ Shatterhand story with *Apache's Last Battle* (or *Old Shatterhand*, 1964), *Half Breed* (1966) and *Winnetou and Shatterhand in the Valley of Death* (1968), a belated attempt by Reinl to revive the series.

With the success of the 'Winnetou' movies, Spanish and Italian production companies decided to capitalise on their popularity by having a stake in the films (with the investment of co-production money) and by casting native stars to give 'international appeal'. Another one of the films' main selling points was their multi-national casts – a fact that was mentioned constantly in their trailers.

If there was one thing the European (and in particular Italian) cinema-going public liked, it was movies packed with big American stars; even better, when the stars started to come to Europe to make movies. Italian, Spanish, German and French directors suddenly had casts normally beyond their wildest dreams, with a seemingly never-ending stream of actors crossing the Atlantic to make everything from horrors to westerns. This transatlantic migration had started with the muscleman epics, which often employed actors like Alan Ladd, Orson Welles and Broderick Crawford in star vehicles.

The Hollywood actors who appeared in European westerns fell into several categories. Some were young TV or movie actors who felt their careers weren't going anywhere in the States (Clint Eastwood and Burt Reynolds). Some had been supporting players in fifties Hollywood productions and wanted their own shot at stardom (Lee Van Cleef, Alex Nicol, Frank Wolff and Charles Bronson). Others' popularity had diminished in America, but they loved the adoration still afforded them by European audiences (Joseph Cotten, Anthony Steel and Jeffrey Hunter). This last type of actor was satirised in Vittorio De Sica's *After the Fox* (1966). Here, a hyperactive, sweet-talking Italian film director, Franco Fabrizi (Peter Sellers) flattered ageing (but narcissistic) matinee idol Tony Powell (Victor Mature) into an appearance in an art-house flick, which was actually a scam to steal 'The Gold of Cairo' (wittily the title of Fabrizi's work-in-progress). But not everyone in Madrid, Yugoslavia, Rome and Almeria were there through circumstance. There were those who were already successful, but followed fashion (or finance) by appearing in the fad. However, it has never been clearly established what possessed Sterling Hayden, William Shatner and James Mason to bother with the genre, as their respective contributions were terrible. Mason best summed up the risk involved: 'When shooting a western in Spain, one should never say to oneself, "Never mind, no one is going to see it", because that will be just the film the Rank Organisation choose to release in England'.

Spaghetti westerns were predominantly Italian productions, or Italian/Spanish co-productions; the directors were usually Italian and the technicians Spanish. The casts were headed by an American star (or a European under an anglicised pseudonym), with multinational co-stars and supporting players. If the French or West Germans invested money, they would want one of their own stars in the cast to ensure popularity in their home market. For UK/US audiences the craze was delayed until 1967, when distributors like United Artists, Avco Embassy and Columbia began buying the rights to Italian westerns that had already been successful in Europe, and releasing them in the UK and US. The Italian western output of 1964–67 quickly swamped cinemas, sometimes at the rate of two or three a week, with the entire *oeuvre* of some actors being condensed internationally to a few months. Moreover, several actors' spaghetti western careers were finished before their films even made it to the States.

Many spaghetti westerns were shot in Italy on rented studio sets and sound stages, and at locations in the countryside around Rome. There were three main western town sets in the vicinity of Rome: at Cinecitta Studios, Elios Studios and Dino De Laurentiis's studio ('Dinocitta'). The Cinecitta town set was erected in 1964 at the studio complex known as 'Hollywood on the Tiber'. Elios Studios (on the Via Tiburtina) was founded in 1962 by Alvaro Mancori; in 1964 a western village set was built for *Jim il Primo* (also called *The Last Gun*), starring Cameron Mitchell. This set was the most frequently used Italian town setting; later an adobe Mexican village was added, which can be seen in *Texas Adios* (1966). At Dinocitta, De Laurentiis built a western set, surrounded by lush grassland, for his production of *The Hills Run Red* (1966). There were several sites in Lazio and Abruzzo, which were used for location scenes; many of the low-budget westerns were shot entirely in this Roman 'west'. Familiar locations include a gorge at Tolfa, the quarries at Magliana, the landscape of Manziana around Bracciano Lake, the Abruzzo National Park and the Nature Reserve at Tor Caldara.

The most distinctive spaghetti western locations were in Spain. Like the Italians, the Spanish constructed several western sets. Balcazar Studios in Barcelona erected their own town set at Esplugues De Llobregat, for the series of Spanish westerns filmed in Aragon. The main centres of western film-making in Spain were Madrid and Almeria. To the north of Madrid, two western towns were constructed: the 'Fractured Jaw' set at Colmenar Viejo (sometimes referred to as 'Aberdeen City') and a 'western village' at Hojo De Manzanares (built in 1962 for the 'Zorro' movies) in the Hojo de Manzanares Mountains. Many location scenes were filmed in the surrounding area, including the rock formations at La Pedriza (in the Guadarrama Mountains), the reservoir at Santillana and the landscape of Manzanares El Real.

The Andalusian province of Almeria has become most associated with spaghetti westerns. Almeria is Europe's only desert, a stark, barren land that has suffered centuries of erosion. The most inhospitable areas are the Tabernas badlands, standing in the shadow of the Sierra Nevada. The distinctive Almerian landscape is defined by dried-up gullies and riverbeds, the grey Miocene clay and treeless plain rising into the hills and sierras: the Sierra Alhamilla and the Sierra de Los Filabres.

A western set was built near Tabernas in 1965 to make *For a Few Dollars More* (1965); throughout the seventies, the set was known as 'Yucca City', but it's now called 'Poblado Del Oeste' and 'Mini Hollywood', a tourist attraction with wild-west shows staged for the tourists. At La Calahorra, the town of 'Flagstone City' was built beside the railway line to film *Once Upon a Time in the West* (1968). These sets, built for prestigious productions, were left standing after filming was completed, so the sets reappeared in many lesser films. To the north of Mini Hollywood, 'Texas Hollywood' was constructed in the early seventies – half clapboard western town, half Mexican pueblo. In 1970, a huge fortress was built to the west of Texas Hollywood for the American production *El Condor*. That same year Dino De Laurentiis built a cavalry fort near Malaga for *The Deserter* and a whitewashed fortress prison (Fort Presidio) in the vicinity of Tabernas for *A Man called Sledge*. Two ranch sets were constructed near Tabernas, at Las Salinillas and 'Rancho Leone' (which is open today to visitors). The coast at Cabo De Gata and San Jose, and villages like Los Albaricoques in the Sierra De Gata, were used for location scenes; the whitewashed villages looked totally authentic, with the only reflection of modern life being the occasional telegraph pole. By the late sixties, Almeria was overrun with film crews shooting westerns, war movies, Arabian adventures and epics: according to director Andre De Toth, stagecoaches chased Rolls-Royces and Indians chased Tiger tanks because they read the wrong call-sheets in their hotel lobbies.

Early spaghetti westerns imitated the 'Winnetou' films, with the most successful being *Buffalo Bill, Hero of the Far West* (1964) and *Seven Hours of Gunfire* (1965). Both films feature 'Buffalo Bill' as the protagonist and concern unscrupulous bad guys running guns to the Sioux. *Buffalo Bill* was an Italian/West German/French co-production shot mainly in Italy (though some location shooting was done in Spain near La Pedriza, Manzanares El Real). Ex-muscleman Gordon Scott (as Bill) was packed into a buckskin outfit and saddled with a goatee beard, a sidekick called 'Snacks' (Ugo Sasso) and a clippety-clop theme tune. But the film had a good cast, including Piero Lulli and Mario Brega as Red and Big Sam (two pawns in the gunrunning game), a big finale (an attack on US Fort Adams) and effective use of the Italian settings. The town set at Elios Studios was used as 'Indian Creek', and a Sioux camp was cheaply constructed at the picturesque Monte Gelato falls in the Treja Valley, where the Indians pay for their repeating rifles with 'yellow sand' and get tanked up on firewater, before going on the rampage.

Marginally the better film, *Seven Hours of Gunfire* (released in Italy in January 1965) was a Spanish/Italian/West German co-production. It begins with Bill Cody as a child who hero-worships Bill Hickok, a fearless messenger who works for the 'Poney Express' (as it's spelt on a sign outside a way station). Years later Buffalo Bill and Wild Bill Hickok, along with Calamity Jane (played by Gloria Milland) unite to stop Red Cloud's Sioux levelling the settlement at 'Custer' (represented by the set at Hojo de Manzanares) with their newly acquired firearms. During the quixotic story, Buffalo Bill (played by 'Clyde Rogers' – American actor Rik Van Nutter under an assumed name) falls for a padre's daughter Ethel (Elga Sommerfield), while Hickok (Adrian Hoven) courts 'Calam' (portrayed as Doris Day in a very bad mood). Using the Winnetou films as a model (and with the sunny Spanish scenery holding its own with Yugoslavia), Cody was teamed with Frank North (Mariano Vidal Molina), the white leader of the friendly Pawnee tribe, who sides with the 7th Cavalry for the slam-bang finale: an ambush of Red Cloud's warriors. The gun-runners are played by a trio of talented Spanish actors (Antonio Molino Rojo, Alvaro De Luna and Lorenzo Robledo), while it is difficult to dislike a film that so shamelessly rewrote history.

Two drifters, Blondy and Tuco, arrive in a Confederate ambulance at the San Antonio Mission in *The Good, the Bad and the Ugly* (1966), and Donald S. Bruce arrives at Cortijo de los Frailes 30 years later.

In the final battle (a last stand in Custer), factual accuracy is thrown to the wind, as Hickok shoots Red Cloud and is then killed himself, with no sign of 'Aces and Eights'; Hickok was actually shot in the back during a poker game in 'Saloon No. 10', Deadwood City (1876), while Red Cloud died peacefully in 1909. Poetic licence aside, the film is entertaining, though inferior to Reinl's films.

Historical accuracy was never the Italian western's strong point. Many of the later films deployed factual characters and events (from the James Gang and the American Civil War to Pancho Villa and the Ku Klux Klan) with scant regard for the facts. In the Spanish/Italian *The Man Who Killed Billy the Kid* (1967, and also called *A Few Bullets More*) the action was accurately set around Silver City and Fort Sumner and correctly portrayed Billy as a right-handed draw (the 'left-handed gun' myth was due to a famous photograph of him being printed in reverse). Directed in pacy fashion by Julio Buchs, it recounted the legend of 'Billy the Kid', who was born Henry McCarty and used the pseudonyms 'William Bonney', 'Henry Antrim' and 'Kid Antrim'. Billy was played by Karl Hirenbach, who shared the outlaw's penchant for aliases (including 'Peter Lee Lawrence', 'Arthur Green' and 'Arthur Grant'), though the reasons behind the subterfuge were equally deceptive. Impressively shot around Madrid and Almeria in 'Totalvision', the finale saw Billy killed not by his nemesis Pat Garrett, but by his old friend (now a Regulator in the Lincoln County War) Mark Travers, at the very moment Billy was about to go straight. Billy was presented as a black-leather-clad, blond-haired archangel (complete with religious overtones on the soundtrack), while the Tunstall/Murphy range war was a ferocious, messy inter-gang feud.

And so it happened that the Italians and Spanish began making westerns, however inaccurately based on frontier history. Initially European audiences approached these nascent spaghetti westerns gingerly, but in 1964 another archangel was about to drift into town, who would change forever the way westerns were made.

SPAGHETTI WESTERN TOP TENS

Professor Sir Christopher Frayling:
Christopher Frayling is the Rector of the Royal College of Art, London, and a writer, historian and broadcaster. His books include *Spaghetti Westerns: Cowboys and Europeans from Karl May to Sergio Leone* and *Clint Eastwood* and *Sergio Leone: Something to Do with Death.*

Once Upon a Time in the West (1968)
The Good, the Bad and the Ugly (1966)
The Big Silence (1967)
For a Few Dollars More (1965)
Django Kill (1967)
The Big Gundown (1967)
Django (1966)
My Name is Nobody (1973)
A Professional Gun (1968)
A Bullet for the General (1966)

Alex Cox:
Alex Cox is a broadcaster, writer and director of such films as *Repo Man*, *Walker*, *Sid and Nancy*, *Straight to Hell* and *Revenger's Tragedy.*

The Big Silence (1967)
A Bullet for the General (1966)
Django Kill (1967)
For a Few Dollars More (1965)
Once Upon a Time in the West (1968)
The Hellbenders (1967)
The Big Gundown (1967)
Requiescant (1967)
Django (1966)
The Good, the Bad and the Ugly (1966)

Tom Betts:
Tom Betts is the editor of the fanzine *Westerns All'Italiana*, published in Anaheim, California since 1983.

Once Upon a Time in the West (1968)
For a Few Dollars More (1965)
The Good, the Bad and the Ugly (1966)
The Big Gundown (1967)
Death Rides a Horse (1967)
Bandidos (1967)
The Big Silence (1967)
The Forgotten Pistolero (1970)
I Want Him Dead (1968)
Sartana the Gravedigger (1969)

Howard Hughes:
Howard Hughes is the author of *Spaghetti Western*s and *The American Indian Wars*.

The Good, the Bad and the Ugly (1966)
Django (1966)
The Big Gundown (1967)
For a Few Dollars More (1965)
The Big Silence (1967)
Sabata (1969)
Navajo Joe (1966)
They Call Me Trinity (1970)
A Professional Gun (1968)
The Hills Run Red (1966)

1

'Life Can Be so Precious'

— Sergio Leone's *A Fistful of Dollars* (1964)

A Fistful of Dollars (1964)
original title: *Per un Pugno di Dollari*
Credits
DIRECTOR – 'Bob Robertson' (Sergio Leone)
PRODUCERS – 'Harry Colombo' (Arrigo Colombo) and 'George
    Papi' (Giorgio Papi)
SCREENPLAY – Sergio Leone, Duccio Tessari, Jaime Comas,
    Fernando Di Leo, Tonino Valerii and Victor A. Catena
DIALOGUE – Mark Lowell and Clint Eastwood
ART DIRECTOR, SET DECORATOR AND COSTUMES – 'Charles Simons'
    (Carlo Simi)
EDITING – 'Bob Quintle' (Roberto Cinquini)
DIRECTOR OF PHOTOGRAPHY – 'Jack Dalmas' (Massimo Dallamano)
MUSIC – 'Dan Savio' (Ennio Morricone)
Interiors filmed at Cinecitta Film Studios, Rome
Techniscope/Technicolor
An Italian/Spanish/West German co-production.
Jolly Film (Rome)/Ocean Film (Madrid)/Constantin Film
    (Munich)
Released internationally by United Artists
Cast
    Clint Eastwood (Joe, the Stranger); Marianne Koch
    (Marisol); 'Johnny Wells', Gian Maria Volonte (Ramon Rojo);
    'W. Lukschy', Wolfgang Lukschy (Sheriff John Baxter);
    'S.Rupp', Sieghardt Rupp (Esteban Rojo); 'Joe Edger', Josef
    Egger (Piripero); Antonio Prieto (Don Miguel Rojo);
    Margherita Lozano (Consuela Baxter); 'Pepe Calvo', Jose
    Calvo (Silvanito); Daniel Martin (Julio); Fredy Arco (Jesus);
    'Carol Brown', Bruno Carotenuto (Antonio Baxter); 'Benny

Reeves', Benito Stefanelli (Rubio); 'Richard Stuyvesant', Mario Brega (Chico); Jose Canalejas (Alvaro); 'Aldo Sambreli', Aldo Sambrell (Manolo); Umberto Spadaro (Miguel); Jose Riesgo (Mexican Cavalry captain); Jose Halufi, Nazzareno Natale and Fernando Sanchez Polack (members of Rojo gang); Bill Thompkins, Joe Kamel, Luis Barboo, Julio Perez Taberno, Antonio Molino Rojo, Franciso Braña, Antonio Pico and Lorenzo Robledo (members of Baxter gang) with Raf Baldassare, Manuel Peña, Jose Orjas, Juan Cortes and Antonio Moreno

*   *   *

Though the westerns made by Sergio Leone and Clint Eastwood in the mid-sixties are forever called spaghetti westerns, the Spanish contribution to the genre has often been ignored. The German-made, Yugoslav-shot 'Winnetou' stories may have awakened European producers' interest in westerns, but Leone's movies would have looked very different if they hadn't been shot in the beautiful locations around Madrid and the deserts and sierras of Almeria. Among the expatriate American actors who found themselves sweating in temperatures that topped 110 degrees in the summer, Almeria was affectionately known as the 'Armpit of Europe'. This sandblasted landscape had a reputation as a place where washed-up 'stars' went to die in the cheapest international adventure co-productions. But no one in Spain could have foreseen the impact Leone was about to have on their film industry when the director arrived there in spring 1964 with an actor dressed in a blanket.

The Spanish had been making westerns since 1962, often co-producing with the French. These exotic action movies were based on the Zorro legend. Whilst not being particularly popular outside Spain, they did prove two things: Spain could look passably 'western' and stories with a Hispanic flavour could be made cheaply on their own doorstep. The handful of Zorro films made in the early sixties are interesting period pieces. The heroes are highly camp, the villains surprisingly brutal and the quick-fire action ensures they are nothing less than entertaining. Frank Latimore often played Don Jose de la Torre (a.k.a. 'El Zorro' – 'The Fox'). Most interesting is the friction between the local gringos and Mexicans, which is at the heart of the original Zorro stories. The villains are usually gringo, but the treachery and murder that escalates the violent situation in 'Old California' has clear parallels with the Italian westerns that followed in their wake.

Sergio Leone had spent the late fifties assisting Hollywood film-makers on Rome-shot epics. Since then, his only steady work had been to collaborate on screenplays with other budding directors, like Duccio Tessari, Sergio Corbucci and Sergio Sollima. Among his assignments was some second-unit work on the chariot race in *Ben Hur* (1959), though to hear Leone tell the tale you would think he had driven the chariots. Leone then directed *The Last Days of Pompeii* (1959) and *The Colossus of Rhodes* (1960), both reasonable successes. Soon afterwards he was fired from the second unit of *The Last Days of Sodom and Gomorrah* (1962) for taking excessively long lunch breaks. Temporarily unemployed, Leone wrote a western provisionally entitled *The Magnificent Stranger* (released as *A Fistful of Dollars*), collaborating with Jaime Comas, Victor Catena, Tonino Valerii, Duccio Tessari and Fernando Di Leo. There is no writing credit at the beginning of the film, only 'Dialogue by Mark Lowell' (the English translator). Some sources mention a writer named 'G. Schock', which was a Germanic-sounding pseudonym for the writers, to please the West German investors. Interestingly, the name 'Jaime Comas' appears on a gravestone in the finished film.

The plot of Leone's film was inspired by Akira Kurosawa's *Yojimbo* (1961), which was released in Italy as *La Sfida Del Samurai* ('The Challenge of the Samurai'). In *Yojimbo*, a nameless ronin (played by Toshiro Mifune) arrives in a shantytown ruled by two rival families. The factions' business interests are different (one sells saki, the other silk), but both want control of the area. By skilful manipulation, the yojimbo ('bodyguard') hires himself to each gang until the conflict is resolved with both groups being annihilated, leaving the wanderer to move on. Kurosawa's movie is a comic strip version of his earlier, more serious works, injecting sidelong humour and humanitarian observations into a jokey, hokey but nevertheless brutal narrative. Leone retained all the major characters intact, adapting them to a 'westernised' (as in 'wild west') version of the Japanese prototypes. In *A Fistful of Dollars*, Gonji (the tavernkeeper) became Silvanito; Hansuke (the watchman) became Juan De Dios (the bellringer); Kuma (the coffin-maker) became Piripero and the nameless ronin became a nameless gunfighter.

In Leone's adaptation, the gangs in the Mexican village of San Miguel are distinguished as Gringo and Mexican (like the Zorro films), but are still two families – gunrunning Sheriff John Baxter (a weak-willed lawman), his wife Consuela (who really runs the show) and their slow-witted son Antonio, against a trio of Mexican brothers: the liquor-selling Rojos. Although the eldest of the Rojos is named Don Miguel (or Benito in the Italian version), he wields no power in the clan, which is led by his sadistic brother, Ramon. The stranger tells Silvanito, 'The Baxters over there, the Rojos there and me right in the middle. Crazy bellringer was right, there's money to be made in a place like this.' The stranger plays both ends against the middle, intensifying the rivalry, until in the finale the Rojos massacre the Baxters. A problem with a 'westernised' version of *Yojimbo* was that the original final showdown pitted the hero, armed with a sword and a throwing knife, against the villain Unosuke (Tatsuya Nakadai) with his pistol – the only firearm in town. Leone's adaptation pits the stranger, with his Colt .45 and a piece of railcar strapped to his chest, against Ramon's Winchester 73 carbine, with its greater range and chamber capacity; but again the inferior weapon prevails.

The main differences between *Yojimbo* and *Fistful* are the motives, characters and scenes added by Leone. The hero siding with the bad guys in order to destroy them owes much to the 'Zorro' movies, while gunrunners and liquor merchants were a regular ingredient of early Italian/Spanish cowboy and Indian fare. A gold robbery and the stranger's location of the loot during a cemetery shootout (a detective story element) was suggested by the adventures of the Continental Op in Dashiell Hammett's *Red Harvest* (called *Piombo e Sangue* or 'Lead and Blood' in Italy) and the western-set *Corkscrew*. Both these stories feature a lone hero caught in a faction-riven town. Hammett was best known for his tough, precise style that pared every detail to the minimum; in Hammett's world, the rule of thumb was 'trust no one', and Kurosawa's hero seemed to agree. Interestingly, in spring 1962, an article in *Film Quarterly* titled 'When the Twain Meet: Hollywood's Remake of *The Seven Samurai*' (which compared Kurosawa's original with John Sturges's *The Magnificent Seven*) closed with news that 'a minor United Artists producer' was soon to remake *Yojimbo* in the US as a western, but the film never happened.

By 1964, Leone had convinced Jolly Film (Italy), Constantin Film (West Germany) and Ocean Film (Spain) to put up $200,000 to make a film provisionally entitled *The Magnificent Stranger*. He wanted Henry Fonda as the stranger, but Fonda was far too big a star. The title of the film was clearly based on *The Magnificent Seven* (or *I Magnifici Sette* on its Italian release), so Leone approached two of the *Seven* stars: Charles Bronson judged the script the worst he had ever read and James Coburn was too expensive (wanting $25,000 when only $15,000 was available). Rory Calhoun (the star of *The Colossus of Rhodes*) also turned Leone down. Folklore has it that Richard Harrison, an ex-AIP actor working at Cinecitta, suggested Leone should try Clint Eastwood. The story is fanciful, but however Leone found Eastwood it was a happy accident. Previously reduced to earning a living digging swimming pools and as a lifeguard, Eastwood's screen career began in the fifties, on contract at Universal. He played the pilot who napalmed the giant *Tarantula* (1953) and also appeared in 'the lousiest Western ever made' (*Ambush at Cimarron Pass* – 1957). He was currently playing Rowdy Yates in the CBS TV series, *Rawhide*.

Leone watched an episode of *Rawhide* entitled 'Incident of the Black Sheep', wherein Rowdy escorts an injured sheep farmer (guest star Richard Baseheart) and his flock to a nearby town and suffers the same prejudicial treatment that he, as a cattleman, had meted out on the sheepherder. Leone thought that six-foot-four-inch Eastwood stole every scene, with his laid-back acting style. Eastwood wasn't enthusiastic about a remake of a Japanese action film near Madrid, but his wife Maggie thought it was 'wild' and 'interesting'. Eastwood found the script unintentionally funny as it was written in a strange version of American slang. But the fee was attractive, as was the trip to Europe (somewhere he'd never been) and so he agreed, providing he could alter his dialogue. Moreover, once his dialogue was pruned, $15,000 wasn't a bad salary for standing, squinting into the sun in Spain. Even so, the fact that he was the cheapest actor available for the role wasn't lost on Eastwood – especially when Leone had the stranger telling Don Miguel 'I don't work cheap'.

Eastwood had seen *Yojimbo* and saw in Mifune a very different acting style – a strength of character through silence, coupled with a dynamism in the action sequences. He realised that such a scruffy, stubbled style would be well suited to a new kind of antihero. Eastwood had experimented with his character to a certain extent on *Rawhide*, even adopting his soon-to-be trademark stubble in episodes such as 'Incident of the Phantom Bugler'. But after five years on the series he was sick of his clean-cut image, exemplified by a series of health tips in *TV Guide*. He was equally tired of the thin plot material and the lack of scope in Rowdy's character. He claimed that his costume on *Rawhide* 'stood up by itself' and out of boredom he would put lip-gloss on his horse to liven up the monotony. It was clear that it was time for a change of scenery.

Covering all markets, the multinational production companies behind *Fistful* bankrolled a cosmopolitan cast of German and Italian co-stars and Spanish extras. German actors Wolfgang Lukschy, Sieghardt Rupp and Josef Egger are all higher in the credits than Spaniard Pepe Calvo, due to the West German backing for the film. Lukschy was Colonel-General Alfred Jodl in *The Longest Day* (1962) and the German-dubbed voice of John Wayne and Gary Cooper. Though German actress

The Stranger in town (Clint Eastwood) and Silvanito the bartender (Pepe Calvo) in familiar surroundings. Sergio Leone's *A Fistful of Dollars* (1964).

Marianne Koch speaks only in three scenes and sings in another, she gets second billing, for what amounts to a cameo role as Marisol, a Mexican peasant woman with jet-black hair and Cleopatra eyeliner. Koch was a popular actress in Europe at the time, occasionally appearing in British and West German thrillers and jungle adventures. She often adopted the pseudonym 'Marianne Cook', though some of the early advertising material for *Fistful* in Italy christened her 'Marianne Kock'.

Italian Gian Maria Volonte (cast as Ramon Rojo) was billed as 'Johnny Wells' in the titles, 'John Wels' on posters and 'Johannes Siedel' in Germany. Thirty-one-year-old Volonte was a stage actor who toured from the age of 22 with an actors' caravan around Italy, playing the classics. His fiery temper left him banned in Italy after an argument over a production of *Crime and Punishment*, so he finished up in genre movies like *Hercules Conquers Atlantis* (1961) and *Journey Beneath the Desert* (1961). Margherita Lozano had appeared in Luis Buñuel's *Viridiana* (1961), while both Antonio Prieto and Daniel Martin had appeared in an interesting Spanish film, *Los Tarantos* (1964), which detailed a tragic love affair between youngsters from rival gypsy families. It was *Fistful* that formed Leone's stock company of actors, and Benito Stefanelli, Mario Brega, Antonio Molino Rojo, Lorenzo Robledo and Aldo Sambrell all appeared in Leone's later westerns. Stefanelli also supervised the stunt work and was a translator.

Eastwood and his stunt-double Bill Thompkins arrived for the 11-week shooting schedule (from late April to June 1964). Some sources claim that Eastwood was also billed as 'Western Consultant', but it is Thompkins (billed by his full name, W.R. Thompkins) who is credited as 'Technical Adviser'. He also had a bit part in the film (he's the Baxter gunman in the green shirt) and did Eastwood's nighttime riding scenes, shot by the second unit in Almeria. The low-budget production was a world away from Hollywood. There were pay strikes, faulty power generators and no sanitary facilities. According to Leone's assistant, Tonino Valerii, the rental on the western town set still hadn't been paid months after the film was completed. Eastwood was amazed at the Italians' lack of western knowledge, pointing out that coonskin hats weren't suitable for a Mexican setting. While on location, Leone spotted a tree he thought would be perfect for the hanging tree at the beginning of the film, so the tree was dug up and relocated.

The San Miguel town set was the Hojo De Manzanares 'western village' near Colmenar Viejo, north of Madrid. The large adobe church was converted into the wooden Baxter house. At the opposite end of the street, a false front was super-imposed on an existing saloon building to become the Mexican Rojo residence, with a fake wall and gateway erected to make the property look like a *hacienda*. Franco Giraldi was Leone's second unit director, and he later used the town set for *Seven Guns for the MacGregors* (1965), in the scene where the water tower in the main street was blown up for the finale. It is interesting to see how other directors used the same set. In *Minnesota Clay* (1964), *Left-handed Johnny West* (1965) and *In a Colt's Shadow* (1966), the street is bustling with market stalls and locals going about their daily business, whereas in *Fistful* it is deserted. The graveyard was near the town set, while the Rio Bravo river (where Ramon's gang attack a Mexican Army convoy) was at Aldea Del Fresno (the 'Village of the Ash Trees') on the River Alberche. The desert riding sequences were shot in Almeria; the house where peasant girl Marisol was imprisoned by the Rojos still stands in San Jose – it is now a hotel called El Sotillo. The stranger's ride into the outskirts of San Miguel was filmed in the Spanish village of Los Albaricoques. Other sets, costumes and props were from the Zorro movies. A mine, where Zorro undergoes his 'transformation', reappears as the stranger's hideout. The bullet-ridden suits of conquistador armour that decorate the Rojo's house had once adorned the Californian governor's residence, while the Mexican courtyard and interiors were part of Casa De Campo, a rural museum in Madrid already used as a marketplace in *Zorro the Avenger* (1962).

The sunny locations are beautifully photographed by Massimo Dallamano. Unfortunately, some of the evening scenes are filmed day-for-night using filters. This is understandable on the low budget, but they cheapen *Fistful*'s look. Where filters were not used, the night scenes were more stylish, with Dallamano using torches and firelight to good effect. When the stranger is introduced to Ramon in a sunny courtyard, pieces of white fluff float across the scene, giving an arty, paradoxical 'snow' effect, while during a hostage exchange the cameraman uses dead leaves blowing in the wind, an image borrowed from *Yojimbo*.

Leone was not the most organised director, but Eastwood deemed the shoot on *The Magnificent Stranger* 'fun', with Leone wearing a cowboy hat and toy pistols on set and acting out the parts between takes. As was the custom for European westerns, the entire film was shot silent, so that it could be dubbed into various languages afterwards. On set the different nationalities could speak their native tongues, making it confusing for Eastwood, who didn't even speak Italian; some of the pauses in Eastwood's dialogue with foreign actors were a result of him making sure that they had finished their piece. Non-recording of sound would also result in the amplified soundtrack that Leone experimented with for the first time here. The crunch of boots, a whistling wind or a tolling bell could create an atmosphere even before any music was added. Traces of the poor English script remain in the English print ('This looks like the work of the Baxters'; 'He will bring you to your room'), but Eastwood seems to have erased most of the script that Bronson found so off-putting.

There was an ongoing argument between Leone and his star as to who was responsible for the stranger's unusual outfit. Eastwood claimed that he arrived in Rome with the entire costume in his luggage, but Leone said that he 'transformed' Rowdy Yates into the stranger. Though the boots, spurs and gunbelt were unwitting donations from *Rawhide*, it is presumed that the stubble, poncho and cigar were Leone's and designer Carlo Simi's idea, Eastwood being a non-smoker. Leone was particularly pleased to see Marlon Brando sporting a poncho in *Southwest to Sonora* (1966), noting that even great American stars were imitating his style (he had forgotten that Brando wore one in *One Eyed Jacks* in 1961). The poncho became synonymous with Eastwood, even though he only wears it for the opening scenes and the final shootout. The limited budget meant he only had one of everything on set throughout the shoot. Eastwood's clothing and props were one of the main features of the film. He was unshaven, he rode a scruffy-looking mule and permanently held a cigar between his teeth. His gestures were slow and deliberate – his head slowly rising to stare at a bad man, the poncho flicked over his shoulder for speed on the draw. But however slow his mannerisms were, his speed with a pistol was unsurpassed. As the posters claimed – 'He's probably the most dangerous man who ever lived'.

With James Bond, Eastwood's stranger is the prototype antihero of the early sixties. Steve McQueen and James Coburn had pioneered the strong, silent type in westerns (Coburn uttered a mere 14 words in *The Magnificent Seven*), but it took Eastwood to create a new breed of enigmatic gunslinger. Bond is suave and brutal, but also a ladies man and obviously contemporary, while Eastwood has very little to do with the opposite sex in the 'Dollars' films. In *Fistful* he saves Marisol from Ramon, alluding to a moment long ago when he knew someone like her, but there was no one to help. Other aspects from the Bond films are the frequent shootouts and the hero's dry sense of humour. Eastwood's deadpan asides contrast well with Volonte's cold Ramon Rojo. In the finale, the stranger cockily quotes Ramon's favourite Mexican proverb to the bandit, 'When a man with a .45 meets a man with a rifle, you said the man with the pistol's a dead man. Let's see if that's true.' The dark wit ties-in with the atmosphere of death in San Miguel: the village widows; the tolling Angelus bell summoning the stranger to town; the dead rider with 'Adios Amigo' scrawled across his back; the wreath where tavernkeeper Silvanito's roulette wheel used to be ('That too was murdered'); and the coffin the stranger uses for his clandestine exit from town. And in a cynical moment Ramon makes peace with the Baxters, reasoning, 'Life can be so precious. It's foolish to risk losing it every minute,' just after he's massacred two troops of cavalry and stolen a fortune in gold.

How the stranger survives the inferno of San Miguel is largely down to Silvanito and Piripero, who work well as comic relief. Silvanito tries to frighten the stranger out of town and warns him to keep away from Marisol, Ramon's girl. The tavernkeeper throws away his shotgun in the final frame of the movie, disgusted that he has been drawn into the conflict. The undertaker Piripero is happy to be the only person in town to have regular work and takes the violence a lot less seriously. Business has never been so 'healthy' and the ongoing gag about the coffin-maker's prosperity is a good example of Leone's black humour. Piripero sneaks the stranger out of town, steals him back his gunbelt and some dynamite, but can't watch the final shootout; he's not entirely convinced of the stranger's invincibility. He even gives Eastwood a name, calling him 'Joe', but promotional material preserved the mystique of the character, always referring to him as 'the man with no name'.

The success of these two characters is down to two excellent performances from Jose 'Pepe' Calvo (Silvanito) and 'Joe Edger' (Piripero). Calvo was a Spaniard who had been in the industry since the early fifties, appearing in some of the earliest spaghettis, including *The Terrible Sheriff* (1963), a case of truth in advertising, which managed to incorporate the super-strength magic potion from *Asterix*. Calvo's likeable performance in *Fistful* is enhanced by his resemblance to Gepetto, the genial puppet-maker in *Pinocchio*. Austrian Edger (real name Josef Egger), an even more eccentric performer, was born in 1889. He was 75 when *Fistful* was shot and Leone's sequel, *For a Few Dollars More*, was his last film appearance. He looks like a grizzled, skinnier Walter Brennan – an irascible old-timer with a cackling laugh and an old-fashioned sense of justice. These two eccentrics, plus the mocking bellringer, give the locals an earthiness, contrasting with Eastwood's supercool hero.

Eastwood and Leone both knew what they wanted from the stranger's character. The other actors in the movie are far more expressive (Volonte was a stage actor) and this, coupled with the sudden violence, the sound effects (gunshots, horses neighing, rifles being cocked, the whistling wind, a cat screeching) and Ennio Morricone's score, creates some explosive scenes. In the middle of the action, Eastwood is

'My mule don't like people laughing': The stranger guns down the opposition in *A Fistful of Dollars* (1964); Clint Eastwood (with Antonio Molino Rojo and Lorenzo Robledo) on the western set at Hojo De Manzanares.

always impassive. In each of the Leone films his character would slip up and pay the consequences; in the first two a considerable beating, in the third a very bad case of sunburn. But it made his character more human, in contrast to his superhuman ability with a gun. It also ensured that the hero being tortured was a staple ingredient of the spaghetti-western formula and a feature of Eastwood's later films. One of the main complaints about *Fistful* was the violence, resulting in a plethora of cuts, and even by today's standards the 97-minute uncut version is brutal. In the full version, Eastwood's beating is much longer: he is punched, kicked, has tequila poured in his wounds and a cigar butt stubbed out on his hand. This beating exemplifies two things about his tormentors. Firstly, it takes the whole gang to beat him up, as he is more than a match for them individually. Secondly, it defines the distinction between the stranger's intelligence and the stupidity of the locals. Chico, the Rojo's dumb, fat henchman stamps on the stranger's left hand, when he shoots with his right.

Much of the appeal of Eastwood's character lies in his mercenary motivation and his laid-back style. He has no qualms about collecting money for killing, can easily outwit his opponents and his marksmanship is far superior to the bootleggers and gunrunners. As one critic said, the hero is no longer the best shot, but the best shot is the hero. He is also emotionless – critics termed it 'wooden'. When Eastwood smiles in *Fistful*, it is never a righteous smile, but rather a sneer of satisfaction, as when he knocks Chico out with the storeroom door. At drama school Eastwood was told, 'don't just say something – stand there', and it was with the stranger rather than Rowdy Yates that he achieved this. On set, there were communication problems, as neither Eastwood nor Leone spoke each other's language and had to rely on interpreters. But as Eastwood pared down his own dialogue he had the perfect milieu to experiment with the 'dynamic lethargy' that became his trademark.

As an intruder to the community, the stranger is conspicuous by his appearance. He attempts to look Mexican, but still looks out of place among the riff-raff of San Miguel. His 'welcome' to town epitomises the locals' insular attitude to strangers. Three Baxter men (Lorenzo Robledo, Antonio Molino Rojo and Luis Barboo) confront him as he rides into town, one cackling, 'It's not smart to go wandering so far from home'. The trio laughs at the stranger as he is told that he could find work as a scarecrow, Robledo adding, 'The crows are liable to scare him, maybe'. The stranger doesn't go for his gun as the trio draw theirs and spook his mule with gunshots. The animal speeds off down the street and the stranger grabs the sign outside Silvanito's tavern to stop himself being thrown. The scene has an epilogue when the stranger impresses Don Miguel (and proves that he is not scared of crows) by gunning down four of the Baxters (the aforementioned trio, plus Julio Perez Taberno) because: 'My mule don't like people laughing. Gets the crazy idea you're laughing at him.' These scenes are like nothing previously seen in a western. The hero is taciturn yet humorous, the villains particularly offensive and the gunplay larger than life. Baxter's gunmen wear classic western garb (straight out of a Hollywood wardrobe department), which contrast with the stranger's poncho.

The wisecrack by Eastwood at the end of the scene is memorable. Before the duel, the stranger orders three coffins from Piripero, but finds himself gunning down four men. 'My mistake,' he tells Piripero, as he walks back down the street, 'four coffins.'

The Christian religious symbolism and folklore superstition often associated with Italian westerns also began with *Fistful*. The stranger's mule, his beating and his 'resurrection' point towards an Easter subtext, as does the raucous replay of a 'Last Supper' at the Rojos' *hacienda* before the bloodletting. The peasant family (Julio, Marisol and their son Jesus) are later saved by an 'angel'. The desert landscape could easily be the Holy Land, and though there is a church in San Miguel, we never see a priest, only a bellringer and an undertaker – all that matters in such a godforsaken place. As the stranger notes, 'Never saw a town as dead as this one'. Silvanito is more concerned with superstition and ghosts. He tells the stranger that the grave chosen for the ruse with the soldiers is a bad choice, as it belongs to the only man to ever die of pneumonia in San Miguel (rather than 'lead poisoning'). During the annihilation of the Baxters, Consuela curses Ramon, hoping the bandit will die spitting blood. Her prophetic wish comes true in the finale, when the stranger appears to be an indestructible ghost, goading Ramon with the mantra, 'The heart Ramon. Don't forget the heart. Aim for the heart or you'll never stop me.'

Of all the film's accomplishments, the most innovative was the soundtrack and Ennio Morricone's groundbreaking composition is still popular today. In 1965 it won the Italian Film Journalists' Silver Ribbon for 'Best Score'. Morricone had been at school with Leone (at the Institute of Saint Juan Baptiste de la Salle) and became a pop-song arranger in the early sixties, having graduated from the Santa Cecilia Conservatory in Rome. Morricone maintains that he drifted into film-scoring: 'I thought a filmmaker must call me because he thinks what I write is fine…so it happened that a director called me, then another, and another'. He scored some of the earliest spaghettis, including *Gunfight in the Red Sands* (1963) and *Pistols Don't Argue* (1964), but Leone wasn't keen on Morricone's previous scores. Morricone had prepared an arrangement of Woody Guthrie's folk song 'Pastures of Plenty' ('To pastures of plenty, from dry desert ground. We come with the dust and are gone – with the wind') with Peter Tevis on vocals. Leone liked this much better. The arrangement used a variety of whip-cracks (like Frankie Laine's title songs to *Rawhide* and *Bullwhip*) and electric guitar lines, strung along a repetitive acoustic guitar riff. Morricone removed Tevis's vocals and rearranged the piece in collaboration with Leone. *Fistful*'s main theme is structured like a pop song. A whistler takes the 'verse' melody, while a guitar leads the 'chorus'. After the first verse, which is simply the whistler accompanied by an acoustic guitar, a series of sound effects (whiplashes, gunshots and bells) are incorporated, along with the Alessandroni Singers chanting 'We defy' and 'With the wind' (from 'Pastures of Plenty'). Alessandro Alessandroni, the leader of the choir named I Cantori Moderni (The Modern Singers), also provided the guitar playing and whistling on the track. This extraordinary sound, coupled with Lardani's title sequence, make for a startling beginning to the movie. Whining ricochets herald Clint Eastwood's name, while animated action scenes from the film (an effect called rotoscope) play in silhouette in the background.

Morricone uses a piano riff, drums and flute trills to accentuate the stranger's actions and dialogue, while the other important theme is the slow trumpet piece played by Michele Lacerenza (backed by the choir and a strummed guitar). Subsequently much copied and owing plenty to the trumpet-led 'Deguello', this style of 'mariachi' trumpet playing became a cliché of Italian westerns, Lacerenza himself using it in his own scores. Morricone put much more effort into his work for Leone, so that every scene has a different composition (or variation on a theme), with the melody taken by a whistler, guitar, harmonica or flute. Other composers simply reused the same main theme over again. Consequently, Morricone's sound-track albums contain a small proportion of the music recorded and sometimes pieces that don't appear in the film at all.

The producers of *Fistful* were cautious: they were aware that they had an 'Italian western' on their hands, so the cast and crew adopted Americanised pseudonyms – not for the export market, but to conceal their identities for Italian release. It was better if domestic audiences thought the film a genuine American one. Leone called himself 'Bob Robertson', Morricone 'Dan Savio', while cast-members took similar measures. Leone's pseudonym was particularly creative. His father, Vincenzo Leone had earlier directed films under the name Roberto Roberti – Leone's *nom de plume* was literally Bob Robert's son. Most of the German performers didn't bother to, due to the success of the 'Winnetou' films. For audiences to believe the movie was a Karl May spin-off could only be beneficial. No reason was given for Leone's change of title from *Il Magnifico Straniero* to *Per Un Pugno di Dollari*, though this intro-duced a reference to Howard Hawks's *Rio Bravo*, which was shown in Italy as *Un Dollaro d'Onore* ('A Dollar of Honour'). Leone managed to slip *Rio Bravo* into *Fistful* – it's the name of the river where the gold robbery takes place. Eventually the producers decided that *The Magnificent Stranger* was perhaps a little too derivative of *The Magnificent Seven*. Its eventual Italian release title, *Per un Pugno di Dollari* ('For A Fistful of Dollars') sounded better, suggesting brutal action and money.

Trendsetting Italian production company Jolly Film (with Spanish-based Tecisa) had already financed and released a spaghetti western in 1963. *Gunfight in the Red Sands* was the story of gunman Riccardo Martinez (nicknamed Gringo), who returns home to find his father murdered and their gold strike stolen by a trio of local Americans (disguised as Mexicans). Inevitably Gringo tracks the killers down, and in a final showdown faces the corrupt, Mexican-hating sheriff in the main street of Carterville (the 'San Miguel' set). *Red Sands* cast-members Daniel Martin, Jose Calvo and Aldo Sambrell appeared in *Fistful*, though one actor who failed to make it into *Fistful* was the film's star, Richard Harrison. If Eastwood was catlike and grace-ful, Harrison was lumbering and ponderous. Most of the participants in *Red Sands* used pseudonymous – some were unimaginative ('Ald Sambrell'), some misleading

('Telly Thomas'). Ennio Morricone's early score was reedy and weak, using only a few instruments and no choir. Having not been particularly successful with *Red Sands*, Jolly were hoping for a greater return on their next western ventures.

Jolly and Constantin made another western concurrently with *Fistful*, called *Pistols Don't Argue* (also known as *Bullets Don't Argue*) starring 54-year-old Rod Cameron. Cameron starred as Pat Garrett, the Sheriff of Rivertown, who has his wedding day interrupted when Billy and George Clanton rob the local bank. Garrett tracks them to Mexico and most of the film is devoted to the trio's trek back across the desert (Devils Valley) and their battle with a Mexican bandit gang. *Pistols* was very old-fashioned (the US cavalry ride to Garrett's rescue at the climax), and with hindsight it seems incredible to think that the producers had a higher regard for this film than *Fistful*. The only interesting aspects of *Pistols* were the locations (including the town set, which Leone reused) and Morricone's score. Without Leone's visuals to inspire him, the music is average, but does hint at a talent to compose a catchy tune. *Pistols* has a traditional title song ('Lonesome Billy', sung by Peter Tevis), but it introduces the villainous Billy, rather than the hero. Packed with clichés and awful rhymes, the lyrics read: 'A rough man who plays with danger, to whom trouble was no stranger'. No wonder Leone wanted a lyric-free title theme.

'When a man with a .45 meets a man with a rifle': the stranger (Clint Eastwood) faces Ramon in the finale to *A Fistful of Dollars* (1964).

After the *Fistful* shoot, Eastwood returned to the US, still believing he appeared in *The Magnificent Stranger*, and presumed that he would never hear of it again. *A Fistful of Dollars* was released in Italy in September 1964, with no publicity, but soon became a huge countrywide hit. *Pistols Don't Argue* was released two weeks before it, and has been little seen since. Leone's film received its Rome premier in November and went on to outgross the two big hits of the year: *My Fair Lady* and *Mary Poppins*. In an interview, Sophia Loren asked an American journalist who was this 'Clint Eastwood', the latest star in Italy, who was giving Marcello Mastroianni a run for his money. Eastwood then read a piece in *Variety* on the popularity of Italian westerns in Europe, due to the outstanding returns on *A Fistful of Dollars*. Having checked a couple of days later, he suddenly realised that it was his stranger who was the magnificent success.

By 1971 *Fistful* had grossed over three billion lira in Italy. Its runaway success resulted in a slew of imitations and rip-offs in the period 1965–67. The most successful examples (*Django*, *The Hills Run Red* and *Django Kill*) all owed something to *Fistful*, but literally dozens of variations appeared. *Fistful* started to make an impact in Italy in 1965, but it was in 1966 that the floodgates really opened. Titular derivatives included *For a Fist in the Eye* (1965 – a comedy starring Franco Franchi and Ciccio Ingrassia), *Ramon the Mexican* (1966), *El Rojo* (1966 – starring Richard Harrison) and many films with 'dollars' in the title. Duccio Tessari used several aspects of *Fistful* in his own westerns. These include the shots of the bell tower and the significance of coffins and funerals, which Tessari reused in *The Return of Ringo* (1965). The incredible appearance of Eastwood through the dusty dynamite explosions was restaged in *Return* when Ringo materialises in the middle of a sandstorm. In *Fistful* Silvanito uses inanimate objects to illustrate the central conflict in town: a jug represents the Baxters, a bottle for the Rojos (the liquor merchants) and a cork is the stranger; Ringo in *A Pistol for Ringo* (1965) demonstrates his escape plan to bandit leader Sancho using a bowl of fruit on a tablecloth map.

By far the most obvious *Fistful* derivatives were the 'Stranger' quartet (1966–75) starring Tony Anthony. In *A Stranger in Town* (1966 – also called *For a Dollar in the Teeth*), Anthony copied Eastwood's mannerisms, while director Luigi Vanzi reused Leone's plot. Anthony's costume even incorporated the trademark poncho, as he faced a bandit named Aguila (the Eagle), played by Frank Wolff. Significantly, *Stranger* was an Italian/US co-production, but the film worked better as a very poor parody of *Fistful* (even down to the railcar breastplate finale) and was an unexpected hit at the US box office.

The next film, *The Stranger Returns* (1967 – also released as *Shoot First, Laugh Last* and *A Man, A Horse, A Gun*) was an acid-trip of a western, powered along by Stelvio Cipriani's score, complete with whip-cracks, electric guitars and echoing screams. Far more polished than its predecessor, *The Stranger Returns* told how the stranger tracked down a goatee-bearded bandit named 'En Plein' ('dead centre' –

he never misses). The bandits have stolen a solid-gold stagecoach and Anthony tracks them down to the town of Santo Spirito. He is captured, dragged around town behind the stagecoach and then plays 'matador' to the stagecoach's 'bull', as the bandits try to run him over. If *The Stranger in Japan* (1969) was self-explanatory (an East-meets-West scenario), then *Get Mean* (1975) certainly wasn't. Here, the stranger travels to Spain into a surreal medieval world where the Baxters and Rojos became the Barbarians and the Moors. The 'Stranger' films were advertised by MGM as 'The living and dying-end in excitement!' and made Anthony a world-wide star.

A Fistful of Dollars was abridged for its international release, like all Leone's subsequent films. Various versions of the film exist for the UK and US market, usually involving one or more of the following omissions or abridgements: the stranger's beating; the barrel-crushing sequence; Ramon hitting Silvanito with a Winchester; Esteban spitting in the barman's ear; Ramon and Esteban's death scenes; and Silvanito having his mouth burned by a cigar. The Baxter massacre was chopped to pieces. The uncut version of the slaughter is a full-blown shootout, the camera lingering on the laughing Rojo boys and the burning bodies lying in the street, while the death of Consuela is sometimes missing completely. In addition to these cuts, Monte Hellman shot an explanatory pre-title sequence for the film, shown only on US TV. Here, the stranger (an Eastwood stand-in) is released from prison by the governor (Harry Dean Stanton) provided he cleans up San Miguel in sixty days, which gave Eastwood's hero an added motivation that he didn't need.

Though *Fistful* was released in West Germany and Spain in 1965, legal problems concerning *Yojimbo* ensured that it didn't make it to the US until January 1967. Kurosawa claimed copyright infringement on his original story and was allowed distribution rights in Japan as compensation. The international rights were secured by United Artists, who gave it an expensive, eye-catching publicity campaign. The advertisement lines read, 'This is the first motion picture of its kind, it won't be the last!', an accurate prediction, as they already had the sequel to release later that year. Eastwood's stranger was dubbed 'the man with no name' in the US and the UK. Elsewhere he was known as 'The fastest draw in Italian cinema'. In Italy he was 'Joe, il Straniero' or 'Il Cigarillo', while in South America he was 'Los Pistolero con Los Ojos Verde' ('the gunman with green eyes'). But American critics pre-dominantly hated Eastwood and his violent, badly dubbed adversaries. Judith Crist in the *New York World Journal Tribune* called *Fistful* a 'cheapjack production' that 'misses both awfulness and mediocrity', while Andrew Sarris in *The Village Voice* thought that 'the dialogue must have been written between cocktails on the Via Veneto'.

The 'Man With No Name' epithet stuck with Eastwood throughout his career. A review of *Two Mules for Sister Sara* (1970) even billed him as 'the nameless drifter, Hogan'. American and British critics largely chose to ignore *Fistful*'s release, few recognising its satirical humour or groundbreaking style, preferring to trash the shoddy production values, shaky sets and the dubbing (described as a 'Mexican mummerset'). But it was obvious that Eastwood's stranger had struck a chord with the public – *Fistful* took an impressive $3.5 million on its first US release, even though it had an 'X' rating. Crowds flocked to see him, making the hero who 'sold lead in exchange for gold' a worldwide phenomenon, ensuring that Eastwood would never dig swimming pools, bomb giant spiders or act with a horse wearing lip-gloss ever again.

2

'It's a Matter of Principle'

— Duccio Tessari's *A Pistol for Ringo* (1965)

A Pistol for Ringo (1965)
original title: *Una Pistola per Ringo*
Credits
DIRECTOR – Duccio Tessari
PRODUCERS – Luciano Ercoli and Alberto Pugliesi
STORY AND SCREENPLAY – Duccio Tessari
SET DRESSING AND COSTUMES – Carlo Gentili
EDITING – Licia Quaglia
DIRECTOR OF PHOTOGRAPHY – Francisco Marin
MUSIC COMPOSER – Ennio Morricone
MUSIC CONDUCTOR – Bruno Nicolai
Interiors filmed at PC Balcazar Productions, Barcelona
Techniscope/Technicolor
An Italian/Spanish co-production
Produzioni Cinematografiche Mediterranee (Rome)/
    Producciones Cinematograficas Balcazar (Barcelona)
Released internationally by Miracle Films (UK)/Embassy
    Films (US)
Cast
    'Montgomery Wood', Giuliano Gemma (Ringo, alias
    'Angel Face'); 'Hally Hammond', Lorella De Luca (Miss
    Ruby); Fernando Sancho (Sancho); Antonio Casas (Major
    Clyde); Nieves Navarro (Dolores); 'George Martin', Jorge
    Martin (Ben, the sheriff); Jose Manuel Martin (Pedro);
    'Pajarito', Murriz Brandariz (Tim, the deputy); Pablito
    Alonso (Chico, the Mexican boy); 'Paco Sanz', Francisco
    Sanz (the colonel); Juan Casalilla (Mr Jenkinson, the
    bank director); Juan Torres (Henry, the bank clerk);
    Nazzareno Zamperla and Jose Halufi (Sancho's

henchmen); Franco Pesce (Quemado storekeeper); Duccio Tessari (bandit)

*   *   *

While *A Fistful of Dollars* outgrossed all-comers at the Italian box office, Leone's scriptwriter Duccio Tessari embarked on his own western project. Tessari was already a screenwriter and director of some repute. He had directed the action-packed *Sons of Thunder* (1962 – also called *My Son the Hero*) and co-written the best of the muscleman 'sword and sandal' pictures, including Leone's *The Colossus of Rhodes* (1960), Sergio Corbucci's *Romulus and Remus* (1961) and Vittorio Cottafavi's *Hercules Conquers Atlantis* (1961). He also contributed to the scripts for two horror/epic hybrids – Sergio Corbucci's *Goliath and the Vampires* (1961) and Mario Bava's *Hercules in the Haunted World* (1961). The first starred one-time Las Vegas lifeguard Gordon Scott (as Goliath) battling Kobrak the Vampire, who is aided by an army of faceless zombies. *Hercules in the Haunted World*, with Reg Park (an ex-Mr Universe), saw Hercules pitted against Lico (Christopher Lee), a satanist who has bewitched Hercules's lover, Deianara. Wildly plotted, it is an amazing 90 minutes, with Hercules fighting a stone demon (an extra in a rubber suit) and flattening airborne ghouls as they emerge from cobweb-draped coffins. Tessari proved with this type of film that he was adept at scripting way-out fantasies, but when he began directing, he tempered this outlandish approach.

After his epics, Tessari directed two James Bond derivatives, including *The Sphinx Smiles Before Death* (1964), before contributing to the *Yojimbo* rewrite on *Fistful*. He then co-wrote Franco Giraldi's comedy spaghetti western, *Seven Guns for the MacGregors* (1965). The film reused the San Miguel set from *Fistful* (here named 'El Rojo' in honour of Leone's movie) and some of Leone's cast, noticeably Antonio Molino Rojo as a sheriff who looks remarkably like John Baxter. *Seven Guns* details the exploits of an elderly family of Scottish pioneers and their seven sons, but makes sure the comedy is finely judged, poking fun at the genre, without resorting to outright parody. This is illustrated by the opening sequence, where a raiding party of Mexican bandits attack the aged ranchers while their sons are away. Expecting easy pickings, the bandits soon find themselves completely outwitted, one commenting, 'Sure ain't been working out the way we figured'. The bandits storm the house, but the seven sons ride back to save their folks; the Mexicans find themselves trapped in the house and are subsequently wiped out. This scene exemplifies Tessari's attitude to the western. Not only is there the violence of the reinvented west of Leone, but also a charm to the humour. Later, Mexican bandit leader Santillana 'relaxes' by watching his men drag a rancher through a fire, burning him to death, while one of his gang complains, 'These Gringos are much too soft'.

When Tessari began work on *A Pistol for Ringo*, his first western as director, he took a different approach to Leone. Instead of concentrating on a single hero, who appears in virtually every scene, Tessari would have several main characters. He also proved Leone wrong; the prominent female protagonists in the 'Ringo' films add to the narrative, rather than slowing down the action, as Leone claimed. Writing a plot for Ringo, Tessari worked by himself and the story was more involving than *Fistful*. In the days leading up to Christmas, a Mexican bandit gang led by Sancho clean out the Quemado bank. As they escape, Sancho is wounded, so they hole-up in a nearby ranch and take the owners (Major Clyde and his daughter Ruby – the sheriff's fiancée) hostage. With the siege a stand-off, the sheriff hires adventurer Ringo to infiltrate the ranch, save the captives and recover the money. Deceptively simple when reduced to such a résumé, this premise could have been the plot for a hackneyed Hollywood 'B-western'. But it was Tessari's emphasis on character, rather than action, that set his film apart.

Tessari's script (like the original *Fistful* script) is packed with familiar western language, including a deputy's immortal opinion of Ringo's marksmanship – 'That was mighty fancy trigger-work'. This time Tessari stuck to his guns and let the clichés stay in the finished film; Eastwood had edited such poeticisms from the *Fistful* script. At one point, Ringo offers his 'kingdom for a gun', only to be told that Shakespeare has beaten him to the quote. Tessari has an old Texas saying as a credo for the movie – 'God created men equal, it was the six-gun that made 'em different' – though the proverb is misquoted. The actual maxim is 'God created man, but it was Sam Colt's revolver that made him equal'.

Tessari used a character name familiar from classic American westerns. The name 'Ringo' had cropped up many times, notably in *Stagecoach* (1939) and *The Gunfighter* (1950). Tessari wanted to call Eastwood's character in *Fistful* Ringo, but Leone vetoed it. Tessari also recalled real-life gunslinger Johnny Ringo, who was one of the deadliest shootists of all time. He had a serious drinking problem (which Tessari chose to ignore) and was well educated – he was known to quote Shakespeare (as he does in Tessari's film). But Johnny Ringo was a bad man and was involved in the ambush on Virgil Earp in Tombstone, shortly after the gunfight at the OK Corral. In John Sturges's 1957 version of the gunfight, John Ireland played Ringo.

For the starring role of Ringo (also known as 'Angel Face'), Tessari hired a young actor already established as a spaghetti-western star – Giuliano Gemma. Gemma had appeared in a towel in the background of the Roman baths sequence of *Ben Hur* (1959) and in Luchino Visconti's *The Leopard* (1961). Then he landed the lead in Tessari's action-packed epic *Sons of Thunder* as Krios, the youngest and most acrobatic of the Titans. Gemma also appeared in pedestrian muscleman movies like *Revolt of the Praetorians* (1964), which featured Richard Harrison as a mysterious avenger who terrorises the neighbourhood wearing a wolf mask. By then, Gemma had made some of the first Italian westerns – *One Silver Dollar* (1965) and *Adios Gringo* (1965). In both films he played a wronged man who must identify and track down those responsible. Both were pretty average films, though they did merit international release and Gemma made a competent enough hero.

He was romantically teamed in both vehicles with Ida Galli (or 'Evelyn Stewart') and both films' entire casts are pseudonymous – Gemma's cover being 'Montgomery Wood'. In these two films, Gemma honed his screen persona. He was very much the Burt Lancaster of Cinecitta movies (Lancaster was his idol). Gemma diffused any situation with a broad grin and frequently indulged in acrobatics and fisticuffs. It was during these early westerns that Gemma perfected his trademark way of mounting a horse, grabbing hold of the saddle horn and hoisting himself aboard in one smooth movement.

Tessari's other lead was 49-year-old Fernando Sancho as bandito Sancho. Spanish-born Sancho had already made over one hundred films in his native country before he was cast in *A Pistol for Ringo*. Between 1944 and 1965, he played all sorts of roles, including several small parts in big-budget international blockbusters shot in Spain. He was a madman (to Jeffrey Hunter's Jesus) in the epic *King of Kings* (1961) and a brutal Turkish sergeant in *Lawrence of Arabia* (1962). He also surfaced in Italian genre movies, including a *Lawrence of Arabia* parody: *Toto of Arabia* (1964) and *Sons of Thunder*. But he was ideal for westerns and appeared in several of the earliest examples. Sancho went on to amass an impressive list of credits, nearly always as a bandit (and often named 'Sancho').

Back in 1964, Sancho initially made the biggest impact as General Ortiz in Sergio Corbucci's *Minnesota Clay*. For the first time Corbucci showed an interest in a self-proclaimed Mexican general, who lives in squalor, but who also has the out-of-place trappings of wealth scattered around him, like a demented pirate king. Ortiz has a huge treasure-chest full of jewels and a golden throne. This was matched by the general's appearance – an overly decorated army jacket, a bandoleer, a droopy moustache and sombrero. Sancho's 'pirate swagger' owed much to an earlier Cinecitta fad, initiated by Gianna Maria Canale's *Queen of the Pirates* (1960) – swashbuckling adventures set in the Caribbean. Franco Giraldi then cast him in *Seven Guns*, and it was clear Sancho had found his niche. He again appeared in his general's outfit (by now a trademark), but there was a strong element of sadistic humour introduced into the character. Sancho took a western staple and created the Italian western villain, *par excellence* – a fat, greedy Mexican bandit who laughs when he shoots people; low-budget spaghetti westerns caught on to this character very quickly. One thing was sure – whatever role Sancho played over the next few years, you could guarantee he would be full of holes by 'The End'.

Tessari cast Sancho's lieutenant from *Minnesota Clay*, Jose Manuel Martin, in the same capacity in *Pistol* and gave him all the best lines. Martin was a supporting player who featured in many westerns, including *Django Shoots First* (1966) – in which he appeared briefly as a bounty-hunter named Ringo. Lorella De Luca, who played Ruby, had appeared in muscleman epics, like *Sign of the Gladiator* (1958 – co-scripted by Leone), usually as a princess or slave-girl; she debuted in Fellini's *The Swindle* (1955), had a stint as a showgirl on an Italian quiz show (*Il Musichiere*) and then moved into Italian films, becoming the popular epitome of the 'sweetie' style.

Angel Face: Giuliano Gemma as gunfighter Ringo in Duccio Tessari's *A Pistol for Ringo* (1965).

Her biggest hit was *Poor But Handsome* (1957), but her popularity waned in the early sixties. Spaniard Antonio Casas played the ageing aristocrat Major Clyde. Following an injury when playing football for Athletico Madrid, Casas turned to acting in 1942. He appeared in some of the early spaghettis: *Ride and Kill* (1963) and *Minnesota Clay*.

Tessari filled out the other roles with a variety of character actors, including stuntman Nazzareno Zamperla and Jose Halufi. Spanish character actor 'Pajarito' (real name Murriz Brandariz) portrayed the ex-Confederate deputy Tim, while perennial villain Paco Sanz had a cameo as the evil, cigar-smoking colonel, whose only solution to the siege is to send for the cavalry. Youngster Pablito Alonso gave the least embarrassing performance by a child actor in a spaghetti, while small roles were taken by Franco Pesce (later the undertaker in the 'Sartana' movies), Juan Torres (a regular in Balcazar productions) and Tessari himself (as one of Sancho's gang).

Tessari based his setting, the town of Quemado (meaning 'sunburnt' in Spanish), on a real town situated in New Mexico towards the western border with Arizona. Tessari's Quemado was the Producciones Cinematograficas Balcazar 'wild west' town set at Esplugues De Llobregat, near Barcelona. The film was a co-production deal between PC Balcazar and the Rome-based Produzioni Cinematografiche Mediterranee. The location scenes were shot in the *ramblas* (dried-up riverbeds) of Almeria and in San Jose, around the Spanish *hacienda* used for Major Clyde's ranch – the *finca* ('country house') of El Romeral. The windmill on the hill in San Jose (used for the sheriff's HQ) still stands, though the sails have long since rotted away.

Ringo is a less serious performance than Gemma's early westerns, and he certainly looks confident in the role. In an interview Gemma described Ringo as a little like Krios in *Sons of Thunder*, stating that he was simply in a different costume and a different setting – the character was essentially the same. This exemplifies how easily the production staff and cast could move between genres without changes in motivation or acting style. As with all film crazes the actors, plots and sets were often the same – only the names changed. Gemma could be called Ringo, Gringo, Arizona, Brett or Gary but he would still be the same character. Far from belittling Gemma's acting, this reiterates how underrated the performers at Cinecitta were. Gemma was as convincing in a 'sword and sandal' fantasy as in his western roles, with his appeal transcending genres.

Apart from Ringo, Tessari deployed five main characters: Ben, the sheriff; his fiancée, Ruby; her father, Major Clyde; bandit leader, Sancho; and his girlfriend, Dolores. The sheriff is a rarity for the Italian genre – an honest, incorruptible lawman. Spanish actor Jorge Martin portrayed him in the Hollywood mould, square-jawed and law-abiding. He is engaged to Ruby, but she's an eastern girl, he's a frontiersman (unfamiliar with her civilised ways). Moreover, he comes across as none too bright, unused to the double-dealing, violence and betrayal the situation calls for – which luckily is Ringo's forte. Ruby's childlike innocence is a gradual revelation, with Tessari initially presenting her as a cliché (in this case the 'sheriff's girl'), but slowly unveiling more of her temperament, from the scenes of quiet domesticity to her contribution to the action-packed finale. Ruby (called Ruth in some prints) loves the sheriff, but later cannot acknowledge that her father can also fall in love, especially with a peasant bandit's girl. Even so, she slowly falls under the spell of a charming gunman. Early on, Ringo tells her jokingly, 'If you're thinking of kissing me, don't', something that obviously doesn't appeal to her in the least. Later Ruby does kiss him, beguiled by his easygoing manner, while Gemma pulls his best 'gee shucks' expression to the camera.

Widower Major Clyde 'lives in a dream world' and represents the bourgeoisie. There are references to his stint in the Lancers, and he is much travelled around Europe. The major attempts to 'civilise' Dolores, treating her to the finer things in life. The final straw for Ruby is seeing the señorita in one of her mother's dresses, making Dolores's 'transformation' complete. This was a spaghetti-western variant of Hitchcock's *Vertigo*, though an even more contemporary reference was the scene in *My Fair Lady* (a huge hit in Italy) in which Eliza (Audrey Hepburn) descends a staircase, now transformed into a lady. Tessari's homage even had Fernando Sancho standing in for Rex Harrison and the major impersonating Pickering. Sancho and Dolores are the antithesis of the major and Ruby – amoral brutality to their 'genteel' domesticity. Sancho's bandita Dolores is fascinated by 'civilisation', but never able to comprehend it.

A key aspect of Tessari's work is his employment of American western clichés. By making his characters archetypes from Hollywood movies (the 'honest sheriff', the 'sheriff's girl', the 'greedy Mexican bandit' and his sneering sidekick), Tessari approaches *Pistol* as an homage to American westerns. Tessari has a lot of fun staging familiar western situations and enjoys the interplay between the characters. He also likes making his 'walking clichés' behave in unusual ways. Ignorant bandits, with no idea of etiquette, dine in luxury – the question not being which item of cutlery to use, but which hand. The land-owner, usually a hardened veteran of the frontier, a man at one with the land, in Tessari's hands is a cultured and cowardly aristocrat, a man at one with Dom Perignon. The Hollywood sheriff's girl is a school-ma'm or young Quaker woman who falls in love with the hero and bolsters a subplot involving the hero hanging up his guns and settling down. He 'realises the error of his ways' and she domesticates him. But Tessari is not interested in the normal resolution of these hackneyed plot devices. In *Pistol*, Ringo doesn't 'get the girl'. Instead, he gets a pistol.

Ringo is an easygoing gunman who just seems to find trouble. He finds it easy to kill, though only in self-defence. Throughout his stay at the ranch we learn some autobiographical details. He committed his first killing aged seven and his father fought in the Civil War, but like the heroes of *The Good, the Bad and the Ugly*, his father switched sides to his own advantage. Ringo lives by a personal maxim, the oft-repeated 'It's a matter of principle'. This credo seems to be his excuse for everything – from playing cards to blackmail – but there is an irony in the phrase, as he is unprincipled in his pursuit of dollars; he saves the hostages for a percentage of the stolen money. The hero having a catchphrase runs through Tessari's *oeuvre*. Gregor MacGregor (Robert Woods), in *Seven Guns*, has the motto, 'If my hunch is right', while in *The Return of Ringo*, Ringo says 'I'll explain later', throughout the film.

Compared to the succinct hero of Leone's film, Ringo is mighty talkative, especially when he first arrives at the ranch. The bandits ask him for his gun and he answers, 'I don't even own one'. He tells the gang that he was in jail for horse-stealing, but he escaped because he didn't like the food. His boyish looks and self-effacing manner make his story all the more convincing, and like Eastwood's stranger, he can manipulate the gang to his own ends. But he is caught and beaten – even though his elaborate plan seems infallible, Sancho is smarter. Ringo looks like a traditional western hero, though his mannerisms include a shrug of the shoulders (an expression of Italian 'machismo' more often associated with gangsters) and a flashier style of riding. Another feature borrowed from American westerns was the fact that Ringo drinks only milk, just like James Stewart's deputy in *Destry Rides Again* (1939). In jail Ringo asks for a glass of milk, but the deputy offers him a slug of whisky. Ringo declines, claiming that liquor 'deadens the eye and makes your hand shake', a sentiment that recalls the clean-cut cowboy heroes of the forties and fifties dispensing their home-spun philosophies (even to stars like Eastwood, offering health tips) and it is this kind of stereotype that both fascinated and amused Tessari.

Uniquely for spaghetti westerns, *Pistol* takes place within a definite time-scale, beginning on the morning of 23 December 1894 and ending with the bandits' chaotic escape attempt on Christmas Day morning. Each day is clearly mapped out, with the murders of the *rancheros* by Sancho and his men 'punctuating' the days. The killings are imaginatively done, with each more ingenious than the last, including a round of 'Mexican roulette'. Bandit Pedro lines up the farm hands and tells them, 'The sun's going down. That means one of you is gonna die.' He says that he will let fate decide who it is, while another bandit loads a revolver with one bullet. 'He don't know,' sneers Pedro, 'I don't know, you don't know. No one can be blamed.' But these scenes jar with the more traditional aspects of the story.

The Christmas setting is effective, as it is not a time of year usually associated with westerns. Cowboys walking down the street carrying Christmas trees and presents is incongruous and unique to the film. The opening scene of *Pistol* establishes the seasonal setting, whilst illustrating Tessari's sidelong view of the genre. Two cowboys (Chuck and Hank) stand face to face in the main street of Quemado. They walk towards each other, but instead of drawing, they shake hands and wish each other 'Happy Christmas'. The Christmas setting also adds pathos to the story. Tim comments during the siege, 'It's Christmas, day after tomorrow. What a beautiful way to celebrate,' while earlier a Mexican boy has been overjoyed to see visitors arriving for Christmas, only to discover that the *rancheros* are suddenly on their 'visitors' death list. The idea of executing innocent people during Christmas is macabre, especially among the bright decorations in the *hacienda* (tinsel, baubles, bunting and a tree). Ringo is even compared to Jesus, when he wakes up on Christmas morning in a stable.

Like the clichéd characters, clichéd Hollywood western situations appear – old chestnuts such as, 'we'll head them off at the pass', or 'the cavalry will arrive in the nick of time and save the day'. But Tessari always hits the audience with the unexpected. The bandits are headed off at the pass, but they are not apprehended and return to the ranch to get Ringo, while the cavalry promised from Crystal City never appear. Though the sheriff doesn't really want the cavalry to show up, the threat of their arrival is a fine tension-builder, echoed in Ennio Morricone's imaginative, suspenseful score.

When the bandits first ride into the ranch, they trample a green pasture and scatter the sheep herd. This shot is a visualisation of the 'shattering' of the ranch's tranquillity, leading to the breakdown of relationships between Sancho and Dolores, and the major and Ruby. Tessari draws parallels between the ranch's peaceful existence and the brutality of the bandits. He also contrasts the Mexicans' and aristocrats' differing customs, providing him with plenty of opportunity for humour, however understated. The evening meals present a severe culture-clash. On the first occasion the two groups eat together, Pedro looks at the major's evening attire

Fernando Sancho in his most memorable role: as a bandit leader holding a ranch to ransom, in Duccio Tessari's *A Pistol For Ringo* (1965).

and comments 'You're dressed like a gravedigger, that means it's time for dinner'. The bandits dance on the dinner table, while the major attempts to raise the tone by playing a gramophone record. Ringo waltzes with Ruby, while in the background the bandits ape their movements in an exaggerated, pantomimic way. But the one aspect of Christmas that unifies the two groups is the carol-singing.

There's plenty of humour in *Pistol*. Some of the gags are obvious, while others are barely noticeable; in Tessari's films much happens on the edge of the frame, or in the background. Moreover, *Pistol* is an ensemble piece. The interaction between the actors is relaxed, which makes the comedy sequences work. The humour in *Pistol* is verbal, visual and at times slapstick. Tessari even manages to include a pie-in-the-face gag. Sancho uses a doily as a sling and has a bloody hole in the back of his jacket, giving him the look of a walking corpse, while Tim says that being involved in the siege is better than spending Christmas with his relatives. The miserly bank director is even used for a seasonal joke. He chides one of the desk clerks for being late, only for the clerk to be told by a colleague that Christmas always makes their boss grumpy (in a western version of Mr Scrooge). His grumpiness is punished later: when Sancho blows up the safe, the director is buried under the wreckage of his own furniture. In the San Jose sequence (actually shot in San Jose, Andalusia), Ringo says he killed the four Benson Brothers in self-defence and that he has witnesses. But in a brief shot we see a poncho-draped peon slumped against a wall (an archetypal sleepy Mexican) lower his sombrero and make no effort to support Ringo's claim; a subtle, yet humorous, example of the friction between Americans and Mexicans.

For *A Pistol for Ringo*, Morricone reverted to a more traditional approach to scoring westerns. Having revolutionised the genre with *Fistful*, he realised that for Tessari's film to be successful, he must reinforce the director's references to American westerns. The most obvious example of this is the title song, 'Angel Face', performed by Maurizio Graf, with lyrics by Gino Paoli. Paoli was a well-known songwriter who sometimes crooned his own compositions, including 'Sapore Di Sale' from *Il Successo* (1964). He had an affair with Stefania Sandrelli, but when they split up Paoli tried to shoot himself and miraculously survived. Like most of Morricone's songs in spaghetti westerns, 'Angel Face' is sung in English (even in the Italian print), but the lyrics are largely unintelligible – sounding akin to an American ballad, but making no logical sense. Later examples by Morricone and others considerably improved on this style and managed an effective synthesis of spaghetti-western-style music and descriptive, appropriate lyrics. Graf's 'Find a Man' (co-written by Alessandroni) from Enzo Castellari's *Johnny Hamlet* (1968) went beyond the usual banal cowboy-song ethics and achieved something like frontier poetry: 'If a dreamer grows wise when he opens his eyes. Shadows in a dream will always seem more real than all men's lies. Find a man who's true at heart and love him till he dies.' These phonetic title-songs epitomise the Italian westerns' attitude to authenticity. If it looks or sounds right, then it must be authentic, even if, after closer inspection, it is only a rough approximation of the genuine American article.

The tune to 'Angel Face' is a western pop song, incorporating a simple acoustic guitar riff, the Alessandroni choir (intoning 'This was Angel Face'), a rattling drum-kit, syncopated strings and a chiming electric-guitar solo. The accompanying lyrics include the phrase: 'Ringo had an Angel Face, but whenever Ringo loved, Ringo fought'. A better-known instrumental version of this tune appears on many of Morricone's compilation albums, usually under the title 'A Gun for Ringo', with an electric guitar and strings playing the vocal line. Ruby even plays a version of the theme on the piano. But it is the title sequence, cut to the vocal version, that is most memorable. Under the credits we see the bandit gang splashing across the Rio Grande as the upbeat theme brings the picturesque sequence to life. The 'Ringo' songs are Morricone's best attempts at western ballads in the American tradition because they capture the mood of Tessari's films so well.

Morricone gives the hero a brief signature theme on an oboe or trumpet, like in *Fistful*, while ominous strings tell us that Sancho and his men are up to no good in Quemado. Morricone adds tension, an element of time running out, by using a banjo or plucked strings playing a two-note 'tick-tock' effect. Another piece, used on Christmas morning as the bandits prepare to leave, is almost identical to the shootout music from *Fistful*, with a Spanish guitar and choir backing a trumpet solo (again provided by Michele Lacerenza). Morricone also uses visible sound. A honky-tonk band plays 'Silent Night', while the bandits prefer the lazy mariachi trumpet of 'Bamba Bambina'. This fiesta music reinforces the contrast between the Gringos and Mexicans. The aristocrats are associated with classical compositions, as in the scene where Major Clyde plays a waltz on his gramophone, which he bought from 'a Mr Edison'.

A Pistol for Ringo made an excellent profit domestically when it was released in May 1965. Such was the film's huge success that the theme song went to number one in the Italian charts. *Pistol's* popularity also provided Italian producers with a new name to splash on billboards to attract punters. Rushed out, unofficial sequels included *$100,000 for Ringo* (1965), *Ringo and Gringo against Everyone* (1966), *Two R-R-Ringos from Texas* (1967) and even a musical comedy: *A Woman for Ringo* (1966), starring Errol Flynn's son, Sean and the 19-year-old Bayona Twins, Pili and Mili, a Spanish pop-singing duo. The movie is very much in the mould of other spaghettis filled with musical numbers – unwatchable.

Several changes were made to *Pistol* for its English-language release, and there was even more humour in the original Italian print. The English release also cut the scene where Ringo removes the bullet from Sancho's shoulder. This scene explains why Filipe, one of Sancho's cohorts, wears a bandage on his hand thereafter: Ringo breaks it against the table with a goblet. All English versions omitted the carol-singing and the opening fake duel, and some dialogue and names were altered for the English-speaking market. In the finale, when the major throws Ringo his grandfather's antique flintlock, Clyde says it was used at Austerlitz, not Waterloo – a French victory, rather than a defeat, to please a European audience.

Tessari's film also did well in the US in 1966. The US trailer proclaimed: 'Ringo – cool-eyed, quick-draw, fast, fast fastest gun of the West!' – cut to music from the wrong *Pistol* (Morricone's *Pistols Don't Argue*). Gemma's pseudonym couldn't have hurt the takings – 'Montgomery Wood' perhaps reminding cinema-goers of Montgomery Clift and Clint Eastwood, but the main reason seems to be that Americans could appreciate Tessari's light-hearted homage to their own fading genre. In the US in 1965–66 the vast majority of westerns were vehicles for has-beens on their way down, or cheap programme-filling 'B-movies'. It could be argued that *A Pistol for Ringo* belonged to the latter, but it made up for its lack of budget with flair, wit and imagination. The plot zipped rather than plodded, and at least *Pistol* featured a cast that wasn't ready for retirement just yet.

3

'A Man Who Hopes, Fears'

— Duccio Tessari's *The Return of Ringo* (1965)

The Return of Ringo **(1965)**
original title: *Il Ritorno di Ringo*
Credits
DIRECTOR – Duccio Tessari
PRODUCERS – Luciano Ercoli and Alberto Pugliesi
STORY AND SCREENPLAY – Duccio Tessari and Fernando Di Leo
ART DIRECTOR – Juan Alberto
COSTUME DESIGNER – Rafael Borque
EDITOR – Licia Quaglia
DIRECTOR OF PHOTOGRAPHY – Francisco Marin
MUSIC COMPOSER – Ennio Morricone
MUSIC CONDUCTOR – Bruno Nicolai
Interiors filmed at PC Balcazar Productions, Barcelona
Cinemascope/Eastmancolor
An Italian/Spanish co-production
Produzioni Cinematografiche Mediterranee (Rome)/ Rizzoli Film
    (Rome)/ Producciones Cinematograficas Balcazar (Barcelona)
Released internationally by Golden Era Film Distribution
Cast
    'Montgomery Wood', Giuliano Gemma (Captain Montgomery
    Brown, alias 'Ringo'); 'Hally Hammond', Lorella De Luca
    (Hally Fitzgerald Brown); Fernando Sancho (Esteban Fuentes);
    Nieves Navarro (Rosita); Monica Sugranes (Elizabeth Brown);
    Antonio Casas (Carson, the sheriff): 'George Martin', Jorge
    Martin (Francisco 'Paco' Fuentes); 'Pajarito', Murriz Brandariz
    (Morning Glory); Victor Bayo (Jeremiah Pitt, the tavernkeeper);
    Jose Halufi (grave-digging bandit); Juan Torres (Mimbres
    bartender); Tunet Vila (Mimbreno Apache medicine man)

               *   *   *

With Sergio Leone, Duccio Tessari was the most important figure in the development of Italian westerns during their first years of European success. Tessari co-scripted the prototype for the genre (*A Fistful of Dollars*), co-wrote the first successful spaghetti-western comedy (*Seven Guns for the MacGregors*) and began the sub-genre of Italian westerns based on Hollywood's classics (*A Pistol for Ringo*). If *Pistol* had drawn on the fast-moving series westerns of the thirties and forties, Tessari's next film, *The Return of Ringo*, quoted directly from John Ford (*She Wore a Yellow Ribbon* and *The Searchers*), John Sturges (*The Magnificent Seven*) and Howard Hawks (*Rio Bravo*).

The Return of Ringo was also a thinly veiled reworking of the story of Odysseus's return to Ithaca following the Trojan War. Leone claimed that Homer was 'the greatest writer of Westerns'; Tessari took this a step further, creating a truly mythical west. Tessari had always been interested in myths and monsters, but tales of the cyclops and journeys to Hades don't easily adapt to the western genre. Having already worked on mythological stories (for Leone, Corbucci and Cottafavi) and rewritten a Japanese samurai tale (for Leone), he saw in *The Odyssey* the potential for another western adaptation. Homer's *The Odyssey* tells how Odysseus, having spent nineteen years away (ten at war and nine finding his way back), returns to Ithaca, his island home. The last third of *The Odyssey* concerns Odysseus discovering that much has changed in his absence. His house has been taken over by ruffians and his wife Penelope and son Telemachus believe he is dead. Odysseus's guardian, the goddess Athene, disguises Odysseus as a beggar and he hides out with Eumaeus, a herdsman, to plot the recovery of his home, his family, his wealth and his kingdom. Penelope is about to remarry and organises an archery competition to decide who will be the lucky brigand. Odysseus (still dressed as a beggar) enters and wins. Finally Athene reveals Odysseus's true identity, to the terror of the suitors. In the showdown, Odysseus, with the aid of the goddess and a small band of allies (including his son and the herdsman) massacre the suitors, who are largely unarmed, leaving the hero reunited with his wife for the fade-out.

There are some obvious inconsistencies, but *The Return of Ringo* is nothing less than a transposition of the events of *The Odyssey* from Ancient Greece to a Mexican border-town. In *Return*, Unionist captain Montgomery Brown (known as Ringo) returns to his hometown of Mimbres after the Civil War. He discovers that following a gold strike, two villainous Mexican brothers Esteban and Paco Fuentes have killed his father, Senator John S. Brown, and taken over his house. Moreover, Paco plans to marry Ringo's wife Hally, who with her daughter Elizabeth is being kept prisoner. Ringo, with help from an alcoholic sheriff, a florist named Morning Glory (who shelters Ringo), Jeremiah Pitt (a tavernkeeper) and a mysterious Apache medicine man, sets about recovering what is rightfully his. Ringo/Odysseus, Hally/Penelope and Paco/the suitors are the most obvious matches for Homer's protagonists, but many of *The Odyssey*'s incidental characters have their counterparts in *Return* – Eumaeus/Morning Glory and Telemachus/Elizabeth, the daughter

Ringo has never seen. However, Tessari often blends them together to create new characters.

The director's borrowings extend to some of *The Odyssey*'s most striking images – in particular the description of the hero's reappearance as Odysseus the warrior. On the threshold of the portal, Odysseus is transformed by the goddess from a beggar into his majestic self. In translation, Ringo appears framed in the doorway of a church in his cavalry uniform, his appearance made all the more awesome by the swirling dust that surrounds him. Tessari's treatment of the final confrontation is noticeably different from *The Odyssey*, the fight being much fairer – in keeping with star Giuliano Gemma's image. Italian western audiences would be disappointed, not to say surprised, if the final reel consisted of good-guy Gemma massacring a bunch of unarmed opponents.

Tessari re-called most of the leading players from *Pistol*, with Paco Sanz and Jose Manuel Martin the only notable absentees. Giuliano Gemma was Ringo; Lorella De Luca his wife; Fernando Sancho a villain and Nieves Navarro a fortune-teller, while 'Pajarito' was Morning Glory, a more eccentric version of his deputy, Tim in *Pistol*. Both actresses had a vested interest in the film's success: De Luca was married to Tessari and Navarro to producer Luciano Ercoli. Sancho was subbed as the main villain by Jorge Martin (as the evil Paco) and Antonio Casas portrayed a washed-up sheriff with a drinking problem and a tremor.

Gaining in confidence, following *Pistol*'s profitable run, Giuliano Gemma used his real name in the credits, his pseudonym 'Montgomery Wood' appearing in brackets. In his westerns, Tessari often named protagonists after the actors who played them. In *Pistol*, Fernando Sancho played bandit Sancho. Here Montgomery Brown is played by 'Montgomery Wood' and Hally Brown is played by 'Hally Hammond'/De Luca. In *Seven Guns for the MacGregors* Tessari even named bandit villain Santillana after the reservoir at Manzanares El Real, near where the film was shot.

By making the hero of *Return* a vengeful Italian western hero, rather than a Hollywood gunman like Angel Face, much of the levity of *Pistol* is lost. *Return* is a much darker film and the characters are more tragic. That said, if Tessari was now directly challenging Leone's perception of the west, he was confronting it on his own terms. He continued to cast women in prominent roles, to use clichéd characters and to wallow in sentimentality when the moment demanded, and the result was a surprisingly assured film, highlighted by a multi-layered structure and a cleverly ironic narrative.

Immediately after completing *A Pistol for Ringo*, Tessari wrote and shot this semi-sequel in Spain during the summer of 1965, this time co-writing with Fernando Di Leo. *Return* is a marked improvement on *Pistol*, though it's obvious the budget wasn't huge. The same town set from *Pistol* was deployed and a close look at the church tower reveals a wooden cut-out bell. Like *Rio Bravo*, Tessari's film is exceptionally 'town-bound' for much of the story, with relatively few trips out to the surrounding countryside. The town of Mimbres was the Balcazar Studios set

(Esplugas City) near Barcelona, also used in *A Dollar of Fire* (1966) and *The Long Days of Vengeance* (1966). This Catalan studio was co-founded by Jose and Francisco Balcazar; the set was used in many of the so-called 'Butifarra' westerns (named after a Catalan sausage) shot in the deserts and sierras of Aragon. Location scenes include Ringo's emergence from the desert, the Indian's hut, the Brown mansion sequences, the river and the tavern – all filmed in the vicinity of Barcelona and further west near Fraga, Huesca.

Effectively, Tessari and Di Leo (via *The Odyssey*) inverted the most popular spaghetti-western plot of the time – the 'stranger in town' scenario from *A Fistful of Dollars*. To everyone else in the film, Giuliano Gemma's hero is a Mexican drifter from the hills, alone in an unfamiliar New Mexican settlement called Mimbres. To the audience, he is the blond captain introduced at the beginning of the film. Virtually every aspect of *Return*'s script is ambiguous, as Ringo gradually becomes reacquainted with his friends. He is well disguised and looks so ordinary that no one recognises him, though he seems somehow familiar – a true everyman, or perhaps a nobody.

Even the title, *The Return of Ringo*, has two meanings: *The Return of Ringo* to the screen (following his adventures in *Pistol*) and also to his hometown. Di Leo's involvement in the script seems to have ironed out the derivative 'Americanisms' from *Pistol*, and the dialogue is more cryptic. Giuliano Gemma doesn't waste a word here, in contrast to his garrulous earlier edition of Ringo. His character is in fact very different from *Pistol*'s Ringo. His reuse of Sancho's beautiful silver Colt .45 from *Pistol* implies that Gemma is the same character, but at the beginning of *Return* Ringo is in the Union army and blond – 'Angel Face' was neither. *Return* is an in-name-only sequel to *Pistol*. The Alessandroni Singers croon 'Ringo's Son' during *Return*'s title song, but the film is set in 1965, which pre-dates the setting of *Pistol* by 29 years.

Antonio Casas gives a career-best portrayal as Sheriff Carson. Tessari cleverly used Casas's haggard features to good effect, his hangdog expression captured the depression of the alcoholic far better than Tessari's inspiration: Dean Martin's much younger character, Dude the Deputy in Howard Hawks's *Rio Bravo* (1959). Dude is known by the locals as 'Borrachon', Spanish for 'Drunk'. He has become a wreck after a failed love affair, which is more romanticised than the loneliness of Casas's interpretation – a man driven to drink though fear. The sheriff can keep his hand steady only by using his white neck-scarf as a primitive pulley to draw the liquor-glass to his lips, and the sheriff's star represents nothing – an empty symbol of law and order. The sheriff is certainly the most pitiful character in both the 'Ringo' films, though in the end he regains his dignity, when Ringo gives him hope. Ringo tells him, 'Nobody wants to die, sheriff, but being afraid means dying every day. A man who isn't afraid, can only die once.' In a key moment, the lawman steadily pours a full glass of whisky back into the bottle, without spilling a drop – echoing a moment in *Rio Bravo* (at a similar emotional turning point) when Dude's tremor has stopped and he's able to hold a gun again.

The Return of Ringo's intricate plot falls into three separate 'sections'. Each section begins with the hero revisiting his hometown, firstly as a beggar, then as a corpse (in a ruse engineered by Paco) and finally as a soldier. The second 'return' of Ringo is particularly well handled, with the arrival of a coffin (apparently containing Ringo's body) and a bogus funeral. The script is full of ambiguities (Ringo is still very much alive) and Ringo's headstone is even used as a joke. It reads: 'Died for the Union'; Ringo died not only for the Union army, but also to facilitate the union in marriage between Hally and Paco. As Ringo is reacquainted with his old friends, it is only the Fuentes brothers who are unaware of the avenger in their midst. On the wedding day, the 'joke' is solely on them. The wedding sequence, like the funeral, is full of contradictions. Hally wears a black mourning gown and veil, not one of the townsfolk is present to see the happy occasion, the tolling bell sounds like a death-knell and the church is full of coffins. This atmosphere makes Ringo's final reappearance in the sandstorm even more effective, as the wedding becomes a funeral – Paco's.

The one character who could unmask Ringo is the gypsy fortune-teller Rosita, an interesting addition to Homer's scenario. If Tessari's comments about Greek tragedy are to be believed, then Rosita stands in for the oracle that Italian musclemen were fond of visiting. When Ringo realises that resistance against the Fuentes is useless, he symbolically leaves his pistol in Rosita's bedroom. This leaves him (like Angel Face in *Pistol*) unarmed through the middle section of the film. Just before the final confrontation, Ringo returns to the fortune-teller to retrieve his gun. She reads the tarot cards and predicts that Ringo and the town will

'Welcome to Mimbres, stranger': Ringo (Giuliano Gemma) is greeted in Mimbres by some of the Fuentes's handiwork in Duccio Tessari's *The Return of Ringo* (1965).

be soon be different. As Ringo leaves her room she asks him, 'But don't you want to know the future?' only to receive the confident reply, 'It doesn't matter, I know it'. By now Ringo has begun to doubt her 'supernatural' powers and later he sets her up. In the most bizarre image in the film, Rosita watches from a rocking chair on a veranda, while Ringo guns down a bunch of Fuentes men sent by her to rescue Esteban. Rosita stares straight ahead, avoiding eye contact with Ringo. She didn't see that coming.

By concentrating on the hero throughout, the film highlights the talents of Gemma. His performance in *Return*, as two different characters, draws together the American and Italian aspects of the film. In the opening scenes when he rides out of the desert, he looks like an 'All-American' good guy, clean-shaven and blond. He's dressed in classic 7th Cavalry garb (even down to the bright yellow neckerchief) and looks like he's walked straight out of John Ford's *She Wore a Yellow Ribbon* (1949). But the Hollywood atmosphere doesn't last long, and when Ringo changes his clothes, the tone of the film changes too. The dashing young cavalry captain leaves the stage until the finale, when he reappears in his uniform and wedding ring. Ringo dyes his hair brown, grows a beard and disguises himself as a poncho-clad Indio (a mountain-dwelling Indian), as Tessari parodies the equivalent scenes in *A Fistful of Dollars*, when the stranger hits town.

As Ringo rides into Mimbres, the only sounds are the howling wind (blowing straw and dust), creaking signs and a rocking chair. He witnesses a shooting, sees the sheriff fail to intervene in the quarrel, meets one of the chief villains (who offers him a job) and is 'welcomed' to town by a local eccentric ('Welcome to Mimbres, stranger'). Many details of *Fistful* are alluded to in this episode. Ringo's poncho and stubble, the amplified wind and creaks on the soundtrack, a powerless lawman, a 'humiliation' by some local toughs and the offer of a job, while florist Morning Glory stands in for Juan De Dios, greeting the stranger. Later, Morning Glory (who is kept busy making funeral wreaths) echoes Silvanito, when he tells Ringo: 'You're staying in Mimbres? You like flowers, you don't carry a gun…you must be crazy.' Gemma adopts some of Eastwood's mannerisms (pausing to light a cigar outside the saloon) and adds some of his own (including an ever-present nervous tic under his left eye). Unfortunately his grey-striped peon's 'pyjamas' and straw hat make him look rather less cool than Eastwood. But although Ringo 'acts tough' in front of the Fuentes, the repeated close-ups of his eyes betray his fear.

Return resembles *Fistful* in tone, but Tessari still includes some clichéd moments (for instance, a whisky glass sliding along a bar top) and occasional sight gags. The name 'James Brown' appears on one of the gravestones, while nearby John Brown's body lies a-mouldering in the grave. This trend was first apparent in *Seven Guns for the MacGregors*, where the name 'Buster Crab' was scrawled on the wall of a prison cell, a reference to the thirties actor Buster Crabbe, star of Saturday morning serials *Flash Gordon* and *Buck Rogers* – characters noted for their daring escapes.

As with *Pistol* and *Sons of Thunder*, Tessari manages to stage plenty of acrobatic stunts for ex-stuntman Gemma – jumping off buildings into haystacks, bounding over wagons and hanging upside-down outside his daughter's window. Other noteworthy action sequences are the opening gunfight in a desert cantina (an ambush by Paco's men), the shootout following the judge's funeral (when the three chief mourners are shot dead outside the saloon) and the exciting finale, when the Mexicans wheel out the antique machine-gun (christened 'Butterfly'). Tessari juxtaposes the action with some well-played, tender love scenes (between Hally and Ringo) and the tragic moment when Ringo discovers his father's gravestone in the cemetery.

Tessari also uses natural sounds and long periods of silence, but it is the opening sequence that is most startling – a nod to the classics of John Ford. Beginning with a static shot of an empty desert met by clear, blue sky, it slowly becomes apparent that a rider is emerging in the distance from the heat-haze. As the rider (Ringo) approaches, Tessari cuts to a close-up of Gemma (in full cavalry uniform and Quick-draw McGraw hat) stopping to drain his canteen. These introductory shots of Gemma are the best references to Ford's style achieved by an Italian director.

But the villainous Fuentes brothers are unmistakably Italian. Jorge Martin, as graceful, bourgeois Paco (Don Francisco, in the Italian dialogue) is subtly menacing, sustaining the edgy tension with Ringo. Fernando Sancho, as hefty, swaggering Esteban, repeats his bandit role from *Pistol*. The brothers wear matching Mexican suits (one in medium, one in extra-large) and Esteban wears a red rose in his buttonhole – echoing Tessari, who always directed with a carnation in his lapel. Paco is the more intimidating of the duo. Though he doesn't hurt Hally, he keeps her imprisoned in her own house (a variation on the hostage situation in *Pistol*) and there are threats of violence against her daughter, Elizabeth. During the wedding, Hally hesitates before saying 'I do', and Paco urges her to remember that Elizabeth is waiting for them at home. Earlier, during a feast at the Brown mansion (Villa Brown), Ringo manages to slip away from the party. He tries to take a music box from Hally's bedroom, but is caught for 'stealing' from his own house. As punishment, Paco pins Ringo's gun hand to a table with a hunting knife, crippling it, which leaves Ringo facing the Fuentes 'single-handed' for the finale.

After such a well-paced build-up, it is only in the action-packed climax at Villa Brown that Tessari's style falters. This is due to the introduction of Ringo's irritatingly cute daughter Elizabeth, played by Monica Sugrane. The scenes detailing Ringo's nostalgic reacquaintance with his bedroom and attic, full of family heirlooms, are filled with touching details. It is the only place in Mimbres where nothing has changed. But when Ringo breaks into the nursery to save Elizabeth, the combination of Monica Sugrane's 'acting' and Gemma's mugging nearly spoils the exciting shootout.

The immediacy of Ringo's dilemma throughout the film is emphasised by the title song, which is performed in the first person as a plea by the hero for help from the locals. Maurizio Attanasio wrote the words, Morricone the music and Maurizio Graf again garbled the lyrics:

> I have looked in the faces of my old friends.
> But nobody looks at me as my old friend.
> You must remember who I am.
> If you see a man with downcast eyes and ragged clothes.
> Walking through your village, don't shun him.
> The liar who told my sweetheart that I was dead.
> To take my place you shall pay for this base lie.

The music that accompanies this song is more downbeat than *Pistol*'s. The tune is in a mournful minor key, with the soothing Alessandroni Singers, a strummed guitar and a tired, march-like drum rhythm. The choir harmonises on the verse with 'Gone forever…now there is Ringo' and on the chorus with 'Ringo's Son'. The piece has a world-weary feel, an atmosphere of assignation that matches the story. But the music to *Return* isn't a patch on the intricacies of *Pistol* – virtually the whole score being based around the main theme tune, voiced by a variety of instruments (violin, guitar, harp, music box). At other times, Morricone uses a series of menacing compositions with sustained piano notes, syncopated strings, bells and drums. There is also a rewrite of Mussorgsky's 'Night on the Bare Mountain' in the scene where Ringo is tempted to shoot his wife (he suspects she has been unfaithful), until he sees his little daughter for the first time. Mussorgsky's piece detailed a Black Mass and the music adds an elemental quality to the scenes, especially when cut to shots of a little girl picking flowers.

The poignant trumpet piece at Ringo's 'funeral' is similar to themes in *The Good, the Bad and the Ugly* and *The Hellbenders* (with their Civil War connotations). The funeral sequence is accompanied by a Last Post – a heavenly choir and a lone trumpet, played by Morricone's regular trumpeter, Michele Lacerenza. At the subsequent feast, Rosita sings a love song 'Mi Corazon' ('My Heart') before dancing to Morricone's 'La Bamba di Barnaba', a folk song with a virtuoso harp solo played by Anna Palombi. Through these compositions, Morricone again captures the mood of Tessari's west – a blend of 'downbeat, threatening and desperate', with a hint of 'religious epic' and 'fiesta' thrown in for good measure.

The Return of Ringo was released successfully in Italy in December 1965. It was the third-biggest hit of the year, behind *For a Few Dollars More* and *A Pistol for Ringo*. As a result of the 'Ringo' films' success, Gemma's *One Silver Dollar*, *Adios Gringo* and *Fort Yuma Gold* (1966) also made a fortune in Italy, as did *$100,000 for Ringo* (1965), starring Richard Harrison and Fernando Sancho. The latter saw Ringo (Harrison) returned from the Civil War to find his wife dead and his son raised by Apaches.

Return was released internationally in 1970 by Golden Era, but was much less successful than its predecessor on the UK and US markets, even though other Gemma westerns, like *Day of Anger* (1967), were big hits there. Some English prints

Captain Montgomery Brown (Giuliano Gemma) and his 'widow' Hally (Lorella De Luca) in *The Return of Ringo* (1965).

alter the title sequence; instead of the Fordian opening, the titles play out on a plain black background, with our first glimpse of Ringo being his entrance into the tavern. The dubbed English dialogue is very similar to the original Italian text, though Rosita's sexuality is accentuated in the Italian print. In the English version, Pajarito is named Morning Glory, after a species of trailing vine, whose flowers open in early morning but close with the midday sun. In the original Italian version he's called Forget-Me-Not (referring to the fact that no one remembers Ringo) and is referred to as Myosotis, the name of the genus the flower belongs to.

Gemma was the first 'home-grown' Italian western star, and his domestic popularity equalled the two top draws of the period, Eastwood and Van Cleef, while Sancho was assured a lucrative career in the genre – he made eight westerns in 1966 alone. Tessari meanwhile wrote Cinecitta-genre films for other directors, like *The Lady from Beirut* and *The Balearic Gold Operation* (both 1966), and the western *A Train for Durango* (1967). Gemma became something of a lucky charm for Tessari and appeared in many of the director's later films, from horror and war films to safari adventures and more westerns, though their later spaghetti collaborations fell well short of their achievements on the 'Ringo' films. An example was the comedy western *Alive or Preferably Dead* (1970) – shamelessly retitled *Sundance and the Kid* for certain gullible markets. Tessari and Gemma also worked together on a spy film called *Kiss Kiss-Bang Bang* (1967), which featured 'Ringo' regulars Martin, Pajarito, De Luca, Navarro and Casas. The title was another attempt by the Italians to cash in on the Bond movie franchise, as 007 was known throughout Europe as 'Mr Kiss Kiss Bang Bang'.

Gemma continued exploring his 'Ringo' persona with his next films: *Fort Yuma Gold* (1966), *Arizona Colt* (1966) and *The Long Days of Vengeance* (1966). Michel Lupo's *Arizona Colt* (also called *The Man from Nowhere*) represented the ultimate, big-budget take on the 'Ringo' films. Gemma (as gunman 'Arizona Colt'– 'Fine state, fine pistol') was again pitted against Fernando Sancho as El Gordo, leader of a gang known as the Sidewinders. The film was as violent (Gemma is kneecapped and shot in both hands) as it was inept (at one point, a shot of a stork stands in for a vulture). *The Long Days of Vengeance* (based on '*The Count of Monte Cristo*') was a definite attempt by Gemma to shake the Ringo image, even though the film was subtitled *Faccia D'Angelo* ('Angel Face') and co-starred Pajarito and Nieves Navarro.

In 1966 Maurizio Lucidi directed a very tough remake of *Return* called *My Name is Pecos*, with Robert Woods as the Mexican hero, returning after a long absence to his hometown of Houston. The most notable aspect of Lucidi's film was that The Animals didn't sue composer Lallo Gori over his title song, 'The Ballad of Pecos' (sung by Bob Smart). It's almost a note-for-note copy of their cover of 'The House of the Rising Sun'.

The influence of the official 'Ringo' films was so great that when Audie Murphy went to Barcelona to make *The Texican* (1966), the title was changed to *Ringo il Texano*. It was a US/Spanish co-production with Murphy playing Jess Carlin, out to avenge his brother's death at the hands of Rimrock town tyrant Luke Starr (Broderick Crawford, looking and sounding like Orson Welles). The rest of the cast was made up of Spanish actors, including Antonio Casas, Frank Braña, Aldo Sambrell and Antonio Molino Rojo. To further reinforce the Ringo connection, the film was shot at Balcazar Studios, while the barman in the Silver Ring saloon was played by Juan Torres, reprising his role from *Return*; the painting of the naked girl hanging behind the bar had previously decorated Rosita's room in Tessari's movie. *The Texican* represents the ideals of three decades of western movies. From the forties there is a singing cowboy; from the fifties there is five-foot-seven-inch Audie Murphy standing on boxes during his dialogue scenes, and from the sixties there are the Spanish locations and cast, and brutal violence.

But copies like this never came close to the original brace of 'Ringos', which proved that there was room for differing Italian perspectives on the western myth – without the only motivation being money, the only hero being a monosyllabic, materialistic bastard and the only woman being a whore. Though neither *Pistol* nor *Return* have aged as well as the 'Dollars' trilogy, they still represent an important development in sixties westerns, and in Gemma Italian audiences found a perfect foil to the dirty, stubble-faced non-actors who tried to be Eastwood, but ended up driftwood.

4

'Were You Ever Young?'

— Sergio Leone's *For a Few Dollars More* (1965)

For a Few Dollars More (1965)
original title: *Per Qualche Dollaro in Piu*
Credits
DIRECTOR – Sergio Leone
PRODUCER – Alberto Grimaldi (for PEA – Rome)
STORY – Sergio Leone and Fulvio Morsella
SCREENPLAY – Luciano Vincenzoni, Sergio Donati and
Sergio Leone
ART DIRECTOR, SET DESIGNER AND COSTUMES – Carlo Simi
EDITORS – Eugenio Alabiso and Giorgio Serralonga
DIRECTOR OF PHOTOGRAPHY – Massimo Dallamano
MUSIC COMPOSER – Ennio Morricone
MUSIC CONDUCTOR – Bruno Nicolai
Interiors filmed at Cinecitta Film Studios, Rome
Techniscope/Technicolor
An Italian/Spanish/West German co-production.
Produzioni Europee Associate (PEA) (Rome)/ Arturo Gonzales
    (Madrid)/ Constantin Film (Munich)
Released internationally by United Artists
Cast
    Clint Eastwood (Manco); Lee Van Cleef (Colonel Douglas
    Mortimer); Gian Maria Volonte (El Indio); Mara Krup
    (Mary); Josef Egger (Prophet in El Paso); Rosemary Dexter
    (colonel's sister); 'Robert Camardiel', Roberto Camardiel
    (Tucumcari stationmaster); Riccardo Palacios (Tucumcari
    bartender); Jose Marco Davo (Red 'Baby' Cavanagh);
    Lorenzo Robledo (Tomaso); Diana Faenza (Tomaso's wife);
    Francesca Leone (Tomaso's son); Sergio Mendizabal
    (Tucumcari banker); Guillermo Mendez (Sheriff of White

Rocks); Kurt Zipps (Mary's husband); Jesus Guzman
(carpetbagger on train); Tomas Blanco (Santa Cruz
telegrapher): Karl Hirenbach (boy in flashback); Luis
Rodriguez (Guy Callaway); Diana Rabito (Callaway's girl);
Carlo Simi (El Paso bank manager); Dante Maggio (Indio's
cellmate); Enrique Navarro (Sheriff of Tucumcari); Giovanni
Tarallo (El Paso bank-vault guard); Mario Meniconi (train
conductor); Mario Brega (Niño); Werner Abrolat (Slim);
Klaus Kinski (the 'Wild One'); Luigi Pistilli (Groggy);
Benito Stefanelli (Huey); Aldo Sambrell (Cuchillo); Frank
Braña (Blacky); Antonio Molino Rojo (Frisco); Jose Canalejas
(Chico); Nazzareno Natale (Paco); Panos Papadopoulos
(Sancho Perez) with Roman Ariznavarreta, Eduardo Garcia,
Rafael Lopez Somoza, Jose Felix Montoya, Aldo Ricci,
Enrique Santiago and Jose Terron

*   *   *

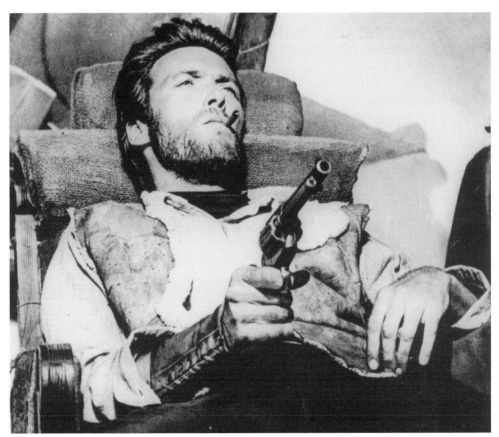

Manco cuts down Indio's gang from the comfort of a barber's chair; Clint
Eastwood in Sergio Leone's *For a Few Dollars More* (1965).

When *A Fistful of Dollars* proved successful, Sergio Leone set to work on a sequel, again with Clint Eastwood's gunslinger in the lead. Leone and Fulvio Morsella wrote a story called 'Two Magnificent Strangers' based on a treatment called 'The Bounty Killer', and it was transformed into a screenplay *Per Qualche Dollaro in Piu* (*For a Few Dollars More*) by Leone and Luciano Vincenzoni. With Tessari now directing his 'Ringo' films, the dialogue for this new film was solely credited to Vincenzoni (though Sergio Donati also worked on it) and the result was even more influential than *Fistful*.

Vincenzoni's western scripts always feature triangular relationships between two ostensibly 'good' characters against one 'bad', and often climax with a three-way shootout in a circular arena. *For a Few Dollars More* establishes this triangle, with its simple plot. Two bounty-hunters, a poncho-clad drifter named Manco and ex-Confederate Colonel Douglas Mortimer, team up to track down an escaped murderer named El Indio. Though Manco infiltrates Indio's gang, he can't prevent the bandits robbing the supposedly impregnable bank in El Paso. The gang hides out in the Mexican village of Agua Caliente, but in an explosive shootout the bounty-hunters wipe out the bandits and the colonel kills Indio. It turns out that the two hunters' motives are very different. Manco is purely after the $67,000 reward, while the colonel wants revenge: Indio raped his sister years before.

After Leone's first western turned in a huge profit, Jolly Film refused to pay him the percentage he was owed unless he made the sequel with them. So Leone teamed up with Alberto Grimaldi, who produced for his own company PEA (Produzioni Europee Associate) – in a co-production deal with Arturo Gonzales (Madrid) and Constantin Film (Munich). With a $600,000 budget, Leone's west expanded dramatically. *Fistful* is an exotic adventure film, set in a nowhere town. *For a Few*, unfettered by the plot confines of *Yojimbo*, is a revision of the 1870s frontier, as Leone addresses the mechanisation and brutality of the post-Civil War west.

In preparing *For a Few*, Vincenzoni studied frontier newspapers of the American west to add authenticity, and discovered that the gunslingers, bandits and lawmen of the real west weren't clean-shaven, honourable men. With the accent on grubby heroes, sudden violence and desolate settings, Vincenzoni incorporated historical place names. El Paso is in Texas; Alamogordo, Tucumcari and Santa Cruz are in New Mexico; Agua Caliente is across the border in Mexico and White Rocks is miles away (in Utah). Vincenzoni's research is echoed in the film, when the Colonel leafs through back copies of the *El Paso Tribune*. The paper's front page (dated June 1876) bears such authentic headlines as 'The Mines', 'Wells and Fargo Arrival' and 'Buffaloes'.

Fifties westerns again influenced Leone, especially Robert Aldrich's action-filled Mexican revolution western *Vera Cruz* (1954). Ex-Confederate Major Trane (Gary Cooper) and black-clad-but-amiable antihero Joe Erin (Burt Lancaster) are the untrustworthy forerunners of Leone's bounty-hunting heroes. They too are after the same quarry – a woman's heart and a cache of gold. *Vera Cruz* was extremely stylised. Lancaster's prolonged death scene (he was able to twirl his pistols and reholster them before falling in the dust) was parodied by a *MAD* magazine cartoon in 1955. After the final gundown, heroic 'Burt Lambaster' goes upstairs, gets a wash, gets changed, freshens up 'and as you're convinced he won, he falls on his face…dead'.

In *For a Few* Leone also draws the distinction between the gringo and Mexican heritage. Tucumcari, Agua Caliente and Santa Cruz are run-down, but White Rocks and El Paso are prosperous and, at last, populated. In the background of the El Paso street sequences, the 'Cosmopolitan Theatre', a Chinese laundry and the offices of the *El Paso Tribune* are clearly visible; the theatre and the laundry also feature prominently in Leone's *Once Upon a Time in the West* (1968). In the Mexican villages, Leone was back in *Fistful* territory. Agua Caliente is as poor and underdeveloped as San Miguel – if not poorer, with no bootlegging or gunrunning.

Leone's increased budget allowed him to hire another 'name' actor to star opposite Eastwood, but he couldn't convince Henry Fonda to take the role of Bible-reading bounty-hunter Colonel Mortimer. Leone tried Charles Bronson ('not interested') and Lee Marvin ('just signed to make *Cat Ballou*'). Leone turned instead to an American actor of Dutch descent called Lee Van Cleef. He was a familiar face to the director from his many villainous roles in fifties westerns: *Rails into Laramie* (1954), *Silver Lode* (1954), *A Man Alone* (1955) and *Gunfight at the OK Corral* (1957). Van Cleef debuted in *High Noon* (1952) and had turned to acting instead of his father's accountancy firm. Notable appearances included AIP's *It Conquered the World* (1956) – a rare starring role in which he was out-acted by a giant cucumber from Venus – and *The Big Combo* (1955) – where he was effective as the gay gunman Fante. Following a car crash in 1959, Van Cleef lost his left kneecap and was told he would never ride a horse again; within six months he was back in the saddle.

Leone screened *High Noon* and was struck by Van Cleef's facial resemblance to Van Gogh. Leone said that he carried 'the same brand of hopelessness, the hint of genius, the same intense eyes, eagle-like nose and clear forehead'. Coincidentally, Van Cleef was earning a living as a freelance artist. Van Cleef hadn't worked in cinema since *How the West Was Won* (1962) and his last feature was the made-for-TV Phil Silvers vehicle, *The Slowest Gun in the West* (1963). Instead he spent his time guest-starring in one-off TV dramas (often with a western theme, like *The Mailbag*) and TV series, including *Cheyenne*, *The Twilight Zone* and even *Rawhide*. Initially, Van Cleef thought that Leone only wanted him for a couple of scenes and was amazed to discover that he was to be the co-star. The money on TV wasn't very good and Van Cleef was relieved, to say the least, when Leone offered him the part of the Colonel, for a fee of $17,000. 'And not a moment too soon,' was Van Cleef's comment on the casting. Leone deliberately used Van Cleef's past association with villainy to great effect in *For a Few*: Van Cleef's malevolence from *A Man Alone*, his hidden Derringer from *Gunfight at the OK Corral*, the arena shootout from *Ride Lonesome* and the pocket watch from *The Bravados*.

After *Fistful*, Eastwood had resumed the *Rawhide* TV series, but his acting style had changed since his association with Leone. Previous episodes had cast him as a juvenile sidekick; Eastwood was now 34, a little old for such antics. The new season began with an episode called 'The Race', in which Rowdy struck out on his own and started a separate herd – an apparent in-joke on behalf of *Rawhide*'s producers at Eastwood's foray into Italian movies. But audience figures were falling and *Rawhide* was axed in December 1965.

The previous spring, Eastwood returned to Italy. For reprising his role as the squinting stranger with no name he received $50,000 and a cut of the profits. Eastwood maintains that his squinting demeanour was simply that his eyes were susceptible to the strong Spanish sunlight. When filming began, he wanted to discard the character's penchant for cigars, as he hated the taste, but Leone convinced him, saying that the cigar was 'playing the lead'. In interviews the actor claimed that the smokes put him in the right frame of mind for the role, terming it, 'kind of a fog', though he kept butts of various lengths on hand to make it look as though he was smoking them.

With Gian Maria Volonte recast as the villain, El Indio (an even more extreme baddie than Ramon Rojo), his gang had to be an equally wild bunch. Mario Brega played Niño ('little child' in Spanish), Indio's right-hand man and drugs supplier; Benito Stefanelli was Huey, a be-whiskered, child-killing gringo, and Aldo Sambrell played Cuchillo (the 'Knife'). Luigi Pistilli appeared as the sceptical Groggy, who realises that Indio is trying to get them all killed. Other roles were filled by Frank Braña, Antonio Molino Rojo, Werner Abrolat and Jose Canalejas, while future Italian western regulars Roberto Camardiel and Riccardo Palacios appeared in bit parts.

But the most remarkable of the henchmen was Klaus Kinski as the hunchback, the 'Wild One'. Kinski appeared in many German films as far back as 1948, playing an assortment of Nazi officers, murderers and psychopaths. The year 1965 was key for him. Leone cast Kinski after the actor had screened *Fistful* in Munich and David Lean also used him as the anarchist Kostoyed, in *Doctor Zhivago*. This led to a flood of offers (Kinski claimed up to thirty a week), of which he chose the highest paid, regardless of quality. Whilst filming *For a Few* he hired an Almerian beach shack and entertained the local gypsies, whom he felt were his soul mates. As 'Wild', Kinski stared, snarled and maniacally twitched through one of his best performances, most memorably in the scene at the El Paso saloon, when the colonel strikes a match on his hump.

For a Few Dollars More was shot in 12 weeks. Most of the interiors were filmed at Cinecitta Studios in Rome. The scene where Eastwood rides into 'Santa Cruz' was also lensed there (on the Cinecitta western town set). Other exteriors were shot in Spain, this time mainly in the Almerian desert in the south: 'Agua Caliente' was a village called Los Albaricoques, while 'El Paso' was designed by Carlo Simi and built especially for the film near Tabernas. The El Paso set bore a resemblance to the western set at Old Tucson, Arizona from *Rio Bravo*, *McLintock* and *Gunfight at the OK Corral*. The El Paso saloon interior was on set at Tabernas, with desert and mountain exteriors shot in the locality. The western town at Colmenar Viejo near Madrid represented White Rocks; the set was built in 1959 for the British western *The Sheriff of Fractured Jaw*. 'Tucumcari' was the re-dressed *Fistful* set at Hojo De Manzanares. During the spaghetti boom the phrase, 'If you've seen one Western town, you've seen 'em all', took on much more significance.

Lee Van Cleef's Colonel Douglas Mortimer isn't a 'whiter-than-white' hero. In an interview, Van Cleef described the colonel as, 'A non-angelic sort of character, who's still on the side of the law', while Leone's concept of the character was John Carradine's shady southern gambler Hatfield in John Ford's *Stagecoach* (1939). Mortimer is more 'modern' than Eastwood's stranger: he keeps a little black book of bounties, opens the safe with special acid (rather than dynamite) and has an arsenal of weapons wrapped in his saddlecloth. His sidearm is a Buntline Special with a 12-inch barrel and a detachable shoulder stock, which slows his draw – so much so that we never see the colonel use it in a quick-draw duel. He leisurely shoots outlaw Callaway at distance, kills the Wild One with a Derringer from up his sleeve and borrows Manco's pistol and gunbelt to face Indio. Van Cleef always

Colonel Douglas Mortimer and his Buntline Special: Lee Van Cleef makes his Italian western debut in *For a Few Dollars More* (1965).

claimed that he was faster on the draw than Eastwood. Eastwood could draw, cock and fire in 0.45 of a second, while it only took Van Cleef 0.125.

Of the two gringos, Colonel Mortimer is the specialist and is a precursor of *Sabata*, another ex-Confederate gunman with an assortment of ballistic surprises. Leone also uses the modern weaponry as an observation on progress, Eastwood's bounty-hunter questioning how the older man can use a 'contraption' like the Buntline Special in their line of business. Previously, the Buntline had featured extensively in the ABC TV series *The Life and Legend of Wyatt Earp* (1955–61), starring Hugh O'Brien. The American trailer publicising *For a Few* christened Van Cleef's character the 'Man in Black' and described him as 'A walking arsenal who uncoils, strikes and kills'. 'Il Colonnello' is certainly the most dangerous of the early Italian western heroes, until the arrival of *Django* in 1966.

Although he still wears his poncho and cobra-handled Colt .45, Eastwood's character had changed considerably from *Fistful*. In *For a Few* he is a bounty-hunter and is even given a name – 'Manco'. In *Fistful* Eastwood is referred to as Joe; *Fistful*'s published Italian script bills him as 'Joe, lo Straniero'. In the English print of *For a Few*, Eastwood's character is called Manco, in the Italian print 'Il Monco'. Various translations have been given for this: the Italian for 'monk' (which is actually *monaco*); the Spanish for 'one-handed' (a more likely meaning, with reference to the leather gauntlet on his gun hand) and even 'Lefty' (in true Hollywood western style). El Indio is Spanish for 'the Indian' and the bandit leader refers to Eastwood's character as 'that monk'. Most likely is the simple fact that Leone or Vincenzoni decided that 'Il Monco' was a good name for Eastwood's hero, and it was anglicised to Manco at the dubbing stage. In the Italian print he is clearly called 'Il Monco' twice, at exactly the same points the English version substitutes Manco. If a religious subtext was intended by Leone this makes *For a Few* as bizarre as *El Topo*, as a monk and a preacher hunt the Prophet and his disciples through a wasteland. Providing Eastwood with a name proved problematic for the English-language release. United Artists went to great lengths to conceal the name, even omitting the line spoken by the Sheriff of Tucumcari ('His name is Manco').

Eastwood's costume in *For a Few* is identical to *Fistful*, with the addition of the leather gauntlet, which looks like it was left over from *The Colossus of Rhodes* (Burt Lancaster had also worn a similar item in *Vera Cruz*). In *For a Few*, it protects Manco's wrist when he fast-draws his pistol and also gives the stranger an identity. When Manco brings prison escapee Sancho Perez to Indio's hideout, he is not wearing it and his reputation seems to be associated with the wrist protector, though it is hardly the most distinctive aspect of his appearance. On the road to Santa Cruz, Manco reveals the gauntlet (and consequently his identity) to the three bandits before killing them. After the El Paso bank robbery Manco hurriedly removes the gauntlet, and when El Indio captures him he tells the stranger to put it back on – there is no point in hiding it any more.

Eastwood's laid-back performance was still pretty emotionless, especially where women were concerned. The scenes in the hotel with the buxom, chess-playing hotel landlady, Mary (she is obviously attracted to him, but he shows no interest) epitomise Leone's attitude to women on screen. Mary is an unwanted distraction from the chase. But promotional stills depict Eastwood and Mary in bed together in the hotel room, so maybe Leone did originally intend a relationship between the two.

Nevertheless, there is more warmth to the stranger than in the previous film, due to the dry humour injected by Vincenzoni and Donati. Vincenzoni (unlike Leone) could speak English, so he had a better understanding of what would work with Eastwood and Van Cleef. The script was more sparing than *Fistful*, with both actors altering their dialogue as they went along. The jokes are an improvement on *Fistful*'s black humour, possibly because there was more scope for them in an original script, rather than their being forced into already-existing scene outlines. At the El Paso bank raid the outlaws' wagon comes down the main street with three bandits inside: two of them are wearing shawls in an attempt to look female, a gag which is acknowledged on screen by Manco. Other sequences are a mixture of gunplay and comedy, as in a macho hat-shooting competition between the bounty-hunters and Manco's apple target practice in Agua Caliente. There are three scenes in El Paso that are played solely for comic value: Manco's relationship with Mexican boy Fernando (a greedy younger version of the stranger); the hotel check-in scene (where Manco ejects a patron from the room overlooking the bank and the pint-sized proprietor offers the departing tenant the bridal suite) and Manco's visit to the Prophet. Here, Josef Egger (from *Fistful*) looks suitably mad, wearing a yellow woolly hat and tatty poncho.

Locations, actors and translations are also used for in-jokes. Agua Caliente is Spanish for 'hot water' and that is where Indio ends up after the El Paso raid, while the stranger mentions that Rio Bravo Canyon is a good place for an ambush (a reference to the riverside massacre in *Fistful*). Leone's daughter Francesca had a cameo in the movie as Tomaso's son, while Carlo Simi played the El Paso bank manager (a building he had designed for the film). Indio says that Agua Caliente looks like a morgue and 'Could become one so easily', then adds, 'Yes, I have many friends here'. There is also some unintentional humour in the film, like the stagecoach that always seems to be arriving in El Paso ('Wells and Fargo Arrival') and the primitive dubbing, where even the English-speaking stars' lips don't match the dialogue track. Outlaw Callaway's poster has two crudely scrawled zeroes after the $1,000 reward and the accompanying likeness of the fugitive clearly shows that he has a moustache. But when Mortimer tracks him down, Callaway doesn't have one and as the colonel pushes the poster under the hotel door the scrawled zeroes are nowhere to be seen.

For a Few features a long, plot-free introduction to the three main characters. The first episode is the colonel's arrival ('This train will stop at Tucumcari'), which is linked to the next by his conversation with the sheriff, who tells him that Manco is also tracking Cavanagh. Already the two bounty-hunters are after the same prey. Only when Indio has escaped does any semblance of a plot materialise, with the appearance of the reward posters and the beginning of the manhunt. The colonel is initially presented as a clergyman, reading the 'good book', though Van Cleef's grimace as he slowly lowers the Bible tells the audience that it is unlikely he's a priest. The first two sequences of *For a Few*, featuring the colonel and the stranger, mirror one other. Mortimer, the older man (normally more wary of 'progress'), uses the railway, while Manco walks into town. Mortimer demonstrates greater intelligence by letting bandit Callaway get out of pistol range and then killing him with the Buntline, while Manco uses brute force (and incongruous karate-chops) to 'apprehend' Cavanagh. Manco even demonstrates a hint of morality when he removes the corrupt sheriff's star and asks, 'Isn't a sheriff supposed to be courageous, loyal and above all honest?'

Leone's sheriffs in *For a Few* are weak, incompetent or crooked; effectively the bounty-hunters have become self-appointed lawmen, motivated by greed rather than justice – their killings legitimised by the reward posters. As the film's opening caption reads: 'Where life had no value, death sometimes had its price. That is why the bounty killers appeared,' which is echoed in the Spanish title of the film, *La Muerte tenia un Precio* ('Death Has a Price').

But the bounty-hunters are positively compassionate when compared to bandit El Indio. From the beginning he is a merciless psychopath – murdering his cellmate in cold blood and ordering his men to slaughter the guards during the jailbreak killing spree. We later learn that he is also a child-killer, a rapist and a drug user (in the original scenario he was called Tombstone). Indio is also extremely cunning, but it is odd that he senses nothing amiss when Manco appears on the scene. From the moment the stranger joins Indio's gang, it suddenly develops a high mortality rate. Initially numbering 14 (plus Sancho Perez, fresh out of jail, makes 15), the bounty-hunters methodically cut down the odds. Manco shoots three on the way to Santa Cruz. The colonel kills the hunchback, then Indio gives them a hand by ordering Niño to knife Slim and shooting Cuchillo himself. Groggy knifes Niño, while the bounty-hunters kill the other six in a gun battle. As the remnants of the gang are wiped out, Indio squashes a beetle scampering across the tabletop and then watches the insect writhe, intercut with the deaths of his men. When they are all dead, Indio flicks the beetle from the table. He was right; Agua Caliente has become a morgue.

The two main themes are the relationship between the bounty-hunters and the vendetta between the colonel and Indio. Mortimer, at 'nearly fifty' (Van Cleef was only forty and was aged for the role), is older and wiser than Manco (in his mid-thirties), and their 'old man and boy' partnership works well. The dapper gentleman from Carolina (complete with waistcoat, pocket watch and tie pin) contrasts with the rougher westerner, though at one point Manco mocks the colonel's

Manco rides into Agua Caliente in *For a Few Dollars More* (1965); Clint Eastwood on location at Los Albaricoques in Almeria.

southern manners. When the pair are released by Niño, Mortimer gestures to Manco, bidding him 'After you'; seconds later Manco politely returns the courtesy. Manco is obviously impressed (but not overawed) by Mortimer – on two occasions saying 'Bravo' to displays of the colonel's marksmanship. The first time (outside the Taberna in Agua Caliente) he means it sarcastically, the second more sincerely. Mortimer has just killed Indio and earned them a lot of money. It is the 'old hand' who is always one step ahead of his younger partner. Though both gunmen figure out that Indio plans to raid El Paso, it is the colonel who does all the detective work and persuades Manco to risk his life by joining Indio's gang. Mortimer even breaks into the storeroom and recovers the money before Manco. This almost has the effect of making Manco look an idiot, but he eventually realises that the colonel has good reason to be so alert: Mortimer's family honour is at stake.

Revenge is the powerful subtext to the story. It becomes apparent midway through the film and is only fully explained at the end. The rape and suicide of the colonel's sister and Indio's memories of the event are Leone's most assured use of a flashback structure. It is presumed that her murder is the reason that Indio is in prison at the beginning of the film. Leone achieves the perfect balance between the flashbacks (two in the original full-length print, one in the cut version), the revelations (a single line from Mortimer referring to his sister) and the act of revenge (with the second flashback coming directly before the final shootout). The vendetta is symbolised throughout the film by the two identical musical pocket watches carried by Indio and Mortimer. At one point Manco asks the colonel, 'Were you ever young?' and Mortimer answers that long ago something happened that made life very precious, as he looks at his sister's picture in the watch lid. Indio's recollections of the crime are a druggy, red-tinted blur, with distorted watch chimes on the soundtrack. Far from being haunted, Leone suggests that Indio enjoys these reminiscences. During the assault, the colonel's sister takes Indio's pistol and shoots herself, to spare herself the shame. Leone links unrelated scenes between Indio and Mortimer with shots of the watch, and before the bank robbery the colonel checks his timepiece, not just to make sure their plan is on schedule, but also to look at his sister's face, reminding himself why Indio must die.

Vincenzoni and Leone also include a range of religious references: Mortimer's preacher garb and Bible-reading; the old prophet (and his revelations); the safe concealed in a drinks cabinet in the bank with its four tall candlesticks (like a church altar); and the bandits' church hideout. Indio's men mingle with the statues around the ruined church, as though the sculptures were members of the gang. The bandits enjoy a meal at a long table, with an icon in the centre and as Tomaso's corpse is carried outside, a statue in the background humorously points 'Way Out'. Indio even relates his 'parable of the carpenter' from the pulpit, accompanied by Morricone's 'Vice of Killing' theme played on an organ.

For a Few has Leone's first experiments with extended shootouts that became synonymous with Italian westerns. In the build-up to his duels, Leone dispensed with conversation and, through a combination of cuts between the individuals (close-ups of eyes, beads of sweat, hands hovering over pistols) and Morricone's score, built the tension to a climax, until the music stopped and the shooting started. As Indio says to one of his opponents: 'When you hear the music finish, begin'. Time is frozen at the moment before the draw and becomes so ritualised in terms of 'realism' as to seem absurd – but it made great cinema. While he was making *For a Few*, Leone's pioneering approach was parodied elsewhere in the film. When Manco arrives in Agua Caliente, three locals walk towards him, as though a showdown is about to take place. Instead the stranger shoots apples from a tree, to demonstrate his gunslinging prowess and to help a Mexican child to gather the fruit, but also sparing the trio's lives.

Leone's style was a great improvement on *Fistful*, though he used the same cinematographer: Massimo Dallamano. The bright colours, never-ending Almeria sunshine and clear, blue skies contrasted effectively with the barren desert, rocky hills and dusty townships. Before the final street fight in Agua Caliente, while the stranger and Mortimer wait outside the taberna, the shots are matched up (like in the duels). Dallamano cuts from a shot of Eastwood's face to the empty street and then back to Eastwood. Exactly the same shots are repeated with Van Cleef. They idly load their weapons, Eastwood sitting on a chair, Van Cleef leaning casually against the wall, and the effect is similar to the long opening sequence of *Once Upon a Time in the West* – the monotony of waiting for the action to begin. Van Cleef even lets out a bored sigh. Eastwood's entrance to White Rocks is also memorable, as he walks up the main street in the pouring rain. Another sequence that stands out (perhaps Leone's perfect fusion of camera style, editing and sound effects) is the scene where Manco and Mortimer look at Indio's reward poster. Manco's eyes are intercut with Indio's $10,000 price tag, while Mortimer reads the legend: 'DEAD OR ALIVE'. Leone then cuts between Mortimer's eyes and Indio's picture, while a fusillade of gunshots explode on the soundtrack. In this simple sequence it is clear that both men are after the bandit, but that their motives are very different.

Leone's strange mixture of humour and extreme violence wasn't supposed to be taken too seriously. His satirical intent was obvious, even in *For a Few*'s curious pre-title sequence. A distant rider in a desert landscape is felled by an unseen marksman. We hear the assassin lighting a smoke and idly humming and whistling (actually voiced by Leone), so we presume that the off-screen gunman is Eastwood. But it is Mortimer who is linked to the humming later in the film, while Indio's men case the bank. The title sequence is imaginatively done, with smoke from the unseen cigar or pipe forming the names of the production staff and later the credits become moving targets on a wire (in particular, the elusive credit to Ennio Morricone), which are obliterated by the gunman.

Morricone's music was the most complex score of the 'Dollars' trilogy, with the incidental themes 'narrating' the entire film. It marked the beginning of Morricone's use of musical riffs, trills or twangs associated with individual characters. Each protagonist has a musical signature: Manco has a flute, the colonel a twang on a Jew's harp and Indio an ominous Rodrigo guitar riff and a tolling bell. The title music is structured exactly like *Fistful*, as a 'pop' arrangement. The first verse features a Jew's harp and a whistled melody (provided by Alessandroni). The second verse adds an echoing drum, a flute, brushed snare and a church bell. By the time the Cantori enter (again with guttural lyrics – 'We defy', 'We say no' and 'We can win'), the tune is in full flow, with drums and the sound of Winchester rifles being levered keeping tempo, while an electric guitar takes the melody for the chorus. Throughout the early part of the film, this theme accompanies Eastwood. In a humorous aside Alessandroni has the choir chanting 'They robbed the bank' during the Santa Cruz robbery chase. Later this theme is replaced by the soaring 'Vice of Killing' – featuring drums, chorus and Edda Dell'Orso's skyscraping soprano solo.

Very little music is associated with the ambiguous colonel (staccato piano notes, drums, twangs or oboe), and what is used has ominous overtones, as we don't know where his allegiances lie. In the Italian print, a bugle plays as the Prophet tells Manco of Mortimer's army career. Indio's marijuana joints are even given a sound effect: Manco smokes cheroots, Mortimer a pipe, but every time Indio lights a reefer, a high-pitched whine appears on the soundtrack. The same sound effect is also used in the scene where Mortimer kills Callaway – it seems killing is a drug too. The main theme associated with Indio is the watch carillon. In the final duel, the chimes become his death-knell. Indio has set up a shootout he can't fail to win. While the colonel looks down at his pistol on the ground and Indio itches to draw, quiet strings (long, sad and mournful) accompany the face-off. Indio looks at the picture of the girl in the watch lid, then at Mortimer and sees a similarity, finally telling Indio who Mortimer is. When a louder watch interrupts the fading chimes and Manco makes his presence known, the gundown music marks the start of a fairer fight. This piece, known as 'Sixty Seconds to What?' (released in Italy as 'La Resa dei Conti' or 'The Settling of Accounts') was originally recorded with lyrics, which were later ditched. 'Sixty Seconds' has already been introduced to us during Tomaso's execution, but the two versions of the piece differ. At the church, the Flamenco guitar passage (played by Bruno D'Amario Battisti) is followed by a blast of church organ (actually Bach's 'Fugue in D Minor'). In the finale, the guitar is followed by a trumpet solo (played by N.Culasso). Soundtrack releases combine these into one long piece, but again Morricone has made a point – organ for church, trumpet for 'arena'.

After Indio's death, the dialogue between Mortimer and Manco explains the revenge motive, reinforced by Morricone's subtle underscoring. Manco looks at the picture in the watch and notes a family resemblance. 'Naturally,' answers Mortimer, 'Between brother and sister.' Manco says that they have become rich, but for Mortimer revenge is enough. Mortimer listens to the chimes, while Morricone's 'Goodbye Colonel' accompanies the scene, again incorporating the carillon, but now with lush strings and chorus. His sister avenged, Mortimer is content and rides into the sunset. A final gag by Leone sees Manco calculating his bounty money, shooting Groggy ('Thought I was having trouble with my adding…it's all right now') and loading the death wagon full of corpses. This shifts the emphasis back to Eastwood (who has been second lead to Van Cleef throughout), as Morricone's title theme swells on the soundtrack, to end the film on a high.

On its release in Italy in December 1965, *For a Few* proved to be an even bigger hit than *Fistful* (it remains Leone's most successful film in Italy) and was ripped off by both big and small productions. Some films poked fun at the title. *For a Few Bullets More* (1967 – also called *Any Gun Can Play*) opens with three gunmen riding into town to face 'the stranger' (George Hilton); the trio are dressed exactly like the most popular Italian western heroes of the time – Manco, Mortimer and Django. *For a Few Dollars Less* (1966 – based on a story by the Corbucci brothers, Sergio and Bruno) was an outright parody of Leone's film. Bank clerk Bill (over-acting comedian Lando Buzzanca, dressed in Eastwood's poncho) joins his cousin 'the general' (Raimondo Vianello, in Van Cleef's Colonel Mortimer garb) to track down Miguel the Mexican (Elio Pandolfi), a tormented outlaw addicted to cocoa

The stranger arouses suspicion when he arrives at Indio's hideout in *For a Few Dollars More* (1965); left to right: Clint Eastwood, Antonio Molino Rojo, Jose Canalejas, Klaus Kinski and Mario Brega.

leaves. In one scene, Bill exits town riding a tatty mule towing a coffin with his girlfriend hidden inside, while the general's gadget-laden coat conceals a selection of pipes and cigars, a soda syphon and a bulletproof vest. Indio's musical watch becomes Miguel's musical cigar box (complete with tiny pirouetting ballerina) and the heroes apprehend the Mexican bandits by gassing them with an aerosol. There's even a reference to Eastwood's distaste for cigars, with Bill refusing to smoke a cheroot, claiming, 'It makes me sick'.

Other Italian westerns concentrated on Mortimer's character: *Django Shoots First* (1966) teamed Django with a Mortimer-type sidekick called Doc (Alberto Lupo) with a switchblade hidden in his cane. Dozens of spaghetti westerns used the frock-coated 'specialist' character, while *Sartana* (1968) and *Sabata* (1969) borrowed the gadgets. The offbeat *Duel in the Eclipse* (1968) featured Lang Jeffries as an Eastwood-style gunslinger dressed in a leopardskin poncho. *Vengeance* (1968) was strongly influenced by Leone, with the poncho-clad half-breed Joko Barratt (Richard Harrison) running down his friend's five killers, while a mysterious Van Cleef lookalike Pinkerton Agent watched from the sidelines. It even included a replay of the hero throwing a sheriff's star into a local's hat with the words, 'Get a new sheriff'. One bit of footage left lying on the cutting-room floor by Leone appeared in *My Name is Pecos* (1966), which bizarrely closes on the opening shot of *For a Few*. In *$10,000 Blood Money* (1966), Django (Gianni Garko) faced an Indio-type villain called Manuel Cortez. Manuel looks incredibly like Indio: director Romolo Guerrieri evidently couldn't afford Gian Maria Volonte, so cleverly cast Volonte's brother, Claudio Camaso, in the role. A further development was actors with variations on Eastwood's western-sounding name (Charles Southwood, George Eastman, Montgomery Wood, Monty Greenwood) and film titles like *Clint il Solitario* (1967 – or 'Clint the Loner') and the shamelessly derivative *A Fistful of Rawhide* (1970).

Many of *For a Few*'s bit players went on to appear in all kinds of Italian films, in anything from starring roles to fleeting glimpses. Hotel landlady Mara Krup turned up in the orgy sequence of *Fellini's Satyricon* (1969). Bank guard Giovanni Tarallo (who enjoyed a giant sandwich in the El Paso robbery sequence) was a starving peasant boy in Pasolini's *Hawks and Sparrows* (1966). But most successful was Karl Hirenbach. He changed his name to 'Peter Lee Lawrence' (after Lee Van Cleef) and established himself as a spaghetti Sherlock Holmes in a series of densely-plotted whodunit mystery westerns, where it was invariably glaringly obvious 'who did it' from the off.

When it came to international distribution, *For a Few* was Leone's last film not to suffer severe cutting for the English-speaking market. This suggests that it is the closest to a 'complete' Sergio Leone film, released exactly how the director intended. *For a Few* was only cut for censorship reasons in the UK and the US, reducing the violence. Minor cuts included the bloody hole in Callaway's head; Indio killing the prison commandant; and the beating of Manco and Mortimer by Indio's gang.

Further cuts occurred in the final flashback. One print removed the sequence altogether, and Indio's face is suddenly tinted red for no apparent reason. In another, the assault is included (and the sound of the fatal shot), but the effects of the bullet are not seen, only the blank expression on the dead girl's face. The cutting of the final flashback is very odd, considering how crucial it is to the story. Even with all these omissions, *For a Few* only managed an 'X' certificate in the UK and the US. Production stills and trailers provide evidence that further scenes were shot, but not included in any released versions. These include Manco folding a reward poster for Red Cavanagh and taking El Indio's reward poster down from the wall, and Indio baptising his Colt. On two occasions Indio caresses and listens to the firing mechanism of his pistol, the same pistol the girl used in the suicide, making the baptism even stranger.

When *For a Few* was released in the US in July 1967, United Artists stuck with their 'man with no name' campaign: 'the man with no name is back…the Man in Black is waiting' and 'As if one wasn't enough…as if death needed a double. It's the second motion picture of its kind! It won't be the last.' Posters featured Van Cleef's arsenal (subtly increased to look even more impressive) and variations added a semi-naked woman draped in a sheet (which had no relevance to the film). To the publicists the films were interchangeable: the United Artists poster for *Fistful* featured Indio and Mortimer from the final duel in *For a Few*. There was little to differentiate the two films for the critics either, but the public ignored the bad press – *For a Few* took $5 million on its initial US release. For some reason, the UK trailer concentrated on the bounty-hunters' patience. The voiceover (by British actor Anthony Dawson) intoned, 'Yes, these men knew how to wait'. Unsurprisingly, critics were unimpressed. The *New York Daily News* noted that the 'sets have an empty look and seem to be as lightly constructed as the plot', while the *New York Times* claimed the film 'endorsed violence, emphasised killer bravado and sought to generate glee, in frantic manifestations of death' – qualities that perhaps attracted audiences to the theatres.

In the 1967 *Western Stars of Television and Film Annual* (published just after the release of *For a Few Dollars More*), much is made of Eastwood's arrival at the UK box office; 'There's Gold In Them Thar Italian Westerns' announced a headline. Noticeably, of all the portraits in the *Annual*, Eastwood is the only hero not clean-shaven and smiling. With Eastwood already a star, Van Cleef's ascendancy soon followed. He was perfect for this new genre and was cast in some of the best Italian westerns of the sixties. Like Eastwood, who reused the same gunbelt throughout his western career, Van Cleef kept two prop ideas from *For a Few*: the pipe (in preference to a cigar), giving his characters a sense of meditative paternal wisdom, and his unusual cross-belly draw holster. After *Fistful*'s success, Jolly Film edited two episodes of *Rawhide* together ('The Backshooter' from 1964 and 'Incident of the Running Man' from 1961) and tried to release them in Italy as *Il Magnifico Straniero*, implying they were new Eastwood releases. Similarly, when *For a Few* surpassed

Fistful's success, Van Cleef's fifties westerns resurfaced in Italy, especially *The Bravados*, *Ride Lonesome* and *High Noon*. The latter, retitled *Mezzogiorno Di Fuoco* ('Noon of Fire'), was advertised with a poster depicting the final shootout (and therefore the central conflict) between the two 'stars', Lee Van Cleef and Gary Cooper. Van Cleef was originally billed twelfth on the cast list. *For a Few Dollars More*, with *The Big Gundown* and *Death Rides a Horse*, represents the best of the mainstream Italian westerns in the period 1965–67, before too much parody, politics or repetition filtered into the formula. Leone now had two western 'icons' in Eastwood and Van Cleef, and their next collaboration would be the greatest achievement of Leone's career.

5

'I Was Away, Too Far Away'

— Sergio Corbucci's *Django* (1966)

Django (1966)
Credits
DIRECTOR – Sergio Corbucci
PRODUCER – Manolo Bolognini
STORY – Sergio and Bruno Corbucci
SCREENPLAY – Sergio and Bruno Corbucci, Franco Rossetti, Jose
    Guittierez Maesso and Piero Vivarelli
ENGLISH-LANGUAGE VERSION – Geoffrey Coplestone
SET DESIGNER AND COSTUMES – Giancarlo Simi
EDITORS – Nino Baragli and Sergio Montenari
DIRECTOR OF PHOTOGRAPHY – Enzo Barboni
MUSIC – Luis Enriquez Bacalov
Interiors filmed at Elios Film Studios, Rome
Eastmancolor
An Italian/Spanish co-production
BRC Produzione Film (Rome)/Tecisa Film (Madrid)
Cast
    'Franco Nero', Francesco Sparanero (Django); Loredana
    Nusciak (Maria); Jose Bodalo (General Hugo Rodriguez);
    Eduardo Fajardo (Major Jackson); Angel Alvarez (Nathaniel,
    the saloonkeeper); 'Jimmy Douglas', Gino Pernice (Brother
    Jonathan); Simon Arriaga (Miguel); 'Erik Schippers', Remo
    De Angelis (Riccardo); Silvana Bacci (Mexican prostitute);
    Lucio De Santis (whipping bandit); Chris Huerta (Mexican
    officer); Jose Canalejas and Raphael Albacin (members of
    Hugo's gang); Ivan Scratuglia, Luciano Rossi and Guillermo
    Mendez (members of the Klan), with Rafael Vaquero

*   *   *

Released in 1966, *Django* was Sergio Corbucci's calling card to European cinema audiences that Leone wasn't the only Italian director capable of rewriting the rules of the western. Corbucci, like Leone and Tessari, was working in popular Italian cinema for over a decade before he became involved in westerns in the early sixties. Previously, he had written and directed comedies for popular comedians like Toto and 'Franchi and Ingrassia', including *Son of the Leopard* (1961) and *The Shortest Day* (1963 – a parody of *The Longest Day*). A diverse director, Corbucci worked as Leone's assistant on *The Last Days of Pompeii* (1959) and helmed *Romulus and Remus* (1961 – also called *Duel of the Titans*), *Goliath and the Vampires* (1961 – co-directed by Giacomo Gentilomo) and *Son of Spartacus* (1962). He also worked on the effective Gothic *Castle of Blood* (1964 – or *La Danza Macabra*) starring Birkenhead-born horror queen Barbara Steele. Corbucci here co-directed with Antonio Margheriti and altered his name on the publicity to 'Gordon Wilson Jnr'.

Corbucci's first western, *Red Pastures* (1963 – also released as *Massacre at Canyon Grande*) featured Robert Mitchum's son, James. Corbucci again adopted a pseudonym ('Stanley Corbett') and shared the direction (this time with Albert Band). *Red Pastures* pre-empted Leone's depiction of two warring gangs in *Fistful*, though in Corbucci's film they quarrel over a spread of land (the red pastures of the title). This early spaghetti western was not filmed in Spain, but near Trieste on the 'Winnetou' sets.

Corbucci made two other westerns before *Django*: the erratic *Minnesota Clay* (1964) and the mediocre *Johnny Oro* (1966 – made before *Django* but released afterwards). Both films contained flashes of brilliance, but were muddied by Corbucci's reliance on Hollywood clichés. Veering wildly between classic westerns and Corbucci's tendency for the bizarre, *Minnesota Clay* was an amalgamation of two films: *A Fistful of Dollars* and the Hollywood western *The Proud Ones* (1956). From *Fistful* Corbucci took the premise of two gangs vying for control of a town. From *The Proud Ones* he reused the plot of a lawman cleaning up a town even though he is going blind. Gunfighter 'Minnesota Clay' ('the greatest shot in the whole world') was portrayed by 46-year-old Cameron Mitchell, who was making a living in Rome. Corbucci hired Mitchell to have an authentic American star for the publicity. The film was a moderate success and Corbucci even distributed the film with his own name on it. He was the first Italian western director brave enough to do so.

Following the breezily inconsequential *Johnny Oro*, in which Mark Damon played a black-clad Mexican bounty-hunter with a solid gold pistol, Corbucci set to work on *Django*, financed by BRC Produzione (Rome) and Tecisa Film (Madrid). It seems producers were none too keen to let Corbucci loose on a film set by himself, reigning him in with co-directors. But when Corbucci did 'go solo', the excesses that had previously been curbed surfaced in all their delirious glory, as Corbucci painted his name in spaghetti-western history in huge, blood-red letters.

Again influenced by *Fistful* and *Yojimbo*, *Django*'s story was written by Corbucci and his younger brother Bruno. Franco Rossetti, Jose Maesso and Piero Vivarelli contributed to the screenplay. A coffin-dragging drifter called Django returns from the Civil War and is caught in a private war between two factions in a bloody border ghost-town; this time north of the Mexican border. The Mexican gang are a group of fugitive renegades, led by sadistic General Hugo Rodriguez, who are lying low during the Mexican revolution. Their enemies are an army of red-hooded Confederate Ku Klux Klansmen, led by ruthless Major Jackson. Django takes on both gangs, with a machine-gun he keeps hidden in his coffin. In an added plot twist (borrowed from *Minnesota Clay*) the major is responsible for murdering Django's wife. Subplots detail the Mexicans needing money to buy machine-guns (so they can return to Mexico) and Django's relationship with Maria, a prostitute in town. Django initially sides with the Mexicans, but eventually double-crosses them. The Mexicans capture him and crush his hands, leaving Django incapacitated for the final confrontation with Jackson in the Tombstone cemetery.

In *A Fistful of Dollars*, the Rojos and the Baxters are liquor and gun merchants: as long as their purposes don't clash, everything is fine. There are no such economics in *Django*. Although neither side appears to trade anything (except lead), there is blood-lust and hatred. The Klansmen are southern fanatics, fighting a prejudicial war against the Mexican peasants. Major Jackson is a racist, blinded by 'the cause', for which he and all his followers will readily die (and eventually do). With his 'southern-fried' logic (that anyone who isn't 'pale-skinned and southern' is trash) and his sadism, he is an all-powerful figure, controlling the surrounding country-side with a religious fervour bordering on insanity. The Mexican bandit gang are sketchily drawn idealists, while the local peons are simply moving targets for Jackson. General Hugo is based on Fernando Sancho's greedy General Ortiz in *Minnesota Clay*. When the Mexicans get the chance to kill the Klan priest, Brother Jonathan, they first humiliate him by severing his ear and making him eat it, in retribution for Jackson casually shooting the peons as though they were game. With the pot already boiling, into this mayhem walks Django, who is like no other previous western hero.

Corbucci's hero was named after jazzman Django Reinhardt. Himself a gypsy, Reinhardt was the foremost purveyor of gypsy jazz (or 'jazz manouche') and a member of the Hot Club of France. He was only 18 when he was involved in an accident that almost ended his life. The story goes (as bizarre as anything Corbucci ever concocted) that on the night of 2 November 1928 he returned to his caravan, which was full of celluloid flowers that his pregnant wife had made to sell the next day at the local cemetery. Django lit a candle and accidentally ignited the celluloid. He escaped, but badly burned the left side of his body and disfigured his fretting hand. After an 18-month convalescence he emerged a better guitarist. Corbucci's Django's hands are crushed by horses' hooves (for stealing the Mexicans' gold), but Reinhardt was clearly the inspiration for the character.

With the ever-present coffin, *Django*'s atmosphere owes much to Italian horror films. Gothic elements include the lurid colour schemes, moody lighting, Grand

Guignol settings and the Klansmen (with their ceremonial cross burning). There is also the deserted, lifeless 'citta di spettro', which resembles a graveyard. The Klansmen's hoods recall Mario Bava's *Kill Baby Kill* (1966); as a coroner arrives in the creepy town of Kernigan, he sees four red-hooded pallbearers carrying a coffin to the local cemetery. The pre-title sequence of Massimo Pupillo's *Bloody Pit of Horror* (1965) features a scarlet-hooded murderer put to death in an iron maiden, only to rise again and possess an out-of-work Cinecitta muscleman actor called Travis Anderson (played by Mickey Hargitay, an out-of-work Cinecitta muscleman). Giorgio Ferroni's *Mill of the Stone Women* (1960) influenced the look of Corbucci's sets and the eerie photographic style. In Ferroni's film, a young art student (Pierre Brice) stays at a secluded windmill in the Dutch canal system. The unsettling décor (weird statuary, Gothic drapes and crucifixes) inspired the clutter of *Django*, with Maria's room and the dilapidated City Hotel echoing Ferroni's macabre attention to detail.

For the title role, Corbucci hired 23-year-old, Parma-born 'Franco Nero' (real name Francesco Sparanero) who had previously appeared in a brace of cheap sci-fi movies directed by Antonio Margheriti – *War of the Planets* (or *The Deadly Diaphanoids*) and *Wild, Wild Planet* (both 1965). He had also played Abel (to Richard Harris's Cain) in *The Bible…In the Beginning* (1966). Mark Damon (star of *Johnny Oro*) was slated to play Django, but Silvia Dionisio (the wife of Ruggero Deodato, Corbucci's assistant director) convinced Corbucci that Nero was a better choice. Nero turned out to be ideal for Django, with his slow, deliberate mannerisms and smouldering looks – whether casting his eye over the heroine, or staring down a villain. His competence at performing his own fight scenes also helped, noticeably in a violent bar-room scrape with Corbucci's regular stuntman Remo De Angelis.

Django deployed the core of Corbucci's western stock company. Gino Pernice (billed as 'Jimmy Douglas') played Brother Jonathan and went on to feature in *The Hellbenders* (1967) and *The Specialists* (1969). Jose Bodalo (who portrayed General Hugo), Guillermo Mendez, Simon Arriaga, Angel Alvarez, Jose Canalejas and stunt coordinator and firearms expert Remo De Angelis (or 'Erik Schippers') all appeared in more Corbucci efforts. Eduardo Fajardo (as Major Jackson) emerged as Corbucci's favourite villain, especially in the director's political spaghetti trilogy. Silvana Bacci carved a niche for herself playing Mexican señoritas and *Django* also marked the film debut of Luciano Rossi, later of *Django the Bastard* and *They Call Me Trinity*. Two exceptionally prolific spaghetti-western players contributed brief cameos to *Django*'s violent opening sequence. Burly Lucio De Santis played the Mexican bandit who tortures Maria, while Ivan Scratuglia was the leader of the Klansmen who gun down De Santis and friends.

Instead of the sun-bleached towns of most spaghetti westerns, *Django*'s was muddy and rain-sodden. The town is the Elios set outside Rome, but look out for an incongruous, high wire fence at one end of the street. Corbucci and Carlo Simi took the street outside the Grafton Store in *Shane* (1953) and based the set around it. Corbucci reduced the main street to a quagmire, though the deep tread marks make you wonder what sort of traffic caused this swamp in a deserted ghost-town. The mud was in contrast to the surrounding arid landscape. The countryside sequences were shot in Spain, north of Madrid near Colmenar Viejo (the watchtower and corral sequences) and La Pedriza at Manzanares El Real, used for the chase sequences around Mexican Fort Cheriba and the scene in which the Mexicans return to Mexico (and are ambushed by the Federales). The fort was near the Santillana reservoir, which is clearly visible in the distance. The remaining scenes were lensed on the coast of Italy, in the wild west of Lazio: the graveyard, the rope bridge and the mud-flats (actually a stretch of beach and an inlet at Tor Caldara, near Anzio). The landscape's bleakness was echoed in the stark interiors. Details such as the stove and the run-down décor recall the street outside, where scaffolding seems to hold most of the town up, whilst other items (potted palms in the saloon or the prostitutes' life-sized sign – 'Open every Night') attempt a more exotic flavour.

In keeping with the desolate setting, Carlo Simi opted for a winter look for the costumes. Django's long Union coat, cavalry trousers and black hat place him as a soldier. The fingerless gloves and scarf make him look like an undertaker. To this strange outfit Corbucci added a belt-feed machine-gun and a coffin, making Django the most distinctive-looking spaghetti-western hero of them all. The Klansmen bear a passing resemblance to the Hammond brothers in Sam Peckinpah's *Ride the High Country* (1962), while other wintry items (scarves, gloves) were borrowed from Andre De Toth's western *Day of the Outlaw* (1959). Costume preparations for Corbucci's movie also involved cutting eyeholes in a lot of red sheets – the hoods were Corbucci's idea, to disguise the ugly-looking extras.

The film was shot by Corbucci's regular cameraman Enzo Barboni in the cold winter of 1965–66. The action sequences were edited for maximum impact, with shots of the machine-gun pouring lead intercut with its bloody effects. Barboni's crisp Eastmancolor photography disguised the film's modest budget with a sur-realistic colour scheme and gave Django a garish look that suited the material. The prostitutes, with their bright dresses and feather boas (in reds, yellows and blues) and the Klansmen, wearing blood-red masks, scarves and hoods, contrast vividly with their drab and decrepit surroundings. Like *Yojimbo*, the first shot of *Django* is the hero walking away from the camera, but here the rain is pouring and the location is rather less exotic – a desolate mud-flat in Italy. Corbucci cuts to Django's boots, trudging through the mud until finally the coffin slides into view, accompanied by the title *Django* in huge red letters.

Like all Italian western heroes, Django is a loner. One of the Mexican bandits refers to him as a 'stray dog', while General Hugo calls him 'The fastest-drawing gringo this side of the border', and 'A thief, a murderer and an outlaw'. Django is a troubled antihero. We learn that he fought in the Civil War (indicating that once he had some ideals), but background information is sparse in the English-language print. Django, like Eastwood's stranger, manipulates the two factions, in particular the Mexicans. It is Django's plan to steal Jackson's gold from Fort Cheriba (across the border in Mexico) – ostensibly for Hugo to buy nine machine-guns from gun-runners in Pecos, though really to force Jackson into the open. Django is already familiar with both villains; Jackson killed Django's wife and Django saved the general's life in prison. This debt is the only reason the general spares Django's life for betraying them, crippling his hands instead. We learn that Django was unable to prevent his wife's death and presume he was away fighting when she was murdered. But it seems Django took a while to get home. During the final confrontation in the cemetery, Django rests his Colt Peacemaker on a wooden cross bearing the name Mercedes Zaro. Beneath her name are the dates 1833–69, which sets *Django* at least four years after the end of the Civil War. It took Django even longer to get back than John Wayne in *The Searchers*. That said, he was walking.

Django is the clearest example of Corbucci's debunking of Hollywood western conventions. In an innovation for western heroes, Django is never seen riding a horse. Corbucci's town has a bizarre community: instead of the expected western inhabitants (the general storekeeper, the blacksmith, the law-abiding townsfolk), Corbucci populates his with what must be the smallest cast ever assembled for a western – Nathaniel, a violin-playing bartender and five prostitutes. Customers are so scarce that they only make money when one of the gangs visits the brothel, and with the conflict raging their patrons are getting fewer. Nathaniel offers the reverse of the undertaker in *Fistful*. He wants Django to get killed quickly, reasoning that then he would lose less custom.

There is no morality in the 'dead city' and religion is thin on the ground. Brother Jonathan, the local priest, is a spineless runt with an Abe Lincoln beard. He spies for the Klan and supports the major's policy of ridding the countryside of Mexicans. Jackson and Jonathan clearly get on like a cross on fire. Jonathan leers as Jackson executes peons, believing the major to be doing God's work. The Lord obviously isn't on Jonathan's side (he probably frowns on cross-burning) and the priest gets his comeuppance in spectacular fashion when he is made to eat his own severed ear, in a bizarre variation of the rite of Communion.

At its best, Corbucci's style was imaginative, intense and cruel. The death of Jonathan is a classic moment in Italian western film-making, with the gore laid on thick. General Hugo draws a huge Bowie knife and laughs at the cornered priest, 'We know just what to do with ears such as yours', before separating Jonathan from his ear. The assistant director on *Django* was Ruggero Deodato, who obviously watched and learned how to stage a bloodbath, as he later made the widely banned and truly repulsive *Cannibal Holocaust* (1979). Corbucci also includes exploitative moments in *Django*. A Mexican girl performs a striptease to distract Hugo's guards and three whores mud wrestle in the street (though two of them are clearly stunt-men in drag).

There is much black humour in *Django*. The only member of Jackson's gang who really needs to wear a mask (but doesn't) is Ringo, an ugly kid with crooked teeth and a scar – a swipe at Tessari's 'Ringo' films, where the virtuous hero had

Original Italian artwork for Sergio Corbucci's *Django* (1966) by Rodolfo
Gasparri, featuring Franco Nero as the coffin-dragging stranger.

youthful good looks; Corbucci's 'Ringo' guns down unarmed Mexican peons. Maria's friend, Amelia, changes dresses just before the Major comes visiting, observing that Jackson 'hates green', 'But he's crazy about red'. Nathaniel says at one point that he 'hasn't got a chance of getting to the graveyard alive'. And though a relationship develops between Django and Maria (played by Loredana Nusciak), she has to pull a Winchester on the hero, so that she isn't left behind when he makes a dash for it. Unlike Hollywood westerners, Django wasn't going to rescue her and it is up to Maria to make sure she gets out of town.

Corbucci's comic-strip directorial style is erratic and it's difficult to isolate definitive examples of his technique. He uses sweeping tracking shots, odd camera angles and his trademark rapid zooms. He even films one dialogue scene through a swinging lamp and takes a hand-held camera into the middle of a fistfight. The initial swift body count sets the tone, but it's the choreography of the later gun-fights, ambushes and beatings that really stand out. The three finest sequences are the one-sided showdown between the Klan and Django in the street, the hand-crushing sequence and the final shootout in the cemetery called 'Tombstone'. The two confrontations between Django and the Klan were shot on similar locations. The street of the town is on a slope, with a large corral gate at the far end, while the graveyard is similarly sited on an incline, with the gate positioned in the distance. Shacks or crosses mark the space between the opponents, but it's still a killing ground.

At the graveyard climax, the only sounds are the whistling wind and the banshee-howl of a coyote, as Django removes the trigger guard from his Colt with his teeth and desperately tries to balance the gun on a cross. It is significant that Corbucci doesn't allow Django to recover for the final showdown. This became important to Corbucci's work – a severely injured man, fearlessly facing his enemies alone. The tension mounts as first five Klansmen arrive at the gate, followed by Jackson. In the cemetery shootout, Django's wife's grave is nearby, accentuating the final reckoning. Having dispatched the major, Django stumbles through the cemetery at the film's close. By this point Django has lost control, as the film becomes a sadistic endurance test; Maria's been badly wounded by the Mexicans and the gold has sunk into a quicksand pit. The title song offers redemption ('After the showers the sun will be shining') though there is little evidence of the sun shining in the final shot.

The music for *Django* was composed by Luis Enriquez Bacalov, an Argentinian who worked in Italian cinema throughout the sixties. Bacalov formed a pop group in the early sixties called 'Luis Enriquez and his Electric Men' (Alessandro Alessandroni was also a member). He then formed his own orchestra and moved into film-scoring. One of his early compositions was the music to Pasolini's *The Gospel According to St. Matthew* (1964). For the opening sequence of *Django*, the music had to reinforce the impact of Corbucci's unique vision. The title song begins with a jagged flourish of electric guitar, followed by syncopated violins, bluesy piano, 'I Cantori' and a baritone vocal belted out by Roberto Fia. The song is attributed to Migliacci/Enriquez (Bacalov sometimes used the writing alias 'Luis Enriquez') and includes the lyrics: 'Django, you must face another day. Django, now your love has gone away. But you've lost her forever, Django.' It also features the most vicious guitar solo to grace a spaghetti western. The blues piano playing and the odd piano effects were a result of Bacalov's initial training in the instrument. Lyricist Franco Migliacci contributed to the popular standard 'Volare (Nel Blu di Pinto di Blu)' which was covered to great success by Dean Martin, and also wrote the Italian version of 'It Had Better Be Tonight' for *The Pink Panther* (1964). On the 45rpm single of *Django* (which was a big hit in Italy), Fia billed himself as Berto Fia, while the English release christened him 'Rocky Roberts'.

The rest of Bacalov's score is equally effective. Django's entrances, with low-angled shots of his boots, are accompanied by the scrape of the coffin amplified on the soundtrack and his 'theme' (on guitar or strings). Sometimes Bacalov uses high-pitched violins ascending the scale and reaching a discordant climax (when Jackson plugs peons from the watchtower), while elsewhere traditional Mexican arrangements dominate: 'Vals De Juana Yimena' and 'Corrido' (which segues into 'El Pajarito'). 'Duello nel Fango' (or 'Duel in the Mud') is led by a doom-laden piano, as Jackson arrives in town at the end of the film to find Django, and in a glaring continuity error walks down the street with five men, then enters the saloon with at least eight (one of whom appears to be a reincarnated Brother Jonathan). Bacalov's two outstanding compositions for the film are the 'Blue Dark Waltz' (a simple guitar lament) and 'La Corsa' – which begins with a flute solo, as Django sits on a fallen tree trunk waiting for the Klan, then suddenly explodes with machine-gun drum rolls, high-pitched flutes and triumphant brass, as the Klan engulf the main street and Django opens his coffin.

Released in April 1966, *Django* was a phenomenon in Italy and turned Nero into a big box-office attraction. The film was also popular in Spain and especially so in Germany. The original Italian-language script is more poetic and informative (we find out that Django was in prison for desertion) and the religious references are more overt. In the Italian print, during the final showdown, Major Jackson shouts, 'In the name of the Father, the Son and the Holy Spirit', as he makes the sign of the cross in bullets on a grave marker, while Django calls back, 'Amen!' when he kills the major. The Italian version also had a longer credits sequence (with more production staff listed), while the English version adds several pseudonyms. The uncut print runs at 87 minutes and was severely criticised in Italy for its extreme violence.

Despite its European popularity, *Django* was unreleased in the UK (because of its violence) and the US (it failed to find a distributor), though Nero says that Jack Nicholson tried to acquire the rights in 1967. Early English-language versions to surface were poorly edited, but they did include a shot missing from most prints of the film – Django and Maria's evocative walk down the muddy street into town. The English-language version of *Django* makes up in violence what it lacks in synchronised lip movement. The English dubbing is atrocious, but Corbucci's strong visual imagination prevails. In his subsequent westerns for Corbucci, Nero used his own voice in the English-language prints, which is just as well judging from the out-of-character, matter-of-fact accent foisted on him here. Nero worked with Corbucci in 1968 on *A Professional Gun* (his best western performance), but only played Django again in the inferior *Django Strikes Again* (1987).

Other actors weren't so particular, and in 1966 Italian studios began churning out 'Django' films that had little to do with Corbucci's original. Like Hercules before him, Django soon had a series of films devoted to his various adventures, though many of the films only used the name to cajole audiences into the cinemas. This is noticeable in such films as *Django Shoots First* (1966) – in which the hero was called Glenn Garvin, 'Django' was an alias – *A Few Dollars for Django* (1966) – which managed to rip off both Leone and Corbucci in the title and then called the hero Regan – and *Django Kill* (1967) – though a fine western, it had nothing to do with other 'Django' movies: Tomas Milian's hero was known only as 'the stranger'. There were 18 movies made between 1966 and 1973 as part of the 'Django' series. In addition to these derivatives, many unrelated items were retitled for the German, French and UK/US market. Twenty-one unrelated movies were rechristened for German release, three for France and eleven for the English-speaking market. Embarrassed by the sheer volume of 'Django' products in cinemas by the late sixties, some legitimate heirs changed their titles inversely – *Django the Bastard*, for instance, became *The Stranger's Gundown*.

Of the 50 films to 'feature' Django, only four are worth viewing: *Django Kill*, *$10,000 Blood Money* (1966), *Django the Bastard* (1969) and the companion piece to Corbucci's original – *Django Get a Coffin Ready* (1968). Of these, *Django Kill* shows few traces of Corbucci's style, while the remaining trio trade on ideas (and even cast-members) from the original. *$10,000 Blood Money* featured Gianni Garko (billed as 'Gary Hudson') as the hero and recast Loredana Nusciak as Django's love interest, here a French saloon-owner named Michelou. Django is a bounty-hunter and the film details one of his adventures – tracking down a bandit, Manuel Cortez, who has kidnapped a rich land-owner's daughter. Django is ambushed, and in the film's most affecting scenes Michelou nurses him back to health. She tries to make him give up bounty-hunting but he refuses. Eventually Cortez kills Michelou in a stage hold-up, triggering a confrontation with Django. This is Garko's finest western and has a bizarre score by Nora Orlandi; it is one of the few spaghettis to feature that fifties sci-fi staple, the theremin.

Django the Bastard (also called *Django the Avenger*) was the best western performance by 'Anthony Steffen' (possibly because he co-wrote it, under his real name Antonio De Teffe). Here Django (Steffen) is a spectral avenger – a soldier back not only from the war, but also from the dead – who takes revenge on three northern officers who betrayed his unit in battle. The film's atmosphere is decidedly unsettling, with Django gradually wiping out the betrayers' gang in a series of moonlit set pieces. Django wears a black poncho, which makes him look like a large bat, and mysteriously appears out of thin air. Noteworthy moments include Django's habit of heralding the deaths of the villains with grave-markers carved with the day's date, and the final lines are particularly effective. Django and the heroine (Rada Rassimov) are left with a fortune, and she, beside herself with joy, says 'We'll be rich forever', to which the 'ghost' replies 'We won't live forever', before vanishing. The film has often been cited as an influence on Eastwood's *High Plains Drifter* (1972). But when Eastwood's film was released in Italy (as *Lo Straniero Senza Nome* or 'The Stranger with No Name'), the ghostly element of the story was axed and the dubbing made it clear that Eastwood was the dead sheriff's brother.

The finest bastard son of Corbucci's original was 1968's *Django Get a Coffin Ready* (also released as *Viva Django*) directed by Ferdinando Baldi, co-written by Rossetti, photographed by Barboni and financed by BRC Produzione. Nero was supposed to star (as part of a three-film deal with BRC), but although he made the next film in the series, *Texas Adios* (1966), the producers brought in Terence Hill for the third film. *Get a Coffin Ready* was a prequel to *Django*, detailing Django's transformation from small-time gunman to avenging coffin-dragger. It featured Hill as Django and retained the gravedigger clothes, the coffin and the machine-gun from the original. At the beginning of *Get a Coffin Ready*, Django is a friend of prospective senatorial candidate, David Barry (Horst Frank). While Django is escorting a shipment of cash, he is ambushed and badly wounded; his wife is killed and Barry is responsible. Five years later, Barry is continuing the robberies, covering

Dying for the Cause: the Klansmen arrive to face Django in the muddy Elios Studios western set for *Django* (1966).

his own responsibility and that of his gang, led by Lucas (George Eastman). Django (now dressed in his trademark Union jacket, coat and scarf) has fully recovered and goes looking for revenge.

Django's vengeance features three scenes that are equal to Corbucci's original. In the first, Django is captured and viciously beaten up by Lucas's men in a barn. Typically for Italian westerns, Django recovers quickly (here by sticking his head in a bucket of cold water, a standard 'cure-all') and escapes. That night, in the muddy street, Django torches the saloon, annihilates the gang and burns Lucas to death in the inferno. Then Barry keeps a date with Django at a deserted hillside cemetery. On his arrival, he finds Django digging Barry's grave, but Django has been double-crossed and the villain's gang appears. Barry's parting words to Django sadistically echo *The Good, the Bad and the Ugly* – 'The dead are in their graves, understand? And you are dead. This is your grave, mister…dig.' Django digs until he unearths a coffin, inside which is his machine-gun. Standing absolutely no chance, Barry and the gang are soon reduced to a heap of corpses. Also of note are the rousing score by Gianfranco Reverberi and the title song 'You'd Better Smile' (sung by Nicola Di Bari).

Along with these semi-official 'Django' sequels, many Italian westerns took Django's outfit and name in vain. A plethora of black-garbed, black-hatted heroes (wearing grey scarves and fingerless gloves) appeared in films like *Today It's Me… Tomorrow You* (1968) and *The Unholy Four* (1969). Django's prop machine-gun was reused in subsequent BRC Produzione releases *Rita of the West* and *Long Ride from Hell*, while in Enzo G. Castellari's *Seven Winchesters for a Massacre* (1967), the gold is hidden in an Indian cemetery in the grave of the Comanche hero 'Django'.

The surreal musical spaghetti western *Rita of the West* (1967) included a witty satire of *Django*. It starred Italian singing sensation Rita Pavone as the feared gunslinger 'Little Rita' ('The famousest gunfighter in the West'). Throughout the movie, Rita faces a series of Italian western heroes and villains including a 'super-bounty killer' named Ringo (who looks exactly like Eastwood's stranger and gets blown apart with a golden grenade) and coffin-dragging Django (who is told at one point that he 'sure do waste a lot of ammunition'). Django (Lucio Rosato) explains how he came by a coffin full of gold ('I went to a lot of trouble for that gold. Whole lot of Mexicans beat on me and crushed my hands') and that he suffered from an Oedipus complex as a child, which explains a lot. What destroys *Rita's* credibility as a spaghetti western are the musical numbers that hurtle out of nowhere to terrorise the audience. The incidental music by Robby Poitevin isn't bad, but the song-and-dance numbers (in their original Italian and choreographed by Gino Landi) don't work at all (sample chorus – 'Howdy, Howdy, Howdy Sceriffo'). It is safe to say you've never seen a western like *Rita*, a film with 'made for domestic distribution' written all over it.

In Europe *Django* was the biggest hit of Corbucci's career so far and it remains his most famous and controversial film. Corbucci's next release was the pedestrian

Johnny Oro (1966), ironically retitled *Ringo and his Golden Pistol* to cash in on the 'Ringo' films. If it had been retitled *Django and his Golden Pistol* it would have probably made more money. With *Django*, Corbucci forged a western landscape so violent, garish and spectacular that it would take some equalling as pure visceral entertainment. But the director was honing his style, and the years 1966–68 would see Corbucci become a major force in the development of action cinema. The style, irreverence and grit that he brought to the western would be widely imitated. As imitated as Leone, in fact, though far less acknowledged.

6

'It's the Reason Why I Live, Why I Breathe'

— Carlo Lizzani's *The Hills Run Red* (1966)

The Hills Run Red (**1966**)
original title: *Un Fiume di Dollari*
Credits
DIRECTOR – 'Lee W. Beaver' (Carlo Lizzani)
PRODUCERS – Ermanno Donati and Luigi Carpentieri
STORY AND SCREENPLAY – 'Dean Craig' (Piero Regnoli)
ART DIRECTOR – Aurelio Crugnola
COSTUMES – Elio Micheli
EDITOR – Ornella Micheli
DIRECTOR OF PHOTOGRAPHY – 'Toni Secchi' (Antonio Secchi)
MUSIC COMPOSER – 'Leo Nichols' (Ennio Morricone)
MUSIC CONDUCTOR – Bruno Nicolai
Interiors filmed at Dino De Laurentiis Studios, Rome
Techniscope/Technicolor
An Italian/Spanish co-production
Dino De Laurentiis Cinematografica (Rome)/CB Films
    (Barcelona)
Released internationally by United Artists
Cast
Thomas Hunter (Jerry Brewster alias 'Jim Houston'); Henry
Silva (Garcia Mendez); Dan Duryea (Colonel Winny Getz);
Nando Gazzalo (Ken Seagall alias 'Ken Milton'); 'Nicoletta
Machiavelli', Nicoletta Rangoni Machiavelli (Mary-Ann);
Gianna Serra (Hattie Gardner); Geoffrey Copleston (Brian
Horner); Loris Loddi (Tim Brewster); Guglielmo Spolettini
(Pedro); Tiberio Mitri (Union cavalry sergeant); Mauro
Mannatrizio (Union soldier); Paolo Magalotti (Stane,
Horner's henchman); Mirko Valentin (Sancho); Goffredo
Unger (Union colonel); Lucio De Santis (Juan); Guido

Celano (blacksmith); Vittorio Bonos (gambler); 'Jeff
Cameron', Nino Scarciofolo (Randall, blond Mendez
gunman); 'Puccio Ceccarelli', Pietro Ceccarelli (bald Mendez
gunman); Osiride Pevarello (bearded Mendez gunman) with
Sandro Dori, Gianluigi Crescenzi, Fiorella Ferrero, Goffredo
Matassi, Piero Morgia, John M. Gaskins and Luigi Scavran

*   *   *

As spaghetti westerns gained momentum throughout 1966 and production companies rushed to release films before public interest faded, more 'serious' Italian
film-makers became attracted to making films in this popular form. No doubt
enticed by the huge profits rolling into the Italian studios' coffers, several directors
relished the opportunity to make thought-provoking movies that would take big
money at the box office, whilst being lauded by the intelligentsia. Carlo Lizzani,
who made westerns under the unusual pseudonym 'Lee W. Beaver', was a case in
point. He began as a militant film critic, then became a documentary film-maker
and was a collaborator on neo-realist films, writing *Germany, Year Zero* (1947) and
Bitter Rice (1948). Given the chance to direct, he chose to make films concerning
the Resistance or clandestine espionage, including *Achtung! Banditi!* (1951) and
The Dirty Game (1965). Lizzani made two westerns in the mid-sixties and *The
Hills Run Red* was the first and best of them. It was financed by Dino De Laurentiis
and Barcelona-based CB Films, with Ermanno Donati and Luigi Carpentieri
producing. CB Films co-financed a *Magnificent Seven* sequel, *Return of the Seven*
(1966), while Donati and Carpentieri were responsible for some of the best and
worst in Italian genre cinema: *The Terror of Dr Hitchcock* (1962), *Maciste in Hell*
(1962) and *Day of the Owl* (1968).

The Hills Run Red was written by Piero Regnoli, under the pseudonym 'Dean
Craig', as a savage revenge western. Following the Civil War, Jerry Brewster and
Ken Seagall (two ex-Confederates) steal $600,000 in Union army cash. As they
head for the Mexican border a Union patrol intercepts them. Brewster and Seagall
agree to draw cards to decide who will escape – Seagall wins and gets away with the
haul, while Brewster is thrown into prison at Fort Wilson. Five years later, Brewster
is released and discovers that his wife is dead and his son is missing, as a direct
result of Seagall's spite. With the help of a mysterious gunman, Winny Getz, he
settles his score with Seagall (now a rich land-owner), is reunited with his son and
falls for Seagall's sister, Mary-Ann.

Hills is convoluted, with subplots, double-crosses and twists. To further com-
plicate matters both Brewster and Seagall use aliases for much of the film – Texan
avenger Brewster adopts the name 'Jim Houston', while Seagall uses his ill-gotten
gains to become rancher 'Ken Milton'. *Hills* also borrows from *Fistful*: here the
inter-gang conflict is a range war, as two factions vie for the fertile pastures around

Austin. Saloon-owner Brian Horner is aided by Brewster in a bid to defeat his nemesis Ken Milton, who wants to run Horner out of town.

Lizzani took fifties revenge westerns as a starting point. These were epitomised by two bodies of work: Anthony Mann's films (mostly with James Stewart in the lead) and the Budd Boetticher-directed, Burt Kennedy-scripted films with ageing Randolph Scott (the 'Ranown' series). Both directors realised the power of landscapes and the suppression of the hero's motives, intelligently adding a psychological element. Instead of the young 'misunderstood' teenagers of many fifties westerns, Mann and Boetticher's heroes were older men, who had suffered a traumatic experience (sometimes the violent death of a family member) and were driven by bitterness, rather than morality. *Hills* is the closest any director has come to an ersatz approximation of Mann's acrimony and brutality – quite simply, this was a Mann western for the sixties. The connection was secured when Lizzani cast two key figures from these films – Dan Duryea (from Mann's *Winchester '73*) and Henry Silva (from Boetticher's *The Tall T*). Lizzani's main reference points were two of Mann's films – *The Naked Spur* (1953) and *The Man from Laramie* (1955). Lizzani's Mannerisms include James Stewart's nightmares (when he calls out his dead wife's name) from the first film, plus the brutality of the totally wired villain, (played by Alex Nicol) and the savage vendetta from the second.

Lizzani cast 59-year-old Dan Duryea, a perennial heavy, as heroic Winny Getz. Duryea was a key figure in Hollywood westerns. His most widely known role was grinning killer Waco Johnny Dean in *Winchester '73* (1950). In addition to big-budget efforts, he also made a series of excellent 'B-movies', mostly for Universal. The best were *Silver Lode* (1954), a clever diatribe against McCarthyism, and *Rails into Laramie* (1954), in which Lee Van Cleef appeared as Duryea's sidekick Ace and title song balladeer Rex Allen dared to rhyme 'Laramie' with 'marry me'. Duryea also had guest-spots on various TV shows, including *Rawhide*. He appeared in a couple of episodes, the best of which was 'Incident of the Prophesy'. Duryea played Brother William, a villainous zealot masquerading as the town priest. Though *Hills* was one of his last screen appearances (Duryea died in 1968), his world weariness suited Getz's persona and the swept-back hair and thin, reedy voice added a touch of class to the proceedings.

A member of Frank Sinatra's 'Rat Pack', Henry Silva played Seagall's demented Mexican henchman Garcia Mendez. Born in Brooklyn of Puerto Rican ancestry, Silva had an unmistakable angular face, with cold, oriental eyes. Elements of Silva's character (his black leather jacket and excessive behaviour) were reminiscent of Hispanic henchman Johnny Cool (William Campbell) in John Sturges's *Backlash* (1956), another western about a crook returning from the Civil War with an unexplained fortune.

Thomas Hunter, as Jerry Brewster, completed the central trio of protagonists, making *The Hills Run Red* one of the few sixties spaghetti westerns with genuine American-born actors battling it out. Usually an American star faced an Italian villain, with a Spanish gang. Hunter's love interest was Nicoletta Machiavelli, as Seagall's naive sister Mary-Ann, blissfully unaware of her brother's malicious past. The second female lead was Gianna Serra, best known for her appearance as a member of James Coburn's exotic home help in *Our Man Flint* (1966). Other actors included Geoffrey Copleston and Paolo Magalotti, both of whom had been involved in spaghetti westerns since the early days. Copleston was responsible for dubbing the English version of *Django*, while stuntman Magalotti had appeared in the 'MacGregor' westerns under the pseudonym 'Paul Carter'.

Lizzani cast Italian smoothy Nando Gazzalo as Ken Seagall, the grubby outlaw who reinvents himself as Ken Milton, gentleman rancher. When we first see unshaven Seagall in his new incarnation as Milton, riding along in a buggy, he is almost unrecognisable, with his smart suit and Douglas Fairbanks moustache. In his next film, *Django Shoots First* (1966), Gazzalo played villainous banker Ken Kluster and reused Milton's debonair wardrobe. The plot of *Django Shoots First* was a variation on Lizzani's film. Gazzalo's character had wrongfully imprisoned his business partner (who turned out to be Django's father) and appropriated his money, only for Django to appear to set things right.

The Hills Run Red was shot in Italy and Spain during the summer of 1966, with the well-chosen locations reinforcing the range war subplot – a contrast between

Jerry Brewster (Thomas Hunter) is released from a five-year stretch in Fort Wilson at the beginning of Carlo Lizzani's *The Hills Run Red* (1966).

rocky hills and lush grassland. 'Austin' was the western set at De Laurentiis Studios, near Rome ('Seven Hills Run Red'). The Mendez blockhouse, the blacksmith's and the Mayflower Ranch were also located in Italy. Part of the opening chase, the riding scenes and the canyon ambush were shot in Spain (at La Pedriza and Colmenar). Fort Wilson was near Madrid, while Brewster's ranch was the MacGregors' farmhouse near Colmenar Viejo.

Elio Micheli's costumes added to the film's success. Silva is dressed entirely in black leather, with a broad-brimmed black sombrero. This arresting outfit owed much to Dirk Bogarde's homosexual bandito, Anacleto Comache, who controlled the Mexican town of Contana in the camp British western, *The Singer Not the Song* (filmed in Torremolinos in 1961). Bogarde's cane-toting, cat-stroking villain was dressed in a black shirt, hat and tight leather trousers. One critic noted that the real star of the film was Bogarde's pants. Hunter and Duryea's duds are more traditional; Brewster wears standard cowboy garb, while Getz (a secret service man travelling incognito) wears mostly black.

Like several spaghettis, *Hills* begins at the end of the American Civil War. Following an unseen payroll robbery, Lizzani gets straight into the action with the pre-title sequence – a chase through the countryside near the Mexican border. Brewster and Seagall are two Texans on the run with a fortune in stolen cash. After his capture and beating at the hands of Union cavalry, Brewster is taken to Fort Wilson for hard labour, and Lizzani's title-sequence montage details the hardships of Brewster's five-year stretch – breaking rocks and standing in a barbed-wire enclosure in the blistering sun. By the end of the titles he appears to be going slightly mad, as he dazedly revolves on the spot in his tiny, darkened cell. Upon his release, Brewster emerges blinking into the daylight, as a soldier smirks, 'What's the matter boy? Sun bother you?' Brewster looks dishevelled as his few possessions are returned to him. These items echo the plot of the film – a photograph of his wife (signifying his family before the war), his gunbelt (symbolising the vendetta) and a pack of playing cards (which represent 'fate'- it could easily have been Brewster who won the cut and escaped).

Ex-comrades Seagall and Brewster behave in similar ways throughout the film. They're both bandits at heart and following the Civil War they both claim to be someone else. In the final nighttime shootout they even use the same trick: Brewster arrives at the *hacienda* disguised in Mendez's leathers, while Seagall/ 'Milton' kills his manservant, dresses him in a smart jacket and uses the corpse as a decoy. Brewster falls for the ruse and Seagall sneers 'This is the second time you've drawn the wrong card'. But Brewster manages to douse the lights, plunging the room into darkness, and kill Seagall in a shadowy gunfight.

The Hills Run Red is a more extreme revenge movie than most, mainly due to manic performances from Hunter and Silva. It is difficult to imagine a more excessive and twisted pair of adversaries. Hunter was an underrated actor. His mannerisms and expressions recall Steve McQueen in *The Magnificent Seven* – cool, yet dynamic

– while at other points he exhibits the power of James Stewart in the Mann westerns, especially Stewart's loss of control when his anger explodes onto the screen. Hunter frequently loses his temper, at one point screaming Seagall's name into an empty landscape after torturing one of Mendez's employees. These primal emotions, coupled with his nightmares, imbue Hunter's character with more than enough evidence for psychoanalysis. His obsessive nature is summed up by his vow of revenge: 'It's the reason why I live, why I breathe'.

Silva is even more unhinged, playing Mendez with all-stops-out. He shouts most of his dialogue and is prone to histrionic outbursts, as in the aftermath of Brewster's fistfight with Los Garcianos, Mendez's gang. Mendez walks towards Brewster and draws his pistol, about to shoot. Brewster tells him to get it over with, but the villain lowers the hammer and laughs. Mendez congratulates the gringo, offers him a job and then applauds, whilst screaming at the top of his lungs, 'Bravo! Bravo!' With this eccentric behaviour, Silva creates one of the most memorable spaghetti-western villains. No one in *Hills* mugged, glared, swaggered and shouted as much as Silva did, but his exhibitionism, whether attempting to out-stare a horse or applauding Brewster's beating, was a *tour-de-force* of ham.

With the two heroes, Brewster and Getz, Lizzani alludes to the 'old man and boy' relationship from *For a Few Dollars More*, though it's de-emphasised here, as we are not sure why Getz is helping Brewster. The youngster asks, 'Is helping your neighbour your calling, maybe?' but we only find out what Getz's 'calling' is in the final scene. Firstly we hear Getz addressed as 'colonel' by a Union officer. Getz then reports that Brewster is dead, but commends 'Houston' for his bravery. Getz is some kind of Army agent (there's a reference to completing his 'assignment') and the insinuation is that the money was stolen from his care. But Getz recognises that Brewster is no longer an outlaw and appoints him Sheriff of Austin. This ending is more sentimental than the similar *dénouement* of Sergio Sollima's *Face to Face* (1967). The closing images are full of optimism, with Brewster and Tim waving goodbye to Getz as Mary-Ann looks on.

Lizzani's sentimentality and the character of Tim could easily have spoiled the film. A child actor in a major role was usually the kiss of death to spaghettis, but Loris Loddi is one of the few exceptions. Blond-haired and cherubic, he appeared in early-sixties epics, including *Cleopatra* (1961); he is the gold-clad little boy by Liz Taylor's side, during her entrance to Rome. Loddi also made westerns, including *$100,000 for Ringo* (1965), *Deguejo* (1966), *Johnny Oro* (1966) and *The Big Silence* (1967). Brewster's relationship with Tim is the sentimental heart of *Hills*, and Loddi's wide-eyed performance is convincing, imbuing the character with a sad innocence rarely seen in the genre. In their first dialogue together, their father-and-son bond is well delineated, even though Tim has no idea who the stranger is. Brewster notices that Tim draws a 'lucky sign' in the air (a circle then a cross) for good luck, which Brewster immediately recognises; Brewster makes the same sign before he cuts Seagall's deck. Tim tells the stranger that his father died a long time ago, adding, 'But he was a great cowboy, even more than you', to which Brewster simply smiles and answers, 'Sure'. Tim also gains much audience sympathy thanks to Mendez's penchant for scaring small children – on two occasions the boy is petrified by Silva's eye-bulging, shrieking performance.

In keeping with Mann's model, the action in *Hills* is often bleak. Many of the sadistic moments are brief, while other shots suggest extreme violence, but show very little – as when Brewster turns a knife in a henchman's stomach. Brewster has a tattoo cut from his arm, but there are no close-ups or blood. The most shocking moment occurs when Getz arrives at the Mayflower Ranch with the patch of tattooed skin pressed in his handkerchief between two leaves – all part of a ruse to convince Seagall that Brewster is dead.

Lizzani comes into his own in a series of impressive set pieces, which gradually become more elaborate. Early action sequences are relatively small-scale affairs, never involving more than a few participants. With the attack on the horse herd, the film picks up pace. This ambush sets up the lively confrontation in the Austin saloon, between Mendez and his gang and Horner's men. Mendez strides alone into the saloon and shouts, 'Hasta la vista', before his men smash the windows, slaughter Horner's gang and trash the bar. Lizzani cuts between the maniacally grinning Mendez and Horner's employees, standing hopefully with their hands aloft, before being mown down. Lizzani later stages a mass shootout in the deserted streets of Austin, with Brewster and Getz alone against Los Garcianos. Preceding this confrontation there is an eerie silence, as a driverless hearse appears and approaches the gang. Once the dynamite starts flying the shootout could easily have become one of those static affairs from the climax of Hollywood westerns, with the entire cast shooting at each other forever from behind boxes and barrels. But here, the action is transformed into a gloriously comic-book confrontation, in which believability takes a back seat to the stunt work and choreography; many of the gang members were played by stuntmen (Guglielmo Spolettini, Paolo Magalotti and Osiride Pevarello).

Ennio Morricone was hired to score *The Hills Run Red*, though to disguise his prolificacy he worked under the pseudonym 'Leo Nichols'. *Hills* features the haunting voice of Gianna Spagnolo, but, as with other post-Civil War spaghettis, Morricone uses trumpets to add a 'military' feel to the title music. The main theme features Spagnolo's approximation of an echoing Red Indian incantation, accompanied by a melodramatic string section, drums and trumpets. This triumphant charge becomes the root of the 'riding theme' throughout the film. *Hills* also features a departure for Morricone: a ballad is used, not as a main theme, but as incidental music. This owes much to Samuel Fuller's *Forty Guns* (1957), in which a lament entitled 'God Has His Arms Around Me' accompanies a tracking shot of a young widow standing on a hilltop beside her loved one's hearse. With their song, Morricone and Lizzani seem to be striving for a combination of parody, homage and pathos. It's called 'Home to My Love' and accompanies Brewster's return to his ranch following his stretch in prison. Morricone wrote the tune and Audrey Nohra provided the lyrics, which for once are completely audible. Sung by Gino, 'Home to My Love' sounds like 'Angel Face' from *A Pistol for Ringo*, but could have appeared in any Hollywood western. Hopelessly sentimental and not to say optimistic, the lyrics include:

I know a girl with golden hair, waiting by the window, all alone.
I know my girl knows how I care. Won't be long my darling, soon be home.
But there's a high wind wailing in the plain, as if I'll never see my girl again.
Hurry home to my love, back home to my darling girl.

For the Italian release of *Hills*, Morricone and Gino also recorded 'Quel Giorno Verra' ('That True Day'), sung to the tune of 'Home to My Love', with new Italian lyrics by Sanjust. The English version of the song echoes the note left by Brewster's long-deceased wife Mary. But the letter also destroys the idealism of the

'Hasta La Vista!': Garcia Mendez and Los Garcianos mow down Horner's men in the Austin saloon shootout from *The Hills Run Red* (1966); Henry Silva (left) at Dino De Laurentiis Studios.

ballad by revealing that, although Mary may have been 'waiting by the window', she did so with an empty stomach, a starving child and the imminent threat of eviction. Fragile instrumental versions of 'Home to My Love' (on strings, guitar or harp) are later associated with Brewster's son, linking him to the ranch.

Morricone's incidental music owes much to his previous work, but by 1966 he was scoring a vast number of films and his writing occasionally became formulaic. More imaginative are the musical sound effects Morricone uses for Mendez. In one scene Brewster lies beaten and Mendez puts a pistol to his head – filmed from a low angle, so that the gun barrel points directly at the camera in close-up. A high-pitched whine on the soundtrack convinces us that Mendez is about to shoot, but instead he lowers the hammer and bursts out laughing. Like *A Pistol for Ringo*, the music also reinforces the cultural differences between the gentlefolk at the Mayflower Ranch and their rough Mexican employees. The aristocrats have a square-dance 'hoe-down', while the Mexican celebrations at the corral (a horseback knife-throwing competition) are cut to fiesta music. In the Austin saloon Morricone sends-up dancehall girl clichés, with atonal Hattie Gardner (Gianna Serra), the saloon singer from hell. She is introduced as 'Fresh from her triumphant successes in Dallas and St Louis' – where presumably everyone is deaf. Morricone also alludes to Mexican serenading cowboys like the 'Cisco Kid'. After Horner's men ambush the horse herd, a survivor arrives at the corral to find the brutally psychopathic Mendez harmonising with his *muchachos* on the Mexican lament, 'Marie Rosa'.

De Laurentiis released *The Hills Run Red* in Italy in September 1966, to great success – it was one of the most popular westerns of the year. Its original title was *Un Fiume di Dollari* ('A River of Dollars'), a tenuous reference to Leone's films. The only river in the film marks the edge of Milton's Territory and provides the setting for one scene. The English title was more effective, with its reference to 'land' (the range war subplot) and 'blood' (Brewster's quest for revenge). The US posters for the film stated: 'This man spent five years thinking about killing his best friend...Finally they meet!' *Hills* was one of six Italian films released worldwide through United Artists in 1967. The others were the first two 'Dollars' movies, a spy spoof called *Operation Kid Brother* (or *O.K. Connery* – both titles making reference to the star, Neil Connery, Sean's brother), *Navajo Joe* and *Matchless*. In part *Navajo Joe*, *Matchless* and *Hills* were showcases for Italian actress Nicoletta Machiavelli. All three were shot at 'Dinocitta' (De Laurentiis's own studio outside Rome) and were scored by Ennio Morricone.

Many Italian westerns tried to capitalise on the success of Lizzani's blending of Mann and Leone, but two films made in 1967 owed a great deal to *The Hills Run Red*. *Dead or Alive* (also called *A Minute to Pray, A Second to Die*) was directed by Franco Giraldi. Using Italian and American finance, it cast two of Mann's villains – Robert Ryan (*The Naked Spur*) and Arthur Kennedy (*Bend of the River* and *The Man from Laramie*) and then squandered them in cameos. The story follows an epileptic outlaw on the run, Clay McCord (played by Alex Cord) and the governor's attempts to persuade him to sign amnesty papers. The film is slowly paced, poorly scripted and shoddily acted. One scene alone hints at what might have been. Two bounty-hunters (Aldo Sambrell and Antonio Molino Rojo) beat up a local priest and tell him that they are going to ambush McCord. The padre tells them 'Thou shalt not kill, my son', to which Rojo replies, 'Unless there's a price on his head. That makes it legal…instead of just fun.' *Dead or Alive* also had two endings for different countries: one happy (McCord is pardoned), one sad (McCord is pardoned, then riddled in an ambush).

Another *Hills* derivative was Domenico Paolella's *Hate for Hate*, which should also have been much better. John Ireland appeared as outlaw hero James Cooper, Antonio Sabato was Miguel, a harmonica-playing Mexican sculptor who dreams of moving to New York, and Mirko Ellis was Cooper's partner, Moxon. After a bank raid, Cooper is captured and sent to do hard labour in a prison camp situated in a swamp, where he catches malaria. Having managed to escape, but prone to blackouts as his quinine runs out, Cooper, with the help of Miguel, tracks down Moxon – who has kidnapped Cooper's wife and daughter. A minor entry for the most part, there are two reasons for seeing *Hate for Hate*. In one scene Cooper faces Miguel in a duel, when the impossible happens – they fire simultaneously, shooting the pistol from each other's hands. Also of note is the opening bank robbery. Moxon takes the staff hostage in the office, while Cooper cleans out the safe. When Cooper returns to the office, he finds all the staff dead. 'I thought I told you, no killing,' he tells Moxon, who sarcastically replies, 'You told me no shooting', as he returns his knife to its sheath.

Lizzani's other western was *Requiescant* (1967 – also called *Kill and Pray* and *Let them Rest*). Here the pace, sentiment and humour of *Hills* was gone, to be replaced with political philosophising; Lizzani and collaborators (no less than five of them) ruminated at length on the church, racism and revolution. Lou Castel appeared as the eponymous hero, the son of a Mexican bandit (but raised by a priest) who comes into conflict with a deranged southern officer Fergusson (Mark Damon, straight out of *Django*). Fergusson keeps his wife in a padded cell, claims that slaves were 'looked after' in the deep south (while northerners exploited them with nominal wages) and steals land from the local Mexican peons with bogus land treaties. Though this sounds an interesting brew, Lizzani's execution of the material was mediocre and misused a talented cast, including its famous guest star (and reportedly co-writer) Pier Paolo Pasolini. Luckily Pasolini managed to forget this episode in his career (wandering around the desert wearing a poncho) and go on to do some of his best work, behind the camera.

Trading on the success of *Hills*, Thomas Hunter appeared in another De Laurentiis western called *Three Golden Boys* (or *Death Walks in Laredo*) immediately after his performance for Lizzani. Made on the same sets as *Hills*, *Three Golden Boys* (an Italian/Algerian co-production) was also written by Piero Regnoli. It features Hunter as a gunman with a four-barrelled pistol, teaming up with a kung-fu expert (the first of many Eastern visitors to the spaghetti west) and a gunslinging French hypnotist (who can make a roulette ball move, even after the wheel has stopped revolving). The heroes are pitted against a toga-wearing villain named Julius Caesar (who lives in an opulent palace, complete with slave-girls and a huge sunken bath) and his army of black-clad Pistoleros. It also features exotic dances performed by grass-skirted slave-girls, to Hawaiian-sounding pop songs.

The Hills Run Red remains an entertaining and atypical addition to the Italian western canon. It is a classic example of how a talented director like Lizzani could absorb the wild west myth and produce a piece of genre cinema; Lizzani says that he made the film solely as a favour to De Laurentiis. *Hills* includes three generations of western actors: Duryea had been active in the genre since the mid-forties, Silva since the fifties and Hunter was the latest addition in the sixties (though his career was short-lived and patchy). *The Hills Run Red* stands as a testament to the Hollywood heroes and directors of the fifties and their values, though Lizzani's sentimental treatment seems at odds with the increasingly violent developments that were overtaking the genre.

7

'Time Was When We'd Pay a Dollar For His Scalp'

— Sergio Corbucci's *Navajo Joe* (1966)

Navajo Joe (1966)
Credits
DIRECTOR – Sergio Corbucci
PRODUCERS – Ermanno Donati and Luigi Carpentieri
STORY – Ugo Pirro
SCREENPLAY – 'Dean Craig' (Piero Regnoli) and Fernando Di Leo
ART DIRECTOR – Aurelio Crugnola
COSTUMES – Marcella De Marchis
EDITOR – Alberto Gallitti
DIRECTOR OF PHOTOGRAPHY – Silvano Ippoliti
MUSIC – 'Leo Nichols' (Ennio Morricone)
Interiors filmed at De Laurentiis Cinematografica Studios, Rome
Techniscope/Technicolor
An Italian/Spanish co-production
Dino De Laurentiis Cinematografica (Rome)/CB Films
    (Barcelona)
Released internationally by United Artists
Cast
    Burt Reynolds (Joe); 'Aldo Sanbrell', Alfredo Sanchez Brell
    (Mervyn 'Vee' Duncan); 'Nicoletta Machiavelli', Nicoletta
    Rangoni Machiavelli (Estella); Tanya Lopert (Maria); Franca
    Polesello (Barbara); Lucia Modugno (Geraldine); 'Fernando
    Rey', Fernando Casado Arambillet (Brother Jonathan); 'Peter
    Cross', Pierre Cressoy (Dr Chester Lynne); Antonio
    Imperato (Chuck); 'Maria Cristina Sani', Cristina Iosani
    (Joe's wife); Valeria Sabel (Hannah Lynne); Mario
    Lanfranchi (Mayor Jefferson Clay); Gianni Di Stolfo (Sheriff
    Regan); Angel Alvarez (Oliver Blackwood); Juan Casalilla
    (Esperanza telegrapher); Alvaro De Luna (Sancho); Lucio

Rosato (Jeffrey Duncan); Simon Arriaga (Monkey); Cris
Huerta (El Gordo); Angel Ortiz (El Cojo); Lorenzo Robledo
(Robledo); Valentino Macchi (Gringo scalphunter); Raf
Baldassare (Tim, one-eyed scalphunter); Raphael Albacin
(Mexican scalphunter); 'Dianick', Dyanik Zurakowska
(Swedish settler on train); Fortunato Arena (townsman), with
Roberto Paoletti and Roderick Auguste

*   *   *

Burt Reynolds famously described *Navajo Joe* as: 'So awful it was shown only in prisons and aeroplanes because nobody could leave. I killed ten thousand guys, wore a Japanese slingshot and a fright wig.' Reynolds's contempt for the film provided him with endless anecdotes for interviews and chat shows throughout his career, though his opinion of the film is rather unfair. *Navajo Joe* was a huge European hit and one of Sergio Corbucci's best movies. Reynolds has mellowed and now he wryly recalls his time in Italy and Spain shooting his first, and last, Italian western.

Italian producer Dino De Laurentiis approached Corbucci with a script with the working title *Un Dollaro a Testa* (A Dollar a Head) by Piero Regnoli and Fernando Di Leo (based on a story by Ugo Pirro). A gang of scalphunters led by the brutal half-breed Duncan earn a living killing Indians for the rewards on their scalps. When the bounties are stopped and Duncan discovers that a reward has been put on his head, the scalphunters go on the rampage, sacking the settlement of Peyote. In league with crooked Doctor Lynne, Duncan and his men steal a $500,000 train shipment bound for the town of Esperanza, but an Indian named Joe intervenes. With the help of a trio of dancehall girls and a servant girl called Estella, Joe whittles down the gang. Joe reveals that his wife was murdered and scalped by Duncan. In the course of his vendetta he annihilates the gang and saves the townspeople's money, but at the cost of his own life.

Corbucci said that *Navajo Joe* was an historically accurate political film about the mass slaughter of Native American Indians, but he addressed it in much the same way he addressed other issues in his westerns – through a hero who kills lots of people. Unlike the German 'Winnetou' westerns, which concerned the Apaches and some lesser-known tribes (the Osages, Utes, Poncas and Assiniboins), the scenarists chose a Navajo protagonist. Cousins of the Apaches, the Navajos were purged from their homeland in 1863. By January 1864 there was no longer a 'Navajo problem', nor indeed much of a tribe; the troops burned their crops and the Indians starved. Corbucci's film takes place during these purges. The scalp bounties were based on fact, but the firearms on display are historically inaccurate; the repeating Winchesters used by Joe and the scalphunters post-date the period by a number of years.

Navajo Joe's main Hollywood influences were Delmer Daves's *The Last Wagon* (1956) and George Sherman's *Comanche* (1956). *Wagon* saw a white trapper named Jonathan 'Comanche' Todd (a psychotic Richard Widmark), out to avenge the death of his Indian wife and children. Daves's film was brutal for its time; in one sequence Todd was crucified on a wagon wheel. Todd's buckskin garb and his accuracy with a tomahawk particularly impressed Corbucci. *Comanche* was the best fifties western to deal with scalphunters; here the hero's blustering sidekick Puffer countered the threat of scalping by wearing a hairpiece (a gag repeated in the 'Winnetou' movies). *The Indian Fighter* (1955) featured Italian actress Elsa Martinelli as a convincing Indian maid, while Esperanza was the den of thieves in the stylish American revenge western *The Burning Hills* (1956). Villainous scalphunter Duncan was based in part on the racist murderer Millard Graff from Marvin H. Albert's 1957 novel *Apache Rising* (filmed in the US in 1965 as *Duel at Diablo*). In *Apache Rising* Jess Remsberg, a bitter army scout, tracks down the Indian-hating Graff (called Willard Grange in the film) to avenge the death of his Indian wife, Singing Sky, who has been scalped beside a river.

Many aspects of Corbucci's early sixties career were synthesised in *Navajo Joe*. In *Romulus and Remus* (1961), Romulus explains his patriotic motivation for resisting the Lord of Albalonga. He is fighting for, 'The place where we were born. The mountains, the rivers, the valleys…our land.' Although Joe's prime motive is revenge, he is also fighting for liberty. His forefathers have lived in the west for generations, a place now populated by prejudiced townspeople and greedy scalphunters. In Corbucci's earlier *Johnny Oro*, the Indians were cast as the villains, with villain Juanito Perez recruiting a war party of Apaches. The Indians attack the town of Coldstone, split a saloonkeeper's skull with a tomahawk and shoot the hero's girlfriend, before being routed by Johnny, his golden pistol and a ton of dynamite.

Corbucci maintains that he was promised Marlon Brando for the role of *Navajo Joe*, but that he was 'unavailable'. De Laurentiis approached ex-stuntman turned TV actor Burt Reynolds because he 'looked like Brando'. He also looked passably Indian, as he was part Cherokee. Reynolds followed the same career path as Clint Eastwood – TV series westerns (in Reynolds's case *Riverboat* and *Gunsmoke*), Italian westerns and on to Hollywood superstardom. Eastwood had been friends with Reynolds for years and attended Reynolds's wedding to Judy Carne in 1964. When Eastwood returned from Italy with a print of *Fistful*, he screened it for Reynolds, who was astonished – 'The look was totally unique, the music was like nothing I'd ever heard before and I was in love with it'. Eastwood introduced Reynolds to De Laurentiis, who needed an actor who could do his own stunts. Reynolds, in the middle of a divorce and just turned 30, accepted and arrived in Rome in April 1966.

Reynolds was raring to go, but De Laurentiis ordered rewrite after rewrite. Reynolds had allowed himself three months before he was due back in the US to begin *Hawk*, a new TV series. Having dieted for the role, Reynolds spent his days sat at Parco Dei Principi and his nights drinking wine, worrying that if he hung around Rome much longer he would be 'too old and fat to play Joe'. As time wore on, Reynolds was in for another surprise. Eastwood had raved about 'Sergio', the magical director who was turning him into a star. The opportunity to work with 'Sergio' was one of the reasons Reynolds signed the contract. When Regnoli and Di Leo finally got De Laurentiis's approval of their sixth draft of the screenplay, shooting was ready to begin. Only then did Reynolds discover that the 'Sergio' directing the film was Corbucci. Reynolds was also under the illusion that the entire cast spoke English, but of course no one did. 'One guy spoke German,' remembered Reynolds, 'One guy spoke French and I would just wait for them to stop talking. I did more pauses than Brando ever did.'

For his merciless villain, Corbucci cast 35-year-old Aldo Sambrell as Joe's nemesis Duncan. Madrid-born Sambrell's real name is Alfredo Sanchez Brell, which he altered to 'Aldo Sanbrell' and 'Aldo Sambrell' for film appearances. Extraordinary prolific, Sambrell was a true product of the Italian western genre. A fine actor, he nearly always played a Mexican gunman, but he played the part very well and remained one of the stalwarts of the genre. Sambrell's characters always ended up dead, but he noted in an interview in 2002: 'They never killed me…I'm still here!' Sambrell debuted in *Gunfight in the Red Sands* (1963) and a plethora of films followed, including Leone's 'Dollars' trilogy. He was also cast as Ramirez, a Calvera-like bandit warlord in the opening sequence of *In a Colt's Shadow* (1966), where his gang attempt to terrorise the township of Casa Grande, but are gunned down by the 'Magnificent Two'.

Corbucci reused some of the *Django* cast, including Simon Arriaga, as the scalphunter Monkey (who shins up telegraph poles) and Angel Alvarez as banker Blackwood (Blackwood was also the family name in Corbucci's *Castle of Blood*). *Navajo Joe* included an early appearance by Fernando Rey, one of Europe's most esteemed actors, who delivered a serene performance as the priest, Brother Jonathan (named Rattigan in the Italian version). Sambrell's gang includes many familiar faces, including Alvaro De Luna (from *Seven Hours of Gunfire*), Valentino Macchi (*Django Shoots First*) and Cris Huerta (*Seven Guns for the MacGregors*).

The scalphunters were teamed with the villain from Gemma's early westerns, French actor Pierre Cressoy, as corrupt Doctor Lynne. Cressoy (billed under the name 'Peter Cross') had been working in France since 1947. He appeared through-out the fifties in Italian epics, where his career reached its nadir in *The Lion of Thebes* (1964). He played the pharaoh Ramissees, though his portrayal was ruined by some ludicrous costumes; in one sequence he looked like a cross between one of the Three Wise Men and a grand wizard of the Ku Klux Klan. Exterior shots of the Egyptian desert were recreated indoors and consisted of a scattering of sand and a rubber plant, while the pharaoh's army appeared to be armed with outsized pickle forks.

Corbucci continued to cast actresses in prominent roles. Florentine-born Nicoletta Machiavelli, as Joe's love interest Estella, was a promising 21-year-old actress hoping to make an impact abroad in Italian genre films. She appeared in *The Hills Run Red*, though she is best remembered internationally as Dominique, one of the trio of French racing drivers in *Monte Carlo or Bust* (1969). The travelling dancehall troupe were played by Franca Polesello (Barbara), Tanya Lopert (Maria) and Lucia Modugno (Geraldine). Modugno went on to appear in *My Name is Pecos* (1966);

Joe (Burt Reynolds) and Destaphanado (without his pinto makeup) in a French promotional still for Sergio Corbucci's *Navajo Joe* (1966).

Polesello could be seen in exploitation fare like *Strangler of Vienna* (1971), a Sweeney Todd variant about a murderous Austrian sausage-maker; and Lopert appeared (in a cross-dressing role) in *Fellini's Satyricon* (1969), as the young Caesar who commits suicide on a beach.

A distinctive feature of the film was the excellent costumes, designed by Marcella De Marchis. The scalphunters are predominantly Mexican and wear a variety of ponchos, bandoleers and sombreros. The dancehall girls are dressed in gaudy outfits (in green, red, gold and black, incorporating lots of sequins), while Indian maid Estella looks stunning in a simple blue sackcloth dress. The best costume was reserved for the hero and Reynolds has never looked better – kitted out in feathers and leathers, and armed to the teeth. Reynolds modestly noted that the cinematography and wardrobe made him look 'tremendous'. This hadn't always been the case, however. Before shooting began, the actor recalled that 'The physical demands of the role didn't frighten me as much as my wardrobe'. No one in the crew seemed to have a clue what real Indians looked like. Consulting a history book, the wardrobe department picked out a Columbus period Indian with feathers and a jockstrap. Reynolds said 'No way', but the Italians took some convincing. As Reynolds states, 'They hacked up an old wig and glued it on my head. I looked like Natalie Wood.'

The shooting schedule took the crew to Rome, then Almeria and Castile. Some of the Esperanza footage was shot at Carlo Simi's Tabernas set (in the scorching temperatures of May 1966); the De Laurentiis Studios town set near Rome was used for other shots of Esperanza (including the church). 'Peyote' was the Colmenar Viejo set near Madrid, with some exteriors also shot at De Laurentiis. The ranch house and corral were near Colmenar. The opening Navajo Indian camp massacre was shot at Tor Caldara in Italy. Interiors were filmed at De Laurentiis Cinematografica, Rome (Dinocitta). The desert, forest and grassland locations were shot at a variety of sites, ranging from Almeria and Colmenar to Torremocha, Castile and the railroad track near Guadix. The train (dubbed the Wells Fargo Express) was the same one that was robbed in *Seven Guns for the MacGregors* (1965). It also appeared in many other spaghettis; the locomotive was the standard prop train on location in Spain.

There was virtually no let-up in the action while making *Navajo Joe*, a fact that wasn't lost on Reynolds, who was so sick of performing stunts that he asked Corbucci to write a love scene between Joe and Estella, to break up the violence. But the idiosyncratic director laughed and answered, 'We have improved the American western by removing all the boring stuff. We have taken out the love scenes and all the talk, talk, talk,' before shouting 'Azione!' and lensing another stabbing. Producer De Laurentiis reasoned that by having a hero who killed more people than Eastwood, then box-office takings would rise accordingly.

The on-screen relationship between Joe and Estella is somewhat overshadowed by the relationship between Joe and his horse. Joe's steed is obedient when whistled, nuzzles his master during dialogue scenes and seems to know where to go when instructed to take the money back to Esperanza. This telepathy between horse and master was reiterated during the making of the film. The Spanish gypsy wranglers had no authentic pinto horses, so Reynolds had an old, tatty grey nag named Destaphanado made-up to look like 'the most beautiful Pinto in all of Spain'. Reynolds said that the horse 'looked like Ricardo Montalban' and maintains that the steed was the best he had ever ridden. In the Italian-shot sequences, Destaphanado had a rather obvious stand-in with different markings. As a parting gesture, Reynolds donated his fee for *Navajo* to Destaphanado's groom, to look after the horse in retirement.

Many of the horses used in spaghetti westerns were less lucky. One of the many horse stunts in *Navajo* strongly resembles a scene in Corbucci's *Minnesota Clay*. Three scalphunters chase a cart with the saloon girls on board. To foil their escape, one of the bandits uses a bolas to stop the horses in their tracks. The rope tangles around the horses' front legs, resulting in the animals cart-wheeling to the ground in a crumpled heap. Exceptionally cruel in its execution, the stunt has little chance of being broadcast today, let alone performed. But in the sixties, before more stringent measures were taken with animal safety, virtually anything was permitted and many actors (notably Klaus Kinski) were injured when they were thrown from untrained horses.

Towards the end of the location shoot a problem arose. Reynolds learned that the commencement date for *Hawk* had been moved forward and he was needed back in the US by the end of June. Corbucci couldn't understand why a TV series was so important, but they compromised. On location at Tabernas, Corbucci filmed Reynolds lobbing dynamite, shooting from a rooftop and generally running amok. These scenes would form the backbone of the big shootout in Esperanza. With Reynolds's performance in the can, he was free to go, while Corbucci shot the rest of the cast for a further six weeks, in Spain and Italy, filling out the remainder of the movie with the train robbery and the other scenes that didn't feature Joe. *Navajo* remains one of the few spaghettis where the money didn't run out, but the star did. The film was then assembled jigsaw-fashion in post-production. The only giveaways are sudden changes of location. The town of Esperanza was 'created' from footage shot in two different countries: in one scene it is surrounded by lush grassland, but by the climax it has relocated to the barren desert. Duncan's gang rides up the street in Italy then arrives outside the adobe bank in Spain – such is the magic of co-produced cinema.

With De Laurentiis's backing Corbucci made a commercial, more accessible film, closer in atmosphere to Leone's films than to the rugged surrealism of *Django*. Cinematographer Enzo Barboni was replaced by Italian-born Silvano Ippoliti, who had photographed several muscleman epics, including *Hercules, Samson and Ulysses* (1963 – which featured Roman soldiers in poorly disguised Second World War German helmets). *Navajo* has a colourful, pop-art sheen and the blue Spanish sky has never looked so beautiful. It was Corbucci's first western shot in Techniscope, and the most competently shot of his films thus far. But the director still had a problem establishing the plot threads at the beginning of his films and bringing the stories to life. The early sequences of many of Corbucci's movies seem unrelated and awkward (a symptom of the director's fast shooting schedules), as though a story is struggling to break through. But gradually his photographic and editing style gels, so that by the climax, the final confrontation makes perfect sense.

Duncan's scalphunters are typically brutal adversaries for a Corbucci hero. When they first appear, mercilessly slaughtering Navajo Indians, it quickly becomes apparent that they are more than just marauding bandits. Beneath the titles the gang rides upriver through a forest, with bloody trophies hanging from their saddles and adorning poles brandished as standards. In the US western *The Scalphunters* (1968), a trapper (Burt Lancaster) sums up the kind of men who hunt down Indians for their scalps: 'Scalphunters…Dirtiest, rottenest trade ever turned a dollar'.

Though Esperanza is under threat from the scalphunters, the townspeople are initially hostile towards Joe, saying 'We don't make bargains with Indians'. Later, when they realise they're in big trouble, race doesn't matter – Joe is welcome to save the town for 'A dollar a head, from every man in this town, for every bandit I kill'. They even agree to make Joe sheriff, but one of the locals points out, 'Time was when we'd pay a dollar for *his* scalp'. When the confrontation comes, the cowardly townsfolk watch as the scalphunters capture and beat Joe. Only outsiders like Estella and the dancehall girls aid the Indian. Though Geraldine dies under Dr Lynne's scalpel, the other two dancers join in the action and help Joe to escape from the gang; they are an antidote to many heroines in Hollywood westerns, looking impressed and fluttering their eyelashes at the hero from the sidelines.

Corbucci went all-out in the violent action sequences, including two big set pieces (an elaborate train hold-up and the showdown between Joe and Duncan's gang in Esperanza) and the final confrontation in the Navajo burial ground. *Navajo* is one of Corbucci's cruellest westerns – featuring scalpings, whippings, a cockfight and death by knife, garrotte and tomahawk. Corbucci loved these excesses, his camera lingering on the victim's agony. This is apparent in the opening sequence. After shooting an Indian girl, Duncan wades across a creek and kneels by her body, drawing his knife. He begins to scalp her, Ennio Morricone's score providing a variety of agonising screams, while Corbucci's camera pans away from the horror as Duncan stands up, brandishing the girl's dripping scalp.

Reynolds's virile performance is one of his best, though he often singles it out as his worst. In his first couple of scenes Reynolds is silent, his powerful screen presence and violent actions speaking louder than words. American publicity for the film ran: 'Silent…Sudden…Violent…*Navajo Joe*'. Reynolds's rippling hero is a direct descendant of musclemen like Goliath and Spartacus. Reynolds's portrayal also works because of his on-screen chemistry with Nicoletta Machiavelli. Though they never kiss, Joe and Estella's relationship is well handled and is one of the strongest aspects of the film. Joe is enigmatic and mysterious, she coy and inquisitive.

His tone with her is gently mocking. Estella chooses to ignore Joe's condescension, seeing through his macho facade and looking for the humanity beneath. Through Reynolds's understated playing, it is obvious that Joe is a compassionate man. He risks his life to stop the slaughter of his own people and surrenders to Duncan in Esperanza, rather than see Estella harmed.

Pierre Cressoy's portrayal of Doctor Chester Lynne is an opportunity to replay his roles from *One Silver Dollar* (1965) and *Adios Gringo* (1965). Lynne is a pillar of the community, who turns out to be a cheap crook. Corbucci carefully conceals the doctor's identity for the first part of the film, and when we first meet him, on the station platform at Esperanza, he is staring at a 'Wanted' poster for Duncan, his partner in crime. No one in town knows of the doctor's criminal past, his time spent in jail, his charade of a marriage to banker Blackwood's daughter and his plan to return to Europe after the robbery.

'A dollar a head': Aldo Sambrell as scalphunter Duncan gruesomely meets his end in *Navajo Joe* (1966).

To offset Cressoy's slippery doctor, Sambrell played the leader of the scalp-hunters as a brooding, violent half-breed. Sambrell's performance remains his personal favourite. Duncan's full name is Mervyn 'Vee' Duncan, but he's known by his surname (rather than the less-than-menacing Mervyn). Like the characters in fifties psychological Hollywood westerns, Duncan gets the opportunity to explain his prejudices. His monologue to Brother Jonathan, poignantly delivered by Sambrell, is presented as his 'confession'. Accompanied by one of Morricone's most emotive themes (a repetitive, cascading acoustic guitar and cor anglais) Duncan tells the priest that he is going to burn down the church with everyone inside, unless Joe gives himself up. The priest preaches racial tolerance to Duncan and begs for mercy; Duncan answers 'Nobody ever had mercy on me'. Triggered by the murder of Duncan's father (who, like Jonathan, was a priest) and the half-breed taunts of his childhood (Duncan's mother was an Indian), he has carried out his revenge on both whites and Indians. Duncan stands beside the pulpit clutching a prayer book, then guns the priest down in cold blood, continuing the cycle of the vendetta.

Both the main characters are fuelled by vengeance. Duncan's revenge for his nightmarish childhood and Joe's vendetta with Duncan. Estella and Duncan are both interested why Joe wants Duncan dead, but Corbucci is ambiguous about Joe's motive. Duncan thinks Joe is a dogged bounty-hunter, eager for cash. Similarly the townspeople think Joe's motivation is money, never questioning why an Indian would want to help a white community. Estella is more persistently inquisitive. Joe and Estella's final dialogue on the outskirts of Esperanza is the most effective and evasive dialogue between hero and heroine in a Corbucci movie. Estella wants Joe to survive (as though she realises he will die in the ensuing showdown) and asks why he hates Duncan so much. 'Someday,' Joe answers, 'when you grow up and don't ask so many questions, maybe I'll tell you.' But this is a Corbucci film and Joe never gets the opportunity to tell her his motive. He does, however, get the opportunity to tell Duncan.

Throughout the film, Joe has left a peculiar interlocking triangular symbol on or near the corpses of Duncan's gang (a 'calling card' lifted from Corbucci's *Son of Spartacus*). In the final face-off in the Navajo cemetery, Duncan discovers why. Joe tears a pendant in the same design from around Duncan's neck; it was stolen from the Indian girl in the opening sequence. Joe wears a matching pendant of two interlocking circles. Joe asks the bandit, 'Do you remember her?' and explains that the necklace once belonged to his wife. In a brutal scene, Joe pins Duncan down and thrashes him with a rifle butt and his fists. Corbucci alternates between close-ups of Duncan's face, becoming a bloody pulp and long shots of the graveyard; simultaneously fascinated and repelled by Joe's terrifying revenge. The final shocking moments are expertly edited. Joe looks for a suitable weapon to finish Duncan off. He spots a tomahawk and dives for it, but Duncan grabs a pistol and shoots him four times; Joe's body twisting with the impact of the bullets as they slam into his back. In a single movement Joe spins and throws the axe (directly at the camera, in a parody of fifties 3D westerns), which splits Duncan's skull. It is a visceral moment, at once exhilarating and saddening, as we realise that Joe is going to die. Though his demise is not shown, the next scene, with Joe's horse arriving riderless in Esperanza with the saddlebag of stolen money confirms it, making the ending most effective.

Navajo Joe is one of Morricone's most instantly recognisable western scores. The main title music fully exploits the depth and power of Alessandro Alessandroni's I Cantori Moderni and the unusual vocal talents of Gianna Spagnolo (who was employed to excellent effect by Nino Rota, during the party sequence of Fellini's *Juliet of the Spirits* – 1965). Spagnolo's ethereal voice adds an exceptionally hard edge to *Navajo* and her style is completely unlike the pure soprano tone of Edda Dell'Orso, Morricone's other regular female soloist.

The title theme begins with Spagnolo's wailing cry: as Duncan scalps Joe's wife, a Native American Indian chant begins on the soundtrack. This is joined by another, then another as Morricone multi-tracks the voices, creating a cacophony which is suddenly stopped by a single booming drumbeat. Out of the silence emerges a jagged electric guitar riff, rising and falling, as heavy tribal drums, Spagnolo's voice, dramatic strings and the choir create a wall of sound behind the ominous guitar and a rolling piano motif. The pounding drums then pick up the pace and are joined by the female section of the Cantori chanting 'Navajo Joe, Navajo Joe', which is 'answered' by the male section. Then Spagnolo enters, her sinuous, almost blues, vocal improvising up and down the scale, while the choir continue their mantra with raw, indiscernible lyrics.

At other moments in the film Spagnolo's voice softens to achieve a religious intensity. When Estella searches for Joe in the Indian graveyard, sparse drums, a quiet flute and Spagnolo's echoing voice creates an eerie mood to the scene among the burial scaffolds and skulls of Joe's ancestors. When Joe corners scalphunter Sancho (Alvaro De Luna) Spagnolo's vocal, accompanied by heavy drumbeats and flute, adds a sense of pagan ritual to the sequence. Joe makes Sancho kneel before him, carves a triangle into his forehead with a knife, then smashes the bandit's skull with a rock. The love theme is more subdued and features the choir literally singing the hero's praises: 'He's like a myth to Indian men'.

One composition dominates when the scalphunters are on screen. It features a death-knell piano riff, sustained strings, drums, blasts of brass, high-pitched whistles, a discordant church organ and a glass-shattering holler from Spagnolo. In the church, a delicate acoustic guitar melody, accompanied by cor anglais and soothing strings, makes scalphunter Duncan's explanation of his violent actions almost sympathetic. In the Peyote saloon, Morricone uses a knockabout bar-room rag to accompany the dancing-girls' amateurish, cheerleader-like routine, using balloons with faces painted on them (a parody of a routine in Fellini's *La Dolce Vita*). But it is the choral title track (missing from the original United Artists soundtrack release) that lingers in the memory, the pounding refrain and wailing rallying cry being the most distinctive ersatz Native American music; a startling juxtaposition of 'The Shadows' and 'The Ghost Dance'.

The film was released in Italy in November 1966 and appeared on the drive-in circuit in the US in late 1967. The Indian hero didn't really take off as a spaghetti-western perennial. Its one influence was on the Italian *Magnificent Seven* rip-offs. These featured a gringo pistolero (usually the big American star of the film) rounding-up a group of 'experts in killing' for a special, invariably highly risky, job. The other members of the group were expendable, with their billing on the posters being a fair indication of their chances of survival. These groups often included an Indian character called Blade or Chato, who was skilled in throwing knives and tomahawks. Similarly, scalphunters rarely reappeared in the genre, one notable exception being *The Fighting Fists of Shanghai Joe* (1973), a kung-fu spaghetti western. It featured a Chinese hero facing a variety of villains, including a cannibal, a gambler, a gunslinging undertaker and a scalphunter named Scalpin' Jack (played by Klaus Kinski). Jack ends up being disembowelled by the knives he keeps in the lining of his jacket, and has his own scalp sent as a gift to his former employer.

Though Corbucci's early films were distributed internationally by MGM (if they were distributed at all), his jump to the international big time and De Laurentiis's

Estella (Nicoletta Machiavelli) attempts to talk Joe (Burt Reynolds) out of facing the scalphunters in Corbucci's *Navajo Joe* (1966).

name on the posters resulted in a distribution deal with United Artists. Despite its violence, *Navajo* was released uncut at 89 minutes, though it gained an 'X' certificate in the English-language version. In the US it was advertised with the tagline: 'Relentless in his vengeance! Deadly in his violence! Navajo revenge slashes, burns...ravages the screen!' The Spanish release title was *Joe El Implacable* ('Joe the Relentless'); the German title was *Kopfgeld: Ein Dollar* ('Head Money: One Dollar'). In subsequent years *Navajo Joe* has been retitled *Red Fighter, Savage Run* and *Navajo's Land*, a title intended to associate the film with Michael Winner's *Chato's Land* (1971), which was influenced by Corbucci's movie. Charles Bronson's portrayal of half-breed Pardon Chato was even more taciturn than Reynolds; Bronson only has two lines of English dialogue in the entire film.

American and British critics were unimpressed with *Navajo*, though Reynolds did garner some good notices. 'Brando-esque Burt Reynolds has the right savage intensity for the vengeance-bound Joe,' noted one critic. Another wit aimed a jibe at Morricone's score, whilst praising the actor's performance – 'The only on-key note in this film is Reynolds'. But though the film grossed well in Europe, it bombed in the US and only made money on rerelease, once Reynolds was famous. Press ads claimed that *Navajo* was TV actor Burt Reynolds's film debut (it was actually his fourth film) and that he'd signed a six-year contract with De Laurentiis. After *Navajo* and his earlier appearance as Quint Asper (the half-breed blacksmith in *Gunsmoke*), Reynolds found himself typecast as Indians. Following *Hawk*, in which Reynolds played a contemporary Iroquois Indian detective – who, the actor claimed, put his ear to the ground to listen for stolen cars – Reynolds returned to Almeria in 1968 to make the pedestrian spaghetti-esque *100 Rifles*. Here he played a half-breed named Yaqui Joe (half-Indian, half-Alabaman 'good old boy') and was reunited with Aldo Sambrell, as vicious Sargento Paletes.

By the beginning of 1969, Reynolds was well and truly sick of playing Native American parts and sent a New Year's resolution to his agent, Dick Clayton – 'The only Indian I haven't played is Pocahontas. I'm tired of shaving my arms – it's easy to get the left, but the right is a bitch.' That said, Reynolds's fine performance as Lewis Medlock in *Deliverance* (1972) was quite obviously indebted to his early, bare chested macho roles. As superstardom beckoned, Reynolds never again had to endure the heat of Spain to earn a dollar, but Corbucci seemed to love the place, returning for his next film, *The Hellbenders*, which featured a coffin that was even more widely travelled than Django's.

8

'In This Life, One Can Die Too'

— Damiano Damiani's *A Bullet for the General* (1966)

A Bullet for the General (1966)
original title: *Quien Sabe?*
Credits
DIRECTOR – Damiano Damiani
PRODUCER – Bianco Manini
STORY AND SCREENPLAY – Salvatore Laurani
ADAPTATION AND DIALOGUE – Franco Solinas
SET DESIGNER – Sergio Canevari
COSTUMES – Marilu Carteny
EDITOR – Renato Cinquini
DIRECTOR OF PHOTOGRAPHY – 'Tony Secchi' (Antonio Secchi)
MUSIC COMPOSER – Luis Bacalov
MUSIC SUPERVISOR – Ennio Morricone
MUSIC CONDUCTOR – Bruno Nicolai
Techniscope/Technicolor
An Italian Production for MCM (Rome)
Released internationally by Avco Embassy Pictures (US)/
　　Warner Pathé (UK)
Cast
　　Gian Maria Volonte (Chuncho Muños, known as 'El
　　Chuncho'); Klaus Kinski (Santo 'the Saint'); Martine Beswick
　　(Adelita); 'Lou Castel', Ulv Quarzéll (Bill Tate, nicknamed
　　'Niño'); Jaime Fernandez (General Elias); Andrea Checchi
　　(Don Filipe); Spartaco Conversi (Cirillo); Joaquin Parra
　　(Picaro 'the Mischievous'); Aldo Sambrell (Lieutenant
　　Alvaro Ferella); Jose Manuel Martin (Raimundo); Santiago
　　Santos (Guapo 'the Handsome'); Valentino Macchi
　　(Durango train driver); Antonio Ruiz (Chico, the Mexican
　　boy); Carla Gravina (Rosario, Don Filipe's wife); Vicente

Roca (clerk in Morelos Hotel); Guy Heroni (Pedrito); Sal
Borgese (bandit)

*   *   *

A Bullet for the General, made by Damiano Damiani in 1966, was the first Italian
western to deal seriously with the Mexican revolution. It was also the first to add a
political slant to the relationship between a gringo outsider and a Mexican bandit,
during their adventures south of the border. Authentic in its depiction of a band of
guerrillas constantly on the move in an effort to stay ahead of government troops,
the film aptly conveyed the powder-keg situation in Mexico in the early twentieth
century. Moreover, it took a serious view of its causes, looking at how they affected
the populace and possible solutions to the insurrection.

Damiano Damiani studied at the Brera Academy of Fine Arts in Milan. He
directed several films, including *Red Lips* (1960), *Arturo's Island* (1962), *Empty Canvas*
(1963 – starring Bette Davis) and a horror film, *The Witch* (1966), starring Gian
Maria Volonte. It was apparent from those early films that Damiani deemed suitable
subject-matter to be isolation, alienation, homosexuality and betrayal, and his first
foray into Italian westerns continued to explore these themes.

A Bullet for the General tells the story of El Chuncho (a Mexican gunrunner),
Santo (his half-brother, a fervent revolutionary and priest) and gringo outlaw Bill
Tate. Following a train robbery, Tate teams-up with Chuncho's gunrunners as they
steal armaments for notorious rebel General Elias. On the way to the general's
hideout, they liberate the town of San Miguel, but only Santo stays on to help the
poorly armed peasants. At an oasis, Chuncho's men are decimated by a Regulare
patrol; Tate and Chuncho soldier on alone to Elias's HQ, but Tate catches malaria.
During Tate's convalescence Chuncho finds a mysterious golden bullet in Tate's
valise. At Elias's camp, Chuncho is sentenced to death for leaving San Miguel, where
the peons have since suffered government reprisals. Santo wants to carry out the
sentence, but during the execution Tate shoots both Elias and Santo. Tate is actually
a hired government assassin; for his contract to kill Elias he earns 100,000 pesos
and Tate offers Chuncho half his fee, as a 'thank you' for leading him to Elias. But
in the Cuidad Juarez railway station, Chuncho at last sees his country as something
worth fighting for. As Tate is boarding a train back to the US, Chuncho guns him
down and gives the money to a Mexican shoeshine boy, yelling 'Don't buy bread
with that money hombre, buy dynamite'.

Bullet's complex schema had more in common with the critically lauded, prize-
winning Italian political cinema of Gillo Pontecorvo and Francesco Rosi than with
the violent action of Leone and Corbucci. More thought had gone into the scenario
for *Bullet* than the average Italian western, and the man who did the thinking was
Franco Solinas. Solinas was an important figure in Italian political cinema. He was
a Marxist writer (active since the fifties), who wrote or collaborated on several key

political films that were lauded as authentic cinematic political statements. His best-known scripts were for Rosi's *Salvatore Giuliano* (1962) and Pontecorvo's *Battle of Algiers* (1966), a faithful depiction of revolution and terrorism.

Made in black-and-white, *Battle of Algiers* is an uncompromising, documentary-like film of the Algerian people's struggle for independence from France between 1954 and 1962. Extraordinary in its simplicity and using mainly non-actors, the film takes the viewer to the heart of a modern revolution. An Italian/Algerian co-production, *Battle of Algiers* details the campaign of terrorism by the Algerian Liberation Army (FLN). It is gripping and all-the-more poignant for one of Ennio Morricone's best scores; written in close collaboration with Pontecorvo, the music evoked the claustrophobic atmosphere of the kasbah, the preparations of the Arab women bombers (as they disguise themselves as Westerners) and the tragedy of the innocents killed in the bomb blasts. Pontecorvo described Solinas's work on the film thus: 'If a famous old film with the same name had not already existed, I should have liked to call *Battle of Algiers*, "The Birth of a Nation". This is the sense of the story, because it tells of the pains and lacerations which the birth of the Algerian nation brought to all of its people.'

Bullet is also about the birth of a nation. More so, however, it is about the birth of a hero. The 'trials' Chuncho has to endure on his path of self-discovery (the various betrayals, the death of his friends and even the death of his brother) are clearly important to Solinas and Damiani. With Tate (the 'Yankee'), Solinas could show the flip side of the revolution through an exploitative character, who understands how the revolution works.

Damiani and Solinas were also influenced by Sergei Eisenstein's unreleased Mexican-shot epic *Que Viva Mexico!* (1931–32), which was only fully realised, as one critic put it, 'in the womb of Eisenstein's mind'. The three fragments that remain (*Que Viva Mexico!*, *Time in the Sun* and *Death Day*) dissect two of Eisenstein's favourite subjects – religion and revolution. In a key sequence of *Que Viva Mexico!* a Mexican peon is recaptured by his master. The shot depicts the peon as Christ, and his two bare-chested compadres (one either side) recall the crucifixion. In a brutal scene they are buried up to their chests and trampled to death by horses' hooves.

Bullet deployed an eclectic international cast. Italian Gian Maria Volonte was cast as El Chuncho. The first two 'Dollars' films had made Volonte a star, but he passed on Leone's offer of the Tuco role in *The Good, the Bad and the Ugly*, preferring to make *Bullet* and Carlo Lizzani's *Wake Up and Kill* (1966), two films that enabled him to make a political statement. Klaus Kinski portrayed Santo; unlike Volonte, Kinski made westerns purely for profit, a neat inversion of their gun-running characters in *Bullet*. Damiani cast Jamaican-born Martine Beswick as Adelita, a señorita who rides with Chuncho ('Adelita' is the heroine of a famous Mexican folk ballad). When Beswick made *Bullet* she had appeared in two Bond movies, *From Russia With Love* (1964) and *Thunderball* (1965), and a brace of prehistoric films made by Hammer Studios: *One Million Years BC* (1966), as Raquel Welch's rock-girl nemesis Nupondi, and *Slave Girls* (1967), as villainous Kari, the leader of a tribe of brunettes who exploit and enslave the local blondes – a political agenda considerably simpler than Damiani's in *Bullet*.

'Lou Castel' (real name Ulv Quarzéll, from Bogota) was the real casting coup. He burst onto the international scene as Alessandro, the epileptic lead in Marco Bellocchio's unrelentingly bleak *Fists in the Pocket* (1965), the powerful study of a dysfunctional family. Alessandro's warped mind concocts a plan to kill the other members of the family, starting with his blind mother, who he leads over a cliff. Castel gave an astonishing performance; completely lost in his own infantile, imaginary world he skilfully took the audience on a surreal journey. Castel was only 23 when he played gringo agent Bill Tate, though his voice was dubbed in the English-language version by William Berger, a much older actor.

Other actors in *Bullet* included Aldo Sambrell (as the officer in charge of an armaments train), Valentino Macchi (as the train driver) and Andrea Checchi (as San Miguel land-owner Don Filipe), while Carla Gravina (Gian Maria Volonte's wife) played the Don's wife, Rosario. Damiani also cast Spartaco Conversi and Jose Manuel Martin in bit parts. Conversi was often billed by a variety of aliases ('Spean Converi', 'Spanny Convery') and became best known as a burly, white-bearded sidekick; he occasionally 'played young' by dying his beard. His turn as gunrunner Cirillo (Eufemio in the English version) was a rare Mexican role – he usually played Anglos. Spaniard Jose Manuel Martin had been involved in domestic cinema since 1952. His first experience of international co-productions was Don Siegel's Spanish-shot melodrama, *Spanish Affair* (1957), of which Siegel said, 'If I knew the Spanish word for "Ech", I'd use it'. Martin's first western roles were as villains in *Minnesota Clay* (1964) and *A Pistol for Ringo* (1965), but from 1966–67 came an avalanche of roles, though they hardly stretched his range. Shrewdly, Damiani cast Martin against type as Raimundo, a downtrodden peon.

Damiani originally wanted to shoot *Bullet* in Mexico, but this proved impossible logistically. Instead it was shot in Almeria in July and August; cinematographer Antonio Secchi (or 'Tony Dry') had just finished working on *The Hills Run Red*. Don Filipe's *hacienda* was the *finca* of El Romeral in San Jose. The fort where Santo grenades the government troops was the monastery of Cortijo de los Frailes ('House of the Brothers'). The train used in the ambush (renamed the 'Nacionale De Mexico') was a local Spanish locomotive; it was also used to ferry around the crew and their provisions. According to Damiani, the only shade the crew had were a few beach umbrellas. Spanish villages and strongholds in the surrounding hills became the Mexican settlements and forts for the action sequences; many of the extras were non-professional actors – locals from the countryside, with speaking parts being given to the more competent among them. The whitewashed village of Polopos represented San Miguel. Guadix railway station doubled for the Cuidad Juarez rail depot; Guadix itself was used for the street scenes. Almost the entire film was set outdoors and the interiors were all on location: the inside of the *finca* and the Morelos Hotel lobby in Cuidad Juarez.

Damiani staged some impressive scenes, including raids on forts and machine-gun shootouts. The set designer on *Bullet* was Sergio Canevari, the art director from *Battle of Algiers*. Several scenes look like photos of the period, especially when the action reaches the Mexican revolutionary camp in the Grande Sierras. Canevari's attention to detail in depicting the peasant lifestyle (señoritas and starving children) and the poorly organised Mexican militia attempts historical authenticity and Damiani termed this realistic approach 'violence verité'.

Mexican history is confusing, as the country was riven with conflicts for years. The revolution of 1910–20 saw the revolutionaries led by Francisco Madero, helped by Francisco 'Pancho' Villa, Venustiano Carranza and Emiliano Zapata. Madero won, but was soon overthrown by General Huerta, who attempted to purge the country of revolutionaries. Most Mexican revolution westerns are set at some point during this hectic ten-year period. *Bullet* takes place between 1915 and 1916, when Carranza switched sides; '*Carrancistas*' (as Carranza's followers were called) executed many of Villa's supporters, and Damiani's film opens with graffiti reading 'VIVA CARRANZA EL PACIFICADOR' ('Long live Carranza the Peacemaker').

Bullet's pre-title sequence establishes Damiani's realistic approach. Four Mexican civilians are lined up to be shot. A group of peasant women and children look on, crying and shouting. One of the condemned men yells 'Tierra e Libertad!' ('land and liberty'), as the firing squad shoot. Three of them are killed outright, while the fourth is badly wounded; he shouts insults at the soldiers (calling them 'cabrons' – bastards), before he is pitilessly shot dead at close range. The camera picks out Tate, in smart suit and trilby, watching the carnage, while an English voiceover (provided by Richard McNamara) sets the scene: 'From 1910 to 1920, Mexico was torn by internal strife. During the entire decade, the vast territory was devastated by bands of marauding bandits. Scenes of this kind were commonplace, as the various factions tried to dominate the others and bring order out of chaos.'

A Bullet for the General concentrates on the relationship between Chuncho and Tate and their differing relationship with Mexico: as native and outsider respectively. The underlying homosexual attraction between them is unusually explicit for a western. Chuncho quickly 'falls for' Tate's professionalism. Chuncho kills one of his own men rather than see Tate harmed, serenades the gringo and nurses him back to health when he catches malaria. Tate is uncomprehending of Chuncho's friendliness and uses their relationship to get to his mark. Chuncho doesn't understand Tate's cold behaviour; soon after they meet, Chuncho notes, 'The boy doesn't drink, doesn't smoke and doesn't want women. What are you interested in?' 'Money,' answers Tate.

Initially Chuncho is an uncouth *bandido*, more concerned with the acquisition of wine, women and pesos than any revolutionary commitment. Chuncho looks like Pancho Villa and Villa's life may have influenced the story. Villa began his career as a bandit, though he eventually sided with the revolution. Importantly, Chuncho doesn't see Elias as a great 'leader', but as a great 'bandit'. Elias's revolutionary activities simply give Chuncho an excuse to do what he enjoys (kill government troops and rob trains) in the name of the revolution, but really for profit.

Volonte's portrayal of Chuncho is different from Ramon Rojo and El Indio in the 'Dollars' films and more than a politicised version of these characters. Chuncho isn't as intelligent or scheming as Leone's bandits. He is unable to calculate the

Poster advertising Damiano Damiani's political western *A Bullet for the General* (1966) on its US release in 1967.

gang's shares of the gunrunning money; Ramon and Indio could probably express it as a fraction. Even when Tate's plan to assassinate General Elias is painfully obvious to the audience, Chuncho still doesn't get it.

Chuncho's half-brother, blond-haired Santo (Spanish for 'saint'), is markedly different – an ardent revolutionary who thinks they give the guns away for nothing. Dressed in a monk's robe strung with bandoleers, he comes across as a bizarre 'Pentecostal pistolero'. Santo is the soul of the film, possessed with the revolutionary vigour that his brother lacks; he accompanies his pronouncements with profound footnotes, supporting his beliefs. When asked by a government-supporting priest why a man of the cloth rides with gunrunners and bandits, Santo answers, 'Christ died between two thieves'. Even Santo would not be so pious as to cast himself as Christ, but he is the character who most resembles a saviour, until Chuncho's timely conversion. By the finale, Chuncho has crossed his brother and Santo leads him into the desert to execute him. Chuncho asks his brother to take his confession; Santo answers that there is no absolution for what he has done. Chuncho says 'You told me God was good, generous', to which Santo humourlessly replies, 'God is, I'm not'.

Chuncho's deteriorating relationship with his brother and his increased political awareness are caused by the manipulative Tate. Despite Tate's apparent naivety (Chuncho christens him 'Niño', Spanish for 'little child'), it is obvious he's a professional gunman. He wears a flashy shoulder holster, is well versed in precision weapons and coolly levels soldiers with a Hawkins machine-gun in an explosive shootout at an oasis. The assassination is well planned; Tate travels on all trains carrying arms out of Cuidad Juarez for two weeks before he makes contact with a rebel band. When the bandits attack the train, Tate stops it, then finds some handcuffs and chains himself up, explaining to Chuncho that he is a wanted man.

Damiani and Solinas use Tate's presence in Mexico as a comment on American imperialism. In the opening scene, Tate walks into the Cuidad Juarez railway station, jumps the queue and buys a ticket to Durango. Chico, a Mexican boy in the queue (Antonio Ruiz from *For a Few Dollars More*), asks if Tate is American, but the gringo doesn't answer. 'Señor,' continues the boy, unperturbed, 'do you like Mexico?' 'No,' answers the gringo, coldly, 'not very much,' as he turns his back on the boy and heads for the platform. Later, having seen the revolution for himself, Tate runs into Chico again at Elias's camp. The Mexican boy is now a revolutionary and repeats the question, 'Now do you like Mexico?' 'I still don't,' smiles Tate. Chico asks why Tate doesn't go back to the US; the gringo says that he makes a living selling guns in Mexico. 'I'd never sell guns to people I didn't like,' reasons Chico. Both the revolutionary forces and the Mexican government Regulares dislike Tate's intervention in their affairs. A peasant revolutionary asks why the US government arms the enemy forces ('I don't associate with the President of the United States,' says Tate), while a Regulare officer describes Americans as 'Not too much heart, but plenty of dollars'.

To offset the central male trio, bandita Adelita adds a human perspective to the horrors of the rebellion. At one point Adelita recounts how she was raped by a rich land-owner, and her bandit lover Pedrito is later killed in an ambush, prompting her to abandon the revolution. In a more humorous vein, she poses as a cigar-smoking prostitute during a raid on a Mexican army stronghold, to plant a dynamite-loaded trunk in the officers' quarters and blow a hole in the fort's defences. Such an action by a woman was unthinkable in Leone's westerns, and was Damiani's equivalent of the Algerian women bombers in *Battle of Algiers*.

Damiani delineated the differences between the various classes in Mexican society. In the sixties a more traditional treatment of Mexico was of a peasant community with the Mexican bandits as outsiders: warlords either terrorising the countryside (*The Magnificent Seven*) or ruling the community with terror-tactics (*A Fistful of Dollars*). In Damiani's film the men in power are rich men – not gunmen, but businessmen. The peasants in *Bullet* are omnipresent; the wallpaper of Mexico, from the opening executions in Cuidad Juarez and the train ride to Durango, to the general's headquarters and the shoeshine boy in the railway station finale. The Mexican characters (everyone in the film, except Tate) represent the polarities of Mexican culture – lowly, illiterate peons; peso-hungry gunrunners; vicious Regulare officers; noble revolutionary generals; crying Mexican women; rich land-owners; hungry children and beggars.

Predictably, the government troops are the villains of *Bullet* – they usually are in Mexican revolution movies. Damiani contrasts their 'valour' with the cruel reality. During a decoration ceremony at a fort, Santo appears on the palisade and unleashes a torrent of abuse at the troops. 'Assassins of Mexico,' he shouts, 'I challenge you, in the name of the Father,' as he produces a grenade and throws it at them, 'and of the Son and of the Holy Ghost, Amen' – each proclamation accompanied by another explosion. We see the army's cruelty first hand. Men and women are left to starve in underground cells without food or water (while their captors drink champagne), revolutionaries are summarily shot and prisoners beaten up; these are the kind of people Tate works for. Ironically, during the opening ambush, the Regulares elicit sympathy. The armaments train is halted by a Mexican captain chained to a cross on the track. The gunrunners are as barbaric as the army, but the guns are too precious; the train keeps going and the captain is flattened in an horrific crucifixion. From the moment Chuncho and Santo are introduced to the story, it is apparent where Damiani's loyalties lie.

With Santo, Raimundo, the one-armed peasant spokesman of San Miguel, is the conscience of the film. The peasants want their land back which has been appropriated by Don Filipe, a rich land-owner and his vain wife Rosario. The don asks the peasants, 'Why do you want to kill me. Is it because I am a rich man?' 'No,' answers Raimundo. 'It is because we are poor men and you've done everything in your power to keep us that way.'

Damiani's presentation of General Elias and his staff makes them look almost holy in their sincerity. If Corbucci had directed *Bullet*, Elias would have been a swaggering, epauletted travesty, rather than the tall, handsome intellectual presented here. Jaime Fernandez's portrayal owes much to Marlon Brando's dignified Emiliano Zapata in *Viva Zapata* (1952). Mexican actor Fernandez had played Zapata in *Lucio Vazquez* (1965) and later appeared in *Emilio Zapata* (1970) and *The Death of Pancho Villa* (1973).

Following San Miguel's liberation, Chuncho finds himself cast as one of these noble-minded types. Gunrunner Cirillo mockingly refers to him as 'General Chuncho' and Chuncho makes a speech to the peons draped in a Mexican flag. His gang are not interested in becoming heroes; only Santo sees how important Chuncho is to the community and Chuncho is tempted to stay. The villagers elect Chuncho mayor, but he nominates a young local boy, the only person in San Miguel who can read and write. Tate quickly realises the gunrunners' trail ends there, so he turns Chuncho's gang against their boss. Tate tells the gang, 'You'll never tear Chuncho away from the applause', while Adelita scoffs, 'He likes the cheers of these drunk peons? I want my money.'

A comic scene shows how inadequately trained the peasants are. Chuncho drills a group of inept peons in the use of brand-new Mauser bolt-action rifles, but the peasants pepper the wall with a scattershot volley, narrowly missing their tutor. 'I'm asking myself why I stay with you,' says a despondent Chuncho. 'The lesson is over, you can kill each other now.' Tate gives Chuncho some advice, as he leaves with the guns: 'They can probably get along without your help…you have to look out for yourself'. When Chuncho discovers that his gunrunners have stolen a precious machine-gun, he uses it as an excuse to abandon the village, leaving Santo to man the barricades with little more than faith.

Chuncho's initial appearance is a clever cinematic trick, which plays on the audience's familiarity with music in westerns. With the Durango train pinned down, a deep timpani drum begins on the soundtrack, as a lone bandit appears on the brow of the hill. Suddenly we realise that the rider, Chuncho, is playing the drums himself – they are attached to his saddle. Thus Chuncho plays his own entrance music. The score was composed by Luis Enrique Bacalov, under Ennio Morricone's supervision. The theme song 'Ya Me Voy' ('I'm Coming'), sung by Ramon Mereles, is a full-blown fiesta (complete with guitars, trumpets and a harp), which plays over the opening train-journey title sequence. We even see a guitarist playing the theme on the back of a flatcar.

The most famous piece from the score begins with a jagged, repetitive guitar riff, which develops into a stately Mexican march (with guitar, drums and trumpets) that sounds like a national anthem. A gentle acoustic guitar version of the piece underscores Adelita's departure in the desert, following her lover's death. For the 'riding theme', Bacalov reuses a tune from *Django*, while violins swoop ominously as the bandits execute soldiers after the train hold-up. Such dramatic compositions are typical of Bacalov, though Morricone's influence is also apparent. As Chuncho and Tate make their way through the Grande Sierras towards the general's HQ, Morricone's trademark high-pitched strings and flute echo on the soundtrack. And each time we get a clue about Tate's assassination plot (for instance, when Chuncho finds the golden bullet in Tate's valise), an eerie flute motif points out its significance. In fact such Morricone-esque touches gave rise to the rumour that he composed part of the score, though his regular collaborator Bruno Nicolai conducted it. Spanish songs enhance the Hispanic atmosphere, but unless you understand a bit

Italian artwork by De Seta for *A Bullet for the General* (1966), featuring (left to right) gringo agent Bill Tate (Lou Castel), gunrunner El Chuncho (Gian Maria Volonte) and revolutionary priest Santo (Klaus Kinski).

of Spanish, some of the finer points are lost. The lyrics sung by the bandits as they ride across the desert, 'Si Adelita se fuera con otro', hint at Tate's real agenda. Like Adelita, Tate is 'going out with another' – in his case the Mexican government.

A Bullet for the General is also known by the titles *Gringo Desperados*, *Tote Amigo* ('Kill Friend') and *Yo Soy La Revolucion* ('I am the Revolution'). The original title for the film is *Quien Sabe?* ('Who Knows?'), while Italian and Spanish release prints are titled *El Chuncho, Quien Sabe?* The significance of the title is arguable. Did it imply 'who knows the future?', 'who knows what's possible?' or more ironically, 'who knows about Tate's plan to kill the general?' In the final sequence, Tate asks why he must die and Chuncho, convinced he is striking a blow for the revolution, replies, 'Quien sabe?' though he realises that he is getting revenge – for his brother, for the peasants of San Miguel and for his gang. The phrase 'Quien sabe?' (used throughout the American southwest and Mexico) invariably implied a philosophical shrug, as much 'who cares?' as 'who knows?', while gringos anglicised it to 'kin savvy?' and applied it to anything they didn't understand.

The prominent use of un-subtitled Spanish dialogue in the English-language print makes the audience feel outsiders, like Tate. The English-language retitling, *A Bullet for the General*, made it crystal clear what the film was about, tying up the main gunrunning plot with the assassination subplot; for some releases of the film, cut from the 115 minutes to 77, there was barely enough time for that. There was also a 108-minute version prepared, which cuts the opening firing-squad sequence and removes the captain crucified on the track.

A Bullet for the General was very successful when it appeared in Italy in December 1966 (a week before *The Good, the Bad and the Ugly*). In the US it was distributed by Joseph E. Levine's Avco Embassy and had an effective poster campaign: 'Like the Bandit…Like the Gringo…A bullet doesn't care who it kills' and 'Nothing can stop the Bandit except the Gringo…Nothing can stop the Gringo except the General…Nothing can stop the General except a bullet!' American critics noted that Damiani had made a rarity – a commercial art film – but opinion was divided; some claimed the film wasn't incisive enough for a political film, nor exciting enough for a western. Damiani was indignant that just because *Bullet* looked like a western, many critics classed it as one. He claimed it was a political film about the Mexican revolution – just as *Battle of Algiers* was not a war film, but a political film about the Algerian revolution.

Later political spaghetti westerns (made between 1968 and 1972) tended to parody *Bullet*, inviting comparisons with Harold Lloyd's *Why Worry?* (1923), where Lloyd's convalescing businessman was inadvertently caught up in the Mexican revolution; and Louis Malle's burlesque *Viva Maria* (1965), which Malle originally wanted to call *Que Viva Maria!* in honour of Eisenstein's film. The more popular political westerns became, the more the American 'Magnificent Seven' series of films embraced a political reading of the gringo–bandit conflict, setting their stories in revolutionary Mexico and integrating political comment into the scenarios. In the last in the series, *The Magnificent Seven Ride* (1972), Chris (Lee Van Cleef) encounters a group of revolutionaries led by a monk. Even though the film was shot in Mexico and the extras are actually Mexican, the whole scene looks phoney – such was the influence of Italian westerns.

The first parody of *Bullet* was *A Train for Durango* (1967 – co-scripted by Tessari). Many of the locations, the producer (Bianco Manini) and even some of the actors (Joaquin Parra, Jose Manuel Martin and Aldo Sambrell) reappeared from Damiani's film. Most memorable is the gringo adventurer, played by Mark Damon, who drives around in a vintage car, negotiates Mexico using an Automobile Club map and looks like a forerunner of Tony Curtis in *Monte Carlo or Bust* (1969).

Damiani's best work was in the field of contemporary-set political cinema. He followed *Bullet* in 1968 with an adaptation of Leonardo Sciascia's novel *Day of the Owl*, casting Franco Nero as the young police inspector Bellodi investigating Mafia operations in Sicily, who encounters a wall of silence. Sciascia's taut novel (originally published in 1961) was a milestone of political literature and Damiani did it justice. Another of Sciascia's novels, 1971's *Il Conteso* (retitled 'Equal Danger' in its English-language translation), became the basis for the finest Italian political film – Francesco Rosi's *Illustrious Corpses* (1976).

Damiani followed *Day of the Owl* with an even more overtly political film (this time concerning police corruption) entitled *Confessions of a Police Captain* (1971). Franco Nero plays Traini, a young district attorney assigned to investigate an assassination attempt with police captain Bonavia (Martin Balsam). The opening scenes see LiPuma, a mentally unstable crook (played by bug-eyed Adolfo Lastretti), released from a mental institution by Bonavia and allowed to murder Dubrozio, a wealthy mobster (with dealings in the construction industry). LiPuma arrives at the hood's offices disguised as a policeman and proceeds to spray the room with a sub-machine-gun. Later LiPuma's girlfriend (Marilu Tolo) is murdered by Dubrozio's henchmen. They shift her body from her flat in a packing case, take her to a nearby building site and cast her in a concrete stanchion that becomes part of Dubrozio's latest building development. *Police Captain* remains Damiani's best and most controversial film.

Of the political spaghetti westerns, *A Bullet for the General* was the most intelligent of all. It was a film about two adventurers' relationships – with Mexico and one another. Damiani only returned to the genre again in 1975 with *Nobody's the Greatest*, a comedy western starring Terence Hill. Gone was the incisive political debate and outcry at the exploitation of the poor, to be replaced by Hill's buffoonery and elaborate comedy chases to the William Tell overture. A genre like the spaghetti western needed film-makers like Damiani to experiment with it, if only to give it kudos with critics. And *A Bullet for the General* was as close to serious political cinema as spaghetti westerns got. Which begs the question, why didn't more film-makers take Damiani's lead? Quien sabe?

9

'There Are Two Kinds of People in the World'

— Sergio Leone's *The Good, the Bad and the Ugly* (1966)

The Good, the Bad and the Ugly (1966)
original title: *Il Buono, Il Brutto, Il Cattivo*
Credits
DIRECTOR – Sergio Leone
PRODUCER – Alberto Grimaldi
STORY – Luciano Vincenzoni and Sergio Leone
SCREENPLAY – Age-Scarpelli, Luciano Vincenzoni, Sergio Donati
    and Sergio Leone
ART DIRECTOR, SET DESIGNER AND COSTUMES – Carlo Simi
EDITORS – Nino Baragli and Eugenio Alabiso
DIRECTOR OF PHOTOGRAPHY – Tonino Delli Colli
MUSIC COMPOSER – Ennio Morricone
MUSIC CONDUCTOR – Bruno Nicolai
Interiors filmed at Elios Film Studios, Rome
Techniscope/Technicolor
An Italian/US co-production for PEA (Rome)/ United Artists
    Studios
Released internationally by United Artists
Cast
    Clint Eastwood (Blondy 'the Good'); Lee Van Cleef (Angel
    Eyes 'the Bad'); Eli Wallach (Tuco Ramirez 'the Ugly'); Aldo
    Giuffre (Captain Clinton); Luigi Pistilli (Padre Pablo
    Ramirez); Rada Rassimov (Maria, prostitute in Santa Anna);
    Antonio Casas (Stevens); Livio Lorenzon (Baker); Antonio
    Casale (Jackson alias 'Bill Carson'); Angelo Novi (young
    monk at San Antonio); 'Molino Rocho', Antonio Molino Rojo
    (Captain Harper, Betterville prison-camp commandant);
    Mario Brega (Corporal Wallace); 'Al Mulloch', Al Mulock
    (Elam, one-armed bounty-hunter); Frank Braña and Claudio

Scarchilli (bounty-hunters in ghost-town); Sergio
Mendizabal (blond bounty-hunter); Nazzareno Natale
(Mexican bounty-hunter); 'John Bartho', Janos Bartha
(sheriff); Sandro Scarchilli (deputy); Jesus Guzman (Pardue,
hotel owner in Santa Fe); Chelo Alonso (Stevens's wife);
Antonio Ruiz (Stevens's son); Enzo Petito (Milton, gunsmith
in Valverde); Victor Israel (Confederate sergeant); Silvana
Bacci (Mexican prostitute); Aysanoa Runachagua (Mexican
hired gun); Lorenzo Robledo (Clem); Romano Puppo (Slim);
Benito Stefanelli, Luigi Ciavarro and Aldo Sambrell
(members of Angel Eyes's gang)

*   *   *

By 1966, Sergio Leone's westerns were so popular that America started to take an interest in his talent, even though none of them had been released there. For his next project, Leone, producer Alberto Grimaldi and writer Luciano Vincenzoni struck a deal with United Artists (UA). UA would put up half of the $1.2 million budget and the film would be made under the tutelage of Grimaldi's PEA. The story, originally called 'Two Magnificent Rogues', was concocted by Vincenzoni and Leone. The comedy writing team of Agenore Incrocci and Furio Scarpelli ('Age-Scarpelli') worked on the screenplay, while Sergio Donati assisted Leone with the dialogue. 'Two Magnificent Rogues' was retitled *Il Buono, Il Brutto, Il Cattivo* ('The Good, The Ugly, The Bad') and Mickey Knox was brought in, to translate the dialogue into English for the dubbed version.

The title, shuffled to *The Good, the Bad and the Ugly* for international release, referred to the three main characters: bounty-hunter Blondy 'the Good', hired gun Angel Eyes 'the Bad' and Mexican bandit Tuco Benedicto Pacifico Juan Maria Ramirez (Tuco for short) 'the Ugly'. The story features their adventures as they trace a cash box containing $200,000 at the height of the Confederate invasion of New Mexico in 1862. Union troops ambush a Confederate payroll wagon; there are three survivors: Stevens, Baker and Jackson – and the gold has gone missing. Angel Eyes finds out about the money when he is hired by Baker to kill Stevens. Meanwhile Tuco and Blondy learn about the cache when they run into mortally wounded Jackson, who tells each of them half the location (Sad Hill war cemetery and the name on the grave where it is buried). But with the American Civil War engulfing the territory, their route is hazardous. Finally, having negotiated burning deserts, blown up bridges, prison camps and artillery barrages, Blondy, Angel Eyes and Tuco meet in the cemetery, with $200,000 the prize for the fastest gun.

The Civil War setting made *The Good* an epic western. The film begins in late 1861 and drifts through to the following summer; the cash was buried at Sad Hill after 3 February 1862, and much of the action takes place in March and April. In early 1862, General Henry H. Sibley led the Confederate forces out of Texas and invaded New Mexico. They reached Valverde in February 1862, then Santa Fe; by-passing the Union forces under General Canby at Fort Craig. When the Confederates attempted to take Fort Union they were defeated at Apache Canyon on 26 March, then decisively at the 'Gettysburg of the West', the Battle of Glorieta Pass at the southern tip of the Sangre De Christo ('Blood of Christ') Mountains on 28 March. The Confederates retreated to Santa Fe through Albuquerque and Peralta, and took a raggedly disastrous route back to their base in San Antonio, Texas in July 1862. Part of their trek took them through the 'Jornado Del Muerto' (the 'Day's Journey of the Dead Man') a 90-mile stretch of 'beautiful sun-baked sand'. Three thousand five hundred Confederates set out on the invasion – five hundred died and five hundred ended up in Yankee prison camps.

Leone had a million-dollar budget, though a quarter of it went on convincing Clint Eastwood to come back to Italy to play Blondy. Following *For a Few Dollars More*, Eastwood had made a cameo appearance in Vittorio De Sica's five-part film *The Witches* (1966). His popularity ensured he received $20,000 and a Ferrari for his brief role as a bored suburban husband; in one scene he reads the Rome cinema listings and considers going to see *Wake Up and Kill*, *The Tenth Victim*, *The Bible* or *A Fistful of Dollars*. Leone recast Lee Van Cleef, this time as the hired killer Angel Eyes; the role had been offered to Charles Bronson, but he had just signed to make *The Dirty Dozen* (1967). For Tuco ('Il Brutto') Leone hired Eli Wallach, bandit chief Calvera from *The Magnificent Seven* (1960). Ironically when Bronson achieved international superstardom in Europe in the late sixties, largely due to his performance as avenging gunslinger Harmonica in Leone's *Once Upon a Time in the West* (1968), his nickname in Italy was 'Il Brutto' – 'The Ugly One'.

Because of the story's episodic structure, the rest of the cast were only required for one or two scenes. Antonio Casas (Stevens), Livio Lorenzon (Baker) and Antonio Casale (Jackson) each appear once, to impart their 'clue' about the gold. Other one-sceners include Luigi Pistilli (as Tuco's brother), Rada Rassimov (as Maria, Jackson's girlfriend), Antonio Molino Rojo (a prison-camp commandant) and Chelo Alonso (Stevens's wife). Alonso appeared in many muscleman epics and had become famous as the 'Cuban H-bomb' at the Folies Bergere in Paris. Stills photographer Angelo Novi has a bit part as a monk. Angel Eyes's gang in the prison camp are Leone's perennial hard men: Aldo Sambrell, Benito Stefanelli, Lorenzo Robledo and Romano Puppo. Puppo and Stefanelli were also involved in the stunt work; Puppo later became Van Cleef's regular stunt-double (here he stood in for both Wallach and Eastwood).

Cinematographer Massimo Dallamano was replaced by Tonino Delli Colli, who had photographed *Toto a Colori* (1952 – Italy's first colour film), *Seven Hills of Rome* (1958 – starring tenor Mario Lanza) and Pasolini's *The Gospel According to St. Matthew* (1964). *The Good* was shot from May to July 1966, firstly at Elios Studios and then in Spain. The Elios set was the first town where Tuco and Blondy trick a sheriff (the street was still waterlogged from the mud of *Django*). The opening ghost-town was specially constructed in the hills in Almeria. The El Paso set near Tabernas played Valverde; when Tuco survives his seventy-mile desert walk, he crosses a rope bridge back into town. The night scene in Santa Anna (in which Maria is thrown into the street by a group of Confederates) was also shot at Tabernas, as was the scene with the Confederate artillery retreating through Santa Fe and Blondy gunning down three Mexican hired guns (Blondy's hotel room was once occupied by Colonel Mortimer in *For a Few Dollars More*). The shelled town of Peralta was shot at Colmenar Viejo, re-dressed to resemble a pile of matchwood. The scene where Blondy saves Tuco from three bounty-hunters was shot near La Pedriza, Manzanares El Real. The railroad station was at La Calahorra, near Guadix. The sand dunes at Cabo De Gata stood in for the Jornado De Muerto. An Andalusian farm close to San Jose, with its distinctive *noria* (waterwheel) was Stevens's farm; a nearby *pueblo blanco* (whitewashed village) was used for Shorty's hanging; and the San Antonio Mission was Cortijo de los Frailes.

The early part of the film was largely lensed in the south, with the deserts and mountains impersonating New Mexico and the Sangre De Christo Mountains. But it was to the north of Madrid, in Castilla-Leon, that Leone staged his Spanish

'The name on a grave': Tuco (Eli Wallach) interrogates 'Bill Carson' (Antonio Casale) in Sergio Leone's *The Good, the Bad and the Ugly* (1966).

Civil War. The hills were greener and the River Arlanza stood in for the Rio Grande. The Battle of Langstone Bridge was shot at Covarrubias, south of Burgos; the bridge was blown up twice: the first time the cameras weren't shooting, the second time Eastwood and Wallach's stunt-doubles nearly got killed in the blast. Betterville prison camp and Sad Hill cemetery were constructed in the same locality, with the huge circular graveyard and chapel being built at Carazo, south of the Arlanza.

The Good, the Bad and the Ugly is impressively staged: exploding bridges, over-populated prison camps and bombardments were unusual in the average 1966 spaghetti western, where often the biggest special effect was a horse falling over. It is the most credible depiction of the American Civil War ever filmed, due to Carlo Simi's settings and costumes. The film looks authentic, from the duster-wearing bounty-hunters in a ghost-town, to two armies of extras (the Spanish army in disguise) fighting over Langstone Bridge. Even the period guns are convincing reproductions: Blondy is armed with a Colt Navy, a Henry rifle with a sharpshooter's telescopic sight (a similar contraption appeared in *For the Taste of Killing* – 1966) and a Sharps rifle (when he rides away on Angel Eyes's horse); Angel Eyes uses a New Model Army Remington, while Tuco has a composite pistol (a Colt Navy handle, a Smith & Wesson chamber and a Colt barrel) strung on a lanyard around his neck.

Leone's presentation of the Civil War owes much to archives of the conflict. The heavy-duty artillery (from Whitworths and mortars to the huge Parrott guns), locomotives, river crossings and wicker and sandbagged earthworks can be found in the work of Civil War photographers Matthew Brady and Alexander Gardner. At the marshalling yard, Brady makes an appearance, taking a picture of several Union officers posing by a mortar, while at Langstone Bridge, a recreation of one of Gardner's photographs (a dead Confederate sharpshooter sprawled on the Gettysburg battlefield) suddenly has Eastwood striding across the background. Pictures taken on the battlefields of Antietam and Gettysburg (especially the wooded 'slaughter pen') are invoked in the aftermath of Leone's Battle of Langstone Bridge. The battle itself is inspired by the fierce three-day engagement at Antietam Creek (where the river ran red with blood) and the futility of Pickett's Charge at Gettysburg. Langstone Bridge looks more like First World War trench warfare, especially when Blondy comments, 'I've never seen so many men wasted so badly'. Leone's cannon mounted on a railway flatcar and the Yankee prison camp look like sepia prints, even if there were no railways in this theatre of war.

Civil War films are also referenced, including Buster Keaton's *The General* (1926) and *Gone With the Wind* (1939). *The General* is Keaton's comic masterpiece, a fast-moving locomotive chase through enemy lines. The finale, the Battle of Rock Bridge, sees the idiot Union commander ordering his train-bound troops across a burning bridge after he assures them 'it's not burned enough', only for the train to swandive into the river. *Gone With the Wind*'s set pieces, especially during the

Atlanta siege, are recalled by Leone, with his wagon trains of refugees and hospitals of blood-sodden amputees. *Gone With the Wind* also includes the celebrated crane shot revealing a sea of wounded soldiers at a railhead; Leone echoes this crane shot when Tuco arrives at Sad Hill, as the camera pulls upward from one gravestone, to reveal a valley full of thousands.

Most of *The Good, the Bad and the Ugly* is set in New Mexico, though Blondy and Tuco cross the Rio Grande into Texas for the finale. The cut English-language print is elusive about exact places and events, and takes place in a timeless, fictitious setting, with a vague approximation of the Civil War as a backdrop, while the Italian version has more facts relating to Sibley's New Mexico campaign. Angel Eyes finds out that Corporal Jackson is now called 'Bill Carson' and is mixed up in the fighting around Santa Fe. The hired gun visits a Confederate fortress and is told that the Battle of Glorieta is raging; if Carson is still alive, he is in the prison camp at Betterville, so Angel Eyes gets a job at the prison camp posing as a sergeant, and lets the Union army locate Carson for him. Tuco and Blondy encounter a Confederate ambulance retreating across the 'Jornado Del Muerto', visit a Confederate bivouac at Galisteo and a monastery hospital at San Antonio. They later travel through the

Il Buono (Clint Eastwood), il Brutto (Eli Wallach) and il Cattivo (Lee Van Cleef) pose for a promotional photograph on the Sad Hill set, during the finale of Sergio Leone's *The Good, the Bad and the Ugly* (1966).

aftermath of Apache Canyon and Canby's Union troops pour through the town of Peralta, under heavy Confederate bombardment. In the Santa Fe sequences, General Sibley even makes a guest appearance; he is accurately depicted riding in an ambulance – he was 'indisposed' (i.e. drunk) for much of the campaign – while the tough, bearded 'Santa Fe Gamblers' ride as his escort.

Leone shows how the war impacts on the territory. In the early scenes we see the catastrophic effects of the war (the 'ugly' side) without seeing any fighting. There is a brief mention of the payroll ambush and Baker's Confederate uniform hanging on a chair (Baker is recovering from a bullet wound, while Stevens walks with a limp). When the action shifts to Valverde and Angel Eyes prises information about Carson from a crippled Confederate 'half-soldier', the stench of death begins to permeate.

Later, soldiers accused of thievery and espionage are mercilessly punished – one carries his own coffin to be shot, another is strapped to the cowcatcher of a locomotive. As the fighting escalates a Union captain (Aldo Giuffre) blocks out the horrors of war by drinking himself into oblivion and dreams of blowing up Langstone Bridge. Blondy and Tuco make his dream come true, but as the crossing explodes, the wounded captain dies.

Leone's view of the war is of a terrible conflict, capable of crippling and killing men for far-reaching ideals, but also the excuse for grotesque black humour. Outside the Valverde saloon, Leone has Angel Eyes's legless informant comment on Carson: 'I'd be scared to be put in his shoes'. Later, Blondy and Tuco pay the price for travelling disguised as Confederates in a Union-held area. As they pass through the corpses of Apache Canyon, they meet a rebel patrol. Tuco waves to them, shouting 'Down with General Grant! Hurrah for General Lee!' – until Blondy realises that they are Unionists, caked in trail dust that makes them appear Confederate grey; in Keaton's *The General*, a Union spy waves to passing Union troops, then remembers he's disguised as a rebel.

The Union prison-camp sequences are the most hard-hitting section of the film. The prison-camp locale, with log cabins, trenches and high fences, recalls the degradation of notorious Confederate prison camp Andersonville (32,000 inmates, 13,000 deaths) and Nazi concentration camps. Leone got away with his criticism of the Fascist death camps by setting his movie in the Civil War, though the implication is clear. 'Sergeant Angel Eyes' is berated by his gangrenous commanding officer, Captain Harper (Antonio Molino Rojo in death-mask makeup) for beating, robbing and murdering the prisoners. Angel Eyes uses the Andersonville example as his defence, but Harper snaps 'I don't give a Goddamn what they do at Andersonville'. In the background to these scenes we see a wagon loaded with prisoners' corpses, a burial party and a prison orchestra and choir performing Morricone's 'The Soldier's Story', while Tuco is beaten to a pulp by thuggish Corporal Wallace (Mario Brega).

Although Leone gives Wallach most screen time, Eastwood's understated performance holds its own. In terms of his 'man with no name' persona, *The Good* is a prequel to the earlier films, as he metamorphoses into the bitter, ruthless stranger. In Eastwood's opening scene, he plays the good samaritan, saving Tuco from three bounty-hunters. Eastwood smiles, quips and has less of the nihilistic killing-machine brutality of earlier incarnations (though he has the same snake grips on his pistol). The con trick Blondy and Tuco concoct, with Blondy turning Tuco over to the authorities, is well handled. As Tuco is about to serve the spaghetti-western

Blondy (Clint Eastwood) finds his head in a noose in Santa Fe; Sergio Leone's *The Good, the Bad and the Ugly* (1966).

equivalent of a 'suspended sentence', Blondy intervenes and shoots the rope, so they can split the bounty. Blondy is only plausible because of the larger-than-life setting; as Eastwood noted, 'In some films he would be ludicrous. You can't have a cartoon in the middle of a Renoir.'

From the moment Tuco drags him into the desert, Blondy changes. This change is reflected in his appearance: from the stylish long coat, broad-brimmed skimmer and patterned hippie shirt he wears at the beginning, to the familiar denim shirt and sheepskin waistcoat he is given on his release from prison. At the Battle of Langstone Bridge, he sees the red harvest of the Civil War first hand and, unlike so many, lives through it. Blondy finds a wounded Confederate in a ruined chapel near Sad Hill and offers the boy a drag on his cigar; the soldier dies, his last breath drifting in a plume of exhaled smoke (a reflection of Belmondo's death in *A Bout De Souffle* – 1959). Blondy, drenched from crossing the river, swaps his battered greatcoat for a brown poncho the soldier was using as a pillow. Now the transformation is complete and Blondy appears at the graveyard dressed as the familiar poncho-clad gunslinger. But though the war has changed him, Blondy finds it in his heart to share the gold with his double-crossing, scheming partner Tuco.

Blondy's partnership with Tuco was the focus for much of the film – in Germany the film was retitled *Zwei Glorreiche Halunken* ('Two Glorious Rascals'). In *A Fistful of Dollars* the central character was Eastwood, in the sequel Van Cleef, but in *The Good* the most important protagonist was Wallach; it remains his most popular role. Wallach's performance as Tuco, a one-man crime-wave, is unusually talkative and expressive. Seldom has an actor been given his head and used it to his advantage so well; in Leone's *Duck You Sucker* (1971) garrulous Rod Steiger overbalanced the film. Before *The Good*, the only Leone characters as animated as Tuco were cackling old-timers and eccentrics, but here the contrast between 'two kinds of people' works well. In the shelled town, during a Confederate mortar barrage, Blondy and Tuco walk down the smoking, cratered street to face Angel Eyes's gang; Eastwood strides out, coolly self-assured, while Wallach twitches along beside him, as though he is being followed by a stalker.

Since Tuco veered spectacularly off the straight and narrow, he has been a busy man, as his litany of crimes attest: murder, armed robbery, rape, arson, perjury, bigamy, deserting his wife and children, derailing a train, impersonating a Mexican general and hiring himself out as a guide to a wagon train, then abandoning the travellers on Sioux Indian hunting grounds. This from a man whose middle name is Pacifico ('peaceful'). Add to this his adventures during the film: swindling local sheriffs, holding up a gunsmith, kidnapping his ex-partner, impersonating a Confederate corporal and blowing up a bridge.

Tuco left home nine years ago; in a poignant moment he is reunited with his brother Pablo, a monk, who tells Tuco that both their parents are dead – 'Only now do you think of them'. Their father died a few days ago: 'He asked for you to be there', says Pablo, 'but there was only me'. When Tuco is accused of deserting his family, he says that back home they had two choices – to become a priest or a bandit. They have chosen their own paths, and when Tuco claims Pablo was too cowardly to be a bandit, the man of God slaps Tuco and then seeks forgiveness. As Blondy and Tuco leave the mission, Leone undercuts the drama: 'My brother, he's crazy about me,' says Tuco, as Blondy looks on disbelievingly, having just witnessed their quarrel. Such moments of uncharacteristic pathos from Eastwood and Wallach suggest Leone aimed to make a more sincere, perhaps even sentimental, film.

'Suspended sentence': The sheriff (John Bartho) whips Tuco's horse, while Blondy fires from the livery stable (background right). This scene from *The Good, the Bad and the Ugly* (1966) was shot at the Elios Studios set in Rome, also used in Corbucci's *Django* (1966).

Eastwood's speed with a gun is still superhuman, but he is not an indestructible hero. Without a gun, he is nothing, while Tuco is much tougher. When Blondy leaves his partner stranded in the desert, he tells Tuco, 'The way back to town is only seventy miles…if you save your breath, I feel a man like you could manage it'. Tuco survives, but when he gets his revenge on Blondy, the fair-skinned Gringo is on the brink of death when a driverless Confederate ambulance appears out of nowhere (with Carson on board) and distracts Tuco's attention. Tuco's treatment of Blondy in the desert is strikingly shot by Tonino Delli Colli. Blondy stumbles along, his face blistered and bubbled, while Tuco trots at a leisurely pace under a pink parasol. Once Blondy has learned half the secret from Carson, there is every reason for Tuco to keep Blondy alive. 'I'll kill you!' snarls Tuco, when Carson has died. 'If you do that,' whispers Blondy, 'you'll always be poor.' The desert ordeal is in place of Eastwood's usual beating, so that he can be resurrected. The ever-present, amplified flies buzzing around Eastwood led Don Rickles (Eastwood's co-star in the later *Kelly's Heroes*) to quip, 'Clint Eastwood, the only man who can talk with flies on his lips'.

During Blondy's convalescence at the San Antonio mission, Tuco attempts to prise the secret out of him and finds a link between them; they are both 'all alone', without family or friends. But the transience of their relationship is always apparent. 'I have you, you have me,' Tuco says of their companionship, 'Only for a little while I mean'. As they rig Langstone Bridge with dynamite, they agree to reveal their respective parts of the secret, but Blondy lies. Moments like this, where Blondy is less than trustworthy, lead us to appreciate the irony of Leone's 'good' and 'bad'; 'the Bad' kills people, but he is also capable of compassion, while the 'Ugly' is the most iniquitous of the trio.

Angel Eyes is Lee Van Cleef's best western villain. 'When I was at school,' Van Cleef remembered, 'My teachers always thought I was unhappy, but this face has let me play some great characters…I look mean without even trying.' He tested for the role of Gary Cooper's deputy in *High Noon* (1952), but the producers wanted him to have a nose job; Van Cleef refused and was cast as a harmonica-playing villain. When Van Cleef died in December 1989, his gravestone epitaph fittingly bore the legend 'BEST OF THE BAD – LOVE AND LIGHT'. 'The Bad', like 'the Good', is initially presented as a stereotype. When Leone freeze-frames on Eastwood as he abandons Tuco in the desert, Eastwood comments, 'Such ingratitude…after all the times I've saved your life' (a joking reference to their rope trick), while a scrawled subtitle reads 'the Good'. When Angel Eyes kills a bedridden Confederate soldier, by holding a pillow across his face and shooting him through it, there hardly needs to be the caption 'the Bad'.

Van Cleef was unhappy with the way Leone developed Angel Eyes. Throughout his film career, Van Cleef lived by a credo – even when he played villains: 'I never kick dogs, I'll never hurt a child, I'll never slap a woman – three things I won't do on film'. In *The Good*, Leone had to get a stuntman to stand in for Van Cleef for

Angel Eyes's beating of Carson's girlfriend Maria. In a revealing scene, Angel Eyes stops at a ruined Confederate fort, where wounded soldiers live on boiled corncobs. A sergeant accuses Angel Eyes of being a draft-dodger, then tells him about Betterville prison camp. For his help, Angel Eyes lets the soldier keep a bottle of whisky; but though the scene is one of the best in the film (with a great set, fluid camerawork and Morricone's moving trumpet theme) it was cut from the English version of the film, making Angel Eyes totally despicable.

Leone's religious symbolism recurred in *The Good*. It is most apparent in the San Antonio Mission scenes; Pablo's room is full of statues and icons. In Valverde, Angel Eyes watches as Blondy is about to free Tuco from a hanging, and comments, 'A golden haired angel watches over him'. For betraying Tuco, the golden-haired angel is dragged into the desert, but there is someone watching over Blondy too, when fate intervenes to save his life. Later, at San Antonio, the Angelus bell tolls, as the now badly blistered angel arrives in an ambulance.

Throughout the film, Blondy has luck on his side. When vengeful Tuco is about to hang Blondy from a hotel-room beam, a mortar scores a direct hit on the hotel and Tuco plummets through the floor. Even though Tuco is smart enough to creep

Angel Eyes (Lee Van Cleef) in Sad Hill cemetery in *The Good, the Bad and the Ugly* (1966).

up on Blondy through the window, the Union army (and pure luck) ruins his plan, leaving Tuco with an empty noose. Both Blondy and Angel Eyes have a supernatural ability to appear out of nowhere. At Sad Hill we see Tuco's arrival and breathless search for the grave, while both Blondy and Angel Eyes materialise like ghosts. Eastwood's first appearance in the film establishes this. Tuco has just been ambushed by three bounty-hunters. One has a reward poster for Tuco and comments that 'the Ugly' has 'a face beautiful enough to be worth $2,000'. 'But you don't look like the one who'll collect it,' says Eastwood's familiar whispering tones. He slides into frame (filmed from behind) and tells the overawed bandit, 'A couple of steps back', as he squares up for the showdown and lights a cheroot.

Leone's staging of the gunfights in *The Good* was more imaginative than *For a Few Dollars More*, with characters often caught off-guard. Al Mulock plays a gunman who is shot by Tuco in the opening ghost-town shootout, only to show up eight months later, minus an arm. When the one-armed bandit surprises Tuco in a bathtub, he gloats for far too long; Tuco shoots him with a pistol hidden under the soapsuds – 'When you have to shoot,' says Tuco, 'shoot…don't talk'. Earlier, Blondy disassembles his gun in a Santa Fe hotel room at an inopportune moment; as he cleans the weapon, three gunmen approach down the corridor. This scene is a familiar Leone duel, but presented in an unusual way. Here the shots of boots, close-ups of eyes and guns being loaded add tension to the scene, while a hand reaches for the door handle, as it would for a gun.

Ennio Morricone's music to *The Good, the Bad and the Ugly* is a series of inspirational compositions – his most famous, enduring score. Each of the title characters has his own signature tune, a five-note 'ah-ey-ah-ey-ah!' answered by 'wah, wah, wah!' Blondy's motif is voiced on soprano flute, Angel Eyes's on the echoing arghilofono, while Tuco's is voiced by members of the Cantori. This association is established by Morricone's spectacular opening title music, performed by the Orchestra Cinefonico Italiana; the piece begins with a hollow drumbeat, with each verse voiced by the characters' instruments – the flute, the arghilofono and the voices (with whistles and harmonica riffs mixed in). For the chorus, the Alessandroni Singers, drums and a blistering electric guitar up the pace, while the tune builds to a rousing climax, as trumpets (doubling as cavalry bugles) cascade and collide. This was cut to Lardani's colourful title sequence, with the Civil War raging in bold pop-art imagery. These brief signature tunes are used throughout the film to punctuate visual and verbal gags, while the main guitar theme scores Blondy and Tuco's adventures.

The music for Blondy's torture in the 'beautiful sun-baked sand' is like the score for a Biblical epic with cello, rolling piano, a gong and wailing cor anglais, which become more discordant as Blondy's condition worsens. Swirling violins that sound like a swarm of flies score Stevens's death, Maria's beating and the shootout in the Santa Fe hotel. A delicate Spanish guitar piece accompanies 'the Bad' as he drifts out of a desert sunset, while a similar melody scores Tuco recalling his childhood.

The Civil War carnage is evocatively described in 'The Soldier's Story', performed by inmates of the prison camp (with hungry-looking extras miming to Alessandroni's Cantori). The lyrics were written by Tommie Connor, though the words evoke the poetry of Rupert Brooke and Siegfried Sassoon. London-born Connor composed many sentimental ballads from the thirties to the fifties. He also wrote 'I Saw Mommy Kissing Santa Claus' and the English words to the German

Bounty-hunter Blondy (Clint Eastwood) lights up a cigar in *The Good, the Bad and the Ugly* (1966).

propaganda song 'Lili Marlene'. Morricone adapted 'The Soldier's Story' lyrics to fit his own composition:

> Bugles are calling, from prairie to shore
> Sign up and fall-in and march off to war
> Smoke hides the valleys and fire paints the plain
> Loud roar the cannons till ruin remains
> Count all the crosses and count all the tears
> These are the losses and sad souvenirs
> How ends the story? Whose is the glory?
> Ask if we dare, our comrades out there, who sleep.

There are three Civil War themes in the film. The beautiful 'Fort' theme (with cor anglais, strings and echoing bugles), used when Angel Eyes arrives at a stockade, as an ambulance materialises out of the desert (complete with Edda Dell'Orso's ghostly soprano), when Langstone Bridge explodes and for the execution of a thief. The marcetta theme, with a whistled melody, harmonica and strings, is used in the prison camp, the railway station and the aftermath of the river battle (the whistling references the Colonel Bogey March from the prison camp in *The Bridge on the River Kwai* – 1957). The third theme is an instrumental version of Connor's ballad, used in the monastery hospital scenes and for the death of the young Confederate in the chapel. While Blondy tends the soldier, Tuco makes his getaway and arrives at Sad Hill; his frantic search for the grave, which becomes a delirious blur of crosses, is scored by Morricone's skyscraping 'Ecstasy of Gold'. It begins with a rolling piano motif and oboe, which builds with the addition of bells, strings, the Cantori, metallic clangs, trumpets and galloping drums, all powered along by Dell'Orso's piercing soprano.

The shootout between the title trio is the most famous moment in spaghetti-western history, and the score is suitably dramatic. The setting is Sad Hill cemetery, with thousands of graves stretching into the distance. Again, Leone was making a point about the huge cost of war; on every grave there is a name (or the legend 'Unknown'), and every name is a life. Tuco unearths Arch Stanton's grave, but to Tuco's and Angel Eyes's surprise the hole actually contains the skeletal remains of Arch. '$200,000 is a lot of money,' says Blondy. 'We're going to have to earn it.' He writes the real name on a stone and places it in the middle of a huge sun-baked arena in the centre of the graveyard. Earlier, a street shootout in a shelled town was scored with eerie percussion, piano and sinister strings, but for the cemetery finale Morricone composed a five-minute bolero of death. As the trio take their places in the arena, the music builds tension, with vicious flamenco guitar (played by Bruno Battisti D'Amario), syncopated strings, castanets, the choir and an exultant trumpet. When they are ready for the duel to begin, Morricone unexpectedly stops the piece.

From out of the silence, crows caw and a musical watch chime alludes to *For a Few Dollars More*. Then a drum roll, a piano riff and a shattering cymbal drive the piece on to the climax, with the trumpet, choir and drums growing in intensity as hands inch towards pistols. Blondy kills Angel Eyes (who falls into an open grave), while Tuco discovers he is packing an empty gun – Blondy has surreptitiously unloaded it. 'You see, in this world there's two kinds of people my friend,' says Blondy, quoting Tuco's credo back to him, 'those with loaded guns and those who dig…you dig'. There's no name on the stone and none on the grave marker either. The gold was hidden in a tomb marked 'Unknown', next to Stanton's. As final revenge (in homage to their earlier partnership), Blondy splits the gold between them, adding, 'seems just like old times'. But this time he rides off, leaving noosed Tuco balancing precariously on a cross. A hollow drum on the soundtrack echoes Tuco's heartbeat; at the moment when Tuco is about to fall, Blondy reappears in the distance and severs the rope, leaving Tuco alive and rich, but stranded.

Though *For a Few Dollars More* is Leone's most popular film in Italy, *The Good* has been the most successful worldwide. It was released in Italy on the day before Christmas Eve 1966 to great acclaim, though some Italian critics commented that the more sentimental moments in the film (Tuco praying to a painting of Christ, Blondy ministering to dying soldiers, Angel Eyes giving a starving Confederate soldier a bottle of whisky) were a dilution of Leone's style and a sell-out to the United Artists money men. Its success in Italy resulted in many rip-offs, parodies and tributes, ranging from the imaginative to the libellous. Mario Mattoli's *For a Few Dollars Less* (1966), known in Spain as *El Bueno, El Feo, El Caradura* ('The Good, the Ugly, the Cheeky'), included a parody of Blondy and Tuco's hanging trick. Leone shot his scenes with Eastwood and Wallach at Elios Studios in May 1966; working fast, Mattoli shot his footage immediately afterwards and released the send-up in August, beating *The Good* to the cinemas by four months.

Three of Enzo G. Castellari's films were heavily indebted to *The Good*: *For a Few Bullets More* (1967) featured three characters in search of hidden treasure, *Kill Them All and Come Back Alone* (1968) was a Civil War heist movie and *Seven Winchesters for a Massacre* (1967) saw poncho-clad Stewart (Edd Byrnes) team up with a gang of Rebel guerrillas to track down a cache of missing Confederate gold. Bequiffed Byrnes was much too lightweight for spaghettis (he had previously duetted with Connie Stevens on the irritating 'Kookie, Kookie, Lend Me Your Comb') and was more Cliff than Clint. Castellari had earlier made *A Few Dollars for Django* (1966) with Anthony Steffen, who was optimistically launched as the Italian Clint Eastwood. Of the Civil War spaghettis, *Massacre at Fort Holman* (1972) and *Fort Yuma Gold* (1966) shared Leone's spirit of adventure, while in *I Want Him Dead* (1968) and *A Bullet for Sandoval* (1969), firing squads, cholera, looting and gravedigging were their cheerful view of the war.

As an antidote to these bleak outings, there was a gleeful Franchi and Ingrassia parody entitled *Il Bello, Il Brutto, Il Cretino* (1967 – 'The Handsome, the Ugly, the Cretinous'), a scene-for-scene send-up of Leone's film. Short, goofy Franchi played inept bounty-hunter 'Il Cretino', debonair Ingrassia played villainous 'Il Brutto', while Mimmo Palmera was vain smoothy 'Il Bello'. The plot included Blondy and Tuco's noose ruse, a prison camp, a pitched battle and a trip into the desert, all played for laughs. They learn of a fortune hidden in the grave of a man named 'Smith' and disguise themselves as Unionists to begin their treasure hunt, but are waylaid by a Confederate patrol. Franchi is convinced the Confederate officer's grey jacket is covered in dust, so he frantically slaps at the sleeve, hoping that it is blue underneath. Finally, the pair arrive at the cemetery (disguised as monks), but discover that 'Smith' is the name on every single grave.

During the English-language dubbing of *The Good, the Bad and the Ugly* some important changes were made. Van Cleef's hired gun is named Sentenza in the Italian script and in the film everyone's lips mouth that name, but Eastwood came up with Angel Eyes, which was substituted in the English version. Eastwood is called Biondo in the Italian print, referring to Eastwood's fair skin. In the dubbing studio Eastwood altered his own dialogue, to retain his character's coolness. Tuco and Blondy find a note left by Angel Eyes that ends with the phrase: 'See you soon, idiots'; on the voice track Eastwood says to Wallach, 'It's for you', while his lips mouth, 'It's for us'. Sergio Donati oversaw the English dubbing, to make sure the dialogue was translated correctly; 'If someone says "pipa",' recounted Donati, 'they [the Americans] are capable of translating "pepper"' [rather than 'pipe'].

There were also problems with the length of the film; UA wanted a film no longer than two-and-a-half hours. From the full 180-minute version, the Italian print cut Blondy sleeping with a prostitute, Tuco watching peons being forced to join the Confederate army in a Mexican village and Tuco recruiting three Mexican gunmen. The 167-minute Italian version includes the 'Bad' visiting a ruined fort, Tuco washing his feet in the desert, Tuco and Blondy visiting a Confederate bivouac, the aftermath of the Battle of Apache Canyon, and Blondy and Angel Eyes's rendez-vous with the latter's gang in a wood. The English-language release removed more scenes, including Tuco robbing a gunsmith and the prison commandant's scene (leaving the film 148 minutes long). Various prints are in existence, including an English-language print with the title-card freeze-frames in Italian.

The Good, the Bad and the Ugly was released in the UK and the US in 1968. The US posters for *The Good* looked like Eastwood's filmography thus far: 'First *Fistful*, then *For a Few*…this time the jackpot's a cool 200,000 Dollars', while another tagline read 'For three men, the Civil War wasn't Hell…it was practice'. The US trailer misidentified Van Cleef as 'the Ugly' and Wallach as 'the Bad'. With its arrival in the US, UA's profits were at an all-time high ($20 million, after tax) and Eastwood became America's fifth-biggest box-office draw. Critics admired Leone and Morricone and their fantastical approach to film-making, referring to the mannered pacing and grandiose shootouts as a 'mocking treacle', but they still sharpened the knives for Eastwood's and Van Cleef's performances.

The huge success of *The Good* broke the spaghetti-western phenomenon to a whole new audience, with some cinemas running 'Dollars' triple-bills. *Fistful* and *For a Few* had been popular, but in the UK and the US crowds flocked in droves to see *The Good*; it was one of the sensations of 1968. In the US, it grossed $6 million.

A novelisation by Joe Millard was published, with a series of eight 'Dollars Western' paperbacks. The book was based on the original Italian script – Blondy is named 'Whitey', and there is more background information. Hugo Montenegro recorded a leaden version of Morricone's theme tune, which went to number one in the UK on 16 November 1968 and stayed there for four weeks (it was toppled by 'Lily the Pink'). The theme has been covered by everyone from Geoff Love to the Grand Fantastic Orchestra (who also recorded a sleazy, sax version of *Django*).

Following *The Good, the Bad and the Ugly*, Leone and Eastwood crossed swords and never collaborated again; Eastwood wanted to pursue a career in the US, while Leone resented Eastwood's huge fee. Leone went on to make the critically revered (but less financially successful) *Once Upon a Time in the West* (1968), but the energy of the 'Dollars' films was gone and his career never recovered the impetus of 1964–66. *The Good, the Bad and the Ugly* remains the high watermark for all concerned; it regularly appears as the highest-ranked western in 'All-time top 100 movie' lists, while *Once Upon a Time in the West* is nowhere to be seen. By 1971, the 'Dollars' trilogy had been rereleased 15 times in the US and *Life* magazine ran a front page with the headline 'The World's Favourite Movie Star Is – No Kidding – Clint Eastwood'. In 1968 Eastwood had won a Golden Laurel award for his action performance as Blondy; his growing popularity in the late sixties was solely due to the Leone westerns and his American western, *Hang 'Em High* (1968). *The Good, the Bad and the Ugly* is the quintessential Italian western – the genius of Leone, Morricone and Eastwood distilled.

10

'We Got Problems ... Even Up in Heaven'

— Giulio Questi's *Django Kill* (1967)

Django Kill – If You Live Shoot! (1967)
original title: *Se Sei Vivo, Spara!*
Credits
DIRECTOR – Giulio Questi
PRODUCER – 'Alex J Rascal' (Sandro Iacovoni)
STORY AND SCREENPLAY – Giulio Questi and Franco Arcalli
ORIGINAL IDEA – Maria Del Carmen Martinez Roman
ASSISTANT WRITER – Benedetto Benedetti
SET DESIGNER – Enzo Bulgarelli
ART DIRECTORS – Jose Luis Galicia and Jaime Perez Cubero
EDITOR – Franco Arcalli
DIRECTOR OF PHOTOGRAPHY – Franco Delli Colli
MUSIC – Ivan Vandor
Interiors filmed at Elios Film Studios (Rome) and Estudios
    Roma (Madrid)
Techniscope/Technicolor
An Italian/Spanish co-production
GIA Cinematografica (Rome) and Hispamer Film (Madrid)
Released internationally by Golden Era Film Distributors
Cast
Tomas Milian (the stranger); Marilu Tolo (Flory); Piero Lulli
    (Oaks); Milo Quesada (Bill Tembler); 'Paco Sanz', Francisco
    Sanz (Hagerman); Roberto Camardiel (Zorro); Patrizia Valturri
    (Elizabeth Hagerman); Raymond Lovelock (Evan Tembler);
    Sancho Gracia (Willy, Zorro's lieutenant); Frank Braña
    (Tembler's henchman); Gene Collins (Collins); Mirella Panfili
    (woman in town); Herman Reynoso (bearded townsman);
    Fernando Villena (member of Oaks's gang); with Miguel
    Serrano, Daniel Martin, Edoardo De Santis and Angel Silva

*   *   *

Invariably referred to as the most gruesome western of all time, Giulio Questi's *Django Kill* has become something of a spaghetti-western myth. The uncut version of the film seems like the most hideous piece of blood-and-sand gunslinger action ever committed to celluloid. The catalogue of violence is extreme: a scalping, a man's chest torn apart by a frenzied mob, a grotesque mass lynching, an implied male rape, a crucifixion, the desecration of a graveyard, a man scalded with molten gold and an entire gang and their steeds obliterated with dynamite. Even years later, *Kill* is ferocious, though not as influential as the equally graphic *The Wild Bunch* (1969), which had a more grisly impact on mainstream westerns. Questi's film is difficult to pigeonhole. It isn't just a western or a horror film, or a splatter film, or a homosexual slant on *A Fistful of Dollars* crossed with *The Fall of the House of Usher*; it is all of these things and more. If *Django Kill* doesn't live up to its 'most violent western ever' tag, it is certainly the weirdest Italian-made western; the most gratuitous piece of gunslinger action to crawl out of Italy in the sixties, and, if a landmark of the genre, what it marks is still a mystery.

Django Kill is the directorial debut of Giulio Questi, a 42-year-old former journalist. His film career began in the fifties making documentaries, and he acted in Fellini's *La Dolce Vita* (1960) as Don Giulio, whose fiancée was played by sixties icon, Nico. Don Giulio is soon to inherit the family castle, which has a cellar full of 'bats, snakes and vampires'. In late 1965 Questi and his writing partner Franco Arcalli were working on a horror/thriller called *A Curious Way to Love* (later released as *Death Laid an Egg*), when they were asked to write and shoot a western in Madrid the following summer. The result was a story entitled *Se Sei Vivo, Spara!* ('If You Live, Shoot!'), one of the most ridiculous spaghetti-western titles ever – on a par with *If Your Left Arm Offends, Cut it Off* (pretty extreme, whatever your arm has done), *Heads I Kill You, Tails You Die* (*Catch-22*, spaghetti-style) and *Cemetery Without Crosses* (which is surely just an empty field). Benedetto Benedetti provided additional dialogue and the screenplay was based on an idea by Maria Del Carmen Martinez Roman, though it was actually another rewrite of *Fistful*. Yet again, a stranger found himself caught between two rival gangs in a nothing town. What could Questi possibly bring to another reworking of this now-hackneyed story?

If Corbucci's *Django* stretched the *Fistful* plot line to breaking point, *Django Kill* broke it. A half-breed stranger and his Mexican friends are betrayed and killed in the desert by a gringo gang, led by Oaks. Having stolen a fortune in gold from the US army, Oaks and his men arrive in a nearby town, but are lynched and slaughtered by the manic townsmen, led by Tembler the saloonkeeper and Hagerman the storekeeper, who then divide the gold between themselves. The stranger is only wounded and is nursed back to health by two Indian medicine men; he arrives in town with his pistol loaded with gold bullets and is drawn into the tangled mystery, as Tembler and Hagerman wrestle with Zorro, a Mexican rancher, for possession of the gold.

In Questi's scenario, the two factions in town are completely outrageous. The Mexicans are a bunch of identically dressed, black-clad gauchos (the Muchachos) led by the sadistic Zorro, who takes pleasure in watching his wild boys eat and drink to excess, before they rape Tembler's son, Evan. Their rivals, the townspeople, are moderate by comparison: Tembler employs a gang of local heavies, while Hagerman is a loner who locks his pyromaniac wife Elizabeth in the attic. The innocent Mexican family from *Fistful* becomes the twisted saloon family of Tembler, his saloon singer lover Flory and dysfunctional son, Evan (though Flory is not Evan's father), while Silvanito and Piripero become a pair of mystical Indians.

Like *Fistful*, *Django Kill* involves a robbery, though the perpetrators are not one of the warring factions, but a third party – Oaks's gringo–Mexican bandit gang. Once the loot goes missing, the stranger tries to locate it, as the gold passes from one group to another like a hot potato; first the army has it, then Oaks, then Tembler and Hagerman – the gold quickly bringing death to whoever owns it. This leaves a trail of bodies, until it is obvious who has the gold when Hagerman is the only one left alive. In the blazing finale, Hagerman's wife sets fire to the house; the gold, hidden in a roof beam, melts and Hagerman is last seen through the flames, descending into hell, his face a mask of molten gold.

Questi's influences were eclectic. He claimed that the Muchachos represented the black shirts of Fascism and that the film was influenced by his experiences fighting Fascists in the countryside as a partisan during the Second World War. The Muchachos were also based on the Pistoleros, a gang from the spaghetti western *Three Golden Boys* (1966); the Pistoleros wore identical black outfits, coupled with tasteful blue scarves. Masked-hero Hollywood westerns provided Questi with the name Zorro, while the stranger's gold bullets and his two Indian saviours echoed the Lone Ranger, who fired silver ammunition and was accompanied by his sidekick, Tonto.

Questi also took inspiration from Spanish horror films. Hispamer Films, the Spanish backers of *Kill*, were more often associated with movies like Jesus Franco's trend-setting *The Awful Dr Orloff* (1962), which featured Dr Orloff and his tall, blind assistant Morpho kidnapping and murdering dancehall girls in an attempt to rejuvenate his daughter's disfigured face. The morbid pair stalk the streets, Morpho following the tap-tap-tap of his master's cane, as they find and kill a victim, hide her in a coffin and transport her body by rowing boat to their castle lair. *Orloff*'s 'do-it-yourself-surgery' and the Gothic elegance (chains, black frock coats, vivid settings, macabre tortures) influenced Questi's style.

Questi chose his cast well – a combination of newcomers and old hands – and employed locals from Madrid (university students, wrestlers and wranglers) as extras. Amongst the new faces were Patrizia Valturri (previously a TV actress) as Elizabeth, Raymond Lovelock (in his film debut) as Evan and Gene Collins (later to co-star with Clint Eastwood in *Kelly's Heroes*) as a member of Oaks's gang. For the hero, Questi chose Cuban Tomas Milian, who had made his western debut in the static *The Ugly Ones* (1966) as Jose Gomez, a Mexican outlaw who escapes from the stagecoach carrying him to prison in Yuma and hides out in New Chacos, an isolated settlement in the desert. *Kill* was Milian's first top-billed role, and the last time he played a gringo-esque lead.

Italian Piero Lulli (who was cast as outlaw Oaks) had appeared in *Duel of the Titans* (1961), *The Hero of Babylon* (1963), *The Spartan Gladiators* (1965) and *Achilles* (1962), a 'tale of Troy' that took historical inaccuracy to new depths, with the Trojan warriors using shields with a horse's-head design on them. Lulli's role as Inspector Kruger in Mario Bava's *Kill Baby Kill* (1966) suggested that he was wasted in a toga. He was subtly menacing as the chief of police in the town of Kernigan, a place in the grip of terror after a spate of mysterious killings in which the victims are discovered with gold coins imbedded in their hearts. Oaks remains Lulli's best role; his cadaverous face was a vulture made man. At once cruel yet cunning, his hooked nose, lanky frame and evil grimace epitomised Questi's house-of-horror-style casting technique.

Paco Sanz, as untrustworthy Hagerman, had appeared as the colonel in *A Pistol for Ringo* and as Consalvo the undertaker in *Yankee* (1966), a comic-strip, Barcelona-shot western directed by Tinto Brass. Spaniard Milo Quesada portrayed his partner Tembler, while Marilu Tolo played Flory. Tolo was an actress who had begun in Cinecitta-genre movies and dabbled in European art-house cinema. Roberto Camardiel had made over twenty-five features in his native Spain, but it was in Italian westerns that he made his mark, initially in vehicles like *Adios Gringo* (1965) and *Left-handed Johnny West* (1965). As Zorro, Camardiel's jovial persona, so amiable in his early westerns, was to become something entirely different; his laugh was chilling, his friendliness threatening, while his round, grinning face and whiskers seemed altogether less than jolly.

Django Kill's Spanish shoot was blazing hot, and money from producer Sandro Iacovoni dribbled through, which infuriated Questi; his bad temper seems to have infused the finished film. The interiors were shot at Elios Studios and Estudios Roma in Madrid. The windblown town was the disguised *Fistful* set at Hojo De Manzanares; Silvanito's cantina became Hagerman's house and the Rojo residence doubled as Tembler's saloon. The town's graveyard was also from Leone's film. Location scenes were staged around Madrid: the army ambush was on the banks of the River Henares, while the desert massacre was shot on a limestone-covered building site near Madrid (complete with deep digger tracks). The exterior of Zorro's *hacienda* was back in Italy, at Villa Mussolini near Rome.

Franco Delli Colli's lush Technicolor cinematography gives the film a stylish look, with sunlight, backlight and dust combining to artistic effect. The sequences in the desert are picturesque, with the white, scorching sand dunes contrasting with the swathes of blue sky, as the stranger and two gringos ride into Oaks's camp. A shootout between Oaks and the stranger in Hagerman's general store is also artfully done; Delli Colli films Milian looking through cobwebs, coloured bottles or a suspended, open-ended wicker basket. A scene where Zorro crucifies the sweaty, near-naked stranger in a cell full of vampire bats and lizards is lit to resemble an El Greco, or Juan Martinez Montanes's crucifixion sculptures. But Questi and Delli Colli are also capable of the unexpected and the inept; one shot of a dead peon rolling down a sand dune is cut into the film upside down, while during the lynching of Oaks's gang, a camera-car's tyre-tracks are clearly visible down the main street.

Django Kill is influenced by various religious idioms, from crucifixion and resurrection, to living hell and reincarnation. The opening shot introduces the half-dead stranger clawing his way out of a grave, his hand reaching for salvation. The Native American Indians believed that the afterlife was a world where buffalo and game were abundant – hence 'happy hunting grounds'. Most tribes didn't believe in hell and thought that the deceased travelled to the next world and lived on as they had on earth. Passage there could be achieved in a number of ways, from climbing a tree, crossing a river or stepping across a magic chain of arrows – but not via a hole in the desert. Only a shaman had the power to communicate with the spirit world. The Indians in *Kill* obviously see the stranger as a shaman. In Indian folklore the shaman would have experienced the other world and returned with a wider knowledge of all things spiritual.

Questi's Indians are not entirely convincing, but are an interesting addition to the story. They chance upon the stranger and dangle some lucky rabbits' feet over his wounds; Indians believed that illness was caused by an evil spirit taking over the victim's body, so the rabbits' feet were Questi's idea of shamanistic ritual. In exchange for nursing the stranger back to health (and casting him several rounds of gold ammunition) the Indians want to know the secrets of the land of the dead ('on other side of river of life'). They ask, 'How is death?' but the stranger never imparts any acquired knowledge. The Indians, in Napoleonic-style jackets, blankets, feathers and beads, look pretty 'hokey' (one even wears a bowler hat), while their dubbed voices are atrocious – one talks like an English gent, while the other sounds like he has sinus trouble.

One interpretation of *Django Kill* is that the stranger's adventures represent the afterlife, though Questi's version of the next world is exceptionally hectic. As Oaks's gang stumble into town, one of them mumbles, 'Sure don't look like heaven'; later, when the stranger falls foul of the bigoted townsfolk, he tells the Indians, 'You see, we got problems my friend...even up in Heaven'. As with many Italian westerns, the hero is a Christ-like figure; he is resurrected, crucified and in one shot resembles Christ on the Via Doloroso – burdened with an outlaw's corpse, rather than a cross.

Another interpretation of the story is that the stranger is back from the dead. Prior to the stranger's execution in the desert, he tells Oaks, 'I don't have to pray for salvation, once I've been killed'. When the stranger unexpectedly appears in town, Oaks shouts: 'You've come back from Hell'; Oaks takes a shot at the stranger, but misses, even though he has just gunned down two of Tembler's men and the stranger seems supernatural, a ghost back to torment his enemies.

The town on the edge of the desert, known by the Indian epithet the 'Unhappy Place', broke new ground in European art-movie weirdness. This is displayed during the gringo gang's arrival in town. Accompanied by an oddly threatening, clockwork musical composition by Ivan Vandor (incorporating bells, bass guitar, drum rattles and strings), they slowly walk down the street, warily observing the extraordinary sights that welcome them: a girl viciously pulls a little boy's hair; a man vomits outside the saloon; an uncle uses his niece as a footstool; a woman bites at an unseen assailant's hand; a young girl swings her skirt as she sings 'A Banjo On My Knee'; the purple hem of a silken dress vanishes behind a stable door; a man licks blood from his thumb and a small crippled animal squeaks in pain. This sequence is the ideal introduction to the creepiest town in Italian westerns.

Throughout this frontier strangeness, Tomas Milian's performance holds the film together. Despite the name 'Django' in the title, Milian's hero is nameless: he signs his name in the hotel register with an 'X' and everyone refers to him as 'the stranger' (though Italian and Spanish prints christen him 'Hondo' and 'Barney'). Milian's method acting works well, with the lack of dialogue compensated by his menacing presence and unshaven scowl. Milian's hero is greedy, unscrupulous and merciless. At the start of *Fistful*, a cackling local tells Eastwood's gunslinger that

'Where's the gold?': The stranger is crucified by rancher Zorro; Tomas Milian in Giulio Questi's *Django Kill* (1967).

he'll become very rich in San Miguel, or else he will be killed. By the end of *Kill*, Milian's stranger is neither rich nor dead, just spent and emotionless as he fails to save the characters he cares about: his Mexican compadres, Evan, the Indians and Elizabeth.

While Eastwood manages to cope with his opponents, Milian's attempts to manipulate the gangs are absolutely chaotic. With more groups in town, the stranger gets the chance to work for everyone. He's a bandit for Oaks, but is double-crossed and killed. Back from the dead, he arrives in town and receives a $500 reward from Tembler for killing Oaks. The stranger then works for Zorro, acting as Evan's bearer when he returns the lad's corpse to town. Finally Hagerman hires him, officially as a bodyguard, but really as a stooge, when Hagerman wants to kill Tembler and get his hands on the rest of the gold. With each new employer, the stranger is promised something (gold, dollars, a steady job, security), but his bosses never deliver.

The hero becomes desensitised to the violence around him. In the desert he is shocked to hear from Oaks, 'I don't divide my gold with no motherless Mexicans'. The stranger reaches for his gun and pulls the trigger, but the chamber is empty; 'Tough luck, half-breed,' sneers Oaks, 'guns don't shoot with no bullets inside'. When the lone avenger hits town he finds his entire ex-gang have been butchered and strung up, like animals in a slaughterhouse. The stranger shields his eyes from the spectacle, but life in the 'Unhappy Place' soon grows on him. In retribution for being double-crossed, he cripples Oaks. In revenge for weak-willed Tembler's apathy towards Evan's death, the stranger blinds one of Tembler's hoods with a broken bottle. And for raping Evan and for his own crucifixion, the stranger blows up the Muchachos and guns down Zorro in a surreal scene, with Zorro's pet parrot warning, 'The time has come, Zorro!'

With *Django Kill*, spaghettis were back in psychological western territory, with a guilt-wracked, tormented central character. The first section of the film (the gold robbery and desert massacre) takes place in flashback, while later the stranger is haunted by recent events. Questi cuts rapidly between snatches of the ambush, the stranger's 'death' in the desert, his compulsive hand-washing and the lynching, accompanied by odd sound-effect montages compiled by Aurelio Pennacchia – distorted gunfire, moans of the dying, thunderous drums and a crescendo of pistol shots.

The hero's relationship with Elizabeth, Hagerman's wife, is Questi's vague con-cession to genre convention. Initially Elizabeth appears to be a woman in peril, like Marisol in *A Fistful of Dollars*; but she's actually a pyromaniac lunatic, locked away like Rochester's wife Bertha in Charlotte Brontë's *Jane Eyre*. In Brontë's novel, Bertha sets fire to her love rival's bed and burns down Thornfield Hall, and Rochester is blinded in the inferno; in Questi's film, Elizabeth acquires of a box of 'The Pioneer's Friend' brand matches, torches the bed she has shared with the stranger and burns down the house, and Hagerman is blinded with molten gold.

Elizabeth's mental disintegration was possibly influenced by Charlotte Perkins Gilman's short story 'The Yellow Wallpaper', in which a woman suffering from 'fatigue' loses her sanity through her constant solitude and a husband who 'knows best'. Eventually she thinks that she can see patterns in the decaying wallpaper, which resemble bars with 'imprisoned women' creeping about behind them; in the climax, the 'women' get out, and the heroine is ready for the sanatorium. In *Django Kill* Hagerman keeps Elizabeth in a room with barred windows so that she begins to doubt her own sanity, but he cunningly allows her out, to waylay the hero. Elizabeth's strange behaviour at the barred window intrigues the stranger (she's actually trying to scare him away), but their doomed romance is never to be. As the house burns down, the stranger watches his lover pirouette in an upstairs window, her hair burnt away, her arms crossed vainly protecting her face. By this point, the stranger is unable to watch the horror. The incessant violence seems to have affected him; it is time he left town.

In contrast to Elizabeth, saloon singer Flory is more like Hagerman and Tembler: greedy and manipulative. Marilu Tolo aptly conveys Flory's lust, in one scene slavering at the mouth as she watches through a keyhole while Tembler and Hagerman argue over the loot. Flory looks more like an opera diva, or a Japanese Noh theatre actress, with her pale face and jet-black bun (recalling a young Liz Taylor). Her saloon song is also unusual, less a boisterous bar room ditty and more a bluesy torch song. Entitled 'My Town', it initially sounds like a paean to the attractions of the shantytown, but becomes something much more sinister. Lines like 'My town is so nice' give way to the ominous: 'I know you'll be staying on forever' and 'Your time may be limited', cryptically foretelling the outlaws' fate.

Although nearly all of the most successful Italian westerns concentrated on a close relationship between two men, few explored the homosexual implications; *A Bullet for the General* (1966) was one of the early minority to do so. But nothing prepared western audiences for *Django Kill*. Zorro's camp gang, the Muchachos, are a fetishistic addition to the genre, dressed in matching embroidered black gaucho outfits and led by Willy (Sancho Gracia). Fatherly Zorro's affections for his gang are not confined to the usual employer–employee relationship; he rewards them with lavish meals and drink. During a feast at the *hacienda*, Zorro encourages the stranger to join in: 'Before you know it, you'll feel you are one of us. The pleasure of food and drink satisfy man's baser senses and opens the way to more refined sensations...like crime.' Zorro later confides in his alcoholic talking parrot, 'It's a pity you don't understand what my Muchachos mean to me. They make me so happy in their black uniforms.' This line would not have been unusual in a psychological melodrama, but in a western it took the genre to pastures new.

While locating the gold, the hero rids the town of Hagerman and Tembler. Pious storekeeper Hagerman (described by Tembler as a 'low-down chiseller') recalls the work of Edgar Allan Poe; he ghosts around town in a frock coat and imprisons his wife. Though Hagerman (called Ackerman in the Italian print) is a merchant, his role in town is more that of a priest: he is referred to as 'Alderman' on occasion in the English-language print. At two points in the film Hagerman's religious zeal boils over and he whips the townsmen into a frenzy, to purge the town of undesirables.

Bill Tembler (called 'Templar' in the Italian print) and his son Evan have a strange relationship. Tembler plans to use the stolen gold to get married to Flory, while Evan hates his stepmother; in a *Psycho*-inspired moment, he slashes her clothes to ribbons. Evan has spent his entire life trying to escape the town, only to find that the outside world is even more inhospitable. He is captured by Zorro and becomes guest of honour at a banquet, but his shame following his ordeal at the hands of the Muchachos leads him to commit suicide; in Questi's original concept Evan was to have died as a result of the assault.

The children in *Django Kill* reflect the savagery in town. Like Sam Peckinpah, Questi includes shots of children behaving oddly; as Oaks's men enter town, the antics of the local kids make a gang of hardened outlaws feel uneasy. They are depicted as victims and voyeurs, but also as perpetrators. In the last shot of the film, the stranger surveys the desecrated graveyard and is startled by two children who are pulling pieces of string tight across their faces – distorting their features in a macabre game: 'I'm uglier than you'. Sick of the wicked town, where even the children are monsters, the stranger turns his back on the 'Unhappy Place' and rides away.

Questi's violent style layers massacre upon massacre, as whole groups of characters are annihilated in the opening half hour. The killing and lynching of Oaks's motley crew is one of the gruesome highlights. A fusillade of gunshots stampedes the bandits' horses, and the townspeople rush the gang, who are summarily shot, drowned, beaten or dragged screaming to the 'necktie-party'. Death by hanging has never been depicted in westerns in such a realistic, horrible way. The gang's bullet wounds are bloated and bruised, their tongues loll out and their necks are grotesquely crooked at odd angles. Left in the desert, and presumed dead by his gringo partners, only the stranger survives this opening holocaust.

The way Questi's camera lingers on the corpses is particularly macabre; he uses images of open graves and unburied corpses throughout the film. This voyeuristic, intrusive style reflects voyeuristic characters in the action, as people spy through windows or keyholes and impassively watch tortures. When the stranger blows up the Muchachos with a horse loaded with dynamite, the scene of carnage is disconcertingly realistic; as the stranger walks through the aftermath of the blast, bits of horses and riders lie strewn about, like an explosion in an abattoir. It is Questi's emotionless attitude to these atrocities that eventually overpowers the viewer.

Ivan Vandor's music to *Django Kill* is a peculiar combination of a twangy spaghetti-western score and horror-inspired pieces. The main theme is nondescript and the opening sand-dunes sequence would have been better served with an understated, ominous piece; instead Vandor deploys an upbeat, lilting guitar groove reminiscent of Stelvio Cipriani's music for *The Ugly Ones* (1966). It begins with a drum roll and cymbal crash, as a bass guitar takes the rhythm, offset by a guitar chord, while another chiming electric guitar plays the melody. Odd effects (flourishes of castanets and a quiet church organ) gradually permeate the piece, as violins rise and take the melody, until a flute trill ends the tune as uneventfully as it began.

Vandor's variations on this composition are much better. An amiable, flute-led version accompanies the Indians' progress through the desert on their wagon and the stranger's arrival in town. An Indian plays the tune on his flute (which later doubles as a poisonous blowpipe) as Oaks's corpse is carried out of the saloon. At Zorro's party, the piece gets slower and more distorted, in an imaginative aural representation of the stranger's gradual inebriation. Elsewhere, Vandor's music recalls the weird scraping violins from *Hercules in the Haunted World* (1961), the atonal jazz improvisations, swirling strings and shrieking voices of *The Awful Dr Orloff* (1962) and eerie bass, harp and bells from *Kill Baby Kill* (1966). These pieces add mystery to shots of Elizabeth stroking the bars on her window or Evan slashing Flory's clothes (a scene that recalls Mario Bava's 1964 fashion-victim

An eye-catching poster for the 1970 UK release of Giulio Questi's *Django Kill* (1967).

classic *Blood and Black Lace*). These horror-style strings are overly dramatic (bordering on the intrusive) and suggest that Dracula will appear at any moment.

When *Django Kill* appeared in Italy in January 1967 there was outrage. One week later an Italian court confiscated the film and withdrew it from circulation until the censors passed an acceptable cut. This resulted in the 117-minute film being pruned to 95 minutes, though subsequent Italian reissues in the seventies restored much of the violence, including an extra shootout between the stranger and the Muchachos at Hagerman's house. Several non-violent scenes were trimmed too: various dialogues between the stranger and the Indians, and two conversations between Tembler and his lieutenant (Frank Braña). Since 1967, the film has been released at many different lengths with various degrees of mutilation, both on-screen and censorial.

When Golden Era Film Distributors released the film in the UK in 1970, with the tagline 'Terror from the Depths of Hell!' the full title was *Django Kill! (If You Live Shoot!)*. An exploitative publicity campaign (including a poster featuring the stranger's hand reaching from beyond the grave) and the US pop-art rotoscoped trailer ('Desperate…Violent…Shocking…If you live Shoot…If you live Kill… Coming soon: *Django Kill*') did not help the film internationally, and it wasn't successful on the UK/US market. The first English version to surface was the hacked-up 95-minute print, with the entire cast (including the parrot) dubbed. This version plays surprisingly well and incorporates all the surreal and macabre elements from the full version. Unusually, the cut version is superior to the full version, with Questi's choppy editing technique remaining consistent throughout. The opening sequences of both editions are a barrage of rapidly edited images; the uncut version then becomes more conventional, while the cut version keeps the action steaming along at a frenetic pace.

Nearly all the deleted scenes and omissions have been restored in a 115-minute English-language print, though it is still two minutes short of the original Italian print. Two key sequences are still missing and both are graphically violent. In the first, Oaks has been badly wounded by the stranger and is laid out on a table in the saloon. During the operation to remove the bullets, the townsfolk discover that Oaks has been 'shot full of gold', and in a frenzy claw at Oaks's chest and gut his belly with a knife. In the second scene, one of the Indians is captured by the lynch mob looking for the stranger; they hold the Indian down and scalp him. This scalping highlights another problem with the film; there are numerous loose ends, including what becomes of the two Indians: in all English-release prints, both vanish mysteriously from the action. This would suggest that there is still footage missing.

To catalogue the differences between the many versions of the film would take an entire book, as some prints add non-violent shots of faces and boots, in place of a couple of seconds of violence. For instance, the German print deleted dialogue scenes, but retained the scalping and operation scenes. Over the years *Django Kill* has had many title changes: *If You're Alive, Shoot* (another literal translation of the Italian title), *Oro Maldito* ('Cursed Gold' in Spain), *Oro Hondo* (seventies Italian reissue), *Gringo Uccidi!* ('Gringo Kill', Italian alternative title) and *Django Kid* (a typo).

Though more violent Italian westerns have been made since, the fullest version of *Django Kill* still has disturbing power. Questi never made another western, having said all he had to say on the genre in one film. But *Kill* is one of the most talked-about spaghetti westerns, with much speculation about a definitive cut. It symbolises the freedom from censorship available to film-makers shooting in Spain in the sixties, and how far the parameters of the genre could be pushed. If *Django Kill* was unsuccessful as a spaghetti western, then that was Questi's intent. Except for the very basic plot and the employment of several stock genre actors, the film owes little to mainstream Italian westerns. *Django Kill* was not supposed to be a conventional western, and the finished film should not be judged as one. What the film has come to represent is another question altogether. It is either a good argument for curbing the excesses of low-budget European art cinema or a fantasy version of *A Fistful of Dollars*, made by someone with a very vivid imagination. As Zorro would say, whatever turns you on.

The stranger stalks Oaks's men in *Django Kill* (1967); Tomas Milian in the 'Unhappy Place' at Hojo De Manzanares.

11

'I Don't Even Respect the Living'

— Sergio Corbucci's *The Hellbenders* (1967)

The Hellbenders (1967)
original title: *I Crudeli*
Credits
DIRECTOR – Sergio Corbucci
PRODUCER – 'Albert Band' (Alfredo Antonini)
STORY – Virgil C. Gerlach
SCREENPLAY – 'Albert Band', Ugo Liberatore and 'Louis
     Garfinkle' (Jose G Maesso)
ART DIRECTOR – Jaime Perez Cubero
EDITOR – Nino Baragli and Alberto Gallitti
DIRECTOR OF PHOTOGRAPHY – Enzo Barboni
MUSIC – 'Leo Nichols' (Ennio Morricone)
Interiors filmed at Cinecitta Studios, Rome and Elios Studios, Rome
Eastmancolor
An Italian/Spanish co-production.
Alba Cinematografica (Rome)/Tecisa Film (Madrid)
Released internationally by Avco Embassy Pictures
Cast
   Joseph Cotten (Colonel Jonas); Norma Bengell (Clare); Julian
   Mateos (Ben); Gino Pernice (Jeff); 'Angel Aranda', Angel
   Perez Aranda (Nat); Maria Martin (Kitty); Al Mulock (the
   beggar); Aldo Sambrell (Pedro); Enio Girolami (Lieutenant
   Sublett); Benito Stefanelli (Slim); Jose Niento (Sheriff);
   'Claudio Gora', Emilio Giordana (Priest of Sundog); Alvaro
   De Luna (Bixby); Julio Peña (Sergeant Tolt); Gene Collins
   (Union soldier counting money); Ivan Scratuglia (gambler in
   Denton Saloon); Claudio Scarchilli (Indian chief); Simon
   Arriaga, Rafael Vaquero and Jose Canalejas (Mexican bandits)
   with Gonzalo Esquiroz and Martin Diaz

*   *   *

When General Lee put quill to paper and signed the Confederate surrender, ending the American Civil War on Palm Sunday 1865, he marked the final defeat of the south and the beginning of the reconstruction era. For the next twelve years the southern populace had to cope with northern-government insurgency measures. Bitter in defeat, many Confederates attempted to prolong the war, with campaigns of guerrilla tactics against the north. These soldiers, essentially 'Rebels without a Cause', were the models for Albert Band and Ugo Liberatore when they concocted their brace of reconstruction-era spaghettis – *The Tramplers* (1966) and its companion film, *The Hellbenders* (1967).

Following Sergio Corbucci's success with *Django* and *Navajo Joe*, Albert Band hired him to direct *The Hellbenders*. They had previously collaborated on *Red Pastures* (1963), when Band co-authored the screenplay and acted as producer. Based on a treatment by Virgil C. Gerlach, *The Hellbenders* was written by Band in collaboration with Liberatore, with added contributions from Jose G. Maesso (who had worked on *Django*). It tells the story of the ex-Confederate Colonel Jonas and his three sons: Ben, Jeff and Nat – known as the Hellbenders. They ambush a Union convoy at Torrid Junction and steal a million dollars in cash, then flee through Texas and New Mexico. They are on their way to their ranch, across the Hondo River, where they plan to use the money to jump-start the American Civil War. To pass unnoticed, they pose as a burial escort, with the money hidden in a coffin and a woman posing as the deceased's widow, but all does not go to plan. In the course of their journey, the coffin is buried at Union Fort Brent and when they go to retrieve it, they dig up the wrong casket. With a corpse instead of a fortune, greed and betrayal take over; on the banks of the Hondo, with their goal in sight, the clan implodes and Jonas, mortally wounded, crawls forlornly to the river's edge.

The Hellbenders was influenced by Albert Band's previous film, *The Tramplers*. Based on the novel *Guns of North Texas* by Will Cook (like *The Hellbenders*, a literary source), *The Tramplers* cast Joseph Cotten as the patriarch of a southern family in post-Civil War Texas. It featured ex-muscleman Gordon Scott, James Mitchum (Robert Mitchum's son) and Franco Nero (in his western debut as 'Frank Nero'). Cotten played Temple Cordine, head of the Cordine family (the Tramplers of the title), who spend their time killing northern interlopers. *The Tramplers* begins with Lon (Gordon Scott) returning to his hometown after the Civil War. He runs into his father and four brothers lynching a Yankee newspaperman and immediately clashes with his father. Temple says that when he returned from the war, the town was full of Yankee shopkeepers and 'Reconstructed varmints in uniforms, wearing badges and enforcing Yankee law'. Temple's wife is worried that her husband has influenced three of her sons beyond redemption and is concerned about Lon and Hobie (Mitchum) – 'I don't want either of you to turn into tramplers like the others'. Hobie simplifies the antagonism within the clan, with echoes of the war (a similar 'brother against brother' struggle): 'Cordine family's like an apple split in two – one half sweet, the other half rotten'. A confrontation is inevitable, and the two groups shoot it out. After the carnage, only Temple and Lon are left alive. Temple calls out for his dead sons, asking Lon, 'Maybe they went home'. 'That's right Pa,' Lon answers, 'they're waiting for us at the ranch.'

The Tramplers establishes a clear view of how the southern populace coped with insurgency measures following the conflict – the appropriation of land, exploitation by shopkeepers and northern law enforcement. Scott was an impressive hero, a sympathetic character to offset the Cordine's excesses; no such equivalent appears in *Hellbenders*. Mitchum turns in an effective, laid-back performance as Hobie, the stubble-faced, two-gunned alcoholic who has lost an arm (which Mitchum attempts to conceal in his shirt); he walks, talks and looks just like his father and gets all the best lines. Some sources note that *The Tramplers* was shot in Argentina. What actually happened was that Band acquired some footage of gauchos driving a huge herd of cattle through the Argentine pampas ('courtesy of Mr John Bryan O'Sullivan and the Argentine Estates of Lovril Limited') and incorporated the stock into his film. This explains why Band's cast never appear in the same shot as the Argentine cattle.

For the follow-up *The Hellbenders*, Joseph Cotten reprised his role as a delusional southern patriarch, here named Colonel Jonas. Though Cotten was best known for his association with Orson Welles's Mercury Theatre projects, he was no stranger to westerns, from *Duel in the Sun* (1946) and *Two Flags West* (1950), to *The Last Sunset* (1961) and *The Great Sioux Massacre* (1965). Amongst the little-known supporting cast are Julian Mateos (Ben), Maria Martin (as Kitty, the first phoney widow) and Brazilian actress Norma Bengell (as Clare, her replacement). Bengell had recently starred as Sonya, the astronaut heroine of Mario Bava's *Planet of the Vampires* (1965). Corbucci favourite Gino Pernice portrays vicious Jeff. Pernice began his fruitful association with Corbucci in 1964, appearing as the leather-boy henchman Scratchy in *Minnesota Clay*. He followed this with his definitive portrayal – Brother Jonathan in *Django*. Spaniard Angel Aranda (full name Angel Perez Aranda) was cast as Nat. Aranda was the only astronaut not to be zombified by the end of *Planet of the Vampires* and an unwilling accomplice to his brother's bank-robbing activities in *Pistols Don't Argue* (1964).

Other roles were taken by Claudio Gora, Benito Stefanelli and Julio Peña. Gora played a priest, an essential character in Corbucci's early westerns. He had worked with Corbucci on *Son of Spartacus* (1962) as the evil Crassus, and also appeared in *The Tramplers*. Stuntman Stefanelli played a bespectacled gambler (and choreo-graphed a punch-up in the Denton Saloon), while Julio Peña played a blind Confederate veteran who nearly unmasks the villains. There were also brief appear-ances by Al Mulock (as a beggar), Aldo Sambrell (a bandit), Jose Niento (a sheriff) and Enio Girolami (a Union officer). Canadian Mulock was beginning to forge a career for himself in spaghettis as a walk-on heavy (he had debuted as such in *The Sheriff of Fractured Jaw* – 1959), while Girolami was the brother of director Enzo Girolami (or 'Enzo G. Castellari') and occasionally appeared in his brother's films.

Many of *The Hellbenders* location scenes were shot among the outstanding rock formations at La Pedriza, Manzanares El Real in Spain. Others were shot near the beach at Tor Caldara in Italy. Such was the limited budget, the coach passes the rocks at La Pedriza twice and through the mud-flats at Tor Caldara three times. The town of Sundog was the Cinecitta western set, with interiors shot at Elios. The

A COFFIN WITHOUT A CORPSE... CRAMMED WITH MILLIONS IN CASH!

JOSEPH COTTEN *in* ALBERT BAND'S PRODUCTION OF **THE HELLBENDERS**

IN COLOR

co-starring

NORMA BENGELL · JULIAN MATEOS
GINO PERNICE · ANGEL ARANDA

Produced by ALBERT BAND
Directed by SERGIO CORBUCCI
Prints by Pathe · An Embassy Pictures Release

Poster for the US release of *The Hellbenders* (1967) in July 1967.

Torrid Junction attack was shot at the confluence of the rivers Alberche and Perales, among the ash-tree forests at Aldea Del Fresno. The River Hondo climax was shot on two separate locations: Tor Caldara near Anzio represented the riverbank campsite, with a river on location near Madrid used as the Hondo. Cotten's stunt-double (Remo De Angelis) performed Jonas's crawl to the river's edge, with Cotten filming his close-ups back in Italy.

Corbucci again used cameraman Enzo Barboni, but this time his visuals are not as arresting as in their previous collaborations. Barboni worked best when the costumes and settings were more vivid. One of his most atmospherically lit movies of the period was the black-and-white shocker *Nightmare Castle* (1965 – also called *Night of the Doomed*). In *The Hellbenders*, Barboni shoots some powerful footage of the carriage on the move, with the hearse looking like Javutich's ghostly coach in Mario Bava's *Black Sunday* (1960). The introduction of the widow is well handled, the camera panning up and silhouetting Kitty (in full funeral regalia, complete with broad-brimmed hat and veil) sitting on the hearse. The vehicle they use to transport the coffin is a classic example of the budget-paring measures that took place in the hectic spaghetti boom years. The side of the hearse bears the legend 'C.S.A. HEADQUARTERS 3RD REGIMENT'. The coach is the same Confederate ambulance Blondy and Tuco meet in the desert in *The Good, the Bad and the Ugly*.

Producer Band's on-set supervision (he reportedly co-directed) curbed Corbucci's excesses and forced him to make a film that did not rely on constant shootouts; the only recognisably Corbucci-esque moment is the opening robbery, with its machine-gun editing and dynamite explosions. Band's control resulted in Corbucci escalating the scenes of tension to breaking point, without resorting to the easy way out – a gunfight or a beating. This is noticeable when the Hellbenders are stopped and searched by the army and the law. Each of the characters the Hellbenders meet on their trek represents a different aspect of the post-Civil War southwest: a sheriff's posse, a priest, a blind soldier, a Mexican bandit gang, the US army, a beggar and a tribe of Indians.

The Hellbenders was the first Corbucci western since *Red Pastures* (1963) that didn't have the hero's name in the title, but there was good reason for the group epithet. *Hellbenders* is the only Corbucci western where none of the characters deserve the audience's sympathy; the film was called *I Crudeli* ('The Cruel') in Italy and dubbed *Los Despiadados* ('The Merciless') in Spain. At the beginning of *Hellbenders*, Jonas tells his sons, 'If they think the war is over because Lee surrendered, they weren't counting on me or any of us Hellbenders'. But the Hell-benders Regiment didn't exist historically and stems from Jonas's Confederates being 'hell-bent' on continuing the war. 'Hellbenders' are actually large, solitary aquatic salamanders, also known as Devil Dogs and Allegheny Alligators. Corbucci's fictitious regiment is symbolised on their badge by a salamander, which appears on the gang's hats, the back of the hearse and on their Texan battle flag – an appro-priately reptilian representation of the group.

Colonel Jonas is a demented zealot, a dreamer detached from reality, but utterly convinced of the feasibility of his plan. His ambitions are fanciful (even for a fanatical colonel with a million dollars to spend) and include the invasion of the north and the formation of a new 'Confederation under God'. Colonel Jonas, ostensibly a southern gentleman, is not honourable by any means – he even shoots a man holding a white flag. Jonas is proud of his Confederate uniform and his sons wear their CSA hats with varying degrees of pride, but the colonel represents the anachronism the 'old south' personifies – an outdated monument.

Cotten galvanises the film; it is a well-judged portrayal, halfway between ranting fanatic (fuming about the 'cause' and how much it should mean to everyone) and snivelling sympathetic. Cotten's forte is his tongue-in-cheek pathos, when telling the Yankee troops the tragic tale of Captain Ambrose Allen's death at the Battle of Nashville (Captain Allen is the name Jonas stole from Nashville cemetery for their fake corpse). Cotten's despondent expression was always used to play characters tinged with sadness. The tyrannical southerners he played in *The Tramplers* and *The Hellbenders* are cruel and manipulative, Cotten's face reinforcing their false sincerity. The only humour in the film arises from Jonas's reverential treatment of the coffin, with any mention of the 'dead hero' being a euphemism for the money. This symbiosis between the corpse and the cash is used throughout the film. Ambrose's dead body represents the defunct Confederacy, in need of revival and hoping one day to rise again. With the contents of the coffin, Jonas hopes his dream will come true.

Jonas is the central character, but the three sons are equally important, counterbalancing their father's commitment and piety with their sibling rivalry. Each of the trio has distinctive traits, though none of them believe as fervently in 'the cause' as their Pa; as Jonas reasons, 'Maybe I believe enough for us all'. The most fanatical of the sons is the sneering, spineless Jeff, played with conviction by Gino Pernice. With his long face and large ears, Pernice could switch in demeanour from placidity to savagery in a moment, and his role in *Hellbenders* fully exploits this. If *Hellbenders* is the ultimate take on the fifties juvenile psychological western (which it resembles in terms of the domineering father-figure and his quarrelsome sons), then Jeff would be played by the young Dennis Hopper, uncontrollable, dangerous, but also cowardly. Angel Aranda as Nat is a different proposition, equally violent, but also possessing the fatal combination of greed and stupidity. Pernice and Aranda are both good actors, but the one that loosely fits the bill of 'hero' is Spaniard Julian Mateos, as Ben. Mateos's performance works well, conveying his turmoil as he decides how far he is willing to follow Jonas. For much of the film he is as obsequious as his brothers. But he is the pacifier, keeping the balance between his father's obsessions and their unpredictability. As a half-brother to the others, Ben never feels completely comfortable with the family unit, as lonely as a member of the group as he would be without them.

During the trip, the gang employ two women to impersonate Ruth Allen, the dead captain's 'widow' – saloon-girl Kitty (who is killed in a frenzy by Jeff when she tries to steal the hearse) and gambler Clare. Alcoholic Kitty makes an unconvincing widow, while Clare is much sharper; it is she who outsmarts the gang and has the money interred in a Union army cemetery, under the auspices of a respectful military burial. Ben's brief relationship with Clare sets him apart from his brothers, who are incapable of such alliances.

The desert landscape is prosaic, making the outsiders' contact with civilisation startling. When the group arrive in the town of Sundog, things begin to go wrong. The local priest wants to hold a memorial service when he recognises Ambrose's name – he was stationed at nearby Fort Brent during the war. Not wanting to arouse suspicion, the Hellbenders accept. In a blackly humorous scene, the congregation honours a coffin full of dollars, while the pastor intones a eulogy to the dead hero: 'And it is written that the ways to our Good Lord are many and multiple. Captain Ambrose Allen, on his way to eternal repose, has come to us, passing-by as it were, for a last farewell.' The moment is both poignant and ludicrous, as the priest and the congregation believe that Jonas and company are do-gooders. Sergeant Tolt, Captain Allen's aide, lives in town on a pension. When he arrives at the service, the old soldier turns out to be blind – a clever ploy by Corbucci to make the cinema audience collude with the Hellbenders, so that Clare is not exposed as an impostor. The priest tells Tolt, 'Fate has brought your Captain back to us for a brief moment' and the veteran begins to cry. The scene is moving and Clare's performance transcends mere role-play. Her sympathy with the blind soldier and her deceased 'spouse' is real. She acts her role not through any sense of commitment to Ben and the family, but out of compassion.

The later sequences at Fort Brent are among the best scenes of Corbucci's career. Having saved the Hellbenders from a gang of Mexican *bandidos* led by Pedro (Aldo Sambrell), Union Lieutenant Sublett offers them the hospitality of the fort; Clare accepts: 'I would like to see the Fort once commanded by my husband'. The scene cuts to the cavalry column and three captured Mexican bandits moving in a slow procession towards the fort. In the fort's parade ground, one of the bandits is put on a horse with his head in a noose. Corbucci unflinchingly captures the whole scene as the horse bolts and the helpless bandit drops to his death. Corbucci includes several details here: the coffins laid out for the bandits, a brief shot of Pedro (turning away in horror at the death of his companion) and a white-coated army doctor (on hand to pronounce the bandits dead). The executions continue, with Pedro the next to swing. In the shade of an archway looking onto the parade ground, the Hellbenders look on, Jeff bandaging his father's injured arm. Clare asks the Union lieutenant to inter Ambrose in the graveyard and Jeff now winds the bandage around his hands like a garrotte. The sequence is well written and acted, Clare commenting, 'Enough running, enough danger, enough fear. My husband deserves a better repose. He belongs here, in a soldier's grave among soldiers.' 'And Fort Brent,' answers the lieutenant, 'will be proud to have him.' The dialogue, powerful enough in itself, is given greater depth by Ennio Morricone's solemn score.

The nihilistic finale on the banks of the Hondo is well staged by Corbucci. All his westerns have strong, unexpected endings, with one final revelation to jolt the audience. Having returned to Fort Brent to retrieve 'Ambrose', the Hellbenders stop by the river to rest the horses. They are in bad shape and tensions are high. Jonas is wounded and Clare has caught pneumonia. In two improbable twists, they

Colonel Jonas in *The Hellbenders* (1967); Joseph Cotten on location at La Pedriza, Manzanares El Real.

are robbed by a beggar (Al Mulock) and then Jeff murders an Indian chief's daughter from a nearby encampment. The arrival of the vengeful Indians results in the family's destruction; Nat and Jeff squabble and shoot each other and Ben gets caught in the crossfire. His sons dead or dying, Jonas drags the coffin towards the Hondo, but it slips and crashes open, to reveal bandit Pedro's grinning face. The grave-robbers forgot there was more than one burial at Fort Brent that day.

The Hellbenders is Morricone's first western score built entirely around the trumpet – the trumpet soloist was Nunzio Rotondo. Morricone (again signing himself as 'Leo Nichols') composed an accompaniment that was nothing like his output of the time. The main themes, dominated by the trumpet (doubling as a bugle) and occasionally voiced by soprano soloist Edda Dell'Orso or electric guitar, are predominantly stately marches – a funeral dirge for a burial party that, rather like the Hellbenders themselves, rarely exceeds a steady canter.

But when the on-screen action occasionally flags, Morricone's score saves the film; it's difficult to imagine *The Hellbenders* being quite so enjoyable without his up-tempo title music. Based on an interesting percussion arrangement, it incorporates a hollow drum, a series of rapid high-hat rolls and a whip-crack (like *A Fistful of Dollars*), which accompanies the credits sequence – a Unionist convoy fording Torrid Junction. The cavalry bugle breezes in with a repetitive, languorous roll, backed by strings, piano riffs and the Alessandroni Singers. This piece is used at various points to score the hearse's progress through the desolate vistas. A more dignified version of the theme is used at Fort Brent, and in the first half of the film Morricone uses discordant sound effects to accompany several tense scenes. These effects include repetitive piano notes, rushes of snare and bongo drums, tapping woodblocks, whips, eerie strings and a ghostly, echoing trumpet. When the group get their first glimpse of the Hondo, the camera pans across the river. An electric guitar plays a simple, dramatic theme as Jonas whispers 'There it is', as though he's saying the words of a prayer. In the finale, as the mortally wounded Jonas reaches the river, Dell'Orso's soprano vividly accompanies the 'Death of the South', as the Hellbenders' flag drifts away downstream.

The Hellbenders was released in Italy in February 1967, but it was a financial disappointment compared to Corbucci's previous successes. When it was released in Spain in November 1967 it was a hit (surprisingly outgrossing *Navajo Joe*), and it was also popular in Germany, where Jonas and his clan were christened 'The Morrisons'.

The Hellbenders, like only a handful of Italian westerns, is a complete one-off, unique in the fact that it was not copied and has no sequels. Its only legacy was that Morricone's entire score was used, uncredited, in the unworthy western *Drummer of Vengeance* (1974). If the plot to *The Hellbenders* wasn't influential on Italian westerns, setting the film in the reconstruction era influenced Tonino Valerii, when he made *The Price of Power* (1969), his powerful, JFK-influenced story of assassination and betrayal in post-Civil War Dallas.

The Hellbenders was distributed internationally by Joseph E. Levine's Embassy Pictures. It was released uncut at 88 minutes (gaining an 'A' certificate, even with the graphic hanging), though it didn't break any box-office records in the UK and the US, suggesting that the film wasn't action-packed enough to please western audiences. The English and American advertising for *The Hellbenders* attempted to promote it as a non-stop adventure. One poster featured the tagline, 'The deadliest convoy that ever gunned its way across the West', while another ran, 'They're hell-bent on the maddest plot ever'. The artwork that accompanied this was misleading, with Cotten pictured lashing the carriage horses (when he never actually drives the carriage – Ben is the teamster) and the coffin bouncing in the back of a flatbed wagon (which looks nothing like the hearse in the film). Other taglines focused on the casket ('A coffin without a corpse…crammed with millions in cash') and the central protagonists – alternately violent and spicy: 'Four desperate men…one wily woman'. Lacking sensationalism, most of the original Italian posters concentrated on the characters of Jonas, Ben and Clare, the artwork being simple portraits.

Whatever the angle, it was unsuccessful and the film was destined for obscurity, which harmed the leading actors' careers more than the supporting cast. For example, Julian Mateos never fulfilled the promise of his starring role here. Instead of playing the lead in spaghettis, he was relegated to second-string parts in international co-productions: *Return of the Seven* (1966), *Shalako* (1968) and *Catlow* (1971). Joseph Cotten made one more obscure spaghetti western, *White Comanche* (1968), co-starring William Shatner, later Captain Kirk in the *Star Trek* series. Meanwhile, Corbucci reverted to his forte – dynamic adventures with larger-than-life heroes. *The Hellbenders* was a failed change of pace and a bold experiment by Corbucci, but he would have to wait a little longer for international success.

12

'The Dogs of Juarez'

— Sergio Sollima's *The Big Gundown* (1967)

The Big Gundown (1967)
original title: *La Resa dei Conti*
Credits
DIRECTOR – Sergio Sollima
PRODUCER – Alberto Grimaldi
STORY – Franco Solinas and Fernando Morandi
SCREENPLAY – Sergio Donati and Sergio Sollima
SET DESIGNER AND COSTUMES – Carlo Simi
EDITOR – Gaby Penalba
DIRECTOR OF PHOTOGRAPHY – Carlo Carlini
MUSIC COMPOSER – Ennio Morricone
MUSIC CONDUCTOR – Bruno Nicolai
Techniscope/Technicolor
An Italian/Spanish co-production
PEA (Rome) and Produzioni Cinematographiche Tulio
    Demicheli (Madrid)
Released internationally by Columbia Pictures
Cast
    Lee Van Cleef (Jonathan 'Colorado' Corbett); Tomas Milian
    (Manuel 'Cuchillo' Sanchez); Walter Barnes (Brokston);
    Nieves Navarro (the widow); Maria Granada (Rosita
    Sanchez); Gerard Herter (the baron, Captain Von
    Schulemberg); Fernando Sancho (Captain Segura); Antonio
    Casas ('Brother Smith and Wesson'); Jose Torres (Paco
    Molinas); Angel Del Pozo (Shep Miller); Roberto Camardiel
    (Sheriff of San Antonio); Tom Felleghi (Mr Miller); Calisto
    Calisti (Mr Lynch, Brokston's secretary); Barta Barry (first
    outlaw); Nello Pazzafini (second outlaw); Luis Gaspar (third
    outlaw); Luisa Rivelli (Lizzie, the prostitute): Fernando

146

Sanchez Polack (Sheriff of Willow Creek); Spartaco Conversi (Mexican prison guard); Lorenzo Robledo (pioneer); Jose Zaldua (Mexican barber); Herman Reynoso (Mormon leader); Angelo Susani (Mexican bordello barman); Silvana Bacci (Mexican prostitute); Antonio Molino Rojo, Benito Stefanelli, Romano Puppo, Luis Barboo and Frank Braña (members of widow's gang); with Lanfranco Ceccarelli

*   *   *

Sergio Sollima's political western *The Big Gundown* is based on a story co-written by Franco Solinas and Fernando Morandi, an assistant director on Gillo Pontecorvo's *Battle of Algiers*. In their story a young lawman is hired by the local dignitaries to apprehend an elderly peasant, who is said to have attacked a young girl. At the climax, though the old man is innocent, the lawman shoots him anyway. In the film version, adapted for the screen by Sollima and Sergio Donati, Jonathan Corbett, an ex-sheriff-turned-bounty-hunter with political ambitions, is hired by Brokston (a Texan railway tycoon in San Antonio) to hunt and capture a Mexican peon named Manuel 'Cuchillo' Sanchez, nicknamed 'Sanchez the Knife'. The Mexican stands accused of raping and stabbing to death a 12-year-old white girl. Through his guile and resourcefulness, Cuchillo manages to elude his pursuer across Texas and escape into Mexico. But when Brokston and Baron Von Schulemberg (his Austrian body-guard) recruit a posse of Mexican *rancheros* to join the hunt, the net closes. Corbett eventually realises that Brokston is shielding his son-in-law, Shep, who is really responsible; Cuchillo was merely a witness to the crime. According to Donati, Sollima changed the ending to Solinas's original story at Sergio Leone's suggestion. In the showdown, Cuchillo kills Shep, then Corbett guns down the Baron and Brokston. Corbett and Cuchillo go their separate ways on friendly, respectful terms.

Sergio Sollima had scripted several muscleman films under the name 'Simon Stirling', including the action-packed *Spartacus and the Ten Gladiators* (1964), where perpetually grinning Roccia (Dan Vadis) defeated the evil Varro (Gianni Rizzo) with a combination of brute force and fancy footwork. Sollima then directed three spy films, including *Passport to Hell* (1965), with George Ardisson as Walter Ross – 'Agent 3S3', who spends the movie battling crime boss 'Mr A', karate-chopping villains and grooving to Kinks records. An attempt to cash in on the British Bond films, it was written by 'Roger Higgins III' (Sollima under an alias) and photo-graphed by 'Charles Charlies' (or Carlo Carlini).

With *The Big Gundown*, Sollima distanced himself from what he called 'Clint Eastwood's cold superhero' of the 'Dollars' trilogy, even though the Italian title for the film, *La Resa dei Conti* ('The Settling of Accounts'), was taken from Morricone's musical watch theme from *For a Few Dollars More* (known on English albums as 'Sixty Seconds to What?'). Sollima wanted to make a film about a character not usually given a voice in westerns; via his David-and-Goliath political adventure story, he had Cuchillo the peon speak up for the downtrodden and exploited, and strike back at the faceless steamroller of big business with his slingshot and throwing knife. In *Gundown*, the social dynamic is between rich liars, who can make false charges stick because of their power, and poor scapegoats, exploited because of their caste; the 'deaf ears' of authority have no time for Cuchillo's pleas. In the course of his flight, Cuchillo hides with various groups of outsiders: a Mexican livery camp, a Mormon wagon train (who are scorned by the Willow Creek townsfolk), a sadistic widow and her tough ranch employees, and an order of monks at a monastery. These groups colour Sollima's presentation of the west.

The Big Gundown was influenced by Hollywood westerns, though manhunts in American westerns rarely had the social comment Sollima deployed. Henry Hathaway's *From Hell to Texas* (1958) influenced Sollima's monastery sequences, Henry King's *The Bravados* (1958) questioned the infallibility of the law, while Herbert Coleman's *Posse from Hell* (1961) deployed some rugged desert landscapes; the last two both featured Lee Van Cleef as the pursued. In the Audie Murphy Hollywood vehicle *Seven Ways from Sundown* (1960) the chase saw Texas Ranger 'Seven' Jones (Murphy) trailing outlaw Jim Flood (Barry Sullivan). In a quarrel, Flood burns down a saloon and Jones is despatched to track Flood down. In one scene, Jones demonstrates his marksmanship by shooting a vulture about to eat his love interest's puppy, then she sends him off on the manhunt with a packed lunch.

Sollima appropriated the blade-versus-pistol duel from *Yojimbo* (1961) for the climax of his story, and businessman Brokston's edgy relationship with his ne'er-do-well son-in-law Shep echoes the spaghetti western *Adios Gringo* (1965), in which wealthy rancher Clayton Ranchester (Pierre Cressoy) protected his rapist son (Massimo Righi) from the law. Sollima also references *For a Few Dollars More*, which seems to have inspired the character of Cuchillo Sanchez. In Leone's film, a member of Indio's gang is a knife-throwing bandit named Cuchillo (Aldo Sambrell) who is wrongly accused of murdering a night-watchman.

Sollima cast Lee Van Cleef in the iconic role of heroic bounty-hunter Jonathan Corbett (following his villainous turn in *The Good, the Bad and the Ugly*) and Tomas Milian as Cuchillo. Walter Barnes was cast as Brokston, the snarling railway tycoon with a penchant for hunting. Barnes had appeared in Hollywood westerns (*Rio Bravo* and *Westbound*) and German 'Winnetou' films (*Winnetou the Warrior* and *Among Vultures*); in *Among Vultures* he played Bauman, 'The Great Bear Hunter'. Sollima cast Fernando Sancho against type as Captain Segura (a crooked Mexican officer in Cuchillo's village) and Nieves Navarro (from the 'Ringo' films) as the lonely widow, who offers Cuchillo shelter at her secluded ranch.

The Big Gundown employs virtually every well-known Italian western supporting player in bit parts. The widow's muscle-bound wranglers consist of the core of Leone's stock company – Benito Stefanelli, Antonio Molino Rojo, Frank Braña and Romano Puppo, while Luis Barboo had appeared briefly in *Fistful*, scaring Eastwood's mule. Lorenzo Robledo played a pioneer who gets punched when he tries to help

Corbett, Antonio Casas appeared as a gunslinger-turned-monk christened 'Brother Smith and Wesson', while Gerard Herter was cast as the monocled, humourless Baron Von Schulemberg, a persona he later replayed as Austrian Colonel Skimmel in *Adios Sabata* (1970).

The authentic Texas–Mexico frontier locations were shot in Spain in late 1966 (after Van Cleef had finished work on *The Good, the Bad and the Ugly*) – in Almeria, around San Jose, in the dunes at Cabo De Gata and in Colmenar and Manzanares El Real. The widow's ranch was a specially constructed set near La Pedriza, Manzanares El Real, while Brokston's San Antonio residence was a studio mock-up. The town of Willow Creek was the set at Colmenar Viejo, while Don Serano's *hacienda*, the base for Brokston's manhunt, was the *finca* of El Romeral; the Mexican village scenes were also shot near San Jose. The big chase sequence through the badlands was beautifully shot by Carlo Carlini in the *ramblas* and sierras of Almeria.

Leone's regular art director Carlo Simi designed the costumes and sets. Corbett is introduced as a stylishly dressed bounty-hunter, with fur-trimmed jacket and high riding boots, while for the lengthy chase he looks like a classic gunslinger in the Wyatt Earp mould: an antihero in a black suit. Already-familiar Van Cleef motifs are incorporated: a pipe, the cross-belly draw holster and Angel Eyes's tooled leather boots from *The Good, the Bad and the Ugly*.

Simi's authentic settings (rough Mexican shacks, muddy Willow Creek) are echoed in the prop armaments on display. Cuchillo has a knife and slingshot, but

Jonathan Corbett (Lee Van Cleef) faces Brokston's posse in the sierras; Sergio Sollima's *The Big Gundown* (1967).

everyone else is armed to the teeth; in an interview, Sollima said that Cuchillo is armed with a knife because 'he's too poor to buy a gun and ammo'. Corbett starts the hunt with a pair of Colts and in the finale chooses a Colt .45 and a Colt Navy from Brokston's gun collection; in the showdown, Corbett kills Brokston at distance with a Colt Lightning slide-action repeating rifle. Van Cleef's two-gun motif (a Colt Navy holstered, a Colt .45 sticking out of his belt) was based on Robert Mitchum's 'town tamer' Clint Tollinger in *Man With The Gun* (1955). Brokston has a high-powered hunting rifle, with exploding dumdum bullets that can 'stop a mad buffalo' and the Baron has a specially designed quick-draw holster (which looks like a stirrup) for his ornate Liege-made pistol.

Jonathan Corbett (sometimes billed as 'Colorado' Corbett, *Colorado* was an alternative title for the film in France) is Van Cleef's most interesting character. He is a believer in law and order, though there are hints early in the film that his belief has flagged in the past. He earns a living tracking down outlaws for reward, but has political aspirations and is about to run for Congress. The posters for his campaign have already been printed and Brokston offers to buy him 'a campaign of high-level proportions'. Transient Corbett used to be a sheriff, though his stake in a gambling operation earned him more money than a lawman's wage. For his solid reputation, Corbett is an inept tracker – completely at odds with Van Cleef's cool screen persona – and his fancy hardware doesn't help him catch Cuchillo any faster. This was a conscious decision by Sollima, who thought it would be better if the lowly character was able to outwit the 'cool superhero', until he is trapped by his pursuers' sheer determination and resources.

Opposite Van Cleef's hunter is his antithesis – Cuban actor Tomas Milian's peon, Cuchillo Sanchez. Cuchillo, unshaven, dirty and dressed in Mexican rags, is the focus of the film; he is one of the disillusioned 'dogs of Juarez', sold out by political promises. In some sequences Milian is a bumbling idiot, clowning around with a young Mormon girl in a river or clumsily avoiding the attentions of a wild bull. These contrast with the moments of confrontation, when Milian is calm and poised – coolly reaching for the haft of his knife, tucked in his collar. Before filming began, Sollima recommended that Milian watch Toshiro Mifune's performance in *Seven Samurai* (1954) as the model for Cuchillo's demeanour.

While on the run, Cuchillo hides out with various groups, but every time Corbett doggedly catches up with him. Their one-upmanship adds much to the film. Cuchillo arrives at an oasis and greedily gulps down water, as Corbett steps from behind an agave. 'Tastes good, eh Cuchillo?' asks Corbett; 'It tasted better a minute ago,' answers the peon. Later, Cuchillo pricks Corbett on the back with a cactus spike and pretends it is a snakebite, convincing Corbett he's about to die so the Mexican can escape.

Cuchillo is perpetually the outsider; the only people to treat him with any respect are Sollima's religious figures – the Mormons and the monks. The monastery is on the border and Cuchillo has fled into Mexico. When Corbett arrives, he learns from

Brother Smith and Wesson that if he crosses the border he is as bad as Cuchillo – the chase becomes personal, the monk adding, 'You must realise the hunt is over'. He eyes the tired-looking Corbett: 'That pistol's been hanging from your belt a long while. In time its weight always changes a man.' But the holy man realises that nothing will change Corbett's mind, even if it means breaking the law; when the lawman crosses the borderline, he crosses the moral line too.

Nieves Navarro delivers her career-best performance, as the lonely, sadistic widow, though she had already played the bad girl in Tessari's 'Ringo' movies. In Tessari's films Navarro's characters had undergone a moral transformation, but in *Gundown* she doesn't alter. A similar widow was played by Magda Konopka (the 'Magnetic Pole', as she was known off-screen) in the spaghetti western *And a Sky Full of Stars for a Roof* (1968). Navarro's widow is introduced watching from a window while two of her wranglers fight; the gladiatorial spectacle is laid on for her entertainment. Her sadistic streak is epitomised by the mind games she plays with Cuchillo. The fugitive wants work and the wranglers are about to send him packing when the widow intervenes. They give him a meal and then put him in a pen with a wild bull ('Old Barney'). When the agile Mexican survives this ordeal, the Widow takes him to her bedroom to recuperate. But because he kisses her without asking ('It must be at my orders…just like the others') he is savagely whipped by the wranglers, again for her gratification; ironically, it is only the arrival of Corbett that saves the Mexican's life.

The Sheriff of San Antonio (played by Roberto Camardiel) legitimises the manhunt by making Corbett a deputy. It will be good publicity for businessman Brokston's public reputation (his planned US/Mexican railway through Texas) and Corbett's forthcoming political campaign. Corbett is not completely unaware of Brokston's publicity-seeking motives, saying, 'I'll bring you the Mexican for a wedding present'. Corbett is unconvinced of working for the law again, but Brokston points out, 'The star can come in handy'. 'And shine brightly on your plans,' smiles Corbett. But Cuchillo steals the star early in the chase; in Willow Creek, the local sheriff notices that Deputy Corbett is not wearing his badge and comments sarcastically, 'Maybe it got too hot to wear'.

As the clues leak out, Corbett finds himself investigating a citizen above suspicion. The key scene occurs when Cuchillo and Corbett end up in Captain Segura's fleapit Mexican jail. Cuchillo says that Corbett is just like all the others, never questioning the facts; Corbett is chasing the wrong man and Cuchillo knows who is really responsible. At Don Serano's *hacienda*, following an argument between Shep and his wife, Shep drunkenly tries to assault a servant girl and the truth finally dawns on Corbett. After the showdown, with the real culprit dead, Corbett and Cuchillo part company near the Mexican border. Corbett begins to apologise; 'Por nada, amigo,' smiles Cuchillo, 'but you never would have got me'.

Brokston's motives for wanting Cuchillo dead have often been misunderstood: in the beginning it is simply a publicity stunt, but in the end he has to protect his family name and an upcoming real estate deal between the Brokstons and the Millers. Brokston's daughter's relationship with Miller's son Shep isn't a marriage; Brokston says that 'It's an option on Miller's land'.

Brokston dominates the second part of *The Big Gundown*, when his passion for hunting intensifies the chase. He has travelled to Africa and India, killing all sorts of animals, but adds, 'There's still one type of animal I haven't hunted…the hunting of man'. In Cuchillo's village, as an exhausted Corbett wanders dazedly through a Mexican 'Death Day' procession, Brokston arrives with his entourage. He has decided to resort to his original idea: to hunt Cuchillo like an animal, with rich land-owner Don Serano's *rancheros*, beaters and hounds as his hunting party. Don Serano doesn't ask questions about the Mexican's guilt, knowing that wealthy connections are worth more than justice.

Corrupt officer Captain Segura holds a grudge against Cuchillo, calling him, 'One of those pieces of trash who stood with Juarez'. He is uncooperative when Corbett tries to enlist the Mexican government's aid in capturing Cuchillo – Sollima's version of American interventionism and Mexican apathy. Corbett tells Segura that in the US a private citizen can help the law, but Segura hates meddling gringos even more than Juarista scum. When Serano's men tear the village apart looking for Cuchillo, Segura does what any knowing government official in his position would do: he goes to bed.

Brokston's bodyguard, the Austrian baron, Captain Von Schulemberg, shares his boss's fetish for firearms and tells Corbett his theory of 'speed over accuracy'. He explains why watching your opponent's eyes is so important in duels, which Sollima uses to comment on Leone's style: the eyes tell you everything – love, hatred, fear. Sollima accentuates this, with repeated close-ups of Van Cleef's eyes throughout the film, which veer from steely-eyed confidence to utter bewilderment. The baron reckons that the moment before an opponent moves his hand to draw, 'His eyes betray him. And you can always read death in them…yours or his.'

Sollima climaxes the film with an exciting chase through sugar cane fields and a shootout in the desert. The posse flush Cuchillo out of the fields with hunting dogs. In the Sierras, Brokston, the baron and the riders scout the hills, while Shep and Corbett manage to corner Cuchillo. But Corbett switches sides and referees a duel between Shep's Colt and Cuchillo's knife. This stylised sequence was choreographed by stuntman Benito Stefanelli. Sollima photographs Cuchillo in a crucifixion pose, with his arms outstretched as he reaches for his blade. Cuchillo wins the duel, planting his knife in Shep's forehead. Brokston and his men arrive and Brokston orders Corbett to kill Cuchillo, but Corbett refuses: 'You thought I'd shoot first and then think'. Brokston snarls, 'You're really too damn smart to be a senator'. The baron and Corbett face each other – Corbett with his Colt tucked in his belt, the baron's Belgian pistol in its sophisticated holster. Sollima's montage-driven duel (accompanied by Ennio Morricone's take on Beethoven's 'Für Elise') proves the baron's quick-draw theory wrong; he fires first, wounding Corbett in the shoulder, but the lawman is more accurate.

With *The Good, the Bad and the Ugly*, *The Big Gundown* is Ennio Morricone's most popular score. The main theme song, 'Run Man Run', is sung in powerful fashion by Joan Baez-esque 'Christy' (real name Maria Cristina Branucci). It begins with Cuchillo's gentle flute theme. Then the strings swell, as the piece ups the tempo and becomes a vocalised version of 'Ecstasy of Gold', complete with the Alessandroni Singers (chanting 'Never!') and stirring brass. The lyrics were written by Audrey Stainton Nohra and read in part:

> Somewhere there is a land where men do not kill each other
> Somewhere there is a land where men call a man a brother
> Somewhere if you keep on running, someday you'll be free
> Run until you know you're free
> Run to the end of the world, 'til you find a place where they'll never lock you in
> Go ahead young man, face towards the sun
> Run man while you can, run man run

The lyrics echo the sentiment of free-thinking brotherly love that places Sollima's film as a precursor of the US-produced, anti-Vietnam, counter-culture films of the late sixties. Quieter instrumental versions of 'Run Man Run' are used throughout, on acoustic guitar, cor anglais and oboe, often accompanying picturesque shots of the landscape. At the Brokston's wedding reception a jazz band even plays the tune on banjo and fiddle. The widow's theme is a threatening, understated flamenco guitar piece that suggests hidden danger, while in a woodland gunfight between Corbett and three bank robbers, Morricone employs a flute and gently tidal strings. In the desert scenes (Cuchillo's arrival at an oasis and the posse scouting the hills) odd, echoing sound effects (voices, strings, piano and gong) are used as a musical collage, with some of the effects achieved by playing the music at half speed (in the manner of Nascimbene's eclipse music from *Barabbas* – 1961). In contrast, Cuchillo's encounter with Old Barney in the bullpen is accompanied by a spluttering, comic piece, with jokey mariachi trumpet, oboe and violin.

Three religious pieces appear in the film – the abrasive 'Death Day' procession chanting, the monks' hymns at the monastery and the strident Mormon choir, who sing as their wagon train pulls out of Willow Creek ('Come and rejoice, let His light be yours…all is well!'); like 'Run Man Run', the Mormon hymn was also recorded in an Italian-language version. Throughout the chase, Cuchillo is associated with a flute trill, while the baron plays Beethoven's 'Für Elise' on the piano. The showdown finale between Cuchillo and Shep is scored with a triumphal march (with brass, piano, drums and trumpets), as Cuchillo reaches down to pick up his knife and the duel begins.

It is the two-part chase music that is most associated with the film. As Cuchillo runs for his life through the sugar cane, scraping violins and a flute pant on the soundtrack. In a moment's silence, as Cuchillo stops to draw breath, he hears the baying hounds. His dismay is emulated in the soundtrack; Morricone deploys layers of multi-tracked percussion, timpani drums and Edda Dell'Orso's pure soprano solo (accompanied by screaming flute blasts and the gutsy Cantori), as the posse tear through the cane. This piece develops into the trumpet 'riding theme' (based on the title song), which stops as Cuchillo heads into the desert. Once in open country, a second, even more ferocious piece begins – with chilling piano chords, jagged guitar and drums, as the hunters get closer to their prey. The Alessandroni Singers, sounding like a raucous version of the Mormon choir, add a religious intensity to the chase. Only in Leone's films have Morricone's grandiose riding themes accompanied such powerful imagery.

The soundtrack was very successful with record buyers, and the film followed suit. When *The Big Gundown* was released in Italy at 105 minutes in March 1967, it was a smash, turning Milian into a star (after the debacle over *Django Kill*) and proving that Van Cleef could pull in audiences without Eastwood. In Italy and Spain it was the biggest hit of Van Cleef's post-Leone career. The film was known as *Der Gehetzte Der Sierra Madre* in Germany and *El Halcon y la Presa* ('The Falcon and the Prey') in Spain; the Spanish distributors abridged the climactic cane-fields chase.

For the UK and US markets *The Big Gundown* was dismembered by Columbia Pictures. They bought the international rights, then edited it down to a 'B-movie' 85 minutes and removed all references to the girl's rape. For other English-language markets they also prepared a 95-minute compromise. The cuts interfered with every aspect of the film – from editing and rearranging the music, to rewriting the dialogue. Virtually no scene escaped unscathed and several were removed altogether, leaving an often-incomprehensible mess.

To take one example: in the opening scene of the 85-minute version, three outlaws (played by Barta Barry, Nello Pazzafini and Luis Gaspar) arrive at a woodland rendezvous. They are on the run after a robbery, but bounty-hunter Corbett has beaten them there. In a brief shootout, Corbett kills all three (without giving them much of a chance) and recovers the money. In the 95-minute version, Cullik, the outlaws' contact, has been lynched by Corbett prior to their arrival (Cullik is clearly visible in the background of the short version, but no reference is made to him). In the full version, the gunfight is scored by Morricone's subdued flute-led gundown music, 'After the Verdict'. In a fair duel, Corbett places three bullets in a row on a log. Each outlaw walks forward to take his bullet. When it's Pazzafini's turn, he cheats and tries to shoot Corbett, but the bounty-hunter kills him, adding, 'He didn't play by the rules'. Corbett gives Barry a choice: 'Rope or pistol'. Barry wants to shoot it out and Corbett kills him too. Gaspar pleads for mercy, but as the lawman goes to check the money sack, the kid draws. Corbett spins and shoots, and Gaspar drops dead (as a faint echo of 'After the Verdict' reappears on the soundtrack).

In the cut version Corbett is a bounty-hunter-turned-'honorary deputy' who mercilessly guns down outlaws; in the full version, he always gives his opponents a chance. In the cut print he is unaffected by his experiences and handles every situation with aplomb, while in the uncut print his pursuit of the murderer teaches him as much about himself as the 'criminal' he pursues, testing his endurance and bringing him close to moral collapse. Corbett is fairer in the uncut print: before a shootout between Corbett and three toughs near a corral, a villain counts to three to 'time' the draw. One of the trio draws on 'two', but Corbett still wins. As the last villain hits the ground Corbett adds, 'and three'. In a deleted scene in the San Antonio sheriff's office, the sheriff tells Corbett that he has tracked down the last desperados in Texas – now he is free to pursue his political career. The sheriff adds that Corbett is a cunning gunman: he doesn't go chasing after outlaws, they come to him – a reference to the opening shootout, but in contrast to his lengthy pursuit of Cuchillo.

The scenes at the widow's ranch suffered badly in the cut in the 85-minute version, Cuchillo steals a necklace from the widow's dresser; in the full version he looks at his reflection in the mirror, feels guilty and puts it back. When Corbett and the widow take tea at the ranch, her seductive advances are more explicit in the Italian version, as she tries to lure Corbett into a liaison. When Corbett leaves

The widow (Nieves Navarro), flanked by two of her wranglers (Frank Braña and Romano Puppo), in a UK front-of-house still advertising *The Big Gundown* (1967).

he tells her that their parting is 'perfetto armonia' ('perfect harmony'); this is re-dubbed in the English language version to the simplistic, 'Thanks for the tea'.

Other scenes missing from the 85-minute print include a Mormon prayer meeting; two monastery scenes (Cuchillo's breathless arrival and Corbett's conversation with Brother Smith and Wesson); a scene in which a dehydrated Corbett is saved by a pioneer in the desert; and the 'Death Day' procession. The scene in which Cuchillo is put in the bullpen is miraculously intact in every version of the film.

Two explanatory scenes are missing from all versions of the film. In the first (at night, early in the chase), Cuchillo steals Corbett's horse and deputy's star. In the second, Corbett kills Cuchillo, but the corpse is actually a brigand named Paco Molinas, dressed like Cuchillo. Molinas was played by Jose Torres; though Torres's name appears in the title sequence of every different print of the film, he is only on screen for seconds, as a corpse over a saddle in Willow Creek.

The UK and US release of *The Big Gundown* in 1968 was a slapdash affair. The trailer features footage not in the English-language release, accompanied by an ominous voiceover: 'Death has many faces...he strikes without pity'. The title sequence features shots of riders – not Brokston's men, but Fernando Sancho's gang (the Sidewinders) from the unrelated *Arizona Colt* (1966). US posters declared 'Mr Ugly Comes To Town!' (in unflattering reference to Van Cleef) and 'Big Action and Big Excitement...*The Big Gundown*'. The cutting seems to have mattered little

After the Verdict: Cuchillo retrieves his knife from Shep's forehead, while Corbett covers his back; left to right: Lee Van Cleef, Tomas Milian and Angel Del Pozo in *The Big Gundown* (1967).

to the film's fortunes; the 85-minute version made over $2 million in the US when it was released in July 1968. The *New York Times* referred to Sollima's 'visual elegance' and 'attention to detail'. Van Cleef and Milian's performances were praised and the general consensus was this was 'a surprise film' – even the dubbing was above average.

Milian was born to portray Cuchillo and he went on to play many 'Cuchillos' throughout his spaghetti-western career. Cuchillo proved so popular with spaghetti-western audiences that many unrelated films featured characters based on Milian's persona: for instance, Jose Torres's knife-throwing Garcia in *Django Get a Coffin Ready* (1968). Milian reprised Cuchillo only once, in Sollima's needless sequel to *The Big Gundown*, called *Run Man Run* (1968). Van Cleef was busy on other projects and Donal O'Brien took the lawman role. This time Cuchillo searches for a solid-gold printing press during the Mexican revolution; the film was chopped into little pieces for an English-language release (from 120 minutes to 85). As the chase proceeds, from pastures to desert and snowscape, Cuchillo is tracked by an ever-growing group of cut-throats – a Mexican bandit gang (who claim to be revolutionaries), a pair of French secret-service agents (working for the Mexican Army), Penny Bennington (a con-artist posing as a Salvation Army sergeant), Cuchillo's girlfriend (who wants to get married) and lawman Cassidy. On a big budget and with a talented cast, *Run Man Run* should have been much better – a Mexican revolution-set *The Good, the Bad and the Ugly* – but Sollima lost the plot along the way.

Though Sollima went on to even greater success with his six-hour mini-series *Sandokan* (1976 – with Kabir Bedi as the swashbuckling hero), *The Big Gundown* is his best-known film outside Italy. The combination of Van Cleef's and Milian's strong roles, the good story (with Van Cleef on hand to make sure true justice prevails) and the memorable music ensured it was a great success, both commercially and artistically. Most importantly, it was a rarity for spaghetti westerns – one with humanity.

13

'I See You're a Man of Your Word'

— Giulio Petroni's *Death Rides a Horse* (1967)

Death Rides a Horse (1967)
original title: *Da Uomo a Uomo*
Credits
DIRECTOR – Giulio Petroni
PRODUCERS – 'Al Sansone' (Alfonso Sansone) and 'Henry
    Chroscicki' (Enrico Chroscicki)
STORY AND SCREENPLAY – Luciano Vincenzoni
EDITOR – Eraldo Da Roma
PHOTOGRAPHY – Carlo Carlini
MUSIC – Ennio Morricone
Interiors filmed at Elios Film Studios, Rome
Techniscope/Technicolor
An Italian Production for PEC – Produzione Esecutiva
    Cinematografia (Rome)
Released internationally by United Artists
Cast
    Lee Van Cleef (Ryan); John Phillip Law (Bill); Luigi Pistilli
    (Walcott); Mario Brega (Juan, Walcott's lieutenant):
    Anthony Dawson (Burt 'Four Aces' Cavanaugh); Jose Torres
    (Pedro); Angelo Susani (Paco); Guglielmo Spoletini
    (Manuel); Franco Balducci (Sheriff of Lyndon City);
    Romano Puppo (deputy); Archie Savage (Union soldier);
    Carla Cassola (Betsy); Bruno Corazzari (barman in Holly
    Springs); Remo Capitani (member of gold escort);
    Nazzareno Natale (bearded member of Walcott's gang);
    Elena Hall (Bill's mother); Felicita Fanny (Mexican girl in
    El Viento); Claudio Ruffini (prison governor); Ignazio
    Leone (drunken priest); Nerina Montagnani (priest's wife);
    Carlo Pisacane (Holly Springs stationmaster); Nino Vingelli

(gambler); with Vivienne Bocca, Richard Watson, Giuseppe Castellano, Giovanni Petrucci, Walter Giulangeli, Mario Mandalari and Ennio Pagliani

*　　*　　*

Death Rides a Horse marked the beginning of a new phase in Lee Van Cleef's career. Having proved with *The Big Gundown* that his name alone could ensure success, he made four films produced by Alfonso Sansone and Enrico Chroscicki. *Death Rides a Horse* was followed by *Day of Anger* (1967), *Beyond the Law* (1968) and the Second World War adventure *Commandos* (1968) – Van Cleef's first attempt at a non-western role in his new incarnation as an international superstar. *Death Rides a Horse* remains the best of the quartet. The director was Giulio Petroni, who loved westerns and whose visual style resembles Leone's, though this look could have been at the behest of the producers, who wanted a made-to-order Van Cleef vehicle.

The screenplay was written by Luciano Vincenzoni. Vincenzoni had fallen out with Leone during the making of *The Good, the Bad and the Ugly*, so he went to work for Petroni, a director he got on well with. In *Death Rides a Horse* Bill, a gunman and Ryan, an ageing outlaw, join forces to track down a bunch of robbers who have used the loot from their robberies to become respectable citizens. The outlaws, including Walcott (now a banker in Lyndon City), 'Four Aces' Cavanaugh (a saloon-owner in Holly Springs) and two Mexican brothers, Paco and Pedro, were responsible for the massacre of Bill's family during a robbery at the Mesita Ranch 15 years previously. When Bill and Ryan face the gang in a showdown in the Mexican village of El Viento, Bill discovers that Ryan was also a member of the gang, but was betrayed to the law by his friends after the robbery and spent 15 years in prison. In a gun battle Walcott and his gang are annihilated, leaving Bill and Ryan to settle their differences.

Vincenzoni reworks his own script from *For a Few Dollars More* and includes many references to Leone's film: the 'old man and boy' relationship (here extended to become almost father and son) and the revenge element (with both heroes wanting revenge on the gang). It is the younger hero, Bill, who suffers a series of flashbacks to the stormy night when the gang killed his father, mother and teenage sister. Vincenzoni also repeats several key scenes from *For a Few*: there's a jailbreak sequence (using a locomotive to pull the bars out); a bank robbery (a nighttime heist by Walcott of the Lyndon City Bank reserve) and a big shootout in a Mexican village. Vincenzoni even repeats the prophet scene, with Bill visiting an alcoholic priest to find out information on villainous Cavanaugh. The key difference to *For a Few* was the finale: Vincenzoni had Bill and Ryan face each other, but Ryan's pistol is unloaded. Though Bill holds Ryan partly responsible for the death of his family, he can't shoot his companion and instead rides away.

Vincenzoni also references two Hollywood westerns in his story. From *The Last Sunset* (1961) he uses the final duel, in which Kirk Douglas faces Rock Hudson with an empty pistol; and before the shootout in El Viento, Walcott's men play a slow Flamenco dirge to wear on Bill's and Ryan's nerves, exactly like the deguello in *Rio Bravo* (1959).

One of the key themes of Lee Van Cleef's best post-Leone spaghetti westerns is corruption and capitalism in the west. Ex-outlaw Walcott has gained a foothold in society and become the head of the Lyndon City Bank reserve. Having negotiated a deal with Senator Carlisle involving the Atchison/Santa Fe Railroad, he steals the senator's million-dollar public works donation. This episode is another example of Vincenzoni using historical sources for his scenarios. Much wheeler-dealing was done to decide a route for the Atchison, Topeka and Santa Fe line involving Cyrus K. Holliday, a Pennsylvania lawyer, who talked Congress into a huge land grant for his grandiose, overreaching scheme.

With Lee Van Cleef slated to play Ryan, the older half of the gunfighting team, Californian actor John Phillip Law was cast in the Eastwood role of his younger partner, Bill. Law (who originally trained as a lawyer) was a film extra at age eight and was coached by Elia Kazan. Law worked in theatre and began in films in Italy, where he produced his best work. The year 1967 was the one that Law's career literally took off, with his famous role as the blind angel Pygar in the De Laurentiis-produced forty-first century sci-fi movie *Barbarella – Queen of the Galaxy*. Its success was attributed to the partially clad Jane Fonda, playing the sexy title role of the 'Five-star Astronominatrix'. Throughout *Barbarella* Law has little to do except look angelic and 'fly' in front of some back-projections. Law's title role in Mario Bava's *Danger: Diabolik* is much better. Bava was a talented director, who could make a rock and a bit of fog look more ominous than a million-dollar special-effects budget. Law portrayed the rubber-suited, Jaguar-driving, comic-book thief with tongue firmly in cheek. The psychedelic, lava-lamp visuals, extravagant Bond-esque situations and a good Morricone score make this Bava's classiest and most financially successful film.

In *Death Rides a Horse* the chief villains are portrayed by Anthony Dawson and Luigi Pistilli. Dawson, not to be confused with 'Anthony M. Dawson' (Italian director Antonio Margheriti's pseudonym) was a lean-faced British character actor, whose forte was cheap villainy. Dawson had two great talents – an ability to die spectacularly (with much flailing, reeling and twitching) and a knack of looking shifty. His most famous appearances were in Hitchcock's *Dial M for Murder* (1953) as the strangler, Swan, and he was evil Professor Dent in *Dr No* (1962). In an ambush, Dent pumps Bond's empty bed full of bullets, but the agent has the drop on him. As the professor points the pistol at 007, Connery utters one of the best lines of the series – 'It's a Smith and Wesson and you've had your six' – before killing Dent and coolly blowing the smoke from the silencer. Dawson then appeared uncredited in *From Russia With Love* (1964) and *Thunderball* (1965) as the unseen villain, Blofeld. He also found himself washed-up in one of the better known Italian swashbucklers, *Seven Seas to Calais* (1962) in the non-pivotal role of Lord Burley, advisor to Queen Elizabeth.

Walcott was Luigi Pistilli's biggest western role, and the only time he played the villain-in-chief in a big budget Italian western. Having debuted in *For a Few Dollars More* (as Groggy, Indio's henchman) and portrayed Padre Ramirez in *The Good, the Bad and the Ugly*, he played a few scattered roles in cheaper efforts – *Texas Adios* and *Dollars for a Fast Gun* (both 1966). Petroni cast Archie Savage as a cashiered soldier who can't get a drink in the Holly Springs saloon. Savage had appeared in *Vera Cruz* (1954), *South Pacific* (1958) and *La Dolce Vita* (1960); he was also a dancer and choreographer, and was responsible for choreographing the dancing girls in *The Last Days of Sodom and Gomorrah* (1962) and *Hercules and the Sons of the Sun* (1964).

Barrel-chested Mario Brega (from the 'Dollars' films) appeared in *Death* as Walcott's mean lieutenant (often billed in cast lists as One-eye, though he clearly has two). Brega's western characterisations hark back to the muscleman epics, where brute force was more important than intelligence. Jose Torres and Angelo Susani played the villainous brothers Pedro and Paco. Torres was prolific in this period (working regularly for directors Sergio Sollima and Giuseppe Vari), while Susani had brief roles in *The Big Gundown* and *Barbarella*, and was a regular (if often uncredited) contributor to spaghettis.

If the supporting casts in spaghetti westerns were beginning to look a little familiar, so were the locations. The Tabernas El Paso set reappeared as Lyndon City (with night scenes shot at Elios Studios), while the Lyndon City railway station sequence (shot at La Calahorra) recalled *For a Few*. The desert and mountain scenes were shot in Almeria and Cabo De Gata. The first town was the Cinecitta western set; Holly Springs was the western village at Elios. The blockhouse desert prison was Castillo De San Felipe. The prison work party, breaking rocks in a quarry, was shot in the Italian gorge at Tolfa, west of Manziana; the nearby homestead set from Giuliano Gemma's early westerns stood-in for the Mesita Ranch.

For the 'slam-bang' finale of the film, the ramshackle El Viento set (with its burned-out church and palisade) was something of a fresh location. The set was located at Las Salinillas in Almeria; the same set reappeared in an even worse state of repair (after Van Cleef and company had shot it up) in several later westerns, including *The Ruthless Four* (1968), in which it convincingly passed as a ruined mission. The name El Viento is a subtle gag from Vincenzoni; the dusty, windblown pueblo translates as 'the wind'. When Bill rides into town, there's a sandstorm, though the effect is actually a rather obvious wind machine on location in Almeria.

The substantial budget allowed for the staging of a large-scale political rally, Walcott's thirty-man gang (who ride impressively through the Almerian landscape) and the mass shootout at El Viento, where Bill and Ryan enlist the help of the local peons to defeat Walcott. The shootout is wreathed in swirling dust, with Van Cleef at his most primal as he cries havoc on Walcott's gang. This set piece bears all the hallmarks of *The Magnificent Seven*, with Ryan standing in for Chris (a role Van Cleef played later in his career in *The Magnificent Seven Ride* – 1972) and Walcott's gang subbing for Calvera's men. The explosive sequence was staged by Eros Bacciucchi, the special-effects master responsible for the Civil War battles in *The Good, the Bad and the Ugly* (Petroni's assistant director was Giancarlo Santi, Leone's assistant on the same film). The Mexican peons make a huge barricade out of the furniture and set fire to an oil-filled ditch, but this doesn't deter Walcott, who blows the barricade to pieces.

In interviews Van Cleef noted that actors had to be tough to make Italian westerns in Spain – 'The horses are wild, the props are real and the locations primitive'. Tall, eagle-nosed Romano Puppo doubled for Van Cleef in some of the more dangerous action sequences, climbing up ladders and jumping through windows. He also performed the Almeria riding shots (filmed by Santi's second unit in the arid *ramblas*) and the scene where Ryan falls through a trapdoor in Walcott's office. Puppo had a small role in the film, as the deputy in Lyndon City. He was a collaborator on all Van Cleef's starring vehicles in the sixties, from *The Good, the Bad and the Ugly* onwards. In each case he was also Van Cleef's stunt-double; Puppo's height and physique closely resembled the six-foot two-inch Van Cleef's. He could speak English and was a useful on-set translator. The two remained good friends, and Puppo was a bearer at Van Cleef's funeral in 1989.

Carlo Carlini's cinematography gives *Death Rides a Horse* two distinct moods. The film begins in Gothic horror territory, with a flash of stock-footage lightning and a roll of thunder, for the rain-sodden attack at the Mesita Ranch. The early scenes hark back to Ryan's confinement in prison; these sequences are claustro-phobic, set mainly indoors (in saloons, offices or cellars) and in busy towns – the urban environment of the businessman. Once Walcott robs the bank and the chase proceeds into the desert, the film moves up a gear and Carlini's craning, zooming camerawork is much better when dealing with the expansive landscapes and dusty villages he shot so inspiringly in *The Big Gundown*.

Petroni's most significant stylistic improvement on *For a Few Dollars More* is his integration of the flashbacks. At the beginning of the film, as little Bill witnesses the massacre and cowers in the shadows, he memorises the killers' distinctive features – Pedro's scar, Paco's earring, 'Four Aces' Cavanaugh's chest tattoo and Walcott's grimace. As the Mesita Ranch is set alight, a mysterious fifth man (wearing a silver skull icon around his neck) saves Bill from the fire. Years later, as Bill tracks down the four villains, red-tinted flashbacks remind him of the crime. Unlike the dreamlike mood of Indio's memories in *For a Few*, Bill's interpretations are a vision of hell, cut to a cacophony from Ennio Morricone. These sudden abstractions precede the deaths of each villain, a device that was repeated in many later spaghettis. When Bill recognises the icon around Ryan's neck he realises that Ryan was also at the ranch that night. Ghostly voices and flutes shriek on the soundtrack, as images of the skull and Bill's face merge and the final part of the mystery falls into place.

Walcott and Cavanaugh are now respectable pillars of the community, and Ryan comments on his old partners' underhand methods: 'You're all alike. Years go by

Lee Van Cleef as avenging outlaw Ryan in Giulio Petroni's *Death Rides a Horse* (1967).

and you all do the same things. Gun in the drawer, knife in the back…lies.' The sneaky villains use modern gadgetry to gain an edge – like the trapdoor in Walcott's office – a nod to technological advances out west that came to the fore in the spaghetti western *Sabata* (1969). Cardsharp Cavanaugh arrived in Holly Springs with nothing but 'a pistol and a pack of cards', and now he runs the lucrative gambling joint. When Ryan arrives unannounced, he finds out that both Walcott and Cavanaugh are 'quick on the drawer'.

The corrupt relationship between 'killing' and 'business' is epitomised by Ryan's reacquaintance with 'Four Aces' Cavanaugh. Cavanaugh (called 'Manina' in the Italian print) wears a smart red dressing gown, Ryan a layer of trail dust. Ryan tells Cavanaugh that the money he spends on hired assassins is a 'bad investment', as though he were talking about a slight fall in stock rather than an attempt on his life. Ryan also says that he was 'sold' to the law and refers to their vendetta as an 'old account'. The outlaws have become rich, respectable and financially astute ('Well established', as Ryan puts it). Cavanaugh's racketeering is organised and his methods brutal, but the sheriff and the judge both conveniently play poker in his saloon.

Petroni's well-paced directorial style ritualises Ryan's release from prison at the start of the film. The sequence begins with Ryan having the shackles removed from his ankles (accompanied by the hymnal chanting of the Alessandroni Singers). Ryan removes his leather work gloves and massages his hands, unblemished by years of swinging a hammer and ready to hold a gun again. As Ryan leaves prison (a sun-bleached fort in the middle of the desert), the doors swing open and Morricone's pulsating riding theme begins, marking the beginning of Ryan's journey of revenge through the wasteland. In the distance he spots a reception committee sent by Cavanaugh to welcome him out of jail; two well-dressed professional guns – incongruous city men in a desert landscape.

Petroni exploits the audience's familiarity with Van Cleef's screen persona and his props: the cross-belly draw holster and Meerschaum pipe. Van Cleef's performances were based to a large extent on extreme understatement – a minimalist, brooding style. Critics wouldn't let this pass for acting, as they reminded him in predominantly unfavourable reviews. It was when Van Cleef diversified (usually involving light comedy and much more dialogue) that his career went off the rails. In the limited field of spaghetti westerns, Van Cleef was a better actor than Eastwood; but Eastwood had the good looks of a leading man, while Van Cleef was blessed with what he himself termed, 'a beady-eyed sneer'.

Whilst being a return to Van Cleef's roots as an outlaw in fifties westerns, Ryan is the clearest example of his 'fallen angel' characterisations. Van Cleef's character ties in with the English release title of the film; the original Italian title (*Da Uomo a Uomo* – or 'From Man to Man') concentrates on the central relationship between Ryan and Bill. In the English-language version, Van Cleef is the personification of Death, stressed by the skull icon Ryan wears around his neck.

When Ryan first arrives at El Viento, his conversation with a village elder hints that the 'fallen angel' is ready to repent. The old Mexican tells Ryan, 'I don't know who you are, but I feel you were sent by God to help us and to protect us against the evil ones'. 'Well actually,' replies Ryan, 'I don't think I'm really in that close a relationship with our good Lord and I don't recall receiving any messages from him. But I am here for personal reasons and it may just be that those reasons coincide with yours.' The peasants see Ryan as a saviour, a role he is uncomfortable with.

John Phillip Law comes across as less an 'avenging angel' and more a vengeful Rowdy Yates; at one point he even refers to the 'women-folk and young uns'. His performance is self-conscious, and he is a much more lightweight hero than Eastwood's Manco in *For a Few*. Bill is constantly being outwitted: he is beaten up and whipped, has his head wedged in a huge grain press, is buried up to his neck in the sand and then has salt pushed in his mouth.

Bill and Ryan first meet shortly after Ryan's release from prison – a result of having been double-crossed by Walcott and friends after the Mesita Ranch robbery. Ryan visits the family graves at Bill's home. In an elegiac sequence, their first conversation hints at Ryan's involvement in the massacre (Ryan commenting, 'I haven't been around here in quite a while') and his guilt at having been unable to prevent it ('I'm sorry. I heard about it some time ago'). Ryan's visit to the ranch ties-in with the 'guardian angel' aspect of the story and later they join forces to catch the gang.

In a variation of the 'old man' and 'boy' scenario, Ryan dispenses advice to Bill throughout their partnership and by the end of the chase the 'son' has learned well. Once Bill knows the location of Walcott's hideout at El Viento he thinks he can go it alone, but he walks straight into a trap. Ryan's arrival at El Viento to save Bill is presented by Petroni as a parody of Eastwood's arrival in San Miguel in *A Fistful of Dollars*, with Van Cleef disguised in a scruffy poncho and leading a moth-eaten mule, as three toughs (including Mario Brega) insult him, before 'biting the dust' (just like the Baxters).

In El Viento, Ryan makes an unusual departure for Italian western heroes: he seems to be getting quite attached to Bill. Vincenzoni's screenplay places an uncharacteristically sympathetic emphasis on Van Cleef's paternal character. At one point Ryan mentions that he wished that he had a son like Bill, a regret not normally associated with spaghetti heroes. This gives an oedipal intensity to their final confrontation. Bill amiably refers to Ryan on numerous occasions as 'Grandpa' and as Bill rides away at the film's close, Ryan watches over him, commenting, 'Good luck son'. Their final showdown in El Viento is Petroni at his best. When all the bandits are dead, Ryan strides into an arena near a burned-out church to face Bill. The whirlwind, an elemental expression of Ryan's and Bill's revenge, subsides, leaving only silence for their final encounter among the hubris of battle – dollar bills, scattered furniture and corpses.

Ennio Morricone's score for *Death Rides a Horse* alternates between the throbbing, incessant riding theme (with chanted lyrics and flute shrieks) and more sombre pieces. The title sequence reuses a piece originally written for *A Fistful of Dollars* – for Eastwood's beating and the Baxters' massacre. It is a threatening atonal composition, occasionally punctuated by a crashing gong, a cascading flute or slow, twanging bass notes. The 'riding theme' is one of the composer's most savage compositions, with two guitars (one strumming a single repetitive riff, the other striking an emphatic chord), a pulsating bass, brushed snare and a stuttering, howling pan-pipe. Over this chugging rhythm, the Alessandroni Singers chant at full volume. Written by Maurizio Attanasio, the lyrics include the lines:

> He'll be coming down the mountain,
> Who'll be the first to seize his gun?
> Who'll be the last to see the ground?
> Who will put flowers on your graves?
> The moment of truth comes.

Another version of this theme, short on lyrics but long on flute, is used throughout the film. Spaghetti-western singer Raoul covered this song in his own inimitable, bellowing style; it was released as a single in Italy (to tie in with the film) but wasn't used in the movie. The Alessandroni Singers are employed effectively – whether adding a ghostly aura to disturbing footage (like the 'serving of the salt' torture of Law), or the angelic harmonies of the 'Notturno Per Chitarra' death song (complete with shimmering Flamenco guitar and castanets). In the Holly Springs saloon, Morricone deploys the ragtime piano piece 'Aces High' from the White Rocks saloon in *For a Few Dollars More*. When Ryan first meets Bill at the graveside at the Mesita Ranch, the scene is accompanied by a reflective piece from Morricone, with strummed guitar and choir. Morricone provides a chaotic piece of 'gundown' music, which was abridged in the final cut of the film. In the recorded version (called 'Imminent Trouble') the choir chant largely unintelligible lyrics (including 'I have seen men without any pity for no one'), while Morricone's lively percussion sounds like Masaru Sato's music for *Yojimbo*. Quentin Tarantino used part of Morricone's *Death* score in his revenge film *Kill Bill* (2003), which also deployed Luis Bacalov's theme from the Van Cleef spaghetti western *The Grand Duel* (1972).

When *Death Rides a Horse* was released in Italy in August 1967 it was one of the top-grossing films of the year. It did well in Spain and also in France (where it was known as *La Morte etait au Rendez-vous*: 'A Rendezvous with Death'). For international distribution, many of the westerns Van Cleef made following his stint with Leone had problems with their lengthy running times: *The Big Gundown* and *Day of Anger* (1967) were butchered, while the overlong *Beyond the Law* (1968) should have been. Even though *Death* contained many violent scenes, it was released uncut at 110 minutes in the US and the UK by United Artists in 1969. Amazingly, it was rated a certificate 'A'; *Day of Anger* wasn't that much more violent, but gained an 'X' certificate. *Death* was another hit for Van Cleef in the US, though it wasn't as popular with critics, already bored with what they saw as Van Cleef's bland screen persona and inexpressive physiognomy.

Though *Death* was a big success, Law never returned to the genre, while Luigi Pistilli alternated western appearances with Mafia thrillers like *We Still Kill the Old Way* (1967) and *Machine Gun McCain* (1968). In the seventies he moved into horror and political films, with Bava's *Bay of Blood* (1971) and Rosi's *Illustrious Corpses* (1976). His life was ended in 1996, when he tragically committed suicide in Milan after a failed love affair.

Bill and Ryan, face to face in El Viento; John Phillip Law and Lee Van Cleef on location at Las Salinillas, Almeria in *Death Rides a Horse* (1967).

Giulio Petroni continued to make westerns throughout the spaghetti boom, directing four more efforts – *And a Sky Full of Stars for a Roof* (1968), *Tepepa* (1969), *Night of the Serpent* (1969) and *They Call Me Providence* (1972). *Tepepa* cast Tomas Milian as a peasant revolutionary and Orson Welles as a Mexican officer in a poor imitation of Sollima's political westerns; Welles worked extensively in Europe as an actor from the fifties onwards, to finance his own directorial projects – hence his unlikely performance as sadistic Colonel Cascoro. *Night of the Serpent* was a Gothic horror western featuring Luigi Pistilli and Anthony Dawson, and *Providence* again featured Milian, this time as a bumbling bounty killer.

Sky Full of Stars (with Giuliano Gemma) is the most interesting of the bunch, mostly for Morricone's little-heard score. The first half of the film is ineptly enacted comedy, but the second half improves, when Gemma finds himself up against the villainous father-and-son team of Samuel and Roger Pratt (played by Anthony Dawson and Federico Boido). The film's opening sequence is memorable. The Pratts attack a stagecoach and kill all the passengers, including a young woman. The gang rides off and the camera dwells on her face, accompanied by Morricone's haunting theme (whistled by Alessandroni). Dust blows across her face, until Gemma's hand appears and strokes the dust from her cheek. Morricone's score also includes a great riding cue (an early version of his *Two Mules for Sister Sara* title music) and a guitar piece (incorporating a Thomas 900 electric organ) that accompanies black-clad Dawson stepping down from the noon train at a desolate railroad station.

Death Rides a Horse marked the end of Lee Van Cleef's most successful period in Europe; not in terms of box-office receipts (*Sabata* considerably outgrossed it

Original Italian artwork by Mauro Innocenti for *Death Rides a Horse* (1967), featuring Lee Van Cleef and John Phillip Law.

in 1969), but in terms of quality. With the exception of *Day of Anger* and *Sabata*, Van Cleef was cast in second-rate star vehicles, with bizarre changes of pace, and some outright disasters – a foregone conclusion whenever Van Cleef attempted comedy. In 1967 Van Cleef was at a crossroads: should he stay in Europe and enjoy the high life, or return to the US and try to build on his comparative fame? Humphrey Bogard once maintained, 'You're not a star until they can spell your name in Karachi', while Van Cleef's agent, Tom Jennings, commented years later, 'Lee was always a bigger star everywhere else than in Hollywood'. With Van Cleef's growing global popularity, they could probably spell his name everywhere – sadly everywhere except Hollywood.

14

'All Men Must Die in Time'

— Sergio Sollima's *Face to Face* (1967)

Face to Face (1967)
original title: *Faccia a Faccia*
Credits
DIRECTOR – Sergio Sollima
PRODUCER – Alberto Grimaldi
STORY – Sergio Sollima
SCREENPLAY – Sergio Sollima and Sergio Donati
ART DIRECTOR – Carlo Simi
EDITOR – Eugenio Alabiso
DIRECTOR OF PHOTOGRAPHY – Raphael Pacheco
MUSIC COMPOSER – Ennio Morricone
MUSIC CONDUCTOR – Bruno Nicolai
Interiors filmed at Elios Film Studios, Rome
Technicolor/Techniscope
An Italian/Spanish co-production
PEA (Rome)/Arturo Gonzales Cinematografica (Madrid)
Released internationally by Butchers Film Company
Cast
    Gian Maria Volonte (Professor Brad Fletcher); Tomas
    Milian (Solomon Beauregard Bennett); William Berger
    (Charley 'Chas' A. Siringo); Jolanda Modio (Maria); Gianni
    Rizzo (Williams); Carole André (Annie); Angel Del Pozo
    (Maximilian De Winton); Lydia Alfonsi (Belle De Winton);
    Aldo Sambrell (Zachary Sean); Nello Pazzafini (Vance); Jose
    Torres (Aaron Chase); Frank Braña (Jason); Paco Sanz
    (Rusty Rogers); Lorenzo Robledo (Agent Wallace); Rossella
    D'Aquino (Elizabeth Wilkins and hotel maid in Purgatory);
    Antonio Casas (outlaw leader); Gerard Tichy (Mayor of
    Silvertown); Rick Boyd (Sheriff of Purgatory); Alfonso

Rojas (First Sheriff); 'Guy Heron', Guy Heroni (Second
Sheriff); Calisto Calisti (Sheriff of Willow Creek); Joaquin
Parra and Guglielmo Spoletini (deputies at way station);
Jose Zaldua (innkeeper); John Karlson (University Dean);
Linda Veras (Fletcher's moll); Osiride Peverello
(blacksmith in Willow Creek); Guillermo Mendez and
Gastone Moschin (gunmen in Puerto Del Fuego);
Ivan Scratuglia, Remo Capitani and Goffredo Unger
(Taylor's gang)

*   *   *

With *The Big Gundown*, Sergio Sollima had added a social-political slant to the gringo–Mexican relationship that was a mainstay of Italian westerns. But his next film was less about the relationship between a lawman and an outlaw, and more concerned with how someone's personality changes when their circumstances and environment are altered. Sollima wrote this new story himself and drafted-in Sergio Donati for a screenplay entitled *Face to Face*. The plot is similar to *Gundown*: Charley Siringo, a lawman working for the Pinkerton's Detective Agency, attempts to apprehend Solomon Beauregard Bennett, a half-breed outlaw. The chase is de-emphasised here and Siringo fades into the background for the early part of the story. While eluding the law, bandit 'Beau' Bennett encounters Brad Fletcher, a tubercular professor of history convalescing out west from Boston, New England.

Face to Face shows the gradual changes that affect the two men's personalities and their eventual exchange of roles. Beau regroups Bennett's Raiders, his outlaw gang, in a haven called Puerto Del Fuego and allows Brad to join them. After a disastrous bank robbery in Willow Creek, planned by Brad, a posse of vigilantes is dispatched from Silvertown to attack the hideout. Thereafter, the professor remakes himself as a brutal bandit, while Beau discovers his conscience. The vigilantes track Beau and Brad into the desert, but Siringo intervenes; in the final three-way face-off Brad and Beau face Siringo. As Brad is about to kill Siringo, Beau shoots the professor. Seeing that Beau has changed, Siringo disfigures the face of one of the vigilante's corpses, to pass him off as Beau. 'The law'll be satisfied with a fake Beauregard Bennett,' Siringo reasons 'Anyhow, the real one doesn't exist anymore'.

Though Beau doesn't resemble any historical outlaws, Sollima based Bennett's Raiders on the James gang and Butch Cassidy's Wild Bunch. In the Italian script of *Face to Face* the Raiders are called the 'Branco Selvaggio' (the Wild Gang), while the hideout of Puerto Del Fuego has its roots in the famous Hole-in-the-Wall Gang epithet applied to Butch's gang; many outlaws sought refuge in Wyoming's Hole-in-the-Wall country, especially Robbers Roost, near Willow Creek. In Sollima's film, Puerto Del Fuego, the name of the rough shacks, hovels and ramadas (brush shelters) huddled in the mountains, translates as 'Pass of Fire'. During a railway hold-up, Bennett's gang don cattle dusters, the long, brown linen coats worn by cattlemen, which were often used by Jesse and Frank James, who impersonated rich cattle speculators during robberies.

The most infamous episode of the James gang's career is echoed in Sollima's scenario. The bungled attack on the Willow Creek Bank bears a striking resemblance to the James gang's Waterloo in Northfield, Minnesota (1876) and the Dalton gang's attempt in 1892 to rob two banks simultaneously in their hometown of Coffeyville, Kansas; despite the Daltons wearing false moustaches and goatees, the locals recognised them instantly. In both robberies the plans descended into chaos, leaving gang members wounded, stranded or bullet-ridden as the townspeople reacted quickly. In *Face*, the meticulously planned heist becomes a bloody fiasco, as Beau is recognised and then Siringo betrays them to the law; Beau is captured, his gang killed and only Brad escapes.

Charley Siringo also had an historical precedent. Pinkerton's did employ a man named Charles Angelo Siringo, whose speciality was posing as a bandit to infiltrate gangs. Siringo joined renegade bands, tipped off the railroad bosses when their stock was to be targeted and then mysteriously vanished – only to reappear to track the bandits down. In *Face* the agent infiltrates Bennett's Raiders by pretending to be an outlaw and the Pinkertons try the same trick later, with Agent Wallace at Puerto Del Fuego. Like his historical precedent, Siringo dupes Beau; during a train hold-up, the agent surreptitiously passes a note to one of the passengers (hidden in a locket) and tells the outlaw that such bravado (returning a keepsake to a lady) will make Beau a legend. The aspects of the story dealing with the Pinkertons have one crucial anomaly. Sollima's film is set during 1863; there is a reference to the Battle of Gettysburg, and Beau packs an authentic-looking brace of period Colt Navy pistols. But the real Charles Siringo didn't join Pinkerton's until 1886. Siringo was a good choice of reference point, as a photograph exists of the agent standing on the set of a William S. Hart silent western – a link between the real wild west and the Hollywood myth.

Face to Face's central character is the professor, and this resulted in the casting of Gian Maria Volonte, then best known for his Mexican-bandit roles. Volonte was an award-winning stage actor, but he was yet to make his mark without wearing a sombrero and a drooping moustache; Sollima gave him the chance and his first top billing. Lee Van Cleef's lawman role went to William Berger. In only his third western, Berger's portrayal of Siringo was his big break. *Face* was a prestigious, well-budgeted production co-financed by PEA, (with Alberto Grimaldi at the helm) and Arturo Gonzales (which was run by Spanish producer Arturo Gonzales Rodriguez) in Madrid. Both companies had been involved in the huge success of Leone's *For a Few Dollars More*.

Sollima recast Tomas Milian, this time as Beau, the fugitive bandit leader on the run. In most spaghetti westerns the bandit leader's gang are a faceless bunch: a collection of sweaty, stubbled faces glaring from under their sombreros. In *Face to Face* Sollima developed an idea first seen in *For a Few Dollars More*, where Indio's men are identified by name and given individual personalities. Here each member of Bennett's Raiders was played by a spaghetti-western 'B-movie' villain, giving his Wild Bunch instant familiarity to fans of the genre. The gang includes Nello Pazzafini (as Vance), Jose Torres (as Aaron Chase), Frank Braña (as Jason) and Angel Del Pozo (as southern plantation owner Maximilian De Winton).

Spanish poster for Sergio Sollima's *Face to Face* (1967), featuring Tomas Milian as half-breed outlaw, Beau Bennett.

Burly Italian actor Pazzafini had appeared in muscleman epics, including Leone's *The Colossus of Rhodes* (as the gong-striker) and *The Lion of Thebes* (1964 – as a wrestler, the mighty Gaor). He also played western villains in *One Silver Dollar* (1965), *Adios Gringo* (1965), *Arizona Colt* (1966) and *Death at Owl Rock* (1967 – in which a manic Pazzafini cut out a witness's tongue). Torres also graduated from high-billed performances as low-budget villains. His best role so far had been the bandit El Diablo in *30 Winchesters for El Diablo* (1965). Frank Braña appeared in *Ride and Kill* (1963), *Adios Gringo* and *For a Few Dollars More*. Rarely trusted to larger roles, this tall, lugubrious actor (with bushy eyebrows) never outstayed his welcome, not even surviving the opening scenes of *The Ugly Ones* (1966) and *The Good, the Bad and the Ugly*. Spaniard Angel Del Pozo had been the traitorous Union Captain Lefevre in Giuliano Gemma's *Fort Yuma Gold* (1966) and Shep, the real villain of *The Big Gundown*.

Face to Face also had a fleeting appearance by Federico Boido, known as 'Rick Boyd', as a sheriff. Boido was a prolific spaghetti-western actor and Federico Fellini used Boido to humorous effect in the stylised Italian awards ceremony of *Toby Dammit* (also called *Don't Bet Heads*), Fellini's contribution to *Histoires Extraordinaires* (1968). English actor Toby (Terence Stamp) is in Rome to make a spaghetti western and is introduced to Boido, his prospective stunt-double; Boido tells Toby, 'I'm very happy to be your double. I have also been the double of Tomas Milian.'

Sollima cast Linda Veras, Gianni Rizzo and a host of familiar faces from Cinecitta-genre films: Aldo Sambrell, Lorenzo Robledo, Antonio Casas and Paco Sanz. Stuntman Goffredo Unger had a small role in the film, as a heavy in Purgatory City (though in a street shootout he clearly gets killed twice). *Face to Face* features two underrated actresses – Lydia Alfonsi and Jolanda Modio. Alfonsi had played the prophetess the Sibyl in the original *Hercules* (1958) and appeared in 'The Telephone' episode of Mario Bava's *Black Sabbath* (1963); since then she had been largely confined to Italian TV films. Modio (sometimes billed as 'Iolanda Modio') was a capable Spanish actress whose best-known appearance was as Marisol in Luigi Vanzi's *Fistful* remake *A Stranger in Town* (1966). Sollima also cast Rossella D'Aquino in two roles: as Boston schoolteacher Miss Wilkins and a hotel maid in Purgatory City.

Face to Face was filmed on location in Spain and at Elios Studios in Italy (with interiors at Elios). The Spanish landscape again became the American southwest, with the mountains, gullies, dunes and dried-up riverbeds being used to good effect. Purgatory City was the San Miguel set at Hojo De Manzanares. The landscape around Manzanares El Real and Colmenar was used in the early part of the film, while the final three-way shootout was shot among the southern dunes of Cabo De Gata. The train station at Purgatory was La Calahorra Station, outside Guadix; the train hold-up was filmed on the Almeria–Guadix railway line. Other desert scenes (including Beau's escape at a way station) were shot in the sierras of Almeria: at Alto De La Morcuera and La Cabrera. The towns of Willow Creek and Silvertown were shot at Elios Studios. A cabin in the woods where Beau recuperates was Cullik's hideout in *The Big Gundown*; these scenes were filmed in the pine forests of the Sierra De Guadarrama mountain range. Two more sets were constructed near Madrid – the De Winton's southern plantation mansion (near Colmenar) and the ramshackle refuge at Puerto Del Fuego (built beneath the rock formations at La Pedriza).

Sollima hired Madrid-born cinematographer Rafael Pacheco De Usa, who worked under the alias 'Rafael Pacheco'. Pacheco has an eye for beautiful lighting effects and his camera is extraordinarily mobile, constantly circling the characters. Pacheco's location photography is equal to many Italian westerns of the time, recalling Massimo Dallamano and Carlo Carlini at their best. Brightly lit desert and mountain landscapes contrast with dark figures and swirling, sunlit dust. A conversation between Brad, Beau and the gang is filmed in a ramada shading a pool table, with shafts of light dappling the scene. Pacheco also lights night sequences effectively: a stormy night at a woodland shack (with tinted lightning flashes), the vigilantes' torch-lit assembly in Silvertown and Siringo lighting a match in a moonlit sheriff's office.

Sollima elicits good performances from his cast; he wrote the role of Beau with Milian in mind. Milian accentuates his method-style moodiness and tones down his clowning, playing the desperado with much understatement as he silently meditates on his gang's next move. Volonte successfully transforms himself from cowardly professor to vicious bandit, while Berger's laconic performance as Siringo was influenced by Lee Van Cleef in *The Big Gundown*; he even wears a fur-trimmed jacket and cross-belly draw holster.

Face to Face was subtler than many political spaghetti westerns. It has little in common with other political films and is much closer to Leone's west. But while Leone could have made *The Big Gundown*, *Face* could never be mistaken for one of his films (being far too talky), even though the landscape, the music and many of the cast are the same. Sollima's films are more personal and character-driven, though *Face* is still concerned with political and social issues: the manipulation of the masses, the changes caused by a brutal environment and the excuses made for senseless violence when linked to history.

In addition to the confrontation between Beau and Brad, the title *Face to Face* also refers to the encounter between east and west. The east–west divide usually saw the eastern 'dude' being ridiculed by the grizzled westerners; Sollima's treatment of the easterner is more serious, making much of Brad's brains, but lack of western know-how. As the Civil War rages off-screen, Brad is not only an easterner out west, but also a northerner down south, as he finds out when he arrives at Max De Winton's Confederate plantation.

In contrast, at Puerto Del Fuego, uniforms, allegiances and politics mean little to the fugitives sheltering there. With the outcasts Sollima depicts the lonely life of outlawry. Most of them are hiding away from a 'modern world' that is unrecognisable, with its telegraph poles and railroads. As Max explains to Brad, the fugitives are 'ghosts from the past'. Brad's optimistic view of the camp ('Happy, alive and free') is markedly different to Max's cynicism ('The dregs of the old romantic frontier'). The 'old romantic frontier' is epitomised by aged outlaw Rusty Rogers (Paco Sanz), an homage by Sollima to the romance of the Hollywood western; his name is a reference to Roy Rogers and perennial sidekicks named Rusty. Rusty has been hiding at Puerto Del Fuego for thirty years and the law has forgotten about him. After the vigilantes' attack, Beau finds Rusty lying gut-shot. Sollima has the old man refer to his demise in strictly Hollywood terms: 'End of the trail for Rusty'.

Sollima has such a strong storyline that the action scenes are barely dwelt upon; instead he uses violence to make social and political comments. This is noticeable with a train robbery and the vigilantes' massacre at Puerto Del Fuego. A train heist, for instance, would usually form a large set piece in a spaghetti western; in some of the lower-budget efforts it could be the premise for the entire film. In *Face* Sollima uses the brief train hold-up scene to demonstrate how Beau is becoming a legendary bandit, when Siringo returns a locket to a passenger. At Puerto Del Fuego, Sollima doesn't show the events of the massacre: the camera pans through the desolation and slaughter, as the laughing, cheering vigilantes torch the huts and drive off the fugitives' cattle. Earlier the professor says, 'Beyond the confines that limit the outlaw as an individual, violence by masses of men is called history'. After the massacre, we see the results of such history-making: the slaughter of the innocents. This is Sollima's presentation of the death of the old west – the reality of history finally catching up with the myth and legend.

At the beginning of *Face*, a stagecoach pulls into the way station where Brad is convalescing. The door springs open and a manacled Beau is pushed out, sprawling in the dust. With his Apache Indian-style haircut, fringed buckskins and unshaven glower, Beau is presented as a savage, brutal bandit, whose only instinct is to kill. During a post wagon robbery, Brad makes Beau feel guilty by reading a stolen letter out loud. The note says that the money enclosed was from an elderly couple leaving their son their life's savings, which Beau has just pocketed. When confronted with reality, Beau changes. At Puerto Del Fuego, Beau is hero-worshipped by Annie, a teenage girl who sees nothing wrong with his brutal behaviour. But later, when a young Mexican boy is killed in the crossfire at Willow Creek, Beau has a change of heart and becomes the outlaw who finally does 'what's right'. Now Brad is the cynical one, when he tells Annie that Beau is 'a hero that doesn't exist'.

In Purgatory City, respected citizen Williams (played by Gianni Rizzo) hires Beau to rid the town of a local tyrant Sam Taylor and his men. Williams is a wheelchair-bound businessman, a character that often appears in Sergio Donati-scripted westerns; similarly powerful yet tragic figures feature in *Dollars for a Fast Gun* (1966) and *Once Upon a Time in the West* (1968). In *Face*, Williams is also on Taylor's payroll, and the two men watch Beau face the gang (outside the Purgatory Hotel) from the comfort of Williams's balcony. Like Brokston in *The Big Gundown*, Williams can

afford to hire minions to do his bidding, though their scheme to capture Beau
backfires and Taylor's men are wiped out.

When Beau and Agent Siringo first meet, the bandit is suspicious – the lawman
seems to know a lot about the gang. Siringo's 'lucky charm' sheriff's star with a

Italian artwork by Morini for *Face to Face* (1967); Gian Maria Volonte as
professor Brad and Tomas Milian as manacled Beau.

bullet hole through it ('From my first sheriff') and his fake wanted poster 'references' are inventive touches. But when Siringo witnesses the arrival of the vigilantes in Silvertown, he realises that law and order doesn't always work. This occurs at exactly the same point as in *The Big Gundown*, when Don Serano's Mexican posse (in the pay of Brokston) arrive at the ranch to start the manhunt. In *Face*, the lawman compares the Silvertown council's actions (and the fugitives' chances in the forthcoming attack) to the US Cavalry massacring the Indians. Siringo watches the vigilante rabble assemble to hear the bounties available on the fugitives at Puerto Del Fuego. Having refused to lead the attack, Siringo watches the sheriff appoint bloodthirsty outlaw Zachary Sean as their guide. Sean is a turncoat, who for amnesty betrays the people who were willing to shelter him – a breach of honour that neither Siringo nor Beau can comprehend. As the cavalcade ride off to Puerto Del Fuego, Siringo throws his cigar away in disgust at how low the law will stoop.

From the opening scene in the Boston University, when Brad lectures his students, education is referred to throughout the film. Brad spends his time learning the ways of the west; his education later extends to learning how to kill and his intellect is handy when he plans the bank robbery. The logic that a safe opens to deposit cash as well as to remove it, impresses Beau's gang. But Brad rejects his university past: in one scene he tears the pages from a history book. The dean tells Brad that with his intelligence he could have gone far, but Brad lacks ambition. During his lecture, Brad tells the class that one day they will have to choose between right and wrong, but out west he forgets the distinction. In fact, Beau provides him with a new credo: only the strongest survive.

As Brad forgets his eastern morals, he also forgets about his illness. The climate out west must agree with him, but Brad knows he is living on borrowed time. He tells his students: 'All men must die in time' – it's just a question of when. The professor yearns to go down in history, and out west he sees the chance to make his mark. Brad tells Beau that it is hard to distinguish between the need to kill for survival and 'the lust to acquire power'. During the story, we see Brad kill three people: a gunman about to kill Beau, one of Beau's men (during a quarrel) and Wallace (another Pinkerton's agent), though there is a pattern to the killings. The first is to save Beau's life, the second is to defend himself, but the third is the most calculated, as his victim is helpless. Here, Brad cold-bloodedly shoots one of his own, an educated university man, his intellectual equal.

After the Willow Creek robbery, Brad relishes his new role as bandit leader and becomes comfortable with his violence and power. He employs a gang of toughs from 'back east' (Chicago, San Francisco and St Louis) and calmly tortures captured Pinkerton Agent Wallace, sent to infiltrate Puerto Del Fuego. Sollima's argument is that ignorant bandits can be excused such sadism, while educated easterners should know better. The conversation between Agent Wallace and Brad is important, as Brad expounds his 'philosophy of violence'. The university-educated Wallace is surprised that a man from Brad's background can become so ruthless: civilised among civilised man, violent among the violent, 'Like a parasite'. The professor answers that with intellect, much can be accomplished out west, 'Where men who are morons have succeeded in usurping the power in the land'. The spy must die so that Brad retains the respect of his ruffians ('Reasons of state,' says Brad). The professor explains that Wallace's execution is not through hate, 'But with compassion'. Brad takes a pistol and blows the agent's brains out.

Sollima cuts from Wallace's death to the lawmen and councillors of Silvertown trying to convince imprisoned Beau to join the side of the law. Sollima uses the scenes to show how Beau and Brad have changed. Beau is sickened by bandit Zachary Sean's brutal plan to knife the guard and escape, while in Puerto Del Fuego Brad shoots a defenceless man through the head. Beau, though he is in the 'civilised' world of Silvertown, doesn't 'change his spots' because of his surroundings.

For *Face to Face*, Ennio Morricone composed an 'all-stops-out' title theme, with the pounding drums recalling the multi-layered percussion of *Gundown*. A church organ takes the melody, and a guitar and harpsichord play a jagged, syncopated riff. Edda Dell'Orso adds her ethereal soprano vocal, while the piece is punctuated by the emphatic boom of a drum, driving the tempo like the timekeeper on a Roman slave galley. This tune accompanies the title sequence, which features rotoscoped animations of the stagecoach carrying Beau to the way station (as though Brad's date with destiny is already unfolding beneath the credits). The Thomas 900 electric organ used in the theme recurs later in the film, adding atmosphere to the suspenseful bank raid.

Sollima, like Leone, gave Morricone's music space, allowing the themes to express more emotion. All Morricone's trademark styles appear on the *Face to Face* soundtrack: the stirring opening theme (and its variations), two poignant themes (a Spanish guitar tune and an elegiac orchestral piece), Siringo's theme (a rhythmic march), the folk dances at Puerto Del Fuego (with harmonica-playing by Franco De Gemini) and the familiar trumpet duel music. The elegiac piece is an early version of a composition later used in *The Mission* (1986). Morricone was fully aware of how to exploit these variations; his scoring here is effortless, creating emotional and shocking effects.

Face to Face was released in Italy in November 1967 and was one of the most successful films of the year. It was also popular in Spain, where it remains Milian's second-best-grossing western, after *The Big Gundown*. In addition to an effective Italian publicity campaign, with posters designed by Morini, a series of evocative black-and-white photographs were taken during the *Face to Face* shoot; they have since been used to theorise that there are scenes missing from the film, but they were solely for advertising purposes. Though *Face to Face* is set in Texas and New Mexico, the film was retitled *Il Etait une Fois en Arizona* ('Once Upon a Time in Arizona') in France; on English rerelease it was known by the equally derivative *High Plains Killer*.

Italian critics speculated that Sollima's wild-west story really concerned the rise of European Fascism, citing Brad's moral disintegration at Puerto Del Fuego (when he exploits and mistreats the fugitives hiding there). Sollima has never made such claims, and critics who concentrated on the political aspects of Brad's transformation largely missed the psychological aspect. Sergio Donati, Sollima's collaborator, thought *Face to Face* was too political: 'I hate films that preach and [with *Face*] Sollima did too much sloganeering', though *Face* remains Sollima's favourite western.

English-language versions were released in 1969. Milian and Berger used their own voices in the English-language print, while the rest of the cast was dubbed. Like *The Big Gundown*, *Face to Face* suffered a 'hatchet job' on international release. In the UK, the appropriately named Butchers Film Corporation decided to carve out 15 minutes of footage from the 107-minute film, leaving the first half of the film with little gunplay and the story with numerous loose ends. The cuts are made even more obvious by Sollima's technique of overlapping dialogue between scenes; in the shorter version, voices snap off mid-sentence or appear from nowhere without relevance to the scenes they accompany. Elsewhere, people recover from bullet wounds instantly and characters appear and disappear without explanation.

There were six major cuts made to *Face to Face* for its English-language release: the scene in a woodland shack (where Beau removes a bullet from his side and Brad has a coughing fit); Brad and Beau's subsequent dialogue in the wood; a conversation between Max's sister and Brad at De Winton's; the shootout between Bennett's Raiders and a posse outside the De Winton's mansion; and the duel between Brad and Beau at Puerto Del Fuego. The gunfight is a major turning point for both protagonists: Brad is capable of drawing on someone with intent to kill (the law of self-preservation) and Beau realises that he is becoming alienated from his own men. The Willow Creek robbery was considerably abridged, while many other scenes were slightly trimmed.

Though *Face to Face* has been more widely screened since its original release, *Gundown* is the better known and more commercially successful of the two, especially in the UK and the US, where *Face* failed to find an audience. In Italy and throughout Europe, it solidified Milian as a top attraction, while continuing to bolster Volonte's popularity and break his typecasting as a bandit/Latino/Mafia-type. The duo appeared together in a thriller, *The Violent Four* (1968); this time on opposite sides of the law. William Berger's career blossomed, and soon after his appearance as Siringo he appeared in Gianfranco Parolini's *Sartana* (1968), which led to his most famous role as Banjo, Lee Van Cleef's roguish partner in Parolini's seminal, acrobatic spaghetti western *Sabata* (1969).

While Milian continued to appear in westerns, cultivating his Cuchillo peon persona into a political icon, Volonte became a rather more serious political symbol. He abandoned the genre that had established his name internationally and embarked on a series of intellectually revered films rooted in Italian politics, which were less financially successful than his westerns. These films, detailing the intricacies of domestic government and business, meant little outside Italy; an export market that would enjoy the simple action of *The Big Gundown* and *Face to Face* wouldn't bother with the contemporary intrigues Volonte was involved in throughout the seventies. It was only his appearance in *Investigation of a Citizen above Suspicion* (1970) that met with worldwide success (even garnering the Best Foreign Film Oscar). *Face to Face* again demonstrated how successful the pseudo-political westerns could be. Though Sollima made one more western (*Run Man Run* in 1968) and several more political films, including *Violent City* (1970 – with Charles Bronson) and *Revolver* (1973 – with Oliver Reed), he never topped his opening salvo of westerns, *Face to Face* representing the intellectual spaghetti western.

15

'I'll Kill You Any Way You Want'

— Tonino Valerii's *Day of Anger* (1967)

Day of Anger (1967)
original title: *I Giorni dell'Ira*
Credits
DIRECTOR – Tonino Valerii
PRODUCERS – Alfonso Sansone and Enrico Chroscicki
STORY – Ron Barker
SCREENPLAY – Ernesto Gastaldi, Renzo Genta and Tonino Valerii
ART DIRECTOR – Piero Filippone
COSTUMES – Carlo Simi
EDITOR – Franco Fraticelli
DIRECTOR OF PHOTOGRAPHY – Enzo Serafin
MUSIC – Riz Ortolani
Interiors filmed at Cinecitta Film Studios, Rome
Techniscope/Technicolor
An Italian/German co-production
Sancrosiap (Rome)/Corona Film (Berlin)/KG Davina Film
    (Munich)
Released internationally by National General Pictures
    (US)/Warner Pathé (UK)
Cast
  Lee Van Cleef (Frank Talby); Giuliano Gemma (Scott Mary);
  Walter Rilla (Murph Allen Short); Andrea Bosic (Abel
  Murray); Lukas Amman (Judge Cutcher); Ennio Balbo
  (Turner, the banker); Jose Calvo (Bill); Christa Linder
  (Gwen); Al Mulock (Wild Jack); Yvonne Sanson (Vivian
  Steel); Benito Stefanelli (Owen, the hired gun); Franco
  Balducci (Slim); Paolo Magalotti (Cross, the deputy);
  Riccardo Palacios (barman in Bowie); Romano Puppo (Harve
  Perkins); Hans Otto Alberty (Sam Corbitt, the barber);

Nazzareno Natale and Sergio Mendizabal (Wild Jack's
henchmen); Virginio Gazzolo (Mr Barton, the gunsmith);
Vladimir Medar (Old Man Perkins); Mauro Mannatrizio
(Mackenzie Perkins) with Giorgio Gargiullo, Anna Orso,
Nino Nini, Eleonora Morana, Giorgio Di Segni and
Christian Consola

*   *   *

The most common criticism of director Tonino Valerii's work is that he has emulated his mentor, Sergio Leone. Valerii's second Italian western, *Day of Anger*, does little to contradict this. After working as Leone's assistant on *A Fistful of Dollars* and *For a Few Dollars More*, Valerii made his directorial debut with *For the Taste of Killing* (1966 – also released as *Lanky Fellow*). The plot adds a clever twist to the standard bounty-hunter picture. A lone gunman named Hank 'Lanky' Fellows makes a living shadowing Union army convoys transporting bank reserves across the southwest. When bandits steal the shipments, Fellows tracks them down and cashes in on the rewards. Fellows was played by American Craig Hill in his first spaghetti western; he went on to star in many more western adventures, including the Civil War revenge film *I Want Him Dead* (1968), his best film.

What sets *For the Taste of Killing* apart from other spaghetti westerns are a memorable score by Nico Fidenco and Valerii's imaginative creation of a Leone-esque atmosphere on a limited budget; Valerii used Carlo Simi's El Paso set as Omaha, with the blockhouse bank again the target for marauding bandits. *For the Taste of Killing* ends with a cynical joke. Fellows collects his reward and then shadows the army convoy into the mountains, where, just like the opening sequence, he spots a bandit gang lying in wait. He levers his rifle (as though to intervene), but then smiles and rides away as the bandits attack the troops.

Its success assured Valerii a better package for his next film, *I Giorni dell'Ira* (literally 'The Days of Anger'). Instead of a little-known star and a bunch of Italian 'B-movie' stalwarts, Valerii was assured two extremely popular leads – Lee Van Cleef and Giuliano Gemma – and an international supporting cast. The financiers behind *Day of Anger* (as the film was titled for English-language release) were the team of Alfonso Sansone and Enrico Chroscicki, fronting their Rome-based company Sancrosiap (an acronym of their names). Many of Van Cleef's mid-sixties films (*Day of Anger*, *Beyond the Law* and *Commandos*) were Italian/German co-productions, though the location shoots were still in Italy and Spain.

Day of Anger is based on the German novel, *Der Tod ritt Dienstags* ('Death Rode on Tuesday') by Ron Barker, but it owed much to Leone's *For a Few Dollars More* and Petroni's *Death Rides a Horse*. It chronicles the parallel rise to notoriety of two men: Scott Mary, an orphan who is treated like an outcast by the respectable citizens of Clifton City, and Frank Talby, a gunman with a hatred of the law. *Anger* is also the clearest example of the 'master gunman and protégé' scenario that became a spaghetti-western staple. The screenplay was written by Ernesto Gastaldi, Renzo Genta and Tonino Valerii. On his released from prison after a ten-year stretch, Talby arrives in Clifton City and takes victimised Scott under his wing. Talby teaches Scott a series of lessons in gunlaw and Scott, exploited by the townspeople's petty prejudices all his life, is an apt pupil. Talby shows Scott how to shoot, makes him feel important, and armed with a new Colt and nine lessons ('The Gospel According To Talby'), lets Scott loose on the town he hates.

Talby has an old score to settle with the 'honest rich bastards' of Clifton City, concerning a $50,000 train hold-up in Abilene. Talby's then-partner Wild Jack was double-crossed by his accomplices from Clifton. Turner, the city banker, knew of the gold shipment; Judge Cutcher was going to provide Jack's alibi; the saloonkeeper Abel Murray was driving the train and rancher Bill Farrell was the commander of the garrison on board. With this incriminating information Talby blackmails the citizens until he becomes an all-powerful figure in town. He uses Scott to get established and brings in some of his old gang members as hired guns. But through Scott's association with elderly Murph Allen, an ex-lawman, Scott sees the error of his ways. In the big shootout, Scott wipes out Talby and his gang, after Murph has been shot down in the street.

By 1967 Van Cleef was a huge star, appearing in the top five list of box-office draws in Europe. His next project again called for him to have a younger, teen-appeal sidekick, and Gemma was the perfect choice for Scott. Muscleman epics, including *Sons of Thunder* (1962) and *Hercules Against the Sons of the Sun* (1964), and sci-fi films like *Battle of the Worlds* (1961 – also called *Planet of the Lifeless Men*) familiarised audiences with Gemma's persona. His appeal led to him being cast as the lead in modest swashbuckling adventures (such as *Erik the Viking* – 1964) and some of the first Italian westerns. Tessari's 'Ringo' films made him a star overnight, but inside eighteen months Gemma took his charming Ringo persona as far as he could and needed a new slant on the eager young hotshot; *Anger* turned out to be the ideal milieu for this change. Scott Mary is an outcast dressed in rags, reduced to sweeping the streets and collecting barrels of sewage from the local businesses. Scott is called a 'bastard' because of his illegitimacy, and his only friends in town are a beggar named Bill, Vivian, the madame of the local brothel and Murph Allen Short, an ex-sheriff reduced to working as a stable hand. Gemma had briefly experimented with this downtrodden characterisation in his previous film, *The Long Days of Vengeance* (1966). Here Gemma, as the hero Ted Barratt, escaped from a chain gang in the desert to track down his father's killers. Virtually unrecognisable, Gemma looks like a cross between Man Friday and Jesus. Luckily, the first villain on his hit list is a barber.

If Gemma had a change of character in *Anger*, Van Cleef was back in familiar territory. American advertising material alluded to *The Good, the Bad and the Ugly*: 'Lee Van Cleef has been dirty, "ugly" and downright mean…Now watch him get violent!' Valerii cast German Lukas Amman as Judge Cutcher and 72-year-old character actor Walter Rilla as stable hand Murph. Rilla had worked in Britain since the thirties and was the father of director Wolff Rilla, who made *Village of the Damned* (1960). Other roles were taken by Italian and Spanish actors, including Ennio Balbo and Riccardo Palacios (reprising his bartender role from *For a Few Dollars More*). Palacios (real name Ricardo Lopez-Nuno Diez) went on to appear in several Van Cleef westerns, including *El Condor* (1970), *Captain Apache* (1971), *Blood Money* (1974) and *Take a Hard Ride* (1975).

Yugoslavian Andrea Bosic (cast as saloon-owner Abel Murray) frequently appeared in westerns, often as the mastermind behind a spate of robberies. Despite his grimace, Bosic could also play sympathetic parts and featured in several non-western productions. These included two Sandokan jungle adventures (with Bosic kitted out in a safari suit and pith helmet), *Romulus and Remus* (1961) and *Danger: Diabolik* (1968). He also made *Master Stroke* (1966) with spaghetti-western star Richard Harrison headlined as 'Master Stroke', a spaghetti-western star (and master of disguise) who is hired by the British Secret Service to break up a spy ring.

There were also many of Leone's actors employed on *Anger*: Al Mulock (unbilled in the Italian version), Benito Stefanelli (also stunts), Romano Puppo (Van Cleef's stunt-double) and Jose Calvo (from *A Fistful of Dollars*). Mulock's role as Wild Jack was one of his last film appearances; he committed suicide in Almeria the following year by throwing himself out of a hotel window in full western costume during the making of *Once Upon a Time in the West*. Franco Balducci appeared in *Anger* as Talby's cohort, Slim. Balducci's early roles included *Romulus and Remus*, *Son of Spartacus* (1962) and Benvolio in *Romeo and Juliet* (1964).

Stuntman Benito Stefanelli was cast as hired gun Owen, who is employed by the dignitaries to kill Talby. Black-frock-coated Owen (called White in the original Italian version) was based on Colonel Douglas Mortimer in *For a Few Dollars More*. Stefanelli successfully transferred from muscleman epics to westerns. On the epics he often worked as the 'Master at Arms', 'Stunt Co-ordinator' and 'Weapons Consultant'. His work on westerns continued this, and he choreographed many bar-room brawls and action scenes. He featured in *Son of Spartacus* (in which he blackened his face as the leader of the leopardskin-clad Iscian warriors) and *The Trojan War* (1961). His western debut was in *Red Pastures* (1963), in which he choreographed his punch-up with James Mitchum. Stefanelli then adopted the pseudonym 'Benny Reeves', appearing as such in *Fistful* and others, before reverting to his own name on *For a Few Dollars More*.

Day of Anger is set in the borderlands of Arizona and New Mexico. Clifton, Arizona is to the west of the Little Burro Mountains; the village of Bowie is about fifty miles further south, while Stafford's roughly between the two. Abilene, the site of the train hold-up, is in Kansas. Location photography was done in Spain, with Valerii using locations he had scouted two years earlier as Leone's assistant. The peasant village of Los Albaricoques (previously Agua Caliente in *For a Few Dollars*

More) became Wild Jack's hideout, Bowie – the exterior of the cantina doubling as its equivalent in *Anger*. Less obvious is the setting used for Bill Farrell's Stafford ranch, which was at El Sotillo in San Jose, from the opening scene of *A Fistful of Dollars*. For *Anger* the two houses were linked by an arch to give the impression of one property. The huge, stone corn-threshing circle where Wild Jack's men drag Talby (actually stuntman Romano Puppo) behind their horses recalls the duel in the circle in *For a Few*.

Clifton City was at Cinecitta Studios in Rome. The western set was considerably revamped for Valerii's movie, with the addition of picket fences and the Judge's grand-looking residence. The saloon was destroyed by fire as part of the action during the film – Talby torches it. This is a rare occurrence in Italian westerns, as the sets were reused so frequently and the cost of repair was a wasteful addition to the budget. Talby builds the .45 Saloon in its place, and Piero Filippone's opulent design incorporates huge wooden carvings of pistols as pillars on the veranda, which gives the town a surreal, cartoon quality for the grand finale.

Day of Anger borrowed from the cheaper Italian 'B-westerns': most of the film takes place on a single town set and the majority of the action is decidedly low-key, with few elaborate set pieces. One exception is a horseback 'joust' between Talby and hired gun Owen, which was choreographed by Benito Stefanelli. The two ride towards each other at breakneck speed, whilst trying to prime muzzle-loading, cap-and-ball rifles; the scene was filmed in a vast Almerian plain, with Romano Puppo doubling for Van Cleef in the long shots. Though Valerii tries to detract from the static plot, this doesn't prevent the Clifton City setting becoming overly familiar. In the sequences at Bowie and at Farrell's Ranch, the atmosphere is unmistakably Leone-esque; the whitewashed buildings, sparse desert, fruit trees and blue sky are much more engaging and hint at what might have been, had Valerii not been overly concerned with events in Clifton.

Van Cleef's first entrance into Clifton City recalls his many appearances as an outlaw in fifties westerns. As he purposefully rides down the street (accompanied by a menacing electric guitar riff), Valerii cuts closer to the mean-looking stranger. Van Cleef had rode threateningly into town many times before – in *High Noon*, *Gunfight at the OK Corral* and *Day of the Badman* – but *Anger* was the first time since his European resurrection. In the Hollywood versions, pounding brass or drums accompanied his ride, filmed as a tracking shot; in *Anger*, the sequence is more stylised, the staccato guitar and camera style more dramatic and Van Cleef's grimace much more ominous.

For *Anger*, Van Cleef abandoned some of his familiar props. Out went the flat-brimmed black hat and cross-belly draw holster, only the Meerschaum pipe remained. When Talby arrives in town, he looks like a down-at-heel gunman, but as he and Scott get established in town, their taste in clothes changes to reflect their standing in the township: Talby goes from shootist to black-suited gambling-house proprietor, while Scott's progression is literally a rags-to-riches tale.

Scott's story recounts his relationships with two men on either side of the law – Murph and Talby. Both are father-figures to Scott and both advise the youngster throughout the film; Murph warns of the dangers of becoming a gunman, while Talby proffers the advantages. Talby teaches the juvenile eight lessons, including 'Never trust anyone' and 'Never leave an opponent wounded'. At the climax, Talby adds a final lesson: when you start killing, you can't stop, this is the last lesson Talby ever preaches.

These lessons encapsulate the code of Italian westerns. This is a feature peculiar to Valerii's work; his westerns, particularly *Anger* and *My Name is Nobody* (1973), are as much about western films as they are about the west itself. Although Talby's creed is cynical, it has a bizarre logic. The man with no name and Django play by these rules, only more traditional western heroes like Giuliano Gemma's Ringo don't. The lessons aspect of *Anger* is only partially successful. When Scott faces Talby's gang, he repeats each of Talby's lessons as he kills his opponents; the confrontation becomes contrived and spoils the irony of Scott using Talby's lessons against his own men.

Original UK/US poster for Tonino Valerii's *Day of Anger* (1967), featuring Lee Van Cleef as Frank Talby.

Ex-lawman Murph is tired of talking about the 'good old days' of the old west. He tells Scott that once a good pistol was worth more than money in the bank, but nowadays gunmen like Talby rely on cheap tricks: Scott must learn them, or risk ending up on Boot Hill. Murph tells Scott that Talby is bad company, and Scott eventually sees that the old man has a point. Following Murph's death, Scott discovers that the old man has bequeathed him 'Doc' Holliday's pistol, which is equal to Talby's. After the final duel, Scott looks at Murph's corpse outside the saloon and says, 'You won, Murph'.

The rotten neighbourhood of Clifton City is something of a departure for Italian western towns. Previously, settlements were either peacefully law-abiding or ruled by a local bandit warlord or crooked businessman. Clifton is neither; it is the quietest town to appear in an Italian western. The overweight sheriff doesn't carry a gun (claiming his star is 'worth more than fancy hardware') and the gunsmith is low on ammunition. The town of Clifton itself is pristine, with no hint of the immorality lurking behind the neat, white picket fences.

Valerii's film incorporates a morality tale subplot. For the Abilene train hold-up to succeed, outlaw Wild Jack has employed four respectable Clifton citizens ('clean hands') to help him. The job works, but the respectable quartet testifies against Jack. As revenge, Talby 'inherits' Jack's vendetta and returns to Clifton in Jack's place to stir-up trouble. With enough information to dirty the clean hands of the townspeople, he establishes himself in town. The real prize for Talby is the judge: Talby needs justice on his side. In the showdown it is Scott alone against Talby, his toughs and the judge. True justice prevails and the judge is one of the first casualties of Scott's newly virtuous gun.

Each of the main characters is identified by his six-shooter. Talby has a customised Colt .45, with two inches of the barrel missing and no sight. Scott and Murph have standard Colts (with seven-inch barrels). In the gunsmiths, Talby deliberately discards three short-barrelled pistols and chooses Scott the longest, slowing down his quick-draw. Previously, Scott has honed his skill with a carved wooden pistol and a holster held up with rope. Hired gun Owen favours specialist hardware, while the sheriff prefers a shotgun – an authentic piece of period detail, as lawmen in the real west preferred 'scatter guns' for close shooting. At one point Talby boasts, 'The weapon that's gonna kill me hasn't been invented yet', a variation on a quote from Dallas Stoudenmire (a Marshall of El Paso in the 1880s), who claimed, 'I don't believe the bullet was ever moulded that will kill me'; like Talby, he was wrong. Not until the final showdown, when Scott uses 'Doc' Holliday's customised gun, does Talby face an equivalent weapon: on equal terms, Scott is faster.

The music for *Day of Anger* was composed by Riz Ortolani, who sometimes signed himself as 'Roger Higgins'. He rose to prominence with his score for Gualtiero Jacopetti's notorious 'shockumentary' *Mondo Cane* (1963), which detailed various unsavoury customs from around the world. Ortolani was nominated for an Oscar for 'More', his hit song from the film, though sickened audiences would no doubt have preferred 'Less'. Ortolani has three styles of scoring: expansive, Hollywood-style string compositions (as in *Beyond the Law*); loose, jazzy workouts (the main title music to *Day of Anger*) and jagged, suspenseful guitar pieces. Ortolani liked the big-band sound, and much of his work features jazz percussion, off-kilter guitar motifs and swathes of wailing brass, resembling Neil Hefti's score to *Duel at Diablo* (1965). *Day of Anger*'s main title music begins with a tumbling, spiky electric guitar riff, punctuated by snare rolls and blasts of brass. Following this fifteen-second barrage, the piece settles down into a catchy groove, with a jaunty guitar melody backed by breezy brass and mellifluous strings, which is cut to the animated title sequence, as gunshots ricochet over the music.

The other prevalent piece is 'To the Last Shot', Ortolani's punchy variation on Morricone's trumpet 'gundown' music from *A Fistful of Dollars*, which is used in the final gun battle through the streets of Clifton City. But it is the recurrent electric guitar riff that is most memorable – whether scoring Talby's arrival in town or a hired gun stepping down from the stage. These discordant strings, backing a guitar riff or rumbling brass, are ever-present in Ortolani's work, whether westerns (*Requiescant* and *Massacre at Fort Holman*), war films (the embarkation scene of *Anzio*) or thrillers (*The Valachi Papers*). Ortolani's score also reinforces the best gag in a film noticeably lacking in humour. As Talby rides through the desert, he is accompanied by the brassy 'riding theme', while Scott (in hot pursuit on a ragged mule) is accompanied by a knockabout, banjo-led version of the same piece.

Even though the European market was swamped with westerns by 1967, a strongly plotted, well-cast film could still be a box-office hit. When *Day of Anger* was released in Italy in December 1967, much was made of the teaming of Van Cleef and Gemma, two of the biggest names in European cinema. Interestingly, their billing differed for separate markets; Gemma was top-billed in Italy and Spain, while Van Cleef starred in the US and the UK (each print's animated title sequence was altered accordingly). The film was named after its literary source in Germany (*Der Tod rit Dienstag*), while in France it was released as *Le Dernier Jour de la Colere* ('The Last Day of Anger') and *On M'Appelle Saligo* (a slang reference, roughly 'They Call Me Bastard'). Business in Europe went through the roof, and it was the equal-top-grossing film in Italy in 1967 with Giuseppe Colizzi's western *God Forgives – I Don't*, starring Terence Hill and Bud Spencer.

When *Anger* was released internationally in 1970, it also made money in the UK and the US, earning $2 million in the US alone. *Day of Anger* circulated in two versions: the uncut 110-minute print and a crudely edited 85-minute version (known variously as *The Days of Wrath* and *Gunlaw*), which lost several scenes of action and plot development, though the beginning and end were generously left intact. In the cut version, the film (like its low-budget cousins) became a series of disconnected action set pieces; in the full version, the action sequences (separated by extended dialogue scenes) represent increased desperation on the part of the town dignitaries to oust Talby's tyrant.

Some scenes were removed for censorship reasons, like the beating inflicted on Scott by Wild Jack. In the cut version Wild Jack packs a considerable punch: from one blow Scott has blood pouring from his mouth, a thick lip and is knocked unconscious (in the full version he has been savagely kicked and punched several times). The horseback duel between Talby and Owen was also trimmed down. Other cuts include Talby's arrival in the Mexican village of Bowie; Scott and Talby's visit to the gunsmith; their target practice outside the barber's; the brief relationship between Scott and the judge's traitorous daughter; Scott being ambushed and his pivotal recovery scenes in a brothel; and the arrival of Talby's four henchmen (who materialise without explanation in the 85-minute print).

If *Anger* borrowed elements from *For a Few Dollars More* and Petroni's *Death Rides a Horse*, it was influential in its own right. The apprenticeship of a youngster to a master gunman reappeared in many sixties and seventies spaghetti westerns, with Massimo Dallamano's *Bandidos* (1967) the best example. After having his hands crippled, shootist Richard Martin (Enrico Maria Salerno) is working as a barker in a travelling circus and teaches an escaped convict how to shoot: apparently for their side-show act, but really to get revenge on the man who shot him in both hands. This apprenticeship was later parodied in *Man of the East* (1972). Terence Hill plays an effete English aristocrat who reads poetry and arrives in California complete with deerstalker, butterfly net and bicycle. Along the way he is taught the ways of the west by a trio of outlaws. Hill's education as a westerner is well spoofed (at one point he warns a villain, 'I'll flatten you like a bookmark'), while the sharpshooting scenes are similarly parodic; when he's taught to quick-draw, Hill observes, 'Speed plus action equals x plus y, or power developed, which you cannot detect, because the energy factor is unknown to us', which added 'gunslinging as science' to the genre.

Another interesting low-budget variation on the master gunman and protégé scenario was Nando Cicero's *Time of Vultures* (1967 – also called *Last of the Badmen*). Here, Frank Wolff (as the master gunman, 'Black' Tracy) hitches up with George Hilton (as the novice, Kitosh). Tracy is one of the most screwed-up Italian western heroes of all time. He dresses completely in black, is epileptic, rides around on a hearse (with his dead mother in a coffin on the back) and is armed with a primitive rocket-launcher. Tracy breaks out of prison so that he can bury his mother on the site of their ranch, and in the finale tracks down the villain Big John (Franco Balducci) and crucifies him to a door.

After *Anger*'s success, Van Cleef's next western, Giorgio Stegani's *Beyond the Law* (1968) was awful, with the actor attempting a comedy western. Van Cleef played Joe Billy Cudlip, a moth-eaten outlaw who steals payrolls bound for Silvertown. Through his relationship with a Czechoslovakian mine administrator (Antonio Sabato), Cudlip begins to change his lawless ways and inadvertently ends up sheriff (complete with Bat Masterson tweed suit and bowler hat), whereupon his outlaw friends disown him. *Beyond*'s best feature is the villain, Burton (Gordon Mitchell in a sinister black cape), who has his eyes on a wagonload of silver. During a community dance his gang sidle into town and take a church congregation hostage. But Sheriff Cudlip galvanises the community and wipes out the bandits in a lively shootout. Also known as *For a Fistful of Silver*, one minute the film is slapstick (complete with comedy banjo on the soundtrack), the next a tough action film. Van Cleef is completely wasted and Bud Spencer looks ill at ease without Terence Hill (and almost unrecognisable without a beard). Clint Eastwood had left Italy as soon as he had finished his third western for Leone; *Day of Anger* was Van Cleef's fifth western in three years, and though they had all been popular *Beyond the Law* saw a fall in takings.

With *Day of Anger*, Gemma had his biggest hit since the 'Ringo' films, but like Van Cleef he saw the need to diversify, shifting from acrobatic action to comedy, with westerns like *Alive, or Preferably Dead* (1969) and the caveman comedy *When Women Had Tails* (1970). His last decent western role came in Tonino Valerii's *The Price of Power* (1969). Gemma had a great affinity with the genre and was one of

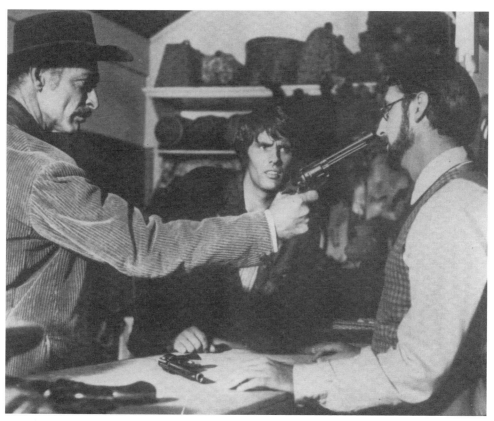

Talby holds up the Clifton City gunsmith, while Scott looks on (left to right: Lee Van Cleef, Giuliano Gemma and Virginio Gazzolo).

the few Italian actors to continue making westerns throughout the seventies and into the eighties, with Lucio Fulci's *Silver Saddle* (1978) and Duccio Tessari's comic-strip *Tex and the Lord of the Deep* (1985). In Italy Gemma was known as 'The King of the Italian Western'; he was one of the biggest stars of the genre – perhaps not as big in the UK or the US, but nevertheless a key figure in sixties westerns. Outside the 'Ringo' films, *Day of Anger* is Gemma's best work, and it is a key film for Van Cleef too. It partly inspired the blackmailing spaghetti western *Sabata* (1969), Van Cleef's international box-office salvation during his fallow period following *Day of Anger*.

16

'Since When Are Wolves Afraid of Wolves?'

— Sergio Corbucci's *The Big Silence* (1967)

The Big Silence (1967)
original title: *Il Grande Silenzio*
Credits
DIRECTOR – Sergio Corbucci
STORY – Sergio Corbucci
SCREENPLAY – Vittoriano Petrilli, Mario Amendola, Sergio and
    Bruno Corbucci
ART DIRECTOR – Riccardo Dominici
COSTUMES – Enrico Job
EDITOR – Amedeo Salfa
DIRECTOR OF PHOTOGRAPHY – Silvano Ippoliti
MUSIC COMPOSER – Ennio Morricone
MUSIC CONDUCTOR – Bruno Nicolai
Interiors filmed at Elios Film Studios, Rome
Eastmancolor
An Italian/French co-production
Adelphia Compagnia Cinematografica (Rome)/Les Films
    Corona (Paris)
Released internationally by 20th Century Fox
Cast
    Jean-Louis Trintignant (Silence); Klaus Kinski (Loco); Frank
    Wolff (Sheriff Gideon Burnett); Luigi Pistilli (Henry
    Pollicut, the Justice of the Peace); Vonetta McGee (Pauline
    Middleton); Mario Brega (Martin); Marisa Merlini (Regina,
    the madam); Bruno Corrazzari (Charlie); Raf Baldassare
    (Sanchez's brother); Spartaco Conversi (Walter, the outlaw
    leader); Carlo D'Angelo (territorial governor); Remo De
    Angelis (sheriff in flashback); Mirella Pamphili (Silence's
    mother); Loris Loddi (Silence as a boy); Mauro Mannatrizio

(Jack, gambler in saloon); Mimmo Poli (Snow Hill dignitary);
Jacques Toulouse (Al, the sheriff); Werner Pochat (first
outlaw); Maria Mizar (outlaw's mother); Marisa Sally
(blonde prostitute); Fortunato Arena (outlaw in earmuffs);
Gino Barbacane (blond bounty-hunter); Claudio Ruffini
(bearded bounty-hunter); Bruno Ukmar (bounty-hunter in
sheepskin coat); Benito Pacifico (stagecoach driver)

*   *   *

By 1967, most Italian western directors realised that to ensure international distribution (and maximum revenue) it would be better if all the main actors spoke English. To an extent, this disguised the films' origins – the unsynchronised dubbing was often their biggest failing. When a spaghetti western was edited together, five dubbed versions would be prepared in English, French, German, Spanish and Italian; any other European-language releases would be subtitled. The Paris-based production company Les Films Corona wanted to make a western with Jean-Louis Trintignant, one of their biggest stars, but he couldn't speak English. This was often surmounted by actors learning their lines phonetically. Bit players were even known to count out loud or recite the alphabet (just to make their lips move), while other directors filmed their actors from the back during dialogue scenes, dispensing with the need for lip synchronisation altogether. But Sergio Corbucci hit upon a foolproof idea – a mute hero.

Sergio Corbucci's *The Big Silence* (also called *The Great Silence*) is Corbucci's most uncompromising western, an inversion of Italian western conventions: a spaghetti western not set in the desert, with Leone's heroic bounty-hunters cast as unscrupulous, amoral villains, who kill the martyred hero in the nihilistic finale. *The Big Silence*'s story was written by Corbucci, who wrote the screenplay with Vittoriano Petrilli, Mario Amendola and Corbucci's brother, Bruno. Clint Eastwood's taciturn hero in the 'Dollars' films became Silence, the mute gunslinger who cripples his enemies by shooting off their thumbs.

In the terrible winter of 1898, Loco and his bounty killers find easy pickings among the starving outlaws hiding in the snowbound mountains of Utah. Pauline, the wife of one of Loco's victims, hires Silence to kill Loco. She has been told he 'avenges injustice and defends the innocent'. But when Silence arrives in the town of Snow Hill, he also has a score to settle with Pollicut, the local Justice of the Peace, who was partly responsible for the death of Silence's parents when Silence was a boy. Loco drowns the Sheriff of Snow Hill in a frozen lake and Silence kills Pollicut, but in the struggle has his gun hand badly burned. Loco and his men round up the starving outlaws (who come to town with the promise of food) and take them hostage in the saloon. Silence goes to face Loco, but one of Loco's men shoots Silence in his uninjured hand and then Loco kills the defenceless man.

Pauline runs to Silence's corpse, takes his pistol and tries to kill Loco, but he shoots her too. Before leaving town Loco's men slaughter the hostages in the saloon – 'All according to the law,' notes Loco.

Though rooted in sixties Italian action cinema, *The Big Silence* owes much to two films: *Day of the Outlaw* (1959) and *Black Sabbath* (1963). The former, directed by Andre De Toth, was a black-and-white snowbound western starring Robert Ryan (as Blaze Starrett). The first half of the film is set in Bitters, an isolated Wyoming settlement, which is disrupted by the arrival of seven outlaws on the run from the cavalry with a stolen army payroll. Corbucci emulated the authentic-looking interiors and stark exteriors, especially when Starrett guides the outlaws through a little-known route in the mountains – ostensibly to save the outlaws, but really to get them out of town. The gang, led by Captain Bruhn (Burl Ives), could easily have appeared in *Silence*; one of the outlaws, Tex (Jack Lambert), clearly influenced face-shrouded Loco. With *Silence*, Corbucci, like Leone before him, took his tiniest favourite moments from fifties westerns. The ending of *Day of the Outlaw* is downbeat; the last two villains die of frostbite, though Starrett does make it back to town.

It was also the 42-minute 'Wurdulak' segment of Mario Bava's three-part film *Black Sabbath* that inspired Corbucci. A nobleman, Count Vladimir D'Urfé (Mark Damon) discovers the headless corpse of Alibek (a Turkish bandit) in the snowbound mountains on his way to Yessey. He takes it to a nearby peasant house, where he finds a family living in fear. Their father, an old man named Gorka (Boris Karloff), has been hunting for the bandit for days and is due back at ten o'clock that night; Alibek is a wurdulak (a vampire): 'a cadaver always seeking blood'. If Gorka hasn't returned by the appointed hour, his family must kill him, as he has been vampirised too. The bell tolls and seconds later Gorka clomps across the rickety bridge with Alibek's head and announces, 'I am hungry'. He seems normal, but his dog howls at his approach, leading the family to be suspicious. It is the detail of Bava's film that informed Corbucci's *mise-en-scène*. Karloff's performance as Gorka, draped in a fur-hooded black cloak, is menacing, and the eerie landscape, with its whistling wind, howling dogs and perpetually drifting fog is suitably creepy. The peasants hang the bandit's head outside the house and the family's little grandson is vampirised by Gorka and then rises from the dead, crying out, 'Mama, I'm cold, let me in', with macabre consequences. The entire story takes place one terrible night, and by dawn everyone is a wurdulak except Vladimir – and he soon will be.

In *The Big Silence* Corbucci also includes the warring factions fighting over a town from *A Fistful of Dollars*, while the downbeat finale is a replay of his own *Minnesota Clay* (though Clay died after defeating the villains). Corbucci never made sequels to his own westerns, though early in his career he directed and wrote 'follow-ups' to other people's – *Goliath and the Vampires* (1961), *Son of Spartacus* (1962) and the retitling of *Johnny Oro* to *Ringo and his Golden Pistol*. The simple explanation for this is that too many characters got killed. *Silence* is the epitome of this, with all the main characters except the villain ending up dead.

Jean-Louis Trintignant had become an international star the previous year, in the tragic love story *A Man and a Woman*. In *The Big Silence* he again found himself in a heart-rending relationship that was doomed from the start, here with black actress Vonetta McGee, making her film debut as Pauline. Klaus Kinski portrayed bounty-hunter Loco, while Corbucci added depth to the drama with some well-chosen supporting players. Villainous Bruno Corrazzari, an Italian actor often compared to Kinski, was cast as Loco's 'heavy', Charlie. Luigi Pistilli was cast as the thumbless Justice of the Peace, Pollicut. Bit parts were taken by established names: Mario Brega (as Pollicut's sidekick Martin), Spartaco Conversi (the leader of the fugitive outlaws), Marisa Merlini (saloon madam Regina), Raf Baldassare (as a wall-eyed bounty-hunter) and Carlo D'Angelo (who sometimes used the pseudonym 'Charles of Angel'). D'Angelo played a corrupt governor who would offer an amnesty to the murderer of his own father 'if he thought it would win him an election'.

Corbucci cast Frank Wolff, usually a villain, as ex-army Sheriff Burnett, a 'rules and regulations' man who plays it by the book. Wolff moved to Rome after parts in three low-budget Roger Corman films – *The Wasp Woman* (1959), *Ski Troop Attack* (1960) and the muscleman film *Atlas* (1960). He started off in fifties 'B-westerns' (he played a moustachioed henchman in Audie Murphy's *The Wild and the Innocent* – 1959), but his breakthrough was in the acclaimed Italian political film *Salvatore Giuliano* (1961). He soon found his niche in spaghetti westerns, and though he cropped up in many forgettable, low-budget productions, he found a degree of fame in some big successes, including *God Forgives – I Don't* (1967 – as the chief villain Bill San Antonio), *Kill Them All and Come Back Alone* (1968 – as Captain Lynch, a traitorous Unionist posing as a Confederate) and *Once Upon a Time in the West* (1968 – as redheaded Irish patriarch Brett McBain). Tragically, Wolff committed suicide in 1971.

Location shooting took place near the ski resort of Cortina D'Ampezzo, in the Veneto region of northern Italy. In one of the most beautiful valleys in the Alps, part of the Snow Hill set was constructed, with Alpine roofs and log cabins. The surrounding hills were used for the other location scenes – the bounty-hunters' shack, the way station, the stagecoach route and the graveyard. In his autobiography, *Kinski Uncut*, Klaus Kinski recalls his on-set affair with actress 'Sherene Miller', while his wife Biggi and daughter (future actress Nastassja) enjoyed sledding in the snow on location. After the Cortina shoot, the crew returned to Italy; the ranch in *Silence*'s flashback was at Bracciano Lake, near Manziana in Lazio. The Elios town set in Rome was used for several Snow Hill scenes, including two night sequences and the build-up to the final duel. The scenes were shot at night so that the fake 'snow' looked more convincing; shaving foam was used to give the street a snow-bound look. For the daylight scenes, the Elios set was swathed in fog, to disguise the fact that the surrounding countryside had no snow.

The Big Silence was shot by Silvano Ippoliti, Corbucci's cameraman from *Navajo Joe*. Ippoliti exploited the tonal contrast between the dark trees, Alpine-style houses and white valleys of fog. His sharp cinematography was at its best on location in the mountains and forests of northern Italy, with panoramas of crisp snow edged with frost-dappled spruce, larch and pine. He shot the film in muted greys and blues, with the camera tracking spectral figures in the mist. In one scene a group of famished outlaws gather around a horse that is about to be their next meal. In another, Loco packs the corpses of his victims in ice along a stagecoach route, so that he can pick them up later; with no respect for the dead, he transports them by strapping the dead men to the stagecoach roof.

With its snowy vistas and well-known cast, *The Big Silence* gives the impression that it had a big budget, though a closer look suggests otherwise. There is a great deal of variety in the film stock, and some continuity errors (especially the amount of snow falling in the town scenes). When Loco drags an outlaw behind his horse with a whip, a rope attaching the whip to Loco's saddle is clearly visible. In the sharpshooting contest between the sheriff and Silence outside the post office, their potato targets hurtle towards them (when the bullet impact would have sent them far away), and as Loco rides to meet his gang he passes an Alpine bird-feeder.

Silence's distinctive rapid-firing pistol is the 1896 9mm Mauser Broomhandle. The wooden holster doubles as a detachable shoulder-stock, which converts it into a carbine. It is self-loading and has a ten-round magazine. The trigger can either be pulled like a normal trigger, or the selector switch altered to 'fully automatic'; on this setting, the pistol fires by itself as long as the trigger is held on. This gives the action sequences an added dynamism; Silence's pistol seems to explode to life, spraying bullets as the bounty killers fall left and right. After Loco has killed Silence he steals the precious Mauser.

Hunting the hunters: Silence (Jean-Louis Trintignant) in the opening sequence of *The Big Silence* (1967).

The costumes, designed by Enrico Job (director Lina Wertmüller's future husband) are equally distinctive. Silence wears a furry collared cape, broad-brimmed hat, headscarf and gloves. Loco wears a long fur coat (as do many of his men) and Pollicut sports a Cossack hat. The bandits in the hills are kitted out with the furry leftovers from Italian epics like *Goliath and the Barbarians* (1959) and *Brennus, Enemy of Rome* (1963).

The stone and wooden houses, though often stark, are cosy shelters from the inhospitable climate. Throughout the film, Corbucci films characters looking out through windows at the oppressive landscape; in their homes they find refuge from the cruel winter, the outlaws and Loco. This is in contrast to *Black Sabbath*, in which Bava often filmed the vampires looking into the peasants' house from outside.

The snowy landscape is threatening in its emptiness. A frozen lake becomes the sheriff's tomb, and scythe-carrying, rag-clothed outlaws emerge from the landscape like phantoms. The film's opening sequence, in the snowbound West Plateau establishes this. Silence rides across a valley, where five bounty killers wait in ambush. Silence senses something is amiss and crows caw in the distance as he slowly removes his glove. In a split second he flips open his wooden holster, draws a machine pistol and mows down the bounty-hunters.

Mutes had appeared in spaghettis as incidental characters, in *Blood at Sundown* and *Requiescant* (both 1967); they often held the key to a mystery and solved the case by pointing the villain out. Loco, Silence and the sheriff begin the film sharing a stagecoach to Snow Hill. Loco knows who Silence is ('The mute who shoots thumbs off'), while the sheriff obviously doesn't; he tries to chat to Silence and when they arrive in town, he hopes that Silence will be more talkative next time. When the sheriff later learns that Silence is mute he remarks, 'You could have told me'.

The only words Silence utters are as a child, played in flashback by child actor Loris Loddi (from *The Hills Run Red*). As his mother is shot, he cries out, 'Mama! Mama!', though the English dubbed voice is being reused from the final scene of Corbucci's *Johnny Oro* (1966). Here, the sheriff's son Stan (played by Loddi again) shouts to his mother when he is taken hostage; in the budget cinema of spaghetti westerns, even the soundtrack cues were reused from film to film.

If Pauline's scars are emotional following the death of her husband at the hands of Loco, Silence's past traumas are more apparent. *The Big Silence* is full of striking imagery, but the scar across the hero's throat is the most unsettling. A scar around a protagonist's throat had already appeared in the spaghetti western *My Name is Pecos* (1966). Here, the villain Clane (Piero Vida) has such a wound and is 'halfway to hell' after a bungled hanging; in the finale Pecos finishes the job and throttles him. In flashback we learn that when Silence was a child, he witnessed his parents' deaths at the hands of bounty-hunters posing as lawmen, though Pollicut was behind the crime. To make sure the little witness did not testify, the phoney sheriff (played by Corbucci's regular stuntman, Remo De Angelis) drew his knife and sneered, 'He'll never talk again'. In a later flashback we learn that Silence tracked down his parents' killers to a bordello, where he shot the sheriff, but spared Pollicut's life, shooting the thumb off his gun hand.

Snake-eyed bounty-hunter Loco resembles Gorka from *Black Sabbath*. A vampire is defined as someone who 'preys ruthlessly on others', and Loco fits the bill, as he stalks through the forests. Loco is a bounty-killer who, according to Leone's westerns, is on the side of the law; Loco even has a little black book of bounties, like Colonel Mortimer in *For a Few Dollars More*. Loco believes he is helping the judicial system by killing outlaws. He refers to their corpses as 'freight' and believes they are 'enemies of God and man'; it is his 'patriotic duty' to exterminate them. But because of the outlaws' circumstances, we pity them, even though they are bad men, and Corbucci asks if it is right that the law-enforcing bounty-hunters should win. Corbucci ends the film with his reply to the opening caption of Leone's *For a Few*, which stated 'Where life had no value, death sometimes had its price. That is why the bounty killers appeared.' Silence's closing caption reads in part: 'The massacre of 1898 finally brought forth fierce public condemnation of the bounty killers, who under the guise of legality made violent murder a profitable way of life'.

Corbucci introduces Loco in stylish fashion. A young outlaw, starving and homesick, returns to his mother's house during a blizzard; his mother has hired a lawyer to plead his case. Inside he is introduced to two legal representatives sitting by the fire. Both wear long fur coats, but they are actually bounty-hunters posing as lawyers. 'You're wise to put your trust in the law, boy,' sneers Loco as his accomplice, Charlie, kills the outlaw. Kinski's face is emotionless as he tells the outlaw's mother, 'It's our bread and butter', while Charlie drags the body outside to collect the blood money. Loco not only indiscriminately takes lives, he also destroys loving relationships – between Pauline and her husband; Silence and Pauline; and Sheriff Burnett and Regina, the saloon madam. By the end of the film, all are dead.

The Big Silence is Klaus Kinski's best western performance. Because he wins, Loco is often singled out as the vilest spaghetti-western villain of all. Jack Palance once observed, 'An awful lot of kids grew up [in the fifties] actually liking the bad

Face-shrouded Loco (Klaus Kinski) on the trail of Pauline's husband, in Sergio Corbucci's wintry Italian western *The Big Silence* (1967).

man and hoping the son of a gun would win – but he didn't. I think it would have been nice if one of them had blasted John Wayne out of his saddle.' Kinski's gargoyle face, framed by the black cowl he wears throughout, is ideal for the malevolent hunter Loco – or 'Tigrero' ('the Tiger') as he is called in the original Italian print.

Loco is quite a subdued role for Kinski; his interpretations were usually fierier. Loco rarely loses his temper, even when Silence tries to goad him into a confront-ation in the Snow Hill saloon. Silence approaches a card game between Loco and his thugs, and throws a lit match and a cigar butt in Loco's whisky glass, but Loco knows Silence's tricks. The mute has a reputation for drawing second but shooting first – always in self-defence. So Loco takes off his gunbelt to face Silence unarmed: Silence is faster with a gun, but is no match for Loco's fists.

Silence is summoned to town by Pauline (called Claudine in some prints) to kill Loco. In a desolate cemetery, at her husband's graveside, she explains why: 'Once my husband told me of this man…he avenges our wrongs. They call him Silence, because wherever he goes, the silence of death follows.' Silence is paid to protect the outlaws in the hills, but when Silence tries to kill Loco he is wounded in the shoulder. Pauline nurses him back to health, and in a night of passion they make love. This intimate love scene is the most tender moment in all Corbucci's westerns; two lost souls, brought together by fate and who face an uncertain future, give in to their emotions as the last act of tragic drama. Before the final showdown, Pauline pleads with Silence, 'You're just one man. I don't want you dead…I love you', but like all Corbucci's heroes, he confronts his destiny.

Outside Leone's films, *The Big Silence* is Ennio Morricone's favourite western score. Morricone's music is Silence's voice and the voice of the landscape. From the echoing violin, bells and unsettling twangs that accompany Silence's ride towards the ambush, Morricone's music is an integral part of the film. The main title music is a lush composition that sounds more like the music to a Euro-melodrama; it incorporates a resonant piano note, delicate guitar riff and a tinkling triangle, as soaring violins and the Alessandroni Singers take the melody. Morricone uses some unusual instruments, including Indian sitars and tabla. The outlaws appear from nowhere in the snowscape and the sitar sound–effects make them seem even stranger. The two 'riding themes' are savage compositions. The first, which accompanies Loco's pursuit of a bandit through the woods, employs a stuttering mariachi trumpet, bells, ear-splitting whistles, the choir and staccato string effects. Its companion piece, as the bounty-hunters ride for Snow Hill recalls the title music to *Face to Face*, with booming percussion, brass, an electric guitar riff and the Alessandroni Singers.

It is the ethereal themes that prove most memorable. In one haunting scene, Silence trudges into a snowbound stage station. In the background he passes a desolate cemetery, where a gravedigger is burying a young outlaw's corpse, while his grieving mother weeps. On the soundtrack, Alessandroni's singers, at their most subdued, wail mournfully. Elsewhere, a stagecoach winds its way through mountainous country, while the sitar, a gentle harp and ghostly voices (the souls of those killed in the mountains) echo the falling snowflakes. Corbucci's love story benefits most from the emotive score. In the scenes between Silence and Pauline, Morricone deploys an effective love theme, with a repetitive echoing piano, eerie tabla and sad gypsy violin. This piece is based on an arrangement of Russi and Costa's 'Scetate' ('Wake Up') that Morricone recorded with Miranda Martino in 1965; Martino had worked on the soundtrack to *Battle of Algiers*. In 1966, this theme became synonymous with Carlo Lizzani's *Wake Up and Kill*, the story of gangster Luciano Lutring, 'Il Solista Del Mitra' ('The First Machinegun of the Orchestra'). Silence and Pauline's love scene was accompanied by a string-laden romantic piece, the layered development of which echoed the changing mood of the sequence (from Pauline bandaging Silence's shoulder, to their lovemaking). A pared-down version of this piece was used in the finale, in which Silence approaches the saloon and faces Loco, linking the couple's brief relationship with its impending demise.

The ending of *Django* was downbeat, but when Corbucci delivered his finished 105-minute cut of *The Big Silence* the producers were not very impressed with the results. Occasionally, spaghetti westerns that had gloomy endings also had upbeat ones filmed too. The producers of *The Big Silence* lacked the nerve to release the western equivalent of *Black Sabbath*, and had Corbucci reshoot another finale. After Loco has shot Silence through the hand, the resurrected sheriff rides in and kills Loco. Silence crashes through the saloon window, shoots the bounty-hunters and frees the hostages. Silence and Pauline are left together for the cheery fadeout, as the gunman unwinds the bandage from his hand to reveal a bulletproof, plate-metal gauntlet. The trailer for the film included much footage from this alternative ending (including an unexplained shot of Silence speaking), but it was never used. Some English-language releases include slight edits for violence (shots of Mario Brega's blistered face and Silence's bloody head wound are cut), while the opening ambush and the saloon massacre are longer in the uncut print.

'The big silence' could also have referred to the reception the film received from stunned audiences throughout Europe. With its snowbound setting and Christmas release, *Silence* was expected to be a big success when it was released in Italy in December 1967, though it was most popular in France and Germany, where Trintignant and Kinski were huge stars. Some prints refer to Snow Hill as Goldstone and Loco as Tiberio, while the German title was the evocative *Leichen Pflastern Seinen Weg* ('Corpses Pave his Path'), shifting the emphasis to Klaus Kinski's character for the German market. Though 20th Century Fox released *Silence* in Europe, it was not able to find a distributor in the US and the UK, and was never shown, even in an abridged version.

The Big Silence's influence can only be seen in a handful of spaghettis. The aptly titled *A Man called Sledge* (1970 – starring James Garner) had a snowy stagecoach hold-up opening, but the action soon headed for the desert. Sergio Merolle's *Taste of Death* (1968), also financed by Les Films Corona, was a snowbound western shot in the Abruzzo National Park, near Rome. Sergio Martino's *Mannaja* (1977 – also called *A Man Called Blade*) featured a tomahawk-throwing hero in a soft-focus, foggy landscape. Tonino Cervi's *Today it's Me…Tomorrow You* (1968) had an autumnal feel, especially the sequences in which bandit Elfago and his Comancheros tracked the five heroes through a leafless, grey forest; the entire film was shot in Manziana, Lazio and was co-scripted by future horror director Dario Argento. Unrelated to *The Big Silence*, the surprise success in Italy of *Call of the Wild* (1972) starring Charlton Heston created a minor fad for snowbound adventure stories in the early seventies, with *White Fang* (1973) and *Return of White Fang* (1974), both starring Franco Nero, proving the most popular.

Silence's horrific neck scar reappeared in Clint Eastwood's *Hang 'Em High* (1968), his American-made follow-up to the 'Dollars' films. It is not known if Eastwood saw *Silence* before he made *Hang 'Em High* (he was in Europe in 1967 on promotional duty), but there are some startling similarities, in particular the scene in which Eastwood walks into a saloon, puts a cigar out in a villain's drink and pulls down his neckerchief to reveal a hanging scar; Silence reveals his scar in exactly the same way, to tell his victim his identity. Silence's Mauser pistol reappeared in Eastwood's *Joe Kidd* (1972), while the snowbound setting was used in *Pale Rider* (1985) and briefly in *Unforgiven* (1992); in the early seventies there was even a rumour that Eastwood was going to remake *The Big Silence*.

The one true heir to *The Big Silence* was *The Specialists* (1969), directed by Corbucci himself. It was the last part of his 'Mud and Blood' trilogy that began with *Django*. Again co-producing with the French, Corbucci cast French pop singer Johnny Hallyday as the Great Hud, a gunman who wears a chain-mail bulletproof vest under his long coat. Hallyday was not a great actor, but the film made up for its shortcomings in pure weirdness. During a fistfight, a villain named Boot has his chest crushed by a heavy cash register, while the hero takes revenge on the townsfolk for not helping his brother, by burning their bank reserve. Amongst Hud's opponents are a bunch of hippies, El Diablo (a bandit with an arm missing), and for once the villain was a woman – the banker's widow, Mrs Pollicut (Françoise Fabian). The bleak, cold setting (it was shot at Cortina D'Ampezzo, after the spring thaw) and ingenious touches lifted this above standard spaghetti-western offerings.

Like *Django* and *Silence*, *Specialists* suffered badly when it came to international distribution. When it was released outside Europe in 1973, it lost over twenty minutes of footage, but thankfully the film's outrageous finale was left intact. El Diablo and his gang ride into Blackstone with the villainous widow in tow. The sheriff is shot and Hud takes the gang on single-handed – catching a few bullets and a pitchfork through his leg in the process. With all the bandits dead, a group of dope-smoking hippies take the whole town hostage and strip them naked, making them lie in the street. During a confrontation between Hud and the hippies, the townsfolk bolt en masse, making a surreal sight – the most excessive western moment ever. The film was renamed in the UK *Drop Them Or I'll Shoot*, a punning title that referred to both gunbelts and trousers; it was not Corbucci's best work, but was certainly his oddest.

The Big Silence, however, was Corbucci's best work, made by a director not afraid to gamble. Trintignant went on to a successful international career, the high-point of which was Bernardo Bertolucci's elegant *The Conformist* (1970), a milestone in Italian political cinema, in which he again played a traumatised character. Meanwhile, European cinema audiences continued to love Kinski, their '*enfant terrible*'. Off-screen he lived to excess, though his opinion of his later spaghettis wasn't very high. 'Westerns,' Kinski remembered, 'One after another. They got shittier and shittier and the so-called directors got lousier and lousier.' He only made them to sustain his extravagant lifestyle; shortly after completing *The Big Silence*, Kinski bought a castle on the Via Appia and a Rolls-Royce Phantom with a built-in bar. Other Kinski roles from this prolific period include Blond ('a killer dressed as a priest') in the western *The Ruthless Four* (1968), and Erich Weiss, one of the international gang after $10 million in diamonds during the Rio Carnival in Giuliano Montaldo's *Grand Slam* (1967 – a film that was originally going to be directed by Sergio Leone). Kinski finally achieved international recognition in a series of films with director Werner Herzog, giving extraordinary performances as obsessives in *Aguirre, the Wrath of God* (1972) and *Fitzcarraldo*

Italian montage still ('*fotobusta*') depicting avenger Silence (Jean-Louis Trintignant), while Loco (Klaus Kinski) loads a stagecoach with 'freight'; Sergio Corbucci's *The Big Silence* (1967).

(1982); only Kinski could play the lead in a remake of *Nosferatu the Vampyre* (1921) and match the original for chills.

Thanks to Kinski's malevolent performance and the winter setting, *The Big Silence* stands as Corbucci's most perceptive and effective contribution to the genre: a ballet of violence in a beautiful landscape. Throughout the film the protagonists seem to be clinging on to life by their fingernails. But in the desolation of snowy Utah, Corbucci has only the fittest survive. Those who can't hold on perish, spilling their blood on the winter's snow, until all that is left is silence.

17

'You Play By the Rules, You Lose'

— Sergio Corbucci's *A Professional Gun* (1968)

A Professional Gun (1968)
original title: *Il Mercenario*
Credits
DIRECTOR – Sergio Corbucci
PRODUCER – Alberto Grimaldi
STORY – Franco Solinas and Giorgio Arlorio
SCREENPLAY – Luciano Vincenzoni, Sergio Spina, Adriano
    Bolzoni and Sergio Corbucci
ART DIRECTOR – Luiz Vazquez
COSTUMES – Jürgen Henze
EDITOR – Eugenio Alabiso
DIRECTOR OF PHOTOGRAPHY – Alejandro Ulloa
MUSIC COMPOSERS – Ennio Morricone and Bruno Nicolai
MUSIC CONDUCTOR – Bruno Nicolai
Techniscope/Technicolor
An Italian/Spanish co-production
PEA (Rome)/Produzioni Associate Delphos (Rome)/Profilms 21
    (Madrid)
Released internationally by United Artists
Cast
    Franco Nero (Captain Sergei Kowalski, 'the Polak'); Tony
    Musante (Paco Roman); Jack Palance (Curly); Giovanna Ralli
    (Columba); Franco Giacobini (Peporte, the arms dealer);
    Eduardo Fajardo (Colonel Alfonso Garcia); Franco Ressel
    (Studs); Vicente Roca (Don Elias Garcia); Jose Riesgo (Elias
    Garcia's brother); Tito Garcia (Garcia's cousin); Joe Kamel
    (Sebastian); Jose Zaldua (innkeeper in Sonora); Guillermo
    Mendez (Mexican officer on train); Remo De Angelis
    (gambler at Curly's); Herman Reynoso (Curly's bearded

henchman); Ugo Adinolfi (land-owner); Juan Cazalilla (mayor); Bruno Corazzari (man in bullfight audience); Antonio De Martino (rodeo dwarf); Alvaro De Luna, Raf Baldassare, Simon Arriaga and Jose Canalejas (members of Paco's gang); with Angel Ortiz, Fernando Villena, Angel Alvarez, Jose Antonio Lopez, Milo Quesada, Paco Niento and Jose Aquinaco

*   *   *

In 1968, Franco Solinas and Giorgio Arlorio wrote *Il Mercenario*, the story of a gringo mercenary mixed up in the Mexican revolution. Gillo Pontecorvo (of *Battle of Algiers* fame) was going to direct. The film was planned as a serious treatment of the Mexican struggle. When Marlon Brando had been in Italy making *Candy* (1968), Pontecorvo tried to interest him in another script, again by Solinas and Arlorio, entitled *Queimada!* The idea concerned a slave revolt on a sugar-cane island in the Antilles, though Brando was uninterested in such a political film. Solinas and Pontecorvo had written it with three actors in mind for the lead role of Sir William Walker, a dandyish English mercenary – Burt Lancaster, Richard Burton and Brando – but none of them were interested. Following the assassination of Martin Luther King, Brando renewed his acquaintance with Pontecorvo and decided to make the film (retitled *Burn!* for international release), which was to be shot in Columbia. Consequently, Pontecorvo had to pass on the western script.

In Pontecorvo's place, producer Alberto Grimaldi brought in Corbucci to direct *Il Mercenario*, retitled *A Professional Gun* in the UK and *The Mercenary* in the US. Corbucci employed Adriano Bolzoni, Sergio Spina and Luciano Vincenzoni to help him adapt the story for the screen. Vincenzoni had become best known for his work with Leone on the 'Dollars' trilogy. Along the way, the serious politics of the story ended up taking a back seat to the humour, as the political message of the film was almost lost amongst the sharp quips and exhilarating action.

A Polish mercenary named Sergei Kowalski (known as the Polak) is hired to guard Mexican silver shipments from the Palo Altos mine (at Los Fresnos in Sierra Palo) to Texas. When he arrives at the mine the exploited workers, led by Paco Roman, have taken over. The Polak teams up with these budding revolutionaries, teaching them to fight as an army, and soon Paco is inadvertently a hero to the Mexican people. But with his fame comes the attentions of the Mexican authorities, with mine-owner Don Alfonso Garcia in command, and an American mercenary named Curly, who sides with Garcia.

There were two crucial alterations made to Solinas's script. In Corbucci's version, when Paco becomes a revolutionary hero, he imprisons the Polak and impounds his money. The Polak is sentenced to death, but manages to escape. Later Paco and Kowalski are reunited, and the Polak tries to convince Paco to make a living as a mercenary. But Paco heads off to continue his own revolution, while the Polak rides away to his next job. In Solinas's original treatment, Paco imprisons the Polak and sentences him to death. The mercenary asks Paco to carry out the sentence, but the Mexican is unable to shoot his friend. Later Kowalski, now employed by the government, is quite able to kill Paco on behalf of the Mexican authorities. Corbucci, wary of the cool reception *The Big Silence* had received, opted for the more upbeat ending. Many of Solinas's political scripts (including *A Bullet for the General, Burn!* and *Tepepa*) close on the death of the Anglo interloper.

Like all Vincenzoni's western scripts, there are three central characters: two good (Kowalski and Paco) pitted against one bad (Curly). In *Professional*, Vincenzoni added a woman to the central trio. During Paco's 'revolutionary activities' Columba, a political prisoner, joins the band and creates friction between the two heroes. Vincenzoni's quick-fire script ensures nearly every scene ends with a visual or verbal punchline. A recurrent gag sees Kowalski striking matches on a variety of rough surfaces: a bandit's teeth, a crook's sideburn, a whore's corset and the sole of a hanged man's boot. Previously jokes in Corbucci's films had been subtler; in *Navajo Joe* the community threatened by bandits live in Esperanza (meaning 'hope').

A Professional Gun is set at the start of the 1910–20 Mexican revolution. The film details lower-class-led revolutionary activity and the influence on Mexico of foreign powers and the ruling classes. In *A Bullet for the General*, an American undercover agent kills a revolutionary hero on behalf of the Mexican government. But his action is also a comment by Solinas on foreign intervention in Mexican affairs. At the start of the Mexican revolution, as the rebellion led by Francisco Madero spread like wildfire across the country, American capitalists owned 17 of the 31 major silver mining operations in Mexico. In *A Professional Gun* Solinas has Paco's rebellion beginning in a US-owned silver mine. The Polak is originally hired to transport the silver to Texas, only to realise that there is more money to be made siding with the peasants.

Early spaghettis had not been overly concerned with the revolution. *Seven for Pancho Villa* (1966) used it as a backdrop, while *Gunfight in the Red Sands* (1963) saw the hero escaping the rebellion and returning home. *A Fistful of Dollars, For a Few Dollars More, Johnny Oro* and *Django* all featured a few Regulare uniforms, though *A Bullet for the General* was the first entire film devoted to the subject.

Louis Malle's French/Italian co-production *Viva Maria* (1965) was the most important influence on *A Professional Gun*. Malle (like Leone) was a huge fan of *Vera Cruz*, and claimed he used it as the model for *Viva Maria*. In Malle's film, Maria Fitzgerald O'Malley (Brigitte Bardot), the daughter of an Irish terrorist, hides out with a circus in a fictitious Latin American country (referred to in some prints as San Miguel). She forms a double-act (The Two Marias) with circus singer Maria (Jeanne Moreau). But through their involvement with Florès (George Hamilton), a revolutionary, and their fight against vicious tyrant Rodriguez (Carlos Lopez Montezuma), they become heroes of the revolution. The larger-than-life villain and the elaborate sight gags (including Bardot sneaking up on a machine-gun with a bomb and an irreverent inquisition scene) were ahead of their time, while the score by Georges Delerue anticipated Morricone's love themes.

In a reprise of *Django*, European superstar Franco Nero was cast as the machine-gun-toting hero of *A Professional Gun*. Since *Django*, Nero had had an affair with Vanessa Redgrave during the filming of the musical *Camelot* (1967) in the US. He had just appeared with Redgrave in Elio Petri's *A Quiet Place in the Country* (1968). Petri's film was produced by Alberto Grimaldi's PEA and Produzioni Associate Delphos, who were also backing *A Professional Gun* (with Madrid-based Profilms 21). Grimaldi thought Nero would be ideal as the Polak. For Paco Roman, Corbucci cast former schoolteacher Tony Musante, having seen his performance in the grim US thriller *The Incident* (1967), in which Musante and Martin Sheen played two delinquents who terrorise the New York subway.

Corbucci's favourite villain Eduardo Fajardo took the Garcia role. Fifty-year-old Fajardo (full name Eduardo Martinez Fajardo) had been working in Spanish cinema for years. His first Italian role came in *Erik the Viking* (1961), and his breakthrough had been Major Jackson in *Django*. Many westerns followed, though he was constantly typecast as an evil rich land-owner and later as a bloodthirsty Mexican officer. Franco Giacobini (previously Hercules's bumbling sidekick Telemachus in *Hercules in the Haunted World* – 1961) played Peporte, one of Paco's gang, who betrays them and becomes a rich arms dealer. Other members of Paco's gang were played by genre regulars Alvaro De Luna, Raf Baldassare, Simon Arriaga and Jose Canalejas. Remo De Angelis worked as a stuntman and had a cameo as a gambler.

Rome-born Giovanna Ralli was cast as Columba. Ralli was attempting to establish herself on the international stage, though she had been acting in Italy since the age of seven. Like Lorella De Luca, she worked for Fellini (*Lights of Variety* – 1950) and became a popular pin-up in the Italian 'sweetie' melodramas of the mid-fifties, but she also portrayed rougher rural characters. Ralli later appeared in several Hollywood productions, including the Italian-shot misfire *What Did You Do in the War, Daddy?* (1966 – with James Coburn), the dark thriller *Deadfall* (1968 – opposite Michael Caine) and the heist film *The Caper of the Golden Bulls* (1966). She also made the American-financed, Spanish-shot political western *Cannon for Cordoba* (1970).

Corbucci was also able to cast Jack Palance, one of the all-time great western villains, as Curly. Palance (the son of a Ukrainian coal-miner) flew a bomber in the Second World War. He was badly burned in a crash, and the resulting plastic surgery gave his lean face an angular, skeletal look, ideal for villainy. His best role came as the whispering hired gun Wilson in *Shane* (1952), though in the late fifties and throughout the sixties he worked extensively in Italy on *The Mongols* (1961), *Barabbas* (1961), *Le Mepris* (1963) and several action-packed war films including *Warriors Five* (1962 – with Giovanna Ralli), *Fall of the Giants* (1968) and *Battle of the Commandos* (1969). His role as Curly, the cold-hearted hired gun, was his first spaghetti western, but Palance found that he enjoyed making westerns in Italy and

Spain. He was once asked why he hadn't won an Oscar till 1991 (as a character named Curly in *City Slickers*). 'What…in spaghetti westerns?' he laughed, though he added, 'But hey, those guys didn't eat spaghetti…they ate caviar'.

On-set high living and the Mexican revolution locale were clear signs that Corbucci's budgets were getting bigger. The large-scale battle scenes (deploying a motor-car, a battery of light artillery, several Browning and Hawkins machine-guns, a train and even a biplane) make this Corbucci's equivalent of *The Good, the Bad and the Ugly*, with the special effects choreographed by Manuel Baquero and Celeste Battistelli. The film's exteriors were shot entirely in Spain, and for once the omnipresent Spanish telegraph poles add an air of authenticity. The Mexican locations around Los Fresnos and Chihuahua were impersonated by Carabaña (where the mine set was constructed, near the River Sacavém), and the desert country and villages near Seseña, Madrid. An ambush was shot among the distinctive sculpted limestone mushroom rocks at Cuidad Encantada (the 'enchanted city') near Cuenca. Several desert sequences were shot in the canyons and sierras of Almeria, while one of the liberated towns was the village of Polopos. A gringo border-town was Carlo Simi's Almeria El Paso set (the blockhouse bank was the exterior of Curly's Casino) and the western set at Colmenar Viejo. The crew travelled to Madrid, then Almeria and completed filming interiors in Rome.

A Professional Gun was colourfully photographed by Alejandro Ulloa. Spaniard Ulloa (full name Alejandro Garcia Alonso Ulloa) filmed many Spanish-shot spaghettis, including Giraldi's two 'MacGregor' westerns, *Kill Them All and Come Back Alone* (1968) and *Massacre at Fort Holman* (1972), and Corbucci's own *Compañeros* (1970).

For the first time, Corbucci adopted a flashback technique to tell his story. Previously his stories had stuttered to life, but here the narrative structure works well. Most of the story consists of the Polak's recollections of his time as a hired gun during the Mexican revolution. The film begins with a 'flash-forward' to the finale – so that almost the whole film takes place in the 'dissolve' of a flashback. This technique had appeared in Solinas's script for *Battle of Algiers*. *Professional* opens with Kowalski watching a circus rodeo in a bullring. One of the performers, a red-nosed clown (actually Paco in disguise) recognises the Polak. A voiceover tells us Kowalski's thoughts: 'So Paco Roman is a clown. Well better a live clown than a dead hero.' The film then recounts how Paco went from 'saviour to clown in six months'.

Franco Nero was in his element as the dryly sarcastic Kowalski. Nero was able to use his own voice in the English-language dubbing, and his whispering, lilting European English is very effective. Over the years Nero's accent has been passed-off as many nationalities; in fact he holds the record for playing the greatest variety of nationalities on screen.

Nero's distinctive costume was designed by Jürgen Henze; he wears a long duster coat, leather gloves and flat-brimmed hat, which, when coupled with his swept-back mane of hair, whiskers and ever-present cigarette, make him look nothing like his previous incarnation as Django. The flat-brimmed hat prompted US critics to compare Nero to a Boy Scout. Kowalski is armed with a Browning Automatic Pistol (which Nero later reused in other political spaghettis) and a Hawkins machine-gun (identical to the one used by Lou Castel in *A Bullet for the General*).

Kowalski's introductory scene in Curly's Casino demonstrates his quietly spoken character. Kowalski catches Studs (Franco Ressel), one of Curly's henchmen, cheating at craps with a pair of loaded dice. 'Do you like milk?' he asks Studs politely, who answers, 'Not too much'. 'A glass of milk for the gentleman,' says the Polak. Kowalski then makes Studs swallow the dice, washed down with milk. When Paco first meets the Polak, the Mexican notes: 'You talk good, like a priest or a high-class crook. The crooks I know, they don't talk funny like you.' When the mine's original owner arrives with artillery, to retake his property, Paco asks the mercenary to help him. 'I am a professional,' answers Kowalski calmly, through the explosions and smoke. 'No cash, no work. Are you a customer?' Paco, with limited options, empties his pockets.

Curly (called Ricciolo, Curl or Elam in various different prints of the film) is a hired killer with a hidden Derringer, a flick-knife and valise full of grenades, who crosses himself after each murder (mimicking Tuco in *The Good, the Bad and the Ugly*). He wears a smart black suit and a carnation in his buttonhole; in a continuity error, Curly plays poker wearing a red carnation and then makes his exit wearing a black one. If Kowalski's selfish motto is 'I'm on my side', then Curly's is 'You play by the rules, you lose'.

Curly loves macabre wisecracks and bizarre killings. When hired gun Studs fails to kill the Polak, Curly asks if Studs is married (he is divorced) or has kids (he has none), before Curly's henchman Sebastian murders Studs with a pitchfork. In a gruesome scene, Curly searches through the rubble of a shattered building. He finds a rebel, badly wounded but still alive, and asks where Paco has gone. The interrogation fails and Curly takes a grenade from his black valise, puts it in the bandit's mouth, pulls the pin and runs for cover. Curly's grenade-filled valise is based on the Hollywood Mexican revolution movie *Bandido!* (1956), in which Robert Mitchum's laid-back gringo mercenary Wilson is similarly equipped.

Rich mine-owner Don Alfonso Garcia (Eduardo Fajardo) and his two brothers represent the ruling classes. They enjoy lavish meals, while listening to 'La Donna E Mobile' from *Riggoletto* on a gramophone. Alfonso is asked if he thinks insurgent Francisco Madero is a threat, but the mine-owner says he's 'nothing'. At that moment Paco and his disgruntled co-workers burst in on the meal and eat their rich employers' dinner at gunpoint. The presentation of the scene is wholly comic; the don is made to eat a boiled lizard that Paco has just been served in his dreadful miner's rations, but despite the jokes, important points are made.

Garcia is also an army colonel, and he begins to resemble General Huerta, the leader of the government forces during the rebellion. Many of the Mexican revolution films of the late sixties and early seventies teamed their Huerta figures with a boot-clicking, monocle-wearing European 'military advisor' in a khaki uniform. In *A Professional Gun* Curly fills this role. It is he who suggests they use a biplane to attack Paco's rebels, but in a memorable scene the Polak coolly shoots down the plane with a Winchester.

The rise of Paco Roman from miner to revolutionary icon (and back again) is the main theme of *A Professional Gun*. He rebels, not through any sense of 'revolutionary conscience', but because he has seen his father and brother die in the mine and doesn't want to meet the same fate. Paco (called Eufemio in the Italian print) begins the film interested only in money – his speciality is 'liberating' banks. But with the Polak's tuition, Paco and his dozen-strong gang ('Paco Roman's

Italian UA picture sleeve single featuring Ennio Morricone's 'Il Mercenario' theme, backed by 'Paco' for *A Professional Gun* (1968). The artwork (left to right) depicts Sergei Kowalski (Franco Nero), Paco (Tony Musante) and Curly (Jack Palance).

twelve apostles') become a force to be reckoned with. His men begin to shout 'Viva Paco!', and the Polak claims he can make Paco as world-famous as Villa or Zapata. The liberated peasants call him 'General Paco' and the 'Pope of Mexico', and even mistake him for Simon Bolivar. Paco stays to help the villagers and the Polak thinks that Paco really believes that he is Bolivar: 'And you've become an idealist...the shortest way to the cemetery'. Paco begins to behave like a revolutionary and deals out his own brand of justice. Peporte, a traitor to the revolution, is brought before Paco. Paco's ex-comrade-in-arms is dressed in an expensive suit, and Paco transforms him back into a peasant by tearing off his jacket and tie and adding a battered sombrero and boot-polish stubble. 'Now I recognise you,' says Paco.

Paco's change of heart stems from his relationship with Columba, a prisoner who joins their gang. Her father was hanged by the soldiers and she wants revenge. She remains suspicious of Kowlaski, saying that her father never stooped to hire a foreigner to kill other Mexicans. Her role in the film is historically accurate. Many women fought in the revolution, the most famous was Coronela Zapatista Maria Chavarria. Columba makes Paco feel guilty for taking the wealth of the towns they liberate. 'A revolutionary is never ashamed of his actions,' she tells Paco, 'a thief is,' which convinces Paco to stay and protect the people from government reprisals. In a key moment, Paco looks at a map of Mexico and tells the Polak, 'See this? It's Mexico. I didn't know it was so big. I've decided to work for Mexico and take back what is ours.'

Corbucci stages the grandiose action sequences with vigour. As the revolutionaries become better equipped, their objectives become more ambitious and Corbucci's set pieces more elaborate. They raid a political prison (with a bank attached), rob a train and take the city of Santa Rosita. These machine-gun shootouts are played for violent laughs: in a typically irreverent Corbucci scene, a mercenary, a revolutionary and a bandita disguise themselves in a religious procession during the Fiesta of Santa Rosita. Columba dresses as Santa Rosita ('the lady with the beard'), a haloed Joan of Arc figure tied to a cross and flanked by a pair of winged angels (Paco and the Polak). Paco's gang carries the float dressed as '*penitentes*' (penitents), in flowing purple robes and giant pointy hoods (called '*capirote*'). When they draw level with the garrison officers, the gang springs into action. The hooded bearers open fire, the angels produce Winchesters and the lady with the beard mows down the troops with a machine-gun.

Like many of Vincenzoni's western stories, the final reckoning takes place in a circular arena; here a Texan rodeo bullring decorated with billboards advertising 'His Master's Voice' and 'Coca Cola'. Paco, now with a price on his head, is hiding from the authorities as a rodeo clown, but the Polak has tracked him down. After the performance, Paco takes a bow, the crowd drift away and the amphitheatre is left empty. As the Mexican is about to leave, Curly appears and captures Paco, but the Polak intervenes. He referees a duel between Curly and Paco with a ringside bell – on the third toll, they both fire and Paco collapses. Paco has only been wounded, and slowly Curly's white carnation begins to 'bleed', as he attempts to cross himself before dropping in the dust.

For this set piece, Ennio Morricone wrote a show-stopping number – a 'bullring symphony', with echoes of Joaquin Rodrigo's 'Concerto De Aranjuez'. As Curly strides into the arena, sustained ominous strings, staccato drums and castanets accompany him. When the Polak appears, his echoing whistled theme appears on the soundtrack, announcing his arrival. As the showdown begins, the sombre trumpet theme becomes a triumphal march, with thunderous drums, the choir, electric guitar and trumpet flourishes. When this powerful theme was released as a 45rpm single (with 'Paco's Theme' on the B-side) it was abridged, and lost the effectiveness of the mannered build-up; it is also almost identical to a theme from Morricone's *Guns for San Sebastian* (1968).

Morricone composed *A Professional Gun* with his conductor, Bruno Nicolai. The title music, 'Paco', is a carnivalesque 'fiesta' theme. The dominant brass (particularly the trumpet) and dramatic bursts of violin are typical of Nicolai's style; some sources claim he wrote it alone, while Nicolai's name has been mysteriously removed from all reissues of the soundtrack. 'Paco' is very upbeat, with Alessandroni's choir in jovial mood, as they intone 'Viva La Revolucion!' and 'Viva Paco Roman!' Though this theme introduces the film effectively (cut to tinted photographs of the revolutionary period), it is best employed in the action sequences. In one scene, Paco and Kowalski load a vintage car with dynamite, prop a machine-gun on the windscreen and drive straight at a battery of cannons, cut to Paco's exhilarating theme.

Morricone and Nicolai here associate characters with individual theme tunes. Paco has 'Paco', the Polak has an eerie whistled theme and Curly has a gloomy church organ and electric guitar motif. Our first view of Kowalski – riding across the desert towards the mine with his machine-gun strapped to a packhorse – features Alessandroni's whistling at its most ominous. Curly's theme (using a Thomas 900 electric organ) is also effective, a requiem for a killer. Another piece, a lilting Straussian waltz entitled 'Curl', was written and recorded as a theme for Palance, but never used in the film, appearing only on the UA soundtrack album. For Paco's clown act, a jazz band plays the 'Blackbottom Charleston Foxtrot' (which actually dates from 1926), while there is much traditional Mexican folk music in the movie. The folksong 'Adelita' is sung by a trainload of Mexican soldiers (recalling the tune's appearance in *A Bullet for the General*), and the lament 'Mexican Dream' (a slow, drunken sing-along complete with whoops and pig squeals) was written and performed by Jose Voltolini.

Corbucci's film was released to massive success in Italy in December 1968. It was also successful in Germany, where it was known as *Mercenario – Der Gefürchtete* ('Mercenary – the Dreaded') and *Die Gefürchteten Zwei* ('The Dreaded Two'). In Spain it was known as *Salario Para Matar* ('Wages for Killing') and *Jaguar*. *A Professional Gun* appeared in the UK in 1970 and was released the same year in the

US as *The Mercenary*, under the UA banner. It has since been rereleased as *Revenge of a Gunfighter*, with Nero's character billed as Bill Douglas. The uncut print runs at 102 minutes. A scene in which traitorous arms dealer Peporte has his penis chopped off was pruned for international release. The uncut print also included a scene where Kowalski explains to Paco the mechanics of revolution using a naked Mexican woman: the rich are the head, the poor are the backside; revolution means trying to bring them together. Some of the violence was also toned down, including the pitchfork murder and the grenade killing, both of which were exorcised from some English-language prints of the film. The US taglines included 'Life Is Cheap…Death Isn't' and 'The Mercenary – He Sells Death To The Highest Bidder…Buy or Die'. With a lot of ballistic hardware on display, the film was by far Corbucci's most successful western on the UK and US markets, and garnered some positive reviews. The *New York Times* said the film was 'technically outstanding' and praised Nero and Palance, but moaned about Morricone's whistled themes, which had 'become trite and should be dropped'. At one point, Paco and the Polak leave Curly stripped naked in the middle of the desert, and the same *New York Times* review noted that Palance was putting on weight during his time abroad.

Corbucci directed two more political westerns, with much less success outside Europe. The first, a partial remake of *Professional*, was called *Vamos a Matar, Compañeros!* (1970), with Nero playing a Swedish arms dealer, sent with Mexican bandit El Vasco (Tomas Milian) to rescue a pacifist from jail in Yuma. Only Jack Palance's pot-smoking villain Wooden Hand John (so called because his pet falcon ate his hand off when John was crucified to a tree) and the action–packed climax in San Bernardino are of note. *What am I doing in the Middle of a Revolution?* (1972) was similarly aimless, with an Italian Shakespearean actor and a priest unwillingly sucked into the revolution. If *Professional* was a satire (both of political films and of Hollywood's treatment of the subject), then *Compañeros* and *What am I?* verged on slapstick.

Following the success of *A Professional Gun*, 'What am I doing in the middle of a revolution?' was also the question on the lips of many actors who found themselves in the celluloid version of the Mexican revolution in the late sixties and early seventies. These big-budget action films included *Villa Rides* (1968), *The Wild Bunch* (1969) and *Cannon for Cordoba* (1970). Star power (Yul Brynner, George Peppard or James Coburn), elaborate armoury (biplanes, steel–plated trains and armoured cars) and superheroics ('One man Against the Mexican army' was the gist of the posters) were the recurrent ingredients. Many of these all–action American films (some of which were shot in Spain, using sets and props previously deployed by Corbucci himself) featured an older generation of Hollywood actors kissing *señoritas* and killing Regulares with no conviction whatsoever. The actors gave the impression that their minds were elsewhere, as they thought about their next round of golf or chat-show appearance – a rather literal expression of the American mercenary's lack of 'revolutionary commitment'.

Robert Mitchum sleepwalked though his role as a biplane-flying gringo in *Villa Rides*, while Yul Brynner looked unusually hairy as Pancho Villa; in one scene he takes a ride in Mitchum's biplane and doesn't lose his wig. Bald Telly Savalas played Villa in *Pancho Villa* (1972), but bypassed the hair problem by having his head shaved in prison in the film's opening sequence; Savalas also crooned the title song, 'We'll all end up the same' (lyrics by Don Black). The film *100 Rifles* (1968) was only noteworthy for good performances by Burt Reynolds, Raquel Welch, Jim Brown and Aldo Sambrell. In *The Five Man Army* (1969) Peter Graves embarked on a mission impossible to rob a steel-plated 'bank on wheels' (a train), while Leone's *Duck You Sucker* (1971 – also called *A Fistful of Dynamite*) was the most disappointing of all. Rod Steiger's overbearing performance as Juan, a peasant bandit (who predictably becomes a revolutionary) ruins the film. Only Morricone's exceptional score (including the mythical nine-minute 'Inventions for John') and James Coburn's appearance as John H. Mallory, a motorcycle-riding IRA dynamiter, make the outing worthwhile. Apart from *A Professional Gun*, only three revolution-set westerns of the era emerged with any dignity: *A Bullet for the General*, the US western *The Professionals* (1966 – starring Burt Lancaster, Lee Marvin, Claudia Cardinale and Jack Palance) and Sam Peckinpah's *The Wild Bunch* (1969). *The Wild Bunch* featured the best machine-gun shootout of the revolution genre, with its fiery 'Battle of Bloody Porch' climax, when the Bunch take on General Mapache's army in Agua Verde. More blank ammunition (90,000 rounds) was fired during the

Imperialism in action: Franco Nero as Captain Sergei Kowalski (the Polak) in Sergio Corbucci's Mexican revolution film *A Professional Gun* (1968).

making of *The Wild Bunch* than was used in the entire ten years of the Mexican revolution.

Following *A Professional Gun*, Corbucci went on to make more westerns, in an even lighter vein. *Sonny & Jed* (1972 – also released as *The J & S Gang*) cast Tomas Milian and Susan George as a pair of romantically involved bank robbers and *White, Yellow, Black* (1974 – retitled *Samurai*) was a knockabout send-up of East-meets-West movies like *Red Sun* (1971). Mickey Knox (the English-language translator from Leone's films) moved into producing, with the Corbucci-esque *Long Live Your Death* (1971 – otherwise known as *Long Live Death…Preferably Yours*), starring Eli Wallach. The film (directed by Duccio Tessari) included Franco Nero as a Russian prince (with shares in Henry Ford), Wallach as Lozoya, a peasant mistaken for the revolutionary hero El Salvador, Eduardo Fajardo as General Huerta and Lynn Redgrave as Mary O'Donnell, a gutsy Irish journalist. The film concerned a fortune in hidden gold, with the location tattooed on two Mexicans backsides (the film was also titled *Don't Turn the Other Cheek*).

Following *A Professional Gun*, Tony Musante stayed in Italy and starred in Dario Argento's horror debut *Bird With the Crystal Plumage* (1969). Jack Palance embarked on his most infamous movie, his portrayal of Fidel Castro in *Che!* (1969 – opposite Omar Sharif as Che Guevara). He donned a false beard and putty nose for the role, but *Che!* bombed; *Newsweek* noted the film 'substituted monkey glands for ideology'. Through a diverse array of roles and sheer prolificacy, Franco Nero became an international sex symbol. His credits included the 1970 adaptation of D.H. Lawrence's *The Virgin and the Gypsy* (Nero was the gypsy); the Gothic western *Keoma* (1976 – in which he shed his Django image with a vengeance); Luis Bunuel's serene *Tristana* (1970); and effective *Dirty Harry*-inspired police thrillers like the stylish *Marseilles Connection* (1973). He also made the western *Deaf Smith and Johnny Ears* (1972), with Anthony Quinn as a deaf-mute gunfighter (Erastus 'Deaf' Smith) and Nero as his sidekick Johnny, set in 1830s Texas.

Corbucci subsequently had several big hits in Italy, and five of his seventies comedies (mostly with Adriano Celentano) appear in the 100 highest grossing Italian films of all time. Not one of his westerns makes the list, though outside Italy he remains best known for them. After *Compañeros*, Corbucci and Nero fell out and never worked together again. In their heyday, they had an ideal partnership: Corbucci once said, 'John Ford has John Wayne, Sergio Leone has Clint Eastwood…and I have Franco Nero'. *A Professional Gun* is Nero's best western, and Corbucci (with a big budget for a change) created his most spectacular film – that was revolutionary in more ways than one.

18

'A Wise Man Keeps His Distance'

— Gianfranco Parolini's *Sabata* (1969)

Sabata (1969)

original title: *Ehi amico...c'e Sabata, hai chiuso!*

Credits

DIRECTOR – 'Frank Kramer' (Gianfranco Parolini)

PRODUCER – Alberto Grimaldi

STORY AND SCREENPLAY – Renato Izzo and Gianfranco Parolini

SETS AND COSTUMES – Carlo Simi

EDITOR – Edmondo Lozzi

DIRECTOR OF PHOTOGRAPHY – Alessandro Mancori

MUSIC – Marcello Giombini

Interiors filmed at Elios Film Studios, Rome

Techniscope/Technicolor

An Italian Production for PEA (Rome)

Released internationally by United Artists

Cast

Lee Van Cleef (Sabata); William Berger (Banjo); Franco Ressel (Hardy Stengel); Linda Veras (Jane); 'Pedro Sanchez', Ignazio Spalla (Garrincha, 'The Little Bird'); Gianni Rizzo (Judge O'Hara); 'Anthony Gradwell', Antonio Gradoli (Fergusson); Nick Jordan (Alley Cat); 'Robert Hundar', Claudio Undari (Oswald); 'Spanny Convery', Spartaco Conversi (Slim); Marco Zuanelli (Sharky); 'John Bartho', Janos Bartha (Sheriff); 'Andrew Ray', Andrea Aureli (Tequila); Romano Puppo (Rocky); 'Alan Collins', Luciano Pigozzi (phoney priest); 'Charles Tamblyn', Carlo Tamberlani (bank manager); Mimmo Poli (Grand Palace Hotel bartender); Franco Marletta (US Army Captain); Gino Barbacane (blond soldier); Franco and Bruno Ukmar and 'Joseph Mathews', Giuseppe Mattei (The Virginian

Brothers); 'R Loddi', Rodolfo Lodi (Father Brown);
Fortunato Arena, Angelo Susani and George Wang (members
of Stengel's gang) with Gino Marturano and Vittorio Andre

*   *   *

By 1969 many Italian producers felt that the western fad had passed, and that with the success of *Bird With the Crystal Plumage* horror films were back in vogue. Not the Gothic horror style of Mario Bava and Antonio Margheriti, but the concrete-and-glass urban nightmare of Dario Argento. Against late-sixties fashion, director Gianfranco Parolini reinvigorated the western with his own peculiar take on the 'west as carnival', epitomised by his 1969 spaghetti western *Sabata*. If Leone's western heroes met their destiny in the arena of death, then Parolini's met theirs in a circus ring. He created a world full of larger-than-life villains, gymnastic set pieces and complicated gadgets. Parolini's protagonists resembled a circus troupe, with acrobats, trick-shooters, knife-throwers, cardsharps and clowns on the bill. Parolini's cinema was carnivalesque in the Fellini sense of the word – Circus Maximus indeed.

Parolini worked as a set designer and assistant director on several muscleman films in the late fifties, before making his directorial debut with *Samson* (1961) starring Brad Harris. Harris was a regular collaborator with Parolini throughout the sixties – firstly on several epics and later in the 'Kommissar X' spy series (1965–68). Parolini made *10 Gladiators* (1963 – with Roger Browne), which was co-scripted by Sergio Sollima, and *79AD* (1962) with Harris. The latter was a partial remake of Leone's *The Last Days of Pompeii* (it was even retitled 'The Last Days of Herculaneum' in France). Esteemed actor Carlo Tamberlani played a character named Furius; no wonder, when he saw the finished film. In 1964, Parolini switched genres and specialised in spy capers, which allowed him to concentrate on well-planned heists and clever gadgetry. Parolini also made an acrobatic superheroes movie called *The Fantastic Three* (1967 – with Harris, Tony Kendal and newcomer Nick Jordan) and a war film called *Five for Hell* (1969), with five GIs on a special mission to break into the German headquarters in Villa Verdi to steal 'Plan K'.

In 1965, Parolini made his western debut with *Left-handed Johnny West*, and for the first time adopted the pseudonym 'Frank Kramer'. It stars 'Dick Palmer' (alias Mimmo Palmera) as Johnny West – 'the great left-hander' – and is shot in Spain on locations used in *A Fistful of Dollars* and *For a Few Dollars More*; Parolini even includes a scene where the hero appears through a series of dynamite explosions. Johnny, with his trusty dog Gypsy, falls foul of the villainous Jackson Twins (played by Mike Anthony in two different costumes). *Johnny West* establishes several of the director's gadget motifs: the hero has a Derringer hidden inside his hat and the villain's cane fires bullets.

Parolini followed this with *Sartana* (1968 – full title *If you Meet Sartana, Pray for your Death*) starring Gianni Garko (or 'John Garko'). Sartana was a character originally played by Garko in Alberto Cardone's *Blood at Sundown* (1967); in Cardone's film Sartana was a psychopathic maniac who resembled Klaus Kinski's Wild One in *For a Few Dollars More*. Parolini's *Sartana* is markedly different. He becomes the hero, a spectral avenger who always has the upper hand. Again played by Garko, Sartana had a look and manner inspired by Lee Van Cleef's Colonel Mortimer (also from *For a Few*). Following a sinister stagecoach robbery, *Sartana*'s complicated plot includes blackmail, bank strongboxes unexpectedly full of stones and much subterfuge, as Sartana tries to outwit an army of villains: Mexican bandit Excellentisimo 'Heneral' Tampico (played by Fernando Sancho), a couple of outlaws – Lasky (William Berger) and Morgan (Klaus Kinski) – and a pair of crooked businessmen (Gianni Rizzo and Sydney Chaplin – son of Charlie). With the help of a coffin-maker named Dusty (Franco Pesce), Sartana wrests the hoard from everyone's grip and rides out of town on a hearse with a coffin full of gold on board. The coffin-maker asks his identity – 'A first-class pallbearer,' sneers Garko.

Sartana was a prototype for *Sabata*. Berger was the hero's ambiguous ally/ nemesis; Kinski was a knife-thrower with bells on his boots; and there was plenty of gadgetry, including Sartana's beautiful silver Sharp's Derringer and a villain with a sword blade concealed in his cane. Parolini also had a brief cameo as a gambler who blows smoke in Sartana's face during a card game. *Sartana* is the best example of a spaghetti shot entirely in the Italian wild west. The town set of Gold Springs is the Elios set, Tampico's *hacienda* is Villa Mussolini, while the location scenes were shot in the gravel pits, quarries and national parks around Rome; these were subsequently reused in *Sabata*.

With his trademark acrobatic heists and gadgets to the fore, Parolini, now in tandem with top Italian producer Alberto Grimaldi for PEA, began work on *Sabata*. The story was written by Parolini and his regular writing partner Renato Izzo. In Daugherty City, Texas, Sabata (a drifting gunslinger) teams up with untrustworthy Banjo (an old friend, with a Winchester hidden in his banjo) and two local layabouts, knife-thrower Garrincha and acrobatic Alley Cat, to confront a trio of thieving businessman: Stengel a rancher, Fergusson the saloonkeeper and Judge O'Hara. The evil trio plan to buy up land the railway needs to pass through Texas. With the aid of a gang of circus acrobats, Stengel and company steal $100,000 from the army, but Sabata foils their heist, returns the money and blackmails the villains with the threat of exposure. Stengel employs a succession of hired guns who try to kill Sabata, and in the climax Sabata, Alley Cat and Garrincha take on Stengel's army at Stengel's fortified ranch.

Parolini's inspirations were unlikely to say the least. The atmosphere of tongue-in-cheek adventure imitated Burt Lancaster's fanciful *The Crimson Pirate* (1952), a tremendously successful and influential film. Lancaster starred as the acrobatic Captain Vallo, who with his mute sidekick Ojo (Lancaster's old circus partner Nick Cravat) runs guns to rebel leader El Libre. It was one of the first Hollywood productions to be filmed in Italy, around Iscia in the Bay of Naples. Elements of

The Magnificent Seven reappeared in *Sabata*, especially Garrincha's knife-throwing skills. Louis Malle's western *Viva Maria* (1965) was set in a travelling circus and included a troupe of acrobats and a rifle that shoots around corners. Tonino Valerii's spaghetti western *Day of Anger* inspired Stengel's attempts to assassinate Sabata. The American musical western *The Fastest Guitar Alive* (1967) featured Roy Orbison as a Confederate spy with a rifle hidden in his guitar. All of these films infused Parolini's work on *Sabata*.

Parolini cast Lee Van Cleef as the hero and William Berger as his sidekick, Banjo. Berger was born in Austria, but went to the US in the fifties, attending the Actors Studio in New York and appearing on Broadway (under the name 'Bill Berger'). In the early sixties he relocated to Rome and briefly shared a flat with the Stones's Keith Richards; Berger even adopted the Stones's counter-culture 'look', with a mop of hair and distinctive Brian Jones sideburns. He made several films, including *The Murder Clinic* (1966 – as a doctor performing skin grafts) and two low-budget spaghettis – *Ringo's Big Night* (1965 – a nocturnal Tessari derivative) and the title role in *El Cisco* (1966 – a hybrid of *Django* and *Zorro*) – before his career took off with his role as Pinkerton's Agent Siringo in *Face to Face*.

Italian actor Pedro Sanchez was cast as Garrincha, the vagabond knife specialist. Sanchez bucked the trend in spaghetti westerns and changed his name from Ignazio Spalla to the Spanish-sounding 'Pedro Sanchez', in imitation of Fernando Sancho. Because of his girth he tended to be cast in Mexican bandit roles usually reserved for Spanish actors, and the new name better suited his image. He debuted in *One Silver Dollar* (1964 – as a Mexican farmer) and followed it up with roles in *In a Colt's Shadow* (1966), *Any Gun Can Play* (1967) and *Johnny Hamlet* (1968).

Linda Veras (as Banjo's girlfriend Jane) had appeared in Jean Luc Godard's *Le Mepris* (1963 – as a siren on the set of Fritz Lang's reworking of *The Odyssey*) and in Sollima's *Face to Face* (1967) and *Run Man Run* (1968). John Bartho (from *The Good, the Bad and the Ugly*) was typecast as the Sheriff of Daugherty City. Nick Jordan (from *Five for Hell*) performed some incredible leaps and somersaults as the mute Indian acrobat Alley Cat. The Virginian Brothers, the villainous acrobats employed by Stengel to rob the bank, were played by three stuntmen – the Ukmar brothers (Bruno and Franco) and Giuseppe Mattei (from *Left-handed Johnny West*). In Brian Fox's novelisation of *Sabata*, published in 1970 to tie in with the film's US release, the acrobats in the story are called the Ukmar Brothers. Franco Ressel played Stengel, a crook with a deadly spike-shooting cane. Stengel's hired guns featured several familiar faces: Spartaco Conversi (as fat henchman Slim), Romano Puppo (also Van Cleef's stuntman), Luciano Pigozzi (as a priestly hitman with a Derringer in his handkerchief), Claudio Undari (or 'Robert Hundar', a regular in Joaquin Romero Marchent westerns) and Marco Zuanelli; Zuanelli played alcoholic hired gun Sharky and had appeared as laundryman Wobbles in *Once Upon a Time in the West* (1968).

Sabata was shot in Italy and Spain early in 1969, with the array of unusual guns being provided by armourers SET-Mancini. The Daugherty City interiors and exteriors were shot at the Elios Studios town set (which since *The Big Silence* had gained a church and a half-built Chinese laundry). The scene in which *Sabata* catches up with the wagon carrying the stolen safe was shot amid the sheer cliffs of the Magliana quarry; the acrobats' hideout was also in Lazio. Stengel's walled ranch was Villa Mussolini, the former summer residence of Benito Mussolini, near

Ballistic surprises: Sabata and his customised Derringer; Lee Van Cleef in Gianfranco Parolini's *Sabata* (1969).

Rome. The more impressive desert locations were shot in Almeria and around San Jose in Spain, including Sharky's whitewashed hovel, the Los Palos water tower rendezvous (shot at Rancho De Las Salinillas) and the windblown desert finale (shot in the sierras above Tabernas).

Parolini's vision of the west is a circus, with the characters representing performers on a grand stage – the prairie and towns of the wild west. Sabata is a circus trick-shooter, Garrincha's the resident knife-thrower and Alley Cat an acrobat. Jane is a showgirl and Stengel a failed magician (he tries to make a safe full of money 'vanish'). Banjo is the novelty turn: a wandering troubadour (with bells sewn on his suit) and a dead-eyed sharpshooter, who combines the two in the most memorable scene in the film. Sabata informs Banjo that the five Clayton brothers are waiting for him in the street. Banjo strides out of the Grand Palace Hotel and walks to face them with only his banjo for protection. The Claytons say that they have been looking for Banjo all over Texas to settle some unfinished business. 'It's sad they have to die so far from home,' muses Banjo. The Claytons go for their guns, but Banjo hits the ground and shoots all five of them with a Winchester hidden in his banjo. 'Right through the heart,' Sabata comments on the hotel balcony; 'he remembers'. 'You knew him?' asks Jane. 'Once,' says Sabata 'we played together'.

Parolini alludes to Banjo and Sabata's past relationship throughout the film, in a variation of Leone's 'old man' and 'boy' scenario, though it is never explained exactly what this relationship was. The suggestion is that they were once outside the law. Banjo says that he barely recognises Sabata, because of his honesty in returning the safe to the army; it is obvious to Sabata that there are richer pickings blackmailing the real culprits. Later, when Banjo turns traitor at a rendezvous in the desert at Los Palos, it becomes apparent that Banjo is still outside the law. 'Me in the south,' he says to Sabata, 'you in the north. We might both have died because of old age. Instead our paths cross again.'

Van Cleef's Sabata persona is a replay of Colonel Mortimer in *For a Few Dollars More*, although this time his only motivation is money. Sabata (a Confederate major during the Civil War) shares Mortimer's penchant for Derringers and fancy weaponry, and dresses like him too. Van Cleef described Sabata in interviews as 'James Bond out West'; he loved the role and laced his performance with a range of sneers, grimaces and Bond-esque quips. Sabata is an easterner 'out west' (there are allusions to his time in St Louis) and his sophistication among the westerners affirms this.

Parolini's westerns are filled with riddles and games. If Leone's *Once Upon a Time in the West* has been compared by critics to a chess game and Vic Morrow's *A Man Called Sledge* (1970) to a hand of poker, then *Sabata* uses both analogies to good effect. When Sabata visits Stengel's ranch to discuss how much the villain is going to pay him to keep quiet, the scene is photographed to suggest a game of chess. The two sit at opposite ends of a long banqueting table laid out for dinner. Stengel places his deadly cane on the table facing Sabata, who warily moves a decanter to shield himself. When Stengel sees this, he moves the cane to improve his aim, but Sabata shifts a jug to cover Stengel's 'move'. All this happens while the pair discuss Sabata's payoff. Throughout the film the 'poker stakes' get higher and higher; Sabata's blackmailing demands become more ridiculous, as each time Stengel refuses to pay up. Stengel would rather hire guns to plug Sabata, but his investments prove costly, as each mercenary fails.

Greedy rancher Hardy Stengel is an improvement on the villains from *Sartana*. His 'mania for grandeur' is echoed in the décor of his ranch house (designed by Carlo Simi), with gold furniture and candelabras. Stengel's favourite reading-matter is Thomas Dew's *Inequality is the Basis of Society*. He recites his favourite passage: 'All men gifted with superior talent and thus with superior powers, must command and use inferior men'. Judge O'Hara (played by Gianni Rizzo, from *Face to Face* and *Sartana*) has second thoughts about their scheme and is the only one to survive Sabata's attack on the ranch, while Fergusson (Antonio Gradoli) remains loyal to Stengel, but is betrayed and shot by his partner.

Stengel particularly enjoys an elaborate duelling game, which he acts out in his own shooting gallery. At either end of the room stand two life-size metal cut-outs of duellists (complete with top hats) with holes through their hearts. The two human duellists stand behind the cut-outs and take pot-shots at each other, except that Stengel cheats and flips a lever that covers his 'heart' with a metal plate (a reference to the breastplate finale in *A Fistful of Dollars*). In the final duel between Sabata and Stengel in the shooting gallery, Sabata finds himself at a disadvantage. He spots Stengel's cane lying nearby and ingeniously tosses a dollar coin, which activates the trigger mechanism and fires a bolt straight through Stengel's heart.

Sabata's gadgets and wisecracks are his trademarks. Apart from his four-barrelled Derringer (with an 'S' on the grips and three extra barrels hidden in the butt) he uses some accurate dollar-coin throwing (be it to activate a pianola or kill a villain) and a long-range Winchester with detachable barrel, to pick off villains at distance. As one robber comments, 'There isn't a Winchester going that can shoot half that distance,' before getting shot. This recalls real-life Civil War General Sedgewick's comment at the Battle of Spotsylvania, as he looked over a parapet wall: 'They couldn't hit an elephant at this dist…'. Later Sabata hits a bell at 600 yards and Garrincha marvels at Sabata's accuracy. 'A wise man keeps his distance,' comments the sharpshooter. Parolini and his writing partner Renato Izzo even borrowed quotes from *Sartana*; one of Stengel's men asks who Sabata is and Garrincha laughs, 'Could be your pall-bearer'. The writers also allude to *The Magnificent Seven*: Sabata watches Garrincha's throwing skill and notes, 'Knife like that'd be better as a friend'. Garrincha beams, 'If it's friends you want, would you like to have two?' and introduces him to Alley Cat.

Banjo is a devious character – a blue-eyed, redheaded drifter who has nightmares about settling down. His relationship with saloon girl Jane provides some humour, with the chemistry between Linda Veras and William Berger adding to their jousting. Jane wants him to stop drifting, but he is 'just passing through'. She wants to travel to Europe and tells him he will never take any money from punters for playing his banjo without killing them. In the finale, Banjo has enough money to move on and Jane packs her bags. But as they are about to depart, the drifter says 'I told you I was just passing through' and rides away alone.

Parolini's massed gunfight at Stengel's ranch was a fitting climax to the film, with Sabata, Alley Cat and Garrincha taking on Stengel's entire gang (and a Gatling gun) with ingenuity, acrobatics, a railway carriage and some well-aimed dynamite. Parolini excels in the action sequences. The opening robbery, in a windblown, gas-lit street, is imaginatively staged. The acrobatic bandits clean out the Daugherty bank with the aid of a seesaw, a trolley and a portable length of railway track. *Sabata* also features the trademark Parolini surprise ending. Turncoat Banjo 'kills' Sabata in a rigged gunfight (earning himself a huge reward from Judge O'Hara) and rides out of town with a wad of dollar bills and Sabata's corpse in a coffin. But Sabata is still alive; when Banjo tries to double-cross his partner, Sabata scatters Banjo's share of the money to the wind and leaves the hapless gunman chasing a whirlwind of dollars through the desert. Parolini had previously used the same effect in a stagecoach robbery in *Left-handed Johnny West*, though the scene emulated the airport finale of Stanley Kubrick's *The Killing* (1956).

The music for *Sabata* is by Marcello Giombini. Giombini scored Mario Bava's Viking horror *Knives of the Avenger* (1965), *Dollars for a Fast Gun* (1966), and provided a very unusual Hawaiian-flavoured score to *Three Golden Boys* (1966). He also composed the music to some of the *Sabata* spin-offs: *Sabata the Killer* (1970) and Parolini's own *Return of Sabata* (1971). *Sabata* is one of the most popular spaghetti-western scores, mainly due to two pieces – the title song and a trumpet-led, funereal bolero that accompanies Sabata's nighttime visit to Stengel's ranch. The title song is voiced in Italian (even in the English print) and consists of the Italian title of the film, 'Ehi amico...c'e Sabata, hai chiuso!' ('Hey friend...Sabata's here, close everything') intoned between a fast-paced, jangly guitar riff, backed by trumpets and Alessandroni's choir. At other points, Giombini uses themes linked to the characters in the film. Banjo's banjo and sleighbells theme; a recurrent church organ (featuring Banjo's performance of Bach's 'Fugue in D Minor'); and several sound-effects, including swirling violins and a springboard twang, to dramatically announce Van Cleef's appearances.

Sabata was released in Italy in September 1969. Terence Hill and Bud Spencer were the stars of the moment, following their trilogy directed by Giuseppe Colizzi (between 1967 and 1969), but *Sabata* struck a chord with audiences all over Europe. In Spain all reference to *Sabata* was gone, with the film retitled *Oro Sangriento* ('Bloody Gold'). Though it owed much to previous Parolini efforts, *Sabata*'s easy-going appeal and a great performance by Van Cleef meant PEA and Grimaldi had one of the top-grossing Italian hits of the year.

The international rights were owned by UA, and it was released at 102 minutes in March 1970, following their success with *Death Rides a Horse*. The only difference to the Italian print was the editing of Linda Veras's bathtub scene. *Sabata* proved to be Van Cleef's most popular post-Leone western in the US and the UK. The UA poster campaign wasn't particularly impressive (it showed Berger firing his banjo, ruining the surprise), though the tagline 'The Man with the Gunsight Eyes comes to Kill!' aptly summed up the straightforward action. Critics generally liked the film, with The *New York Times* calling Van Cleef's hero a cross between 'Judex and Fearless Fosdick' and praising Parolini's cinematographic 'arabesques', comparing the production design to Bava at his best.

Parolini followed *Sabata* with another widescreen western adventure that was more ambitious than its predecessor. Yul Brynner played Indio Black (the title of the film in Italy) who was rechristened 'Sabata' in the US version. The film was retitled *Adios Sabata* for the US market and *The Bounty Hunters* in the UK. Indio Black/Sabata is a mercenary in revolutionary Mexico *circa* 1867. He teams up with 'Blondito' Balantine (played by Dean Reed), Escudo (Sanchez again), Septembre (Sal Borgese – who fires conker-sized ball-bearings from his custom-made boots) and Gitano, an Apache acrobat (Joseph Persaud), to steal Austrian gold from the evil Colonel Skimmel (Gerard Herter). Though Brynner's black-fringed outfit and cool, cigar-smoking professionalism echoed his role as Chris in *The Magnificent Seven*, it owed more to Brynner's performance in the US western *Invitation to a Gunfighter* (1964). Here he played a fancy, black-clad gunman named Jules Gaspard

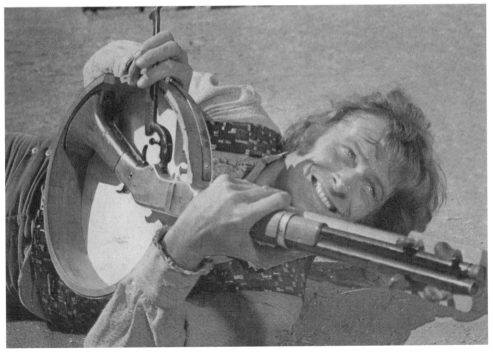

Play Me the Song of Death: Banjo (William Berger) gives a recital in *Sabata* (1969).

D'Estaing, who is hired to clean up a crooked town, only to turn on his employers: in one memorable scene he wrecks their saloon with a hatstand. D'Estaing's poetry-quoting and harpsichord-playing were particularly influential: Indio Black's pronouncements sound akin to poetry and he performs Schubert on the piano. The Mexican setting (revolutionaries, gunrunners and Gatling guns), the great locations (Almeria, Madrid, Cinecitta and Elios), stylish costumes (Napoleonic uniforms and Mexican rags) and gadgets (a model ship that fires real cannons, Sabata's sawn-off Winchester and some less impressive carrier pigeons) made the film another huge hit for the Parolini/Grimaldi team. It also features Bruno Nicolai's best score, incorporating whistles, flute blasts and twangy guitars. Like *Sabata*, *Adios Sabata* was a big hit in the US.

Simultaneously, Sartana, with his snappy catchphrase ('I am your pallbearer') became immensely popular (especially in Germany), and Garko went on to star in his own series of films, usually directed by Giuliano Carmineo. The Carmineo/Garko series was *Sartana the Gravedigger* (1969 – with Frank Wolff and Klaus Kinski), *Have a Good Funeral, Sartana Will Pay* (1970 – with Franco Ressel) and *Light the Fuse…Sartana's Coming* (1971) – the best of the series, in which the final shootout sees Sartana taking on a bandit gang with a church organ that doubles as a cannon.

Several westerns tried to cash in on the success of *Sabata*, but the only genuine sequel was *Return of Sabata*, directed by Parolini in 1971. It was shot entirely in Italy, with two town sets (Elios and De Laurentiis) being used as the setting for Hobsonville. Though slightly fanciful, the gadgets and set pieces in the first 'Sabata' film were plausible; there was nothing completely outlandish about a long-range rifle, a Winchester disguised as a banjo or even a spring-loaded, bolt-firing cane. *Return of Sabata* retained the spectacular atmosphere and gadgets of its predecessor, but went overboard; the entire film resembles an elaborate, stage-managed night in the big top. At one point Sabata is addressed as 'stage manager' and his sidekick 'a clown'. *Return of Sabata* saw Van Cleef reprise his role – this time as a spaghetti secret agent who is working as a circus sharpshooter while he investigates a counter-feiting ring. He arrives in the Texan town of Hobsonville, where an Irish Mafia (sporting some unconvincing ginger wigs) exhort taxes from the locals, ostensibly for town development, but really to finance their money laundering. All the ingredients from the first *Sabata* reappear: Sabata's partner Banjo becomes Confederate Lieutenant Clyde (Reiner Schone); Sanchez becomes the town barker named Bronco; and the villain is the Irish Godfather, Joe McIntock (Gianpiero Albertini). Sabata sides with Bronco and two acrobatic pickpockets (Vasilli Karis and Nick Jordan) to break up McIntock's party, resulting in some entertaining action sequences involving trampolines and seesaws.

The up-tempo title song (again provided by Giombini) celebrated *Sabata* in a way only spaghettis could. It included lines like 'Nine-fingered man' (a reference to Van Cleef's stubby digit, which he injured in a carpentry accident in the late

fifties), 'Four-barrelled Derringer' (his favoured weapon) and a 'Bum ba bum ba
bum bum bum' wordless refrain, all accompanied by a Bollywood backing track.
This time the gimmicky weapons veered into James Bond territory. Sabata deployed
a set of handy cigars – one a magnet for winning at roulette and one a blowpipe for
scaring McIntock. Sabata also had a magnet in his boot heel and a palm gun (the
Protector), and one of the acrobats fired wheel nuts from a catapult strung between

'A wise man keeps his distance': Sabata (Lee Van Cleef) takes aim from the
balcony of the Grand Palace Hotel set at Elios Studios in *Sabata* (1969).

his feet. The circus atmosphere of *Return of Sabata* is established in the memorable opening sequence, beautifully photographed by Parolini's regular cinematographer, Alessandro Mancori. The scene is a western shootout in a coffin-maker's, bathed in swathes of red and green light, as Sabata outguns six stylishly dressed gunslingers. Only when the duel is over do the audience realise they've been watching a Bava-esque circus show, as the six gunmen wipe off their fake blood; this western fantasy becomes the basis for the finale of the film, this time for real. Unfortunately poor distribution, a lacklustre advertising campaign ('The Man with the Gunsight eyes is back!') and extreme cutting (from 102 minutes to 85) led to its failure. Parolini and Van Cleef worked together for the last time five years later on the inferior *God's Gun* (1976), with Van Cleef in the dual roles of peaceful Father John and gunfighter Lewis, and seventies teen idol Leif Garrett cast as the gunslinger's young admirer.

Van Cleef used the huge success of *Sabata* to launch his career back in America, particularly in American productions (by 1969 his fee had reached $400,000 per film). He first attempted this by appearing in an American-financed imitation spaghetti western produced by Andre De Toth called *El Condor* (1970). With a vast budget and a good cast, including Jim Brown, Mariana Hill and Patrick O'Neal, the film was huge in Europe, but was less successful than *Sabata* in the US. Van Cleef made several more spaghettis, including *The Grand Duel* (1972) and *Blood Money* (1974), and tried an assortment of styles, including the comedy *Bad Man's River* (1972), the nadir of his career. He was one of the most travelled stars in the Italian film industry, shooting westerns in Italy, Spain, the US, the Canary Islands and Israel throughout the seventies, but the quality declined. Van Cleef's agent, Tom Jennings, said that the actor's extended stay in Italy irrevocably damaged his Hollywood career, adding, 'I think he could have been a greater movie star, as big as Charles Bronson or Clint Eastwood, had he come back from Europe sooner… but he liked working abroad'. This proved costly to Van Cleef's long-term career, though his output throughout the sixties was a worthy testament to his talent and *Sabata* is one of the last great Italian westerns. It was a film made as the winds of change were blowing through the western sets of Rome – a moment when the killing stopped and the laughter started.

19

'He Keeps Alive With His Colt .45'

— Enzo Barboni's *They Call Me Trinity* (1970)

They Call Me Trinity (1970)
original title: *Lo Chiamavano Trinità*
Credits
DIRECTOR – 'E.B. Clucher' (Enzo Barboni)
PRODUCER – Italo Zingarelli
STORY AND SCREENPLAY – 'E.B. Clucher' (Enzo Barboni)
COSTUMES – Enzo Bulgarelli
EDITOR – Gianpiero Giunti
DIRECTOR OF PHOTOGRAPHY – Aldo Giordani
MUSIC COMPOSER – Franco Micalizzi
MUSIC CONDUCTOR – Gianfranco Plenzio
Interiors filmed at Incir De Paolis Studios, Rome
Techniscope/Technochrome
An Italian Production for West Film (Rome)
Released internationally by Avco Embassy Pictures
Cast
    'Terence Hill', Mario Girotti (Trinity); 'Bud Spencer', Carlo
    Pedersoli (Bambino); Steffen Zacharias (Jonathan Swift);
    Dan Sturkie (Brother Tobias); Gisela Hahn (Sarah); Elena
    Pedemonte (Judith); Farley Granger (Major Harrison); Ezio
    Marano (Weasel); Luciano Rossi (Timid); Remo Capitani
    (Mescal); Riccardo Pizzuti (Jeff); Paolo Magalotti (Major
    Harrison's lieutenant); Ugo Sasso (real Sheriff); Osiride
    Pevarello (Joe, Mormon in general store); Gigi Bonos
    (Mexican innkeeper); Michele Cimarosa (drunken Mexican
    prisoner); Dominic Barto (Mortimer); Alessandro Sperli
    (Jack); Tony Norton (bounty-hunter); Fortunato Arena
    (general storekeeper); Jess Hill (Mormon baby); Gaetano
    Imbro (bearded member of Harrison's gang); Alberto

Dell'Aqua (young blond Mormon); Herman Reynoso
(Mormon 'Brother Lookout'); Lorenzo Fineschi (blond
Mormon); with Vito Gagliardi, Antonio Monselesan and
Franco Marletta

*   *   *

In October 1967, a western was released in Italy that had such a huge impact on
Italian cinema that it resonated throughout the seventies. *God Forgives – I Don't*, a
tough, Almeria-shot spaghetti, was directed by Giuseppe Colizzi. Two gunmen,
Cat Stevens and Hutch Bessy, team up to track down an outlaw, Bill San Antonio,
who has faked his own death, but continues to rob trains. The action sequences
were very brutal: the film opens with a driverless train crashing into the buffers at
Canyon City station, with everyone on board dead. But there was also fine comic
interplay between the two heroes: Cat was an excellent gunman, acrobat, knifeman
and fistfighter (*The Magnificent Seven* rolled into one), while his partner Hutch was
a man mountain, with the strength of ten. These two were played by a pair of pseudonymous Italians – Venetian 'Terence Hill' and Neapolitan 'Bud Spencer'. Via the
'Trinity' films – *They Call Me Trinity* (1970) and *Trinity is Still My Name* (1971) –
Hill and Spencer would go on to dominate Italian cinema for the next decade and
become the most popular domestic comedy duo of all time. The partnership was
formed by chance. When *God Forgives – I Don't* was planned, the original lead was
Peter Martell, but he broke his leg as the film was about to start. It was going to be
called *Il Cane, Il Gatto, Il Volpe* ('The Dog, the Cat, the Fox'); with Spencer already
cast as the 'Dog' and Frank Wolff as the 'Fox', the role of the 'Cat' was offered to
Terence Hill.

Financed by Italo Zingarelli (who had already produced *Hate for Hate* and
directed *The Five Man Army*), director Enzo Barboni cast Hill and Spencer in his
latest project, *They Call Me Trinity*. Barboni wrote the story and the screenplay.
Bambino, a horse-rustler, has escaped from the Penitentiary in Yuma. He's biding
his time, posing as a sheriff in a township where Major Harrison's men (in league
with a bunch of Mexican raiders led by bandit Mescal) are persecuting the pacifist
Mormons. The major wants their lush valley as pasture for his horses. Bambino is
waiting for his henchmen, Weasel and Timid, to plan their next hold-up. Partly out
of decency – and partly to get his hands on the major's horses – Bambino sides with
the Mormons.

Trinity arrives in town and is enlisted by his half-brother to help; Bambino, a
sheriff only because he stole the star from a peace officer he ambushed, appoints
the unpredictable Trinity as his deputy and nervously awaits the impending chaos.
Trinity quickly makes an impression on the major's men, though Bambino is not
impressed by the catalogue of disaster: 'One store destroyed, three heads split like
overripe melons, one man wounded and one castrated…all in two hours! Just two

hours I left you alone.' 'Well you asked me to give you a hand,' notes Trinity. Bambino, Trinity, Weasel and Timid teach the Mormons how to use their fists, and in the finale they defeat their enemies in a huge punch-up. The story contains elements of *Destry Rides Again* (1939), *Shane* (1953), *Rio Bravo* (1959) and *The Magnificent Seven* (1960); Barboni's original script featured only Trinity, but Zingarelli suggested the addition of pugnacious Bambino, on hand to brain the opposition with his lethal punches.

With the feats of strength and lively scuffles, spaghetti westerns were back in muscleman territory ('Bambino the Mighty'), but the muscle-bound beefcake is contrasted with a clever, agile sidekick – a character in the mould of Giuliano Gemma's Krios in *Sons of Thunder* (1962), one of the few Italian mythical heroes to use acrobatics and guile rather than strength to defeat the villains. Contrasting comedy teams had always been popular in Italy, the most obvious example being tall, urbane Ciccio Ingrassia and short, uncouth Franco Franchi, who made parodies of every popular Cinecitta-genre. Even a comedy team like Peter Cook and Dudley Moore were popular in Italy; *Bedazzled*, a moderate grosser in most countries, was the third-biggest money-maker in Italy in 1967 and led to their casting in the Italian caper *Monte Carlo or Bust* (1969).

Previously cast as a lightweight dreamboat, Terence Hill's real name was Mario Girotti, and his family was of German descent. He started his career as a youngster in fifties Italian productions and made his mark as Count Cavriaghi in Visconti's *The Leopard* (1963). He also appeared in one of the best 'Winnetou' movies, *Last of the Renegades* (1964 – also called *Winnetou II*) as 7th Cavalry Lieutenant Merrill. Hill enjoyed a three-year contract in Germany, but it was his gritty role in *God Forgives – I Don't* and his Franco Nero impersonation in Ferdinando Baldi's *Django Get a Coffin Ready* (1968) that revealed his star quality. Prior to his role as Django, Hill made *Rita of the West* (1967), the infamous musical spaghetti. He played Black Stan, the lover of Little Rita, though he tried to blend into the background during the production numbers. For *God Forgives – I Don't*, his first Italian western, Girotti was asked to anglicise his name. 'Terence Hill' was given to him (he was asked to choose from a list of names); he was not inspired by Latin historical authors ('Terenzio') or his wife's maiden name (Lori Hill), as his publicity often claimed.

'Bud Spencer' (real name Carlo Pedersoli) had won a silver swimming medal at the 1952 Helsinki Olympics and subsequently managed to break into acting. Spencer (who named himself after Spencer Tracy) debuted in *Quo Vadis?* (1951). *God Forgives – I Don't* was his first western, though in interviews Spencer maintains that it was he who replaced injured Martell in the film. Following *God Forgives*, he made three westerns without Hill, *Today it's Me…Tomorrow You* (1968), *Beyond the Law* (1968) and *The Five Man Army* (1969).

The huge success of *God Forgives – I Don't* (it was the number-one film in Italy in 1967) resulted in two sequels, inferior in quality, but big box-office hits: *Ace High* (1968) and the pedestrian, circus-bound *Boot Hill* (1969). *Ace High* (retitled

Revenge at El Paso) remains one of the most financially successful spaghettis of all time and teams the duo with a gunman named Cacopoulos (played by Eli Wallach). More boisterous than *God Forgives – I Don't*, *Ace High* features a lighter side to the Hill and Spencer team, with Spencer brawling his way through several knockabout fistfights.

Renowned director of photography Enzo Barboni had shot some of the best spaghetti westerns, working particularly well with Sergio Corbucci on *Django*; in a cutting-room oversight, Barboni can be seen, camera in hand, during Django's bar-room punch-up. Barboni also had aspirations as a director. While photographing *Texas Adios* (1966), he approached Franco Nero with a comedy script he was working on, but Nero wasn't interested in a light-hearted western, so the project was put on hold. Barboni met Hill when he photographed *Rita of the West* and *Django Get a Coffin Ready*, and met Spencer while photographing *The Five Man Army* in 1969. That same year, Barboni adopted the pseudonym 'E.B. Clucher' and made his directorial debut with an autumnal western called *The Unholy Four* (also released as *Chuck Mool*). Influenced by Corbucci's early work, it featured an amnesiac gunman (Leonard Mann) escaping from the State Mental Institution to seek revenge on those who wrongly put him there; here the hero is a 'man with no name' only because he has forgotten it.

When *They Call Me Trinity* was first announced, the leads were Peter Martell as Trinity and Luigi Montefiore (who used the pseudonym 'George Eastman') as Bambino, but Barboni eventually decided on Hill and Spencer for the roles. Barboni filled out his cast with some familiar faces. Steffen Zacharias (from *Ace High* and *The Five Man Army*) played Jonathan Swift, the housekeeper in the sheriff's office. Dan Sturkie (from *The Five Man Army*) played the Mormon leader Brother Tobias. Remo Capitani (a stuntman from Colizzi's westerns and *The Unholy Four*) played mad Mexican renegade Mescal. Farley Granger played southern horse-obsessed rancher Major Harrison (named Harriman in the Italian print) as an effete version of Major Jackson in *Django*. Granger was best known as the star of Hitchcock's *Rope* (1948) and *Strangers on a Train* (1951), and for his appearance in Luchino Visconti's *Senso* (1954). He had been a regular in Hollywood productions until 1955, when he suddenly retired from the screen to concentrate on TV and theatre work. He resurfaced in the late sixties in Italy, and Major Harrison was one of his first comeback roles. *Trinity* also features Terence Hill's 10-month-old son Jess, as the Mormon baby who sits on Trinity's knee.

They Call Me Trinity was shot in Italy; it was financed by Italian-based West Film. Aldo Giordani was hired as director of photography and Barboni includes several authentic background details – locals tanning cowhides in town, the half-built Mormon settlement and a stage-station shack with a cow grazing on the roof – based on period photographs. The town set was at Incir De Paolis Studios, near Rome (also used in *The Five Man Army*); the stage station was in the Magliana quarry, Lazio. The beautiful grassy valley locations were shot in the Parco Dei

Monti Simbruini, to the east of Rome, where the Mormons' camp was constructed. The verdant countryside locations give the film a fine edge, a pleasant change from the stark desert. The same lush woodlands, hills and rock outcrops were later seen in 'Trinity' derivatives like *Panhandle Calibre .38* (1971). The picturesque waterfall where Trinity frolics with Sarah and Judith, two Mormon women, was the Monte Gelato falls in the Treja Valley Park, Lazio; in this scene Trinity claims that he can't swim, though Hill and Spencer used to swim for the same team in Rome.

The two brothers look nothing like each other and therein lies the comedy. Trinity is a comical western hero – a cross between a lethal gunslinger and a beguiling buffoon. He wears a tatty pair of dungarees, a moth-eaten shirt and a low-slung gunbelt, and travels around on a horse-drawn Indian travois – a sort of bumpy, mobile hammock. He is also extremely unhygienic; when Trinity walks into a cantina and brushes himself off, he is barely visible through the dust cloud. He fears no one (from saddle-tramp bounty-hunters to the fastest professional guns), but the thought of responsibility, hard work and the horror of 'settling down' fills him with dread.

His colossal brother Bambino was played by Spencer as a dim-witted bruiser. Theirs is the classic teaming of brains and agility with pigheadedness and brawn, which had already been exploited by Colizzi. Bambino knows what he wants (the major's herd of stallions) and Trinity knows how to get it (by helping out the Mormons). If dim-witted Bambino gets an idea in his head, it is only because Trinity planted it there. Bambino is an indestructible rock, as the toughest punches and slaps bounce off him. He bears a resemblance to the character of Obelix, the comic-strip Gaul who fell into the magic invincibility potion when he was a baby. Obelix's

Bambino (Bud Spencer) and Trinity (Terence Hill) help a Mormon settlement in the hit comedy western *They Call Me Trinity* (1970).

favourite move was the uppercut, while Bambino's speciality is piledriving punches, usually applied to the victim's forehead, as though he is trying to drive his opponent into the ground like a nail.

Comedy westerns had always been popular. Some of the best examples from Hollywood were James Stewart's *Destry Rides Again* (1939), Bob Hope's *The Paleface* (1948) and its sequel *Son of Paleface* (1952) and *Cat Ballou* (1965 – notable for Lee Marvin's drunkard Kid Sheleen). All were successful because they respected genre convention – laughing with the characters rather than ridiculing them. There had even been some comedy spaghettis, ranging from the Franchi and Ingrassia series, to farce westerns like *I Came, I Saw, I Shot* (1968) and *The Bang Bang Kid* (1967 – featuring a gunslinging robot), though even the most serious Italian westerns had some elements of humour. The first successful comedy spaghettis were Franco Giraldi's 'MacGregor' westerns (*Seven Guns for the MacGregors* and *Seven Women for the MacGregors*); and *Django Shoots First* (1966), which featured bar-room brawls and a lightweight hero played by Dutch actor Roel Bos (under the alias 'Glenn Saxson').

The enduring influence on Barboni was Laurel and Hardy's *Way Out West* (1937). Here, the established personas of Stan and Ollie were transposed unchanged into the wild west. They arrive in Brushwood Gulch to deliver an inheritance (a locket and the deeds to a gold mine) to the daughter of their deceased partner, but wily saloon-owner Mickey Finn (played by James Finleyson) tricks them out of it. What makes the film so successful are Stan and Ollie's comedy antics and their musical numbers. On a stagecoach Ollie attempts to strike up conversation with a female passenger: 'A lot of weather we've been having lately'. When they arrive in town, a bunch of singing cowpokes (billed as the Avalon Boys) are airing a gentle toe-tapper called 'At the Ball, That's All' on the porch of Mickey Finn's Palace, and Stan and Ollie do a soft-shoe shuffle on their way into the saloon. Later they perform their best-known song, 'Trail of the Lonesome Pine', while propping up the bar. When the deed is stolen, Stan swears that if they don't get it back, he will eat his hat, but their first attempt fails and Ollie makes him keep his word. 'Now you're taking me illiterally,' comments Stan. But it is the ahead-of-their-time sight gags that made the film so influential. Stan's thumb-lighting, Ollie's neck-stretching, several wacky chases and their aborted attempt at acrobatics involving Ollie, a block and tackle, a mule and a high window.

They Call Me Trinity begins with a sequence based on its equivalent in *Way Out West*. Stan and Ollie make their way towards Brushwood Gulch – with Stan leading the way and Ollie lying on their mule-drawn travois. As they mosey along, the litter gives Ollie a rough ride, first over bumpy rocks in the road and then through a river. In the next sequence Ollie is wrapped in a blanket and there's a washing line strung across the travois, drying his clothes. In Barboni's title sequence, as yawning Trinity is dragged along on his litter by a horse with a good sense of direction, the horse drags him through a river, submerging its passenger. The difference is that Trinity is so laid-back he doesn't 'bat an eye'.

Barboni deployed a parade of western stereotypes (both American and Italian) for his way-out west. Neat and tidy Jonathan Swift – Bambino's put-upon housekeeper in the sheriff's office – is a fastidious version of Walter Brennan's Stumpy in *Rio Bravo*. In fact, the early section of Trinity strongly resembles a parody of Howard Hawks's film, with Bambino as Sheriff John T. Chance and Trinity as his young deputy, Dude. Trinity even features the sheriff's 'nightly scolding' of the rough elements in the town saloon. As Bambino makes his way to the saloon, a local cheerfully offers, 'Evenin' sheriff', to which he curtly replies 'Shut up'. Zacharias's parodic performance as Jonathan enhances such references. He does Bambino's washing and cooking, and is a stickler for cleanliness, refusing to shake Trinity's filthy hand ('Don't want to catch no tetanus'). Zacharias delivers the best lines, provided by Gene Luotto's English translation of Barboni's original script. At one point Jonathan points out that Bambino always seems to be elsewhere when trouble starts – 'I've never met such an unlucky sheriff'.

The major hates the Mormons, and Farley Granger's drawling accent works best when he vents his rage on the farmers. In one scene he tells how, through their faith, they settled in the valley to live in 'dignified poverty'. 'Then good old faith forms a community,' fumes Harrison, 'builds a house that could shelter an army and fills the corrals with livestock.' The major hires Jack and Mortimer, two humourless hired guns (played by Alessandro Sperli and Dominic Barto) to tackle the 'fast deputy'. But Trinity is easily a match for them, humiliating the duo by making them run out of town in their long johns.

Mescal is the ultimate send-up of Corbucci's comical Mexican generals, with his sombrero, cannon-like pistol, bandoleers and an epaulette hanging around his neck. When he raids the Mormon settlement he is offered their meagre food, but demands 'good soup with garlic and mucho vino' for their next visit. Later, when the Major hires him to get rid of the Mormons, he is paid with 20 stallions, but Mescal would prefer it if he could steal the horses; for bandits to work for pay is too embarrassing.

The noble Mormons, led by their stalwart leader Brother Tobias, are righteous, God-fearing people. As Jonathan says, 'All they do is pray and work, work and pray'. When Trinity and Bambino first arrive at the camp, Tobias shouts, 'Welcome brothers!' and Bambino frowns, 'Hey, who told him we were brothers?' Tobias speaks in quotes from the Bible; Trinity falls for Sarah and Judith (two Mormon women he has saved from the major's men); and Tobias describes their rescue thus: 'They were innocent doves surrounded by evil and the Lord heard their prayers and sent you to answer'. Bambino shrugs, 'It was approximately like that'. It is Tobias's own interpretation of the Bible that helps the Mormons win the day. In the finale, the major's gang attack the Mormon camp. In a variation on *The Magnificent Seven*, the farmers have no firearms, but have been trained in fisticuffs by Trinity, Bambino and Bambino's two bumbling cohorts, Timid and Weasel. They dupe the major into ordering his gang to take off their guns (out of respect for the Mormons' non-violent beliefs), then Tobias reads from the Bible: 'In the words of Coeleth, son of David, King of Jerusalem, "There's a time to fight and a time to win!"' which is the Mormons' cue to confront their oppressors.

Barboni's forte is the well-choreographed, action-packed fistfights, with much breakaway furniture and hidden crash mats. In that respect, Trinity's huge stunt crew were the stars of the show. Hill and Spencer performed all their own stunts and fights, while most of the male cast-members were stuntmen, including Osiride Pevarello, Alberto Dell'Aqua and Lorenzo Fineschi (as Mormons) and Riccardo Pizzuti, Gaetano Imbro and Paolo Magalotti (with the major). The punch-ups were choreographed by Giorgio Ubaldi. In the fight between Trinity and two of the major's henchmen in a general store (a parody of the Grafton Store scene in *Shane*), Trinity bangs one man's head against a cash register, which rings up 'Thank You'. In a saloon fracas, Trinity and Bambino face a bunch of the major's men, but Trinity, having started the argument, sits back and watches his brother pummel the gang.

Trinity owes much to cartoons, especially Trinity's speeded-up gunslinging prowess and ridiculously accurate marksmanship. In one sequence, he draws and reholsters his Colt Navy three times before his opponents can twitch. At the chaparral cantina, Trinity devours a huge pan of beans, mopped up with bread and washed down with tequila, then belches loudly. Two bounty-hunters in the cantina check their collection of reward posters and ask his name. 'They call me Trinity,' Hill answers, as the gunmen's jaws drop open. 'The Right Hand of the Devil!' says one, the other adding 'They say you've got the fastest gun around'. 'Is that what they say?' grins Trinity, 'Gees.' As he walks to his travois they aim to shoot him in the back, but without turning around Trinity draws his pistol and kills them both.

Barboni integrates running gags into his films, and *They Call Me Trinity* has two good examples. Trinity arrives in town with a wounded Mexican prisoner (Michele Cimarosa). In an unsanitary operation, Trinity gets the Mexican drunk, Bambino removes the bullet with a red-hot knife and Trinity plugs up the hole with his finger. The anaesthetic proves so popular that the Mexican refuses to budge from the jail for the duration of the film. Another running gag recounts the story of the sheriff (Ugo Sasso) from whom Bambino stole the badge. The sheriff wasn't following Bambino – they just happened to be going the same way – but Bambino ambushed the lawman and stole his star, leaving him for dead. Subsequently, it appears the lawman, now lame in one leg, survived. 'Sheriff' Bambino receives a note from the injured lawman: 'Now he wants me to give him a hand to find me'. Later Timid and Weasel encounter the same sheriff, and Bambino asks if they finished him off: 'Well almost… Timid got him in the good leg, then we broke his crutches.' Jonathan describes the lawman thus: 'Moustache, star on his chest, crutches – a typical crippled sheriff' – a joke at the expense of Hawks's *Rio Bravo* sequel, *El Dorado* (1967) which saw John Wayne and Robert Mitchum hobbling down the street on crutches.

Barboni handles Trinity's fade-out particularly well. With the major defeated, he rides off to Nebraska, in search of pastures new, while Bambino discovers that

Trinity has allowed the Mormons to claim the major's horse herd by branding them with a 'Ten Commandments' motif. Furious, Bambino leaves and Trinity stays on to begin a new life. As Tobias welcomes the 'lost sheep' into the fold, Trinity hears the dreaded words 'labour', 'hard day's work' and 'fatigue', and decides to follow Bambino's dust towards California.

The music to *They Call Me Trinity* was written by Franco Micalizzi, who had previously worked with Roberto Pregadio on his famous whistled western score for *The Forgotten Pistolero* (1970). Trinity's jokey title-sequence travois ride is scored with a light-hearted, catchy theme song, which establishes the mood. The opening shot of Trinity's holstered pistol, dragging through the dust, is accompanied by the sound of a rattlesnake. Then a lazy whistler, an oboe, honky-tonk piano and acoustic guitar begin an idle melody. David King belts out the parodic title song in classic cowboy style:

> You may think he's a sleepy-type guy, always takes his time
> Soon I know you'll be changing your mind, when you've seen him use a gun boy
> He's the top of the west, always cool he's the best
> He keeps alive with his Colt .45
> Who's the guy who's a riding to town, in the prairie sun
> You won't bother to fool him around, when you've seen him use a gun boy
> When you've seen him use his gun.

Have Gun Will Travel: Trinity (Terence Hill) drifts into town in the opening scene of Enzo Barboni's *They Call Me Trinity* (1970).

The piece was written by Franco Micalizzi and Lally Stott. Englishman Stott was brought in to write the English lyrics and also had a hand in the melody; he is billed on the instrumental versions of the theme too. Stott later had a hit in the early seventies with a cover of 'Chirpy Chirpy, Cheep Cheep'. With Alessandroni's whistling, his singers harmonising with lyrics ('Don't! Don't!') and big-band brass and drum-kit, King delivers the song with just the right amount of half-hearted Dean Martin-esque conviction to make it a success. King is billed as 'Annibale' on the Italian soundtrack releases.

Throughout the film a whistled version of the theme accompanies Trinity as he ambles towards his next run-in with the major, while an up-tempo version, with electric piano and 'wah-wah' guitar, scores the brothers' ride to the Mormon camp. The Mormons have a sombre hymnal piece, used as the background score to the climactic fistfight. The major has a trumpet riding theme (with horn, electric guitar and trumpet flourish) and Mescal's bandits have Micalizzi's take on the 'Mexican Hat Dance'. In the waterfall sequence, in which Trinity splashes about with Sarah and Judith, a 'love theme' incorporates mellow guitar, strings and a synthesised pan-pipe. For the scene in which two black-clad hired guns walk menacingly down the main street, Micalizzi composed an effective pastiche – a slow bolero with familiar Don Giovanni strings, electric guitar, rattlesnake maracas and mariachi trumpet.

When *They Call Me Trinity* was released in Italy, just before Christmas 1970, Barboni had a smash hit. In Germany the film was retitled *Die Rechte und Linke Hand Des Teufels* ('The Right and Left Hand of the Devil', in reference to the two heroes), while Trinity was christened Müde Joe (Tired Joe) and Bambino Der Kleine (the little one). In Spain it outgrossed every previous Italian western except *For a Few Dollars More*. Hill and Spencer were already established as a partnership from their Colizzi films, and the film was also lucrative when it had its UK and US release in 1971. It was distributed by Joseph E. Levine's Avco Embassy Pictures, uncut at 106 minutes, and garnered a 'G' rating (all ages permitted). US publicity for the film included the taglines: 'He was on the side of law and order…he was on the side of crime and chaos…he was on any side that would have him!' and 'He was so mean, he shot his horse for smiling', which sat oddly with Hill's persona; if there is one thing Trinity loves, it is his rheumy-eyed horse. Gene Luotto oversaw the dubbing of the English-language print, and the result was way above average for a foreign western. This was aided by Hill, Spencer, Zacharias and the other main actors speaking their lines in English. Even so, critics were divided: some found the film 'good fun', while others considered it uneven and wondered how Hill and Spencer 'earned a crust as actors'.

Trinity's success opened the saloon doors for the unruly mob of comedy spaghettis that followed. Some incorporated the cartoonish fights into kung-fu westerns like *The Fighting Fists of Shanghai Joe* (1973) and *Blood Money* (1974). The most blatant spin-offs included Franchi and Ingrassia's *Two Sons of Trinity* (1972), the 'Carambola' series (starring Hill and Spencer lookalikes Michael Coby and Paul Smith) and

Jesse & Lester: Two Brothers in a Place Called Trinity (1972), with two brothers (a womanising gunslinger and an honest Mormon) arguing over an inheritance. Moreover, many westerns appeared in the early seventies with *They Call Me...* in the title, including *Holy Ghost* (1970), *Cemetery* and *Hallelujah* (both 1971), *Veritas, Providence* and *Amen* (all 1972).

The true heir to *They Call Me Trinity* is Barboni's own sequel with Hill and Spencer, *Trinity is Still My Name* (1971), which sees Trinity and Bambino trying unsuccessfully to become outlaws, while being mistaken for federal agents on a special mission. It is more fragmented than its predecessor, with a series of improvisory set pieces becoming more like a revue. The action includes gunrunning monks, farting babies, comic card games, Trinity and Bambino's appalling table manners in a fancy French eating house and a grandstand finale that descends into a riotous game of American football. This irreverent humour reappeared to great success in Mel Brooks's *Blazing Saddles* (1974), which was retitled in Italy *Mezzogiorno e Mezzo di Fuoco* ('Noon and a Half of Fire'), in reference to *High Noon* (which was retitled *Mezzogiorno di Fuoco*).

The 'Trinity' films are often accused of being childish, meathead entertainment, but Hill and Spencer continued to be hugely popular with young and old audiences throughout the seventies. Among their biggest hits were *All the Way Boys!* (1972) and *Watch Out, We're Mad!* (1973); between 1971 and 1994 they made 12 films together. Their films were never graphically violent, making them suitable for the whole family. This was for obvious financial reasons: the lower the certificate, the wider the range of audience able to see the film.

They Call Me Trinity is the twenty-second most successful Italian film of all time – one place behind *The Good, the Bad and the Ugly*, though their reputations outside Europe are completely different. While *The Good* is praised as one of the greatest westerns of all time, the 'Trinity' films are still treated with critical disdain. Barboni had the last laugh when *Trinity is Still My Name* outgrossed all western opposition in Italy, including Leone's most successful western, *For a Few Dollars More*; it remains the fifth most financially successful Italian film of all time.

They Call Me Trinity is Hill and Spencer's finest vehicle; the duo were under-rated by critics as actors, but equally the directors they worked with were all-important. They followed *They Call Me Trinity* with the swashbuckling *The Black Pirate* (1971), directed by 'Vincent Thomas' (Lorenzo Gicca Palli), which sank like a stock-footage galleon. Hill played a thinly disguised Trinity in two more westerns – *My Name is Nobody* (1973) and *Nobody's the Greatest* (1975) – while Spencer's performance as Coburn in *The Big and the Bad* (1971) owed much to Bambino. But when they were together, and especially in *They Call Me Trinity*, they were like their screen personas – invincible.

20

'The Secret of a Long Life is to Try Not to Shorten it'

— Tonino Valerii's *My Name is Nobody* (1973)

My Name is Nobody (1973)
original title: *Il Mio Nome e Nessuno*
Credits
DIRECTOR – Tonino Valerii
EXECUTIVE PRODUCER – Fulvio Morsella
STORY – Fulvio Morsella, Ernesto Gastaldi and Sergio Leone
SCREENPLAY – Ernesto Gastaldi
COSTUMES – Vera Marzot
ART DIRECTOR – Gianni Polidori
EDITOR – Nino Baragli
DIRECTORS OF PHOTOGRAPHY – Giuseppe Ruzzolini and Armando
    Nannuzzi
MUSIC – Ennio Morricone
Interiors filmed at Incir De Paolis Studios, Rome
Panavision/Technicolor
An Italian/French/West German co-production
Rafran Cinematografica (Rome)/Les Films Jacques Leitienne
    (Paris)/La Societé Imp.Ex.Ci. (Nice)/La Societé Alcinter
    (Paris)/Rialto Film Preben GMB and Co KG (Berlin)
Released internationally by Universal Pictures
Cast
    Henry Fonda (Jack Beauregard); 'Terence Hill', Mario
    Girotti (Nobody); Jean Martin (Sullivan); 'Leo Gordon', Leo
    Vincent Gordon (Red); Neil Summers (Squirrel); 'R.G.
    Armstrong', Robert Golden Armstrong (first gunman with
    bomb); Mario Brega (second gunman); Tommy Polgar (third
    gunman); Steve Kanaly (first fake barber); Geoffrey Lewis
    (leader of the Wild Bunch); Piero Lulli (sheriff); 'Mark
    Mazza', Marc Mazzacurati (Don John); Benito Stefanelli,

Alexander Allerson and Antoine Saint-John (members of the
Wild Bunch); Antonio De Martino (dwarf on stilts); Franco
Angrisano (train-driver); Emile Feist (real barber); Humbert
Mittendorf (carnival barker); Angelo Novi (bartender):
Antonio Molino Rojo (US army officer) with Remus Peets,
Antonio Luigi Guerra, Carla Mancini, Ulrich Muller,
Antonio Palombi and Claus Schmidt

*   *   *

By the early seventies, Italian westerns had diversified to an extreme extent. Some directors continued to be preoccupied with monosyllabic heroes shooting it out with ever-depleting gangs of bandits. Django and Sartana were still gunning for outlaws, though they were unrecognisable from the trend-setting characters that inspired them; Django in particular had seen his entire immediate family wiped out since 1966. More original was Ferdinando Baldi's *Blindman* (1971), which starred Tony Anthony as a blind gunslinger, who survives the entire film on hearing alone. British and American crews travelled to Spain to make imitation spaghetti westerns and even the French joined the craze, with *The Legend of Frenchie King* (1971), a 'baguetti western' starring Brigitte Bardot and Claudia Cardinale. The 'Trinity' films had spawned many imitators, with the finest Italian stuntmen kept busy falling off balconies and hitting each other with breakaway chairs, but the genre was running out of steam in Europe, as thrillers, horrors and comedies ate away at westerns' takings.

Popular Italian cinema had become increasingly self-obsessed since its global success with westerns. Previously it had absorbed the American myths and rein-vigorated them with a fresh approach. But in the seventies its westerns were being treated with a kind of reverence, as the Italians' references became more obscure. Jack Palance portrayed a pot-smoking relative of Dracula in Corbucci's western *Compañeros* (1970); Cuban Tomas Milian played a Mexican revolutionary dressed like Che Guevara in the same film. In the thriller *Violent City* (1970), Sergio Sollima transposed the climax of his manhunt western *The Big Gundown* to modern-day New Orleans (complete with Morricone score); in one scene villainous Telly Savalas watches *Seven Guns for the MacGregors* on TV, in homage to the film's frontier roots. In *Trinity is Still My Name*, Harry Carey Jr (a key figure in the best work of John Ford) had a cameo as the father of Trinity and Bambino. Here his paternal plea was not for his sons to settle down, but to become horse rustlers, get a decent price on their heads and 'do something with their lives'. That was how cynical and mocking spaghetti westerns had become.

As the 'Trinity' films outgrossed Sergio Leone's films (in more ways than one) and made fun of tough western gunslingers, Leone and Tonino Valerii teamed-up for the comedy western *My Name is Nobody*, the most referential western ever made. If Leone and Corbucci's films had referenced Hollywood westerns, then *Nobody* had the last word on the subject. The film is set in the dying days of the west, but it is as much about western films as the historical period.

In *My Name is Nobody*, Jack Beauregard, a 51-year-old gunfighter, has decided that he is going to retire to Europe, and the film recounts his last days in the wild west. But it is the west of 1899 – much has changed and Beauregard feels out of step with the times. On his way to New Orleans to catch the steamer 'Sundowner', he is pestered by a young admirer named Nobody, who wants to see his hero go out with a bang, rather than drift into obscurity. Beauregard's brother (the Nevada Kid) has been killed by his crooked mining partner Sullivan, who is in cahoots with the Wild Bunch, a notorious 150-strong gang of gunslingers. As the days dwindle, it seems Beauregard is going to get his wish and sail away to Europe, but Nobody has other ideas, telling Beauregard, 'A hero can't run away from his destiny'. 'You're sure trying hard to make a hero out of me,' says Beauregard. 'You're that already,' answers Nobody, 'you just need a special act…something that'll make your name a legend.' Nobody stage-manages a confrontation between Beauregard and the Wild Bunch in the desert. Beauregard survives, and Nobody later 'kills' him in the main street of New Orleans. But the duel was a trick to allow Beauregard to retire in peace. Beauregard sails away on the steamship 'Sundowner', while Nobody learns to deal with life as a 'somebody'.

The story is based on 'an idea by Sergio Leone', and it certainly incorporates many of his trademarks, including the 'old man' and 'boy' duo from *For a Few Dollars More*. The script was written by Ernesto Gastaldi, from a story outline written by Gastaldi and Fulvio Morsella (Leone's brother-in-law, business partner and trans-lator, who had also collaborated on the story of *For a Few*). Gastaldi had scripted several Italian Gothic horrors under the pseudonyms 'Julian Berry' and 'Gastad Green', including – *The Terror of Dr Hitchcock* (1962), *The Whip and the Flesh* (1963), *The Virgin of Nuremberg* (1963), *Crypt of Horror* (1964) and *Libido* (1966). He also worked on many westerns, including *Day of Anger*, *The Price of Power* (1969) and *Massacre at Fort Holman* (1972) – all with Tonino Valerii. The story for *My Name is Nobody* was rewritten three times until Leone was satisfied with the result. He was striving for mythical overtones – the title is a reference to Homer's *The Odyssey*: when Odysseus is captured by the cyclops, he is asked his name, and replies 'My name is Nobody'.

In the seven years since *The Good, the Bad and the Ugly*, Leone had directed two more westerns: *Once Upon a Time in the West* (1968) and *Duck You Sucker* (1971). *Once Upon a Time*, Leone's elegy to the frontier, had a well-known international cast, backing from a US studio (Paramount Pictures) and was co-written by Leone, Sergio Donati and two future directors, Bernardo Bertolucci and Dario Argento. Newlywed Jill (played by Claudia Cardinale), an ex-prostitute from New Orleans, arrives in Flagstone City, a half-built boomtown in Arizona and discovers that her husband Brett McBain (Frank Wolff) has been killed by Frank (Henry Fonda), a hired gun in the pay of railway tycoon Mr Morton (Gabriela Ferzetti). Morton wants the land around the McBain ranch (and its precious supply of water) on his railway west to the Pacific. During Jill's stay at McBain's ranch at Sweetwater, she attempts to solve the mystery of her husband's murder and comes into contact with Cheyenne (Jason Robards), an outlaw on the run, and half-breed gunslinger Harmonica (Charles Bronson), who has a score to settle; Harmonica's brother was lynched by Frank many years before.

Filmed from April to July 1968, *Once Upon a Time* addresses the coming of the railway, the economics of the thriving boomtown, the power of the dollar and the death of 'the age of the gunfighter'. The railway brings easterner Jill to the wild west, to a new life and a new beginning, but it also brings Morton, Frank, civilisation and capitalism. The opening and closing scenes are set in two railway stations; Cattle Corner station is a flyblown, clapboard hovel in the desert, while the nascent Sweetwater station is about to be transformed into a boomtown: the next Flagstone City. Throughout the film, Leone includes many visual and verbal quotes from his favourite Hollywood westerns, including *The Iron Horse* (1924), *High Noon* (1952), *Shane* (1953) and *The Searchers* (1956); the hackneyed plot of the railway obtaining valuable land by fair means or foul had been the premise for countless westerns, from *Johnny Guitar* (1954) to *Winnetou the Warrior* (1963). Leone also cast well-known American actors as supporting players – Woody Strode, Keenan Wynn, Lionel Stander and Jack Elam (who was originally to have played the one-armed bounty-hunter in *The Good, the Bad and the Ugly*).

Once Upon a Time in the West was shot in Almeria and the US; Leone even filmed Jill's carriage ride to Sweetwater in the towering cathedral buttes of Monument Valley, Utah – a setting synonymous with John Ford's westerns starring John Wayne. Though the US trailer introduced Bronson's character as 'the man in search of a name', *Once Upon a Time* is a definite change of pace for Leone. It's much slower than the 'Dollars' films, partly due to the rhythm of Morricone's pre-recorded, sedate score: Edda Dell'Orso's majestic 'Jill's America', the wailing 'Man With A Harmonica' and the grating clippety-clop of 'Cheyenne's Theme'. There are no grandiose riding themes, daring escapes or bank robberies, and relatively little gunplay, particularly in the first half. The languid violence (an ambush at Cattle Corner station, the McBain massacre at Sweetwater, a street fight in Flagstone City and the final duel between Frank and Harmonica) and the picturesque, arty compositions are at odds with the exhilarating action of Leone's previous westerns.

Audiences seemed to agree: it was the least successful of Leone's westerns thus far in Italy when it was released in December 1968, though it was hugely popular in France and also Germany (where it was known as *Spiel mir das Lied vom Tod* – 'Play me the Song of Death'). For its UK/US release in 1969, Paramount predictably cut the 161-minute film down by 20 minutes (resulting in some odd continuity errors); Leone and Donati had already pruned the original script, and the vast $250,000 Flagstone City set hardly appears in the finished film. *Once Upon a Time* bombed in the UK/US market, while many other Italian westerns (including Lee

Van Cleef's work for Petroni, Valerii and Parolini) continued to draw huge crowds. Critics, particularly American ones, hated Leone's John Ford locations, his Hollywood western citations and the crawling pace (*Variety* called it 'Tedium in the Tumbleweed'), though the film has since enjoyed a critical revival with the release of Leone's longer, restored version. Leone seemed to lose faith in his work in 1969, and it was to be three years before he directed another film – the political western *Duck You Sucker*, which was even less lucrative in Italy than *Once Upon a Time*, though it was pitted against *Trinity is Still My Name* at the box office in October 1971.

Since *Day of Anger*, Tonino Valerii had directed a political western called *The Price of Power* (which reused Leone's Flagstone City and Sweetwater sets from *Once Upon a Time*) and *Massacre at Fort Holman* (1972 – also called *A Reason to Live, A Reason to Die*), a comic-book 1862 Civil War adventure, in which most of the budget seems to have been spent on dynamite. James Coburn played disgraced Union Colonel Pembroke, who leads seven convicts on a special mission to take Confederate Fort Holman from his old enemy Major Ward (Telly Savalas). The film was picturesquely shot in Almeria (including the grandiose fortress of El Condor) and even the extensive reuse of Riz Ortolani's scores from *Day of Anger* and *Beyond the Law* couldn't spoil the film. The apocalyptic scenes of mass destruction that had previously climaxed muscleman epics (falling masonry, volcanoes and earthquakes) had been appropriated by Italian westerns. Instead of the 'settling of accounts' duel, many spaghettis of the late sixties and early seventies closed with an attack on a fortress, with impressive pyrotechnics to the fore. *Massacre at Fort Holman*, as the title implies, was no exception; for the finale, Valerii loaded up the Gatling guns and pulled the trigger for the explosive assault, with Coburn and company killing everyone in sight.

In *My Name is Nobody*, 68-year-old Henry Fonda was cast as Beauregard and 33-year-old Terence Hill as Nobody, in one of the most unlikely western teamings of all time. Henry Fonda – an icon of the American genre, whose career sprawled across four decades – and Terence Hill, whose biggest successes had been the outrageous 'Trinity' films, the farting, burping travesties of the American myth. The personifications of the old west and the new collide on screen, as the sun sets on a west from which the old-timer wants to escape. In *Once Upon a Time in the West*, Leone cast Fonda as Frank, a heartless hired gun, to prove he could play a villain; in *Nobody* Leone and Valerii cast Fonda to demonstrate that the Hollywood western icon's time had passed. Fonda had appeared in comedy westerns before, but it was usually as an old-timer in red long johns, while his serious westerns were of the nature of *Firecreek* (1968 – described by one critic as 'a geriatric *High Noon*'). But in *Nobody*, Fonda subtly sends-up his statesmanlike position in the genre, from classic films like *The Ox-Bow Incident* (1943), *My Darling Clementine* (1946), *The Tin Star* (1957) and *Warlock* (1959).

The cast reinforces the film's Italian-American origins. Villain Leo Gordon (from *The Restless Breed* and *Man With the Gun*) played miner Red. French actor Jean

Martin (from *Battle of Algiers*) was Sullivan, while his men were played by an array of character actors. R.G. Armstrong had worked for Sam Peckinpah (in *Ride the High Country*, *Major Dundee* and *Pat Garrett and Billy the Kid*), and Geoffrey Lewis (Clint Eastwood's future sidekick) played the leader of the riders. Reptilian Don John and his toothy partner Squirrel were played by Mark Mazza and Neil Summers. London-born Summers was a stuntman in *Duel at Diablo* (1965) and *El Dorado* (1967), then appeared in *The Life and Times of Judge Roy Bean* (1972) as a drunken gunman who puts a bullet through a portrait of Lily Langtry; Steve Kanaly was one of Judge Bean's deputies and also reappeared in *Nobody*. Leone's actors Mario

German picture sleeve single with Terence Hill as 'blue-eyed angel' Nobody in Tonino Valerii's *My Name is Nobody* (1973); this Ariola label release teamed Ennio Morricone's theme music with 'Meine Schuld?' ('My Fault?'), the German title of Morricone's parody of his own musical watch theme from *For a Few Dollars More* (1965).

Brega, Antonio Molino Rojo and Benito Stefanelli had cameos; Stefanelli organised the stunts and is clearly visible riding with the Wild Bunch in the finale.

For *My Name is Nobody*, Leone decided to act as producer (for his own Rafran Cinematografica), with Valerii as director. Like *Once Upon a Time in the West* the film was shot partly in the actual American west. Acoma Pueblo ('The Sky City') in New Mexico, and the San Esteban Del Rey Mission were used for the scenes in a Navajo graveyard; the pueblo dates from AD1150. The gypsum dune fields at White Sands, New Mexico were used for some shots of the Wild Bunch riding through the desert. The opening barbershop shootout was filmed in the New Mexican town of Cabezon, previously used in the climactic shootout of Peter Fonda's acid western *The Hired Hand* (1971). The ghost-town of Mogollon at the bottom of Silver Creek Canyon in New Mexico was used as two sets: Red's shack and the saloon where Nobody first meets his hero. The mining town sprang up in the 1890s, though some buildings (including the general store opposite the saloon) were constructed especially for the film. The final duel between Beauregard and *Nobody* was filmed in Royal Street, in the French Quarter of New Orleans. The harbour where Beauregard catches the 'Sundowner' was also shot in New Orleans. Other filming was done in Almeria; the railway station at La Calahorra was the Golden Plume Limited depot, Cheyenne City was Leone's Flagstone set at Calahorra, while the battle between Beauregard and the Wild Bunch was shot on the plains near the Almeria–Guadix railway line.

My Name is Nobody was shot by two different cameramen – Armando Nannuzzi (in the US) and Giuseppe Ruzzolini (in Spain and at De Paolis Studios, Rome). There are some huge inconsistencies in the film's tone and style; it often appears to be three separate films stitched together. *Nobody* has three distinct tones: the lyrical 'old man and boy' sequences; the more straightforward revenge subplot between Sullivan and Beauregard; and the broad, 'Trinity'-inspired comedy scenes. The mood ranges from touching homage to cruel parody, but never within the same scene, which gives *Nobody* a juddering pace. This was down to a number of factors. Valerii directed most of *Nobody*, but Leone lent a hand and directed the second unit in Spain. Valerii is no Leone, but equally Leone is no Valerii – and neither of them have the comic timing of Enzo Barboni. Over the years the juxta-positions in *Nobody*'s style have been blamed on Valerii, but Leone was co-director, producer and general factotum – perhaps he was losing his touch.

The relationship between 'national monument' Beauregard and his awe-struck fan Nobody is well delineated. Nobody is unable to face the idea that his icon wants to fade away, and their dialogues are the most powerful presentation of the western 'generation gap' scenario. Nobody wants to see Beauregard's heroism written up in the history books, though Beauregard points out, 'You'll be down on earth reading 'em and I'll be up there, playing on a harp'. In the 'hero and fan' dialogues, Hill adds depth to their relationship, as he plays a gunman who 'still believes in fairy tales'.

The revenge motif is interestingly handled. Throughout *Nobody*, Sullivan is worried that Beauregard is going to expose his mining operation (Golden Plume Limited) as a fraud; stolen ore is added to what little comes out of the worthless mine. Throughout Beauregard's last ride across the west, he tries to avoid Sullivan's gang, and the film is punctuated with several showdowns: in a barber's, a saloon and later in Cheyenne City and at a fairground. Nobody presumes that Beauregard's brother has been killed by Sullivan (they were business partners in the mine), but it transpires that Red, another mining associate, was responsible. Red has already been killed, so Beauregard's vendetta is an elaborate red herring.

The comedy sequences sit uneasily with the rest of the film; they were inserted to coax Hill into the role, as the original script was less light-hearted. Nobody arrives in Cheyenne City and the fair is in town ('The Street of Pleasure'). During these scenes, Nobody becomes Trinity: he slaps Sullivan's men around, they shoot it out in a hall of mirrors and Nobody takes part in a drinking and shooting competition in a saloon. While the speeded-up quick-draw and face-slapping is from *Trinity is Still My Name* and the hall of mirrors (dubbed the 'Horror House') owes much to the 'Sabata' films, the shooting challenge drags on for far too long. But it is a deftly edited parody when compared to the scene in a public urinal. Here, Nobody prevents a train-driver from relieving himself by staring at the old man, in a scene that seems to go on forever. Rather surprisingly, Leone was responsible for the saloon and urinal scenes, both of which would have benefited from some editing, but remain in the final version as flabby, unwelcome diversions. It was obvious Leone was competing with the 'Trinity' films, but if the entire film had been of the quality of Hill and Fonda's four central dialogue scenes – discussing the death of the west and the birth of a legend – it would have been a masterpiece. If it had played for non-stop laughs it would have been a 'Trinity' film. As it stands, the film sags badly in the middle.

It is fitting that a film about a living legend, the 'only hope for law and order in the west', should be justified by Henry Fonda's dignified performance. Fonda represents the American western and the films of John Ford and his contemporaries. He is tired of the new west, epitomised by the 'Trinity' films and the violent work of Sam Peckinpah, and wants to get out while he still can. Like Johnny Ringo (Gregory Peck), the aged hero of *The Gunfighter* (1950), Beauregard wants to live down his reputation and have a quiet life – but he can't.

In the west of 1899, violence is more organised, and Beauregard tells Nobody 'It's your kind of time, not mine'. Big business and urban crime are beginning to have an impact on the west, epitomised by Golden Plume Limited, the Sullivan-fronted mining operation. Signs for the company appear throughout (on warehouses in Cheyenne City and at the rail depot) and 'city slicker' Sullivan's glass-windowed office is photographed to suggest the open-plan airiness of a skyscraper. As in Valerii's *Day of Anger* and *The Price of Power*, the respected citizen is in league with a gang of outlaws.

In *My Name is Nobody*, Hollywood western hero Beauregard is pitted against spaghetti-western gunfighters, a situation that is established in the opening sequence. Three gunfighters ride into a deserted town and try to look inconspicuous, as they lock up the local barber and his son. One of them masquerades as the barber, while the other two blend in outside – one milks a cow, the other grooms a horse. Beauregard wanders into the barber's shop to get a shave, but just as the razor is about to touch his throat, Beauregard cocks his pistol – unholstered and pointing at the fake barber. So, to the bemusement of the duo outside, the 'barber' gives Beauregard a shave and the old gunfighter pays him. As Beauregard leaves, the trio spring their ambush, but Beauregard shoots so quickly that the three shots blend as one, killing all three. He releases the real barber and his son, and departs. Mesmerised, the boy blurts out, 'How'd he do it Pa? I only heard one shot.' 'It's a question of speed son,' says the barber. 'Ain't nobody faster on the draw than him?' asks the kid. 'Faster than him?' muses the barber, 'Nobody.' The bad guys resemble their equivalents in Leone's films and Beauregard/Hollywood draws first blood.

The barber's son is Valerii's equivalent of the children in fifties westerns, like Joey in *Shane*, in awe of the hero's sharpshooting and noting 'Gee mister!' at the gunfighter's speed on the draw. But he is also a younger version of Nobody's adulation. 'When I was a kid,' says Nobody, 'I used to make believe I was Jack Beauregard.' Nobody even carries the same Colt Navy revolver as his hero, though Beauregard's is ornately engraved in the traditional vine style.

When Beauregard first meets Nobody in a saloon, the youngster has been asked to deliver a basket (which contains a bomb) to the old gunfighter, on behalf of three of Sullivan's men. 'Only three,' says Nobody dismissively, as he recounts some of Beauregard's most famous exploits, with impressively accurate statistics: '82 was one of your best years,' says Nobody, 'It was in the fall that you really scored – September, Socorro, five.' It is the fact that Nobody wants these exploits written down forever, capped off with a confrontation with the Wild Bunch, that drives him on, often in a selfish manner. The bomb starts to wheeze and whistle, so Nobody tosses it out into the street; as it explodes, smoke from the blast wreathes the room and Nobody announces, 'But you've never taken on 150, all at once'. Nobody says that as a boy, he had a dream: 'An immense open plain – 150 pure-bred sons of bitches on horseback and you facing them…alone'. 'Why only 150?' asks Beauregard. 'The Wild Bunch, they are only 150.' But Beauregard seems unconvinced: '150, who shoot and ride like there was thousands'. He thinks no more of Nobody's comment, until eventually he begins to realise that Nobody is being serious.

Beauregard's date with destiny begins when he arrives in the village of Acoma. In an Indian graveyard he discovers Nobody attending the funeral of Navajo Chief Broken Branch. Nobody finds a grave marked 'Nevada Kid', and Beauregard realises that his brother is dead. 'It's always the best who are the first to go,' says Nobody, but Beauregard is tired of Nobody's wisecracks and tries to scare him off by shooting at his hat. It doesn't work, and Nobody is thrilled to see his hero in action.

after your

SADDLE BLAZES

...what next?

He's out to build a legend
in his own ∧ time!
              good

SERGIO LEONE presents

Henry Fonda • **Terence Hill**

as Jack Beauregard   as "Nobody"

in

**"My Name
is Nobody"**

Executive Producer FULVIO MORSELLA Directed by TONINO VALERII A UNIVERSAL RELEASE · TECHNICOLOR ® PANAVISION ®

PG | PARENTAL GUIDANCE SUGGESTED
SOME MATERIAL MAY NOT BE
SUITABLE FOR PRE-TEENAGERS

'Sergio Leone presents': Universal Studios US poster for *My Name is Nobody*
(1973), featuring Henry Fonda as the legendary gunfighter Jack Beauregard and
Terence Hill as his fan, Nobody.

He holds up his hat – 'Four shots, one hole…just like the good old days'. 'There was never any good old days,' adds Beauregard, noticing that there are two holes in the hat. Their dialogue is interrupted by a thunderous roar, and the duo watch from the cemetery's adobe palisade as the Wild Bunch ride by, a tide of one hundred and fifty duster-clad badmen; it is suddenly obvious why Beauregard is unenthusiastic about making an appearance in the history books.

The Wild Bunch is a significant choice of name for Beauregard's adversaries. Sam Peckinpah's ultra-violent western *The Wild Bunch* (1969) also concerned the end of the west. But Peckinpah's 'bunch' are a group of ageing outlaws, decimated in a chaotic bank robbery in Starbuck. The remnants flee to Mexico and clash with Mexican General Mapache. In the finale, when faced with huge odds (four of them against Mapache's army), their attitude to the confrontation is 'Hell, why not?' as they meet their makers in Agua Verde. Valerii's treatment is noticeably different. This time it is the Wild Bunch who are innumerable, and Beauregard's attitude is, 'Hell, why bother?' 'If you go,' says Hill, 'who's going to be left…Nobody?' 'A man's gotta quit sometime,' says Beauregard, but Nobody reasons that someone like Beauregard's 'gotta go out with style'. There is even a grave marker in the Indian cemetery in Acoma with *The Wild Bunch* director's name on it. 'Sam Peckinpah,' notes Nobody, 'That's a beautiful name in Navajo.'

The visual precedents for Valerii's Wild Bunch ranged from a variety of sources. Samuel Fuller's *Forty Guns* (1957) featured Barbara Stanwyck as Jessica Drummond ('a hard-riding woman with a whip'), who rules the territory with her forty hired guns. In *Tension at Table Rock* (1956) it is the arrival of fifty tough cattle drovers (some wearing dusters) in Table Rock which causes the tension, while in the spaghetti *A Man Called Sledge* (1970) strongbox gold shipments are protected by forty heavily armed 'gold riders'. The villains' duster coats also recall Cheyenne's gang in *Once Upon a Time in the West*.

Though *Nobody* is a comedy western, most of the sequences dealing with Fonda are played straight – as though Nobody is ashamed of his childishness and doesn't want his hero to see his juvenile slapping and gunfighting routines. During his dialogues with Beauregard, Nobody is reflective and respectful; Hill was thrilled to be working with Fonda, and the film remains Hill's personal favourite. Beauregard refers to him as 'My blue-eyed angel who protects me from harm' and American advertising material for the film capitalised on this analogy, with a saddle slung over Nobody's shoulder (resembling a pair of angelic wings) and a smoke ring halo drifting from his cigar.

Though the early part of the film is uneven, the erratic style gels for the two-part finale: an explosive desert battle and the trademark settling of accounts duel. As Beauregard follows the railroad tracks to Kimball to catch the train to New Orleans, Nobody hijacks a locomotive carrying a shipment of Golden Plume gold bars to the Bank of Cheyenne, and the Wild Bunch are despatched to recover the train. Nobody has already told Beauregard 'Sometimes you run smack into your destiny on the very road you take to get away from it,' and demonstrated the impending scenario with a pool table flooded with balls (Nobody's representation of the Wild Bunch). In the middle of an immense plain, Beauregard pauses by the tracks and in the distance hears a roll of thunder. The rumbling becomes more ominous, and on the horizon he sees a huge cloud of dust. Through the heat haze, Beauregard can make out the Wild Bunch, riding to recover the stolen train, but the old man thinks that Nobody's wish is coming true: he has run into his destiny. When the stolen train appears, Beauregard tries to board it, but Nobody is driving; he wants a ringside seat to see his hero go down in the history books. The Wild Bunch's saddlebags are loaded with dynamite and with each direct hit Beauregard decimates the gang in spectacular fashion, while Nobody keeps score. For this scene, Valerii and Leone refer to *The Wild Bunch*, with the explosions slowed down, Peckinpah-style; finally, freeze-frames capture the moment for history, as the stills become the sepia-tinted pages of a history book, with dime-novel captions like 'Men and Horses Butchered by Dynamite'.

The only western actors of comparable stature to Fonda (and thus capable of playing Beauregard) were James Stewart and John Wayne, each of whom would have confronted the Wild Bunch very differently. Stewart would have reasoned with them ('Now wait just a minute'), while Wayne would have given them a political lecture ('Republic, I like the sound of the word. Some words can give you a feeling that makes your heart warm. Republic is one of those words'). Fonda has just the right amount of dignity and resolve. When he stands, Winchester in hand, looking out across the plain, he epitomises the heroic westerner – the hero who stands up for himself, whatever the odds.

After the confrontation, Beauregard says, 'Well now you've got me into the history books, how do I quit?' 'There's only one way,' answers Nobody, 'You gotta die.' Beauregard looks shocked: 'Where?'; 'Where there's lots of people'. In the main street of New Orleans, outside the Cornstalk Fence Hotel, with an excited audience and a photographer again freezing the moment for history, Nobody faces Beauregard. Youth is faster than experience, and Nobody shoots his hero. As the photographer's flash pops, Beauregard is captured forever, on his knees, dying.

But *My Name is Nobody* doesn't close with a Corbucci-esque bleak ending. When we see Beauregard collapse in the street, he is not dead at all: the duel is a ruse to allow Beauregard to enjoy his retirement quietly. In an emotional *dénouement*, bespectacled Beauregard, now wearing a sweater and woolly hat (unrecognisable as the legendary gunfighter), sits in his cabin on the steamer 'Sundowner'. He writes a parting letter to Nobody, warning that he's a 'somebody' now – 'The only way to become a Nobody again is to die'. He hopes Nobody can 'preserve a little of that illusion that made my generation tick'. Not only is this last scene the end of the west, it is also the end of the western. The old man has seen many changes and reasons it is time to leave – the question is can Nobody survive living as a 'somebody'? The remnants of the Wild Bunch are after Nobody, and we see him taking a shave, with the leader of the bunch pretending to be the barber. But the crafty youngster will survive the new west. His thinking is the same as Beauregard's, his methods different (he sticks his finger in the seat of the barber's trousers, like a pistol), but he's still 'preserving the illusion', in his own fairy-tale way. As it says on Beauregard's epitaph: 'NOBODY WAS FASTER ON THE DRAW'.

The score to *My Name is Nobody* was one of Morricone's last contributions to the genre, and also one of his most accomplished. For the title music he composed an instrumental equivalent of the jokey 'Trinity' themes, with a comical recorder, chimes, synthesised 'wah-wah' sound-effects and the Alessandroni Singers' cheery bubblegum refrain. This theme (and variations) often accompanies Nobody's comedy antics. But it is the scenes with Fonda and the Wild Bunch in which Morricone was really successful, referencing his own work, whilst adding to the myth. The galloping Wild Bunch are accompanied by a thundering riding theme, with Alessandro Alessandroni's *A Fistful of Dollars*-style whistling, a 12-string guitar (played by Silvano Chimenti), the Cantori barking raucously (like the theme to *For a Few Dollars More*), screeching pan-pipe and drums. The piece is augmented with excerpts from Wagner's 'Ride of the Valkyries', which adds a mythical yet satirical edge to the bunch's scenes. The Wild Bunch's whistled melody has its roots in 'Quello Che Conta' (sung by Luigi Tenco for *La Cuccagna* in 1962); the sombre theme was reorchestrated by Morricone for *Nobody* with his trademark gusto.

For the battle in the desert, trumpets and the Cantori voice the 'Nobody' theme, the choir putting a triumphant 'Amen' to Beauregard's career. When Beauregard rides sedately into Acoma (and later along the railway tracks), an echo of Edda Dell'Orso's theme from *Once Upon a Time in the West* accompanies his last ride, while his risky visit to the barber uses side drums, cello, synthesised effects and an interminably ticking metronome, adding a sense of time ticking away the end of the Old West. The ticking clock motif (accompanied by a tinkling musical watch) is used in the two duels between Nobody and Beauregard – in the Navajo graveyard and the main street of New Orleans. Bruno Battisti D'Amario adds his familiar savage electric guitar riffs from *For a Few Dollars More*, and Arnaldo Graziosi's rolling piano recalls *The Good, the Bad and the Ugly*, as the piece develops into a parody of Morricone's 'Man With A Harmonica' from *Once Upon a Time*, complete with syncopated strings, scything guitar, the Cantori and Gino Agostinelli's trumpet. Morricone's *Nobody* score is as much a fitting a tribute to the composer's staggering western output as the film is a tribute to the genre.

Nobody was a huge success at the European box office, opening in Italy over Christmas 1973. All Hill's films of this period were huge grossers in Italy, Germany and France, from *Man of the East* (1972 – his third western with Barboni) to the contemporary Hill and Spencer punch-ups (*All the Way Boys!* and *Watch Out, We're Mad!*). In Germany *My Name is Nobody* and *Trinity is Still My Name* won Golden Screen awards for their huge admissions. *Nobody* was so successful that it resulted in a sequel, *Nobody's the Greatest* (1975 – also called *A Genius*), again with

Leone's involvement; he had the original idea and directed the pre-title sequence (in which a farmer is riddled with arrows). Gastaldi and Morsella wrote the story, Morsella acted as producer and Damiano Damiani directed. Here, Nobody is a somebody named Joe Thanks. The best scene sees Doc Foster (Klaus Kinski) 'waiting for somebody' in the Chaco Canyon Saloon (actually the 'Gold Coin' set from *Once Upon a Time in the West*). Doc is humiliated in a duel in the main street, as Nobody's gun draws and fires by itself. With its ecological theme (everyone should be able to live as free as the buzzards), fine cast (Patrick McGoohan, Jean Martin and Miou-Miou), Leone references (Mario Brega and Benito Stefanelli both appear, the latter as a villain called Mortimer) and satirical sequences shot in Monument Valley, the film had some good ideas, but they were spread too thinly over the 117-minute running time.

When Terence Hill directed and starred in *Lucky Luke* (1991), his adaptation of Morris and Goscinny's western comic book, he played the character as Nobody, complete with white duster coat. Luke is quicker on the draw than his own shadow and the way he rids Daisy Town of the evil Daltons strongly resembles Hill's role in *They Call Me Trinity*. Hill returned to White Sands, New Mexico to shoot the film (for his own production company, Paloma Films) and cast Dominic Barto (from *They Call Me Trinity*) as William Dalton and Neil Summers (from *My Name is Nobody*) as Luke's deputy, Virgil. Luke's horse, Jolly Jumper, narrates the entire film, with the voice-over provided by Roger Miller, the Disney voice artist.

My Name is Nobody outgrossed the first 'Trinity' film in Italy and was Valerii's biggest hit, but its success failed to keep Italian westerns popular with the public. After the 'Trinity' films it was difficult to take spaghetti westerns seriously, and the predominantly cheap films that appeared in the early seventies were barely distributed domestically, let alone abroad. In the US and the UK, *Nobody* was slightly trimmed from 117 minutes to 112, but was not very successful when it was released by Universal in June 1974. The posters announced 'Sergio Leone Presents' and featured Hill snoozing against his saddle with the taglines: 'After Your Saddle Blazes… What Next?' (in reference to the hugely successful *Blazing Saddles*), 'Nobody But Nobody, Knows the Trouble He's In!' and 'He's Out To Build A Legend In His Own Good Time'.

By now, spaghetti westerns had come full circle. American and British crews working in Almeria made their own variations on the formula, with a blood-simple mentality that made Peckinpah look subtle. The most excessive of these outings were *The Hunting Party* (1970), a bloody manhunt western with Oliver Reed and Gene Hackman, and *A Town Called Bastard* (1971), with Robert Shaw as a priest and Telly Savalas as a murderous bandit in revolutionary Mexico. Only twilight spaghettis shot in Italy, like *Keoma* (1976 – starring Franco Nero) and *Mannaja* (1977 – starring Maurizio Merli) tried to extend the genre in the seventies with medieval primitivism, but although both films were successful, the genre quietly faded away. Unfortunately, seventies spaghettis dated badly, with flares, chequered jackets, handlebar moustaches and curly perms defining their style.

Valerii never directed another western, and following his foray into production, neither did Leone. Instead, he spent the last years of his life ruining his health during the stressful making and release of *Once Upon a Time in America* (1984). He died in April 1989, aged 60, while two of his contemporaries, Sergio Corbucci and Duccio Tessari, passed away respectively in December 1990 (aged 62) and September 1994 (aged 67): both had been more prolific than Leone, though it is his westerns that have endured. The 'Dollars' films remain the most widely known Italian westerns, as much for Eastwood's presence and Morricone's music. In the US, Leone's films are by far the most popular spaghetti westerns; as Luciano Vincenzoni commented: 'If Leone's films fly at 90,000 feet altitude, the others are moles that travel underground'.

As the seventies progressed, fewer American westerns were made, as other attractions (science fiction, horror, thrillers and kung fu) became popular. Only westerns directed by and starring Clint Eastwood have been big successes world-wide since the seventies, though the hugely popular *Dances with Wolves* (1990) remains the highest-grossing western of all time; perhaps that says more about modern cinema audiences' expectations than it does about the genre. Good westerns (whatever their country of origin) will always be popular, but the genre has been overused: of all the sound films made since 1927, a quarter are westerns.

Sergio Sollima once noted, 'The stories told in western films reflect life as it really is', while Leone claimed his films were 'fairy tales for adults'. Towards the end of *My Name is Nobody*, Nobody tells Beauregard, 'A man who's a man needs someone to believe in'. The reply is movingly eloquent: 'I've met all kinds in my life,' reflects Beauregard, 'thieves and killers, pimps and prostitutes, con men and preachers. Even a few fellers who told the truth. But the kind of man you're talking about…never.' 'Maybe you've never met them,' Nobody replies, 'or hardly ever. They're the only ones who count.' When they made their westerns, maybe Leone, Corbucci, Sollima and company didn't always tell the truth, or even half the truth, but in view of their achievements, it'll do.

BIBLIOGRAPHY

Bergan, Ronald, *The United Artists Story* (Octopus Books 1986)

Bertolino, Marco and Ettore Ridola, *Bud Spencer and Terence Hill* (Gremese Editore 2002)

Betts, Tom (ed.), *Westerns All'Italiana!* (Anaheim, California 1983–present) (memorial issues: Lee Van Cleef, William Berger and Sergio Corbucci)

Botting, Douglas, *Wilderness Europe* (Time-Life Books 1976)

Bruckner, Ulrich P., *Für ein paar Leichen mehr* (Schwarzkopf and Schwarzkopf 2002)

Bruschini, Antonio and Federico De Zigno, *Western All'Italiana-Book II* (Glittering Images 2001)

Bruschini, Antonio and Antonio Tentori, *Western All'Italiana-Book I* (Glittering Images 1998)

Burt, Rob, *Rockerama – 25 Years of Teen Screen Idols* (Blandford Press 1983)

Cole, Gerald and Peter Williams, *Clint Eastwood* (W.H. Allen 1983)

Commager, Henry Steele (ed.), *Illustrated History of the Civil War* (Promontory Press 1976)

Connolly, William, *Spaghetti Cinema* (Hollywood, California 1984–present)

Cotterell, Arthur, *World Mythology* (Parragon 1999)

Crawley, Tony, *Bébé – The Films of Brigitte Bardot* (BCA 1979)

Cumbow, Robert C., *Once Upon a Time – The Films of Sergio Leone* (Scarecrow Press 1987)

De Fornari, Oreste, *Sergio Leone – The Great Italian Dream of Legendary America* (Gremese 1997)

Douglas, Peter, *Clint Eastwood – Movin' On* (Star 1975)

Duncan, Paul, *Film Noir – Films of Trust and Betrayal* (Pocket Essentials 2000)

Elley, Derek, *The Epic Film – Myth and History* (Routledge and Kegan 1984)

Everman, Welch, *Cult Science Fiction Films* (Citadel Press 1995)

Fenin, George N. and William K. Everson, *The Western – From Silents to the Seventies* (Penguin 1977)

Fox, Brian, *Sabata* (Tandem 1971)

Frank, Alan, *The Films of Roger Corman* (Batsford 1998)

Frayling, Christopher, *Clint Eastwood* (Virgin 1992)

— *Sergio Leone – Something To Do With Death* (Faber and Faber 2000)

— *Spaghetti Westerns – Cowboys and Europeans from Karl May to Sergio Leone* (Routledge and Kegan 1981, reprinted I.B. Tauris 1998)

Gallant, Chris (ed.), *Art of Darkness – The Cinema of Dario Argento* (Fab Press 2000)

Gardner, Alexander, *Gardner's Photographic Sketch Book of the Civil War* (Dover Publications 1959)

Guérif, François, *Clint Eastwood: From Rawhide to Pale Rider* (Roger Houghton Ltd 1986)

Hardy, Phil (ed.), *The Aurum Film Encyclopedia – Gangsters* (Aurum Press 1998)

— *The Aurum Film Encyclopedia – Horror* (Aurum Press 1985)

— *The Aurum Film Encyclopedia – Science Fiction* (Aurum Press 1984)

— *The Aurum Film Encyclopedia – The Western* (Aurum Press 1983)

Hart, John Mason, *Revolutionary Mexico* (University of California Press 1997)

Howarth, Troy, *The Haunted World of Mario Bava* (Fab Press 2002)

Hughes, Howard, *Spaghetti Westerns* (Pocket Essentials 2001)

— *The American Indian Wars* (Pocket Essentials 2001)

Johnstone, Iain, *The Man With No Name* (Plexus 1981)

Josephy Jr., Alvin M., *The Civil War in the American West* (Vintage Books 1991)

Kaminsky, Stuart M., *Don Siegel – Director* (Curtis 1974)

Katz, Ephraim, *The Macmillan International Film Encyclopedia* (Macmillan 1998)

Kinski, Klaus, *Kinski Uncut* (Bloomsbury 1996)

Lloyd, Ann (ed.), *Good Guys and Bad Guys* (Orbis 1982)

— *Movies of the Fifties* (Orbis 1982)

— *Movies of the Seventies* (Orbis 1984)

— *Movies of the Sixties* (Orbis 1983)

Lloyd, Ann and Graham Fuller, *The Illustrated Who's Who of the Cinema* (Orbis 1983)

Maltin, Leonard, *2001 Movie and Video Guide* (Penguin 2001)

Masi, Stefano and Enrico Lancia, *Italian Movie Goddesses* (Gremese 1997)

May, Robin, *The Story of the West* (Chancellor Press 1996)

McCabe, Bob, *Clint Eastwood 'Quote Unquote'* (Parragon 1996)

McGilligan, Patrick, *Clint – The Life and Legend* (HarperCollins 1999)

Meyer, William R., *The Making of the Great Westerns* (Arlington House 1979)

Millard, Joe, *The Good, the Bad and the Ugly* (Star 1968)

Newman, Kim, *Wild West Movies* (Bloomsbury 1990)

Nowell-Smith, Geoffrey, *The Companion to Italian Cinema* (Cassell 1996)

O'Brien, Daniel, *Clint Eastwood – Film-Maker* (Batsford 1996)

O'Neal, Bill, *The Pimlico Encyclopedia of Western Gunfighters* (Pimlico 1998)

Parkinson, Michael and Clyde Jeavons, *A Pictorial History of Westerns* (Hamlyn 1983)

Reynolds, Burt, *My Life* (Hodder and Stoughton 1995)

Richie, Donald, *The Films of Akira Kurosawa* (University of California Press 1965)

Robb, Brian J., *Laurel and Hardy* (Pocket Essentials 2001)

Rosa, Joseph G., *Age of the Gunfighter* (Oklahoma Press 1995)

Ross, Jonathan, *The Incredibly Strange Film Book* (Simon and Schuster 1993)

Sciascia, Leonardo, *The Day of the Owl/Equal Danger* (Paladin 1987)

Shipman, David, *The Movie Makers – Brando* (Macmillan 1974)

Simmons, Michael, 'Jazz Manouche', *Acoustic Guitar*, February 1996, no 38

Slide, Anthony, *De Toth on De Toth* (Faber and Faber 1996)

Staig, Laurence and Tony Williams, *Italian Western – The Opera of Violence* (Lorrimer 1975)

Stewart, John, *Italian Film – A Who's Who* (McFarland 1994)

Streebeck, Nancy, *The Films of Burt Reynolds* (Citadel Press 1982)

Thrower, Stephen, *Beyond Terror – The Films of Lucio Fulci* (Fab Press 1999)

Trachtman, Paul, *The Gunfighters* (Time-Life Books 1974)

Tyler, Parker, *Early Classics of the Foreign Film* (Citadel Press 1962)

Verdone, Luca (ed.), *Per Un Pugno Di Dollari – Italian Script* (Cappelli 1979)

Weddle, David, *Sam Peckinpah: 'If They Move...Kill 'Em'* (Faber and Faber 1996)

Weisser, Thomas, *Spaghetti Westerns – the Good, the Bad and the Violent* (McFarland 1992)

Whitman, Mark, *Clint Eastwood* (LSP 1982)

Whitney, Steven, *Charles Bronson – Superstar* (Dell 1975)

Wilkinson, Frederick, *Handguns – A Collectors Guide to Pistols and Revolvers* (1993)

Zmijewsky, Boris and Lee Pfeiffer, *The Films of Clint Eastwood* (Citadel Press 1993)

Plus several useful LP booklets, travel guides, maps of Italy and Spain, press books, documentaries, posters and still sets, and the film website the Internet Movie Database (www.imdb.com).

INDEX

Film titles in bold type denote a chapter devoted to the film; page numbers in bold type denote an illustration.

Ace High 231–232
Achilles 127
Achtung! Banditi! 71
Adios Gringo 19, 36, 89, 127, 148, 174
Adios Sabata 149, 225–226
After the Fox xvi
Age-Scarpelli 107
Aguirre, The Wrath of God 203
Alessandroni, Alessandro 11, 26, 32, 52, 64, 91,
    118–119, 213, 238, 252
  and I Cantori Moderni di Alessandroni (The
    Modern Singers) 11, 27, 32, 36, 52, 64, 91,
    118–119, 144, 153–154, 164, 166, 200, 213, 224,
    238, 252
Alfonsi, Lydia 174
Alive or Preferably Dead 38, 191
All the Way Boys! 239, 252
Alonso, Chelo 108
Alonso, Pablito 22
Alvarez, Angel 60, 84
Ambush at Cimarron Pass 4
Amendola, Mario 194
Amman, Lukas 185
Among Vultures xvi, 148
And a Sky Full of Stars for a Roof 151, 168
Anthony, Tony 14–15, 241
Any Gun Can Play 220
Anzio 189
Apache's Last Battle xvi
Aranda, Angel 138, 141
Arcalli, Franco 125
Argento, Dario 202, 216, 218, 242
Arizona Colt 38, 156
Arlorio, Giorgio 206
Armstrong, R.G. 245
Arriaga, Simon 60, 84, 208
Arturo's Island 95
Asterix 9, 233
Atlas 196
The Awful Dr Orloff viii, 126, 133

Bacalov, Luis Enriquez 64–65, 102, 166
Bacci, Silvana 60
Backlash 72
Bad Man's River 228
Baldassare, Raf 196, 208
Baldi, Ferdinando 67, 231, 241
Balducci, Franco 185, 190
The Balearic Gold Operation 38
Band, Albert 58, 137–138, 140
Bandido! 210
Bandidos xxii, 190
The Bang Bang Kid 234
Barabbas 153, 208
Barbarella: Queen of the Galaxy 160–161
Barboni, Enzo 67, 87, 252

and *Django* 61, 232
and *The Hellbenders* 140
and *They Call Me Trinity* vii, 230–232, 234–239
Barboo, Luis 10, 148
Bardot, Brigitte 207–208, 241
Barker, Lex **xiii**, xvi
Barker, Ron 183
Barnes, Walter 148
Barry, Barta 154
Bartho, John **115**, 220
Barto, Dominic 235, 253
Baseheart, Richard xii, 4
Battle of Algiers 96, 98, 101, 104, 147, 201, 206, 209,
    245
Battle of the Commandos 208
Battle of the Worlds xi, 184
Bava, Mario xi, 18, 127, 133, 138, 140, 160, 167,
    174, 195, 198, 218, 224, 225, 228
Bay of Blood 167
Bedazzled 231
Bend of the River 78
Benedetti, Benedetto 125
Bengell, Norma 138
Ben Hur xi, 2, 19
Il Bello, Il Brutto, Il Cretino viii, 121–122
Berger, William 97, 172, 175, 180, 219–220, 223,
    225
Bertolucci, Bernardo 203, 242
Beswick, Martine 96–97
Betts, Tom viii, ix, xxii, 255
Beyond the Law 159, 166, 183, 189–191, 231, 244
The Bible...In the Beginning 60, 108
The Big and the Bad 239
The Big Combo 43
The Big Gundown vii, xxi–xxii, 56, 146–157, **149,**
    155, 156, 159, 161–162, 174, 178, 181
  abridgements 154–156, 166, 180
  cast and credits 146–147
  influence 157, 171, 176, 241
  inspiration 148
  leading players 148–149
  music 153–154, 179
  plot resume 147
  release 154, 156–157
  shooting locations 149, 175
The Big Silence vii, xxi–xxii, 75, 193–204, **197,**
    199, 203
  abridgements 201
  cast and credits 193–194
  influence 201–203
  inspiration 195
  leading players 196
  music 200–201
  plot resume 194–195
  release 201, 207
  shooting locations 196–197, 221

257

Bird With the Crystal Plumage 216, 218
Bitter Rice 71
The Black Pirate 239
Black Sabbath viii, 174, 195, 198–199, 201
Black Sunday viii, xi, 140
Blindman 241
Blood and Black Lace xi, 134
Blood at Sundown 198, 219
Blood Money 185, 228, 238
Bloody Pit of Horror 60
Bodalo, Jose 60
Boetticher, Budd 72
Bogarde, Dirk xii, 74
Boido, Federico 168, 174
Bolzoni, Adriano 206
Boot Hill 231
Bosic, Andrea 185
A Bout de Souffle 114
Braña, Frank 39, 44, 134, 148, **155**, 173, 174
Brando, Marlon 7–8, 83–84, 93, 102, 206
The Bravados 43, 56, 148
Brega, Mario xviii, 6, 44, **53**, 112, 161, 196, 201, 245–246, 253
Brennus: Enemy of Rome 198
Brice, Pierre xiii, xvi, 60
The Bridge on the River Kwai 120
Bronson, Charles xvi, 4, 7, 43, 93, 108, 181, 228, 243
Brynner, Yul 214–215, 225
Buck Rogers 34
Buffalo Bill, Hero of the Far West viii, xviii
A Bullet for Sandoval 121
A Bullet for the General vii, xxi, 94–105, **99**, **103**, 131, 215
  abridgements 104
  cast and credits 94–95
  influence 104–105, 207, 210
  inspiration 95–96
  leading players 96–97
  music 102–104, 213
  plot resume 95
  release 104
  shooting locations 97–98
Bullwhip 11
Burn! 206–207
The Burning Hills 83
Byrnes, Edd 121

Call of the Wild 202
Calvo, Jose 'Pepe' **5**, 9, 12, 185
Camardiel, Roberto 44, 127, 151
Camelot 208
Cameron, Rod xv, 13
Canalejas, Jose 44, **53**, 60, 208
Candy 206
Canevari, Sergio 98
Cannibal Holocaust 62
Cannon for Cordoba 208, 214
The Caper of the Golden Bulls 208
Capitani, Remo 232
Captain Apache 185
Cardinale, Claudia 215, 241–242
Carlini, Carlo 147, 149, 162, 175
Carpentieri, Luigi 71
Carreras, Michael xii

Casale, Antonio 108, **109**
Casas, Antonio 22, 31–32, 38–39, 108, 148, 174
Castel, Lou 79, 97, **103**, 210
Castellari, Enzo G. 26, 68, 121, 138
The Castillian xi
Castle of Blood xi, 58, 84
Cat Ballou 234
Catlow 145
Cemetery Without Crosses 125
Chato's Land 93
Che! 216
Checchi, Andrea 97
Cheyenne (TV series) 43
Christy 153
Chroscicki, Enrico 159, 183
Cimarosa, Michele 136
Cipriani, Stelvio 14, 133
City Slickers 209
Clayton, Dick 93
Cleopatra 75
Clint il Solitario 54
Coburn, James 4, 8, 73, 208, 214–215, 244
Coby, Michael 238
Colizzi, Giuseppe 189, 224, 230, 233, 238
Collins, Gene 126
The Colossus of Rhodes 2–4, 18, 46, 174
Comanche 83
Commandos xii, 159, 183
Compañeros viii, 209, 214, 216, 241
Confessions of a Police Captain 105
The Conformist 203
Connor, Tommie 119–120
Conversi, Spartaco 97, 196, 220
Cooper, Gary 5, 42, 56, 116
Copleston, Geoffrey 73
Corazzari, Bruno 196
Corbucci, Bruno 58, 194
Corbucci, Sergio ix, xi, 2, 18, 20, 30, 95, 101, 214, 216, 232, 235, 241, 251, 254
  and *The Big Silence* vii, 194–204, 207
  and *Django* vii, 58–69, 137, 201
  and *The Hellbenders* vii, 93, 137–138, 140, 142–145
  and *Navajo Joe* vii, 82–88, 90, 92–93, 137
  and *A Professional Gun* vii, 206–209, 212–216
Cord, Alex 78
Cottafavi, Vittorio xi, 18, 30
Cotten, Joseph xvi, 137–138, 141, **143**, 145
Cox, Alex viii, ix, xxi
Crawford, Broderick xvi, 39
Cressoy, Pierre 84, 89, 148
Crime and Punishment 6
The Crimson Pirate 219
Crypt of Horror 242
La Cuccagna 252
A Curious Way to Love 125

Dallamano, Massimo 7, 51, 108, 175, 190
Damiani, Damiano vii, 95–101, 105, 253
Damon, Mark 58, 60, 79, 105, 195
Dances with Wolves 254
D'Angelo, Carlo 196
Danger: Diabolik 160, 185
D'Aquino, Rossella 174

Daves, Delmer 83
Dawson, Anthony 55, 160–161, 168
Day of Anger vii, 36, 159, 169, 182–192, **187**, **191**, 242, 244
  abridgements 166, 189–190
  cast and credits 182–183
  influence 190, 220, 247
  inspiration 183, 186
  leading players 183–185
  music 188–189
  plot resume 183–184
  release 167, 189
  shooting locations 185–186
Day of the Badman 186
Day of the Outlaw viii, 61, 195
Day of the Owl 71, 105
Dead or Alive 78–79
Deadfall 208
Deaf Smith and Johnny Ears 216
De Angelis, Remo 60, 140, 198, 208
Death at Owl Rock 174
The Death of Pancho Villa 102
Death Rides a Horse vii, xxii, 56, 158–169, **163**, **167**, **168**
  cast and credits 158–159
  influence 183, 190
  inspiration 159–160
  leading players 160–161
  music 166
  plot resume 159
  release 166–167
  shooting locations 161, **167**
Deguejo 75
De Laurentiis, Dino xvii–xviii, 71, 74, 77–78, 80, 82–84, 86–87, 92–93, 160
Deliverance 93
Dell'Aqua, Alberto 236
Delli Colli, Franco 127–128
Delli Colli, Tonino 108
Dell'Orso, Edda 52, 120, 144, 154, 179, 243, 252
De Luca, Lorella 20, 22, 31, **37**, 38, 208
De Luna, Alvaro xix, 84, 91, 208
Del Pozo, Angel **156**, 173–174
De Santis, Lucio 60
The Deserter xviii
The Desperado Trail xv
Destry Rides Again 24, 231, 234
De Toth, Andre 61, 195, 228
Dial M for Murder 160
Di Leo, Fernando 3, 31–32, 82, 84
The Dirty Dozen 108
The Dirty Game 71
Dirty Harry 216
Django vii, xxi–xxii, 46, 53, 57–69, **63**, **67**, 84, 87, 137, 138, 201–202, 207–208, 220, 232
  abridgements 65
  cast and credits 57
  influence 66–68, 79, 125
  inspiration 14, 58–60
  leading players 60
  music 64–65, 102, 123
  plot resume 59
  release 65
  shooting locations 60–61, 67, 108, 115
Django Get a Coffin Ready 66–68, 157, 231–232

Django Kill vii, xxi, 124–135, **129**, **133**, **135**, 154
  abridgements 134–135
  cast and credits 124
  inspiration 14, 66, 126
  leading players 126–127
  music 132–134
  plot resume 125–126
  release 134
  shooting locations 127, **135**
Django Shoots First 20, 54, 66, 73, 84, 234
Django Strikes Again 66
Django the Bastard 60, 66
Doctor Zhivago 44
A Dollar of Fire 32
Dollars for a Fast Gun 161, 176, 224
Donati, Ermanno 71
Donati, Sergio 42, 47, 107, 122, 147, 171, 180, 242–243
Dr No 160
Drummer of Vengeance 144
Duck You Sucker 114, 215, 242, 244
Duel at Diablo 83, 189, 245
Duel in the Eclipse 54
Duryea, Dan 72, 74, 80

Eastman, George 54, 68, 232
Eastwood, Clint vii, xvi, 4, 24, 28, 38–39, 61, 67–68, 84, 147, 154, 160, 164, 194, 202, 216, 228, 245, 254
  and *A Fistful of Dollars* 2, 4–12, **5**, **9**, **13**, 14–16, 19, 34, 44, 46, 83, 129–130, 148, 166
  and *For a Few Dollars More* **41**, 42–47, **49**, 51–56, **53**, 165
  and *The Good, the Bad and the Ugly* 108, 110, **111**, 112–114, **113**, **115**, 116, **119**, 121–123, 191
Egger, Josef 5, 9, 47
Eisenstein, Sergei 96, 104
Elam, Jack 243
El Cid xi
El Cisco 220
El Condor xviii, 185, 228
El Dorado 236, 245
El Rojo 14
El Topo 46
Emilio Zapata 102
Empty Canvas 95
Ercoli, Luciano 31
Erik the Conqueror xi
Erik the Viking 184, 208
The Evil Eye xi

Face to Face vii, 170–181, **173**, **177**, 220, 223
  abridgements 180
  cast and credits 170–171
  historical references 171–172
  influence 180
  inspiration 75, 171–172
  leading players 172–174
  music 179, 200
  plot resume 171
  release 179–180
  shooting locations 174–175
Fajardo, Eduardo 60, 208, 210, 216
Fall of the Giants xii, 208
The Fall of the House of Usher 125

The Fantastic Three 218
The Fastest Guitar Alive 220
Fellini, Federico 20, 54, 86, 91, 174, 208, 218
Fernandez, Jaime 102
Ferzetti, Gabriela 242
A Few Dollars for Django 66, 121
Fia, Roberto 64–65
The Fighting Fists of Shanghai Joe 92, 238
Fineschi, Lorenzo 236
Firecreek 244
A Fistful of Dollars vii, 1–16, **5**, **9**, **13**, 19, 30, 34,
    42–44, 46–47, 51, 53, 55, 62, 83, 101, 108, 114,
    122, 129, 130, 135, 148, 165, 174, 183, 185, 207,
    223
  abridgements 10, 15
  cast and credits 1–2
  influence 14–15, 58–59, 71, 125–126, 195
  inspiration 3–4
  leading players 4–6
  music 11–12, 26–27, 52, 144, 166, 189, 252
  plot resume 3
  release 14–15, 18
  shooting locations 6–7, **9**, 12–13, 45, 127, 186, 218
A Fistful of Rawhide 54
Fists in the Pocket 97
Fitzcarraldo 203
Five for Hell 218, 220
The Five Man Army 215, 230–232
Flaming Frontier xvi
Flash Gordon 34
The Flashing Blade (TV series) vii
Fonda, Henry 43, 242, 244, 247, **249**, 250–252
For a Few Bullets More 53, 121
For a Few Dollars Less viii, 53–54, 121
For a Few Dollars More vii, xxi–xxii, 9, 36, 40–56,
    41, **45**, **49**, **53**, 100, 114, 121–122, 162, 165, 174,
    186, 207, 238–239
  abridgements 50, 54–55
  cast and credits 40–41
  influence 53–54, 75, 147–148, 159, 172, 183, 190,
    199, 219, 222, 242
  inspiration 42–43
  leading players 43–44
  music 51–53, 118, 120, 166, 245, 252
  plot resume 42
  release 53–55
  shooting locations xviii, 44–45, **49**, 109, 161, 183,
    185, 218
For a Fist in the Eye 14
For the Taste of Killing 110, 183
Ford, John 30, 34–35, 38, 45, 216, 243–244, 247
The Forgotten Pistolero xxii, 237
Forty Guns viii, 76, 250
Fort Yuma Gold 36, 38, 121, 174
Franchi and Ingrassia 14, 58, 121–122, 231, 234, 238
Frank, Horst 67
Frayling, Professor Sir Christopher viii, ix, xxi, 255
From Hell to Texas 148
From Russia With Love 96, 160
Fuller, Samuel 76, 250

Garko, Gianni 54, 66, 218–219, 226
Gaspar, Luis 154
Gastaldi, Ernesto 184, 242, 253
Gazzalo, Nando 73

Gazzalo, Virginio **191**
Gemma, Giuliano 19–20, 36, 38, 84, 168, 174, 184,
    187, 231
  and *Day of Anger* 183–184, 189, 191–192, **191**
  and *A Pistol for Ringo* 19, **21**, 22–23, 28, 187
  and *The Return of Ringo* 31–32, **33**, 34–35, **37**, 39
The General 110, 112
Gerlach, Virgil C. 137
Germany, Year Zero 71
Get Mean 15
Giacobini, Franco 208
Gino 77
Giombini, Marcello 224, 226–227
Giordani, Aldo 232
Giraldi, Franco 6, 18, 20, 78, 209, 234
Girolami, Enio 138
Giuffre, Aldo 112
God Forgives – I Don't 189, 196, 230–231
God's Gun 228
The Golden Arrow xi
Goliath and the Barbarians 198
Goliath and the Dragon xi
Goliath and the Vampires viii, xi, 18, 58, 195
Gone With the Wind 110–111
The Good, the Bad and the Ugly vii, xv, xix,
    xxi–xxii, 23, 96, 106–123, **109**, **111**, **113**, **115**,
    117, **119**, 148–149, 157, 159, 161–162, 174, 184,
    209, 220, 239, 242
  abridgements 122
  cast and credits 106–107
  historical references 107–108, 110–112
  influence 68, 121–122, 140, 210
  inspiration 110–111
  leading players 108
  music 36, 118–121, 153, 252
  plot resume 107
  release 104, 121–123
  shooting locations xv, **xix**, 108–110, **115**
Gora, Claudio 138
Gordon, Leo 244
The Gospel According to St Matthew 64, 108
Gracia, Sancho 131
Gradoli, Antonio 223
Graf, Maurizio 26, 36
The Grand Duel 166, 228
Grand Slam 203
Granger, Farley 232, 235
Granger, Stewart xvi
Gravina, Carla 97
Grimaldi, Alberto 42, 107, 172, 206, 208, 219, 224,
    226
Gunfight at the OK Corral 19, 43, 45, 186
The Gunfighter 19, 247
Gunfight in the Red Sands 11–12, 84, 207
Guns for San Sebastian 213
Gunsmoke (TV series) xii, 83, 93

Half Breed xvi
Hallyday, Johnny 202
Halufi, Jose 22
Hammett, Dashiell 4
Hang 'Em High 123, 202
Hardy, Oliver 234
Harrison, Richard 4, 12, 19, 36, 54, 185
Hate for Hate 79, 230

Have a Good Funeral, Sartana will Pay 226
Hawk (TV series) 83, 87, 93
Hawks and Sparrows 54
Hawks, Howard 12, 30, 32, 235, 236
Heads I Kill You, Tails You Die 125
Helen of Troy xi
The Hellbenders vii, xxi, 60, 93, 136–145, **139**, **143**
  cast and credits 136
  influence 144
  inspiration 137–138
  leading players 138
  music 36, 144
  plot resume 137
  release 144–145
  shooting locations 139–140, **143**
Henze, Jürgen 209
Hercules xi, 174
Hercules Against Moloch xi
Hercules and the Sons of the Son 161, 184
Hercules Conquers Atlantis xi, 6
Hercules in the Haunted World viii, xi, xii, 18, 133, 208
Hercules, Samson and Ulysses 87
Hercules Unchained xi
The Hero of Babylon 127
Herter, Gerard 149, 225
Herzog, Werner 203
High Noon viii, 43, 56, 116, 186, 239, 243–244
High Plains Drifter 67
Hill, Craig 183
Hill, Terence xv, 67, 105, 189–191, 224, 230, 231–232, 236, 244, 252–253
  and *My Name is Nobody* 244, **245**, 247, **249**, 250, 253
  and *They Call Me Trinity* 230, 232–233, **233**, 236, **237**, 238–239, 253
The Hills Run Red vii, xxii, 70–80, **73**, **77**, 85, 97, 198
  cast and credits 70–71
  influence 78–80
  inspiration 14, 72
  leading players 72–73
  music 76–78
  plot resume 71–72
  release 78
  shooting locations xvii, 73–74, **77**
Hilton, George 53, 190
The Hired Hand 246
Hirenbach, Karl xx, 54
How the West Was Won 43
Huerta, Cris 84
Hundar, Robert 220
Hunter, Thomas 72–75, **73**, 79–80
The Hunting Party 253

I Came, I Saw, I Shot 234
If Your Left Arm Offends, Cut it Off 125
Illustrious Corpses 105, 167
Imbro, Gaetano 236
In a Colt's Shadow 6, 84, 220
The Incident 208
The Indian Fighter 83
Investigation of a Citizen Above Suspicion 181
Invitation to a Gunfighter 225
Ippoliti, Silvano 87, 197

Ireland, John 19, 79
The Iron Horse 243
It Conquered the World 43
I Want Him Dead xxii, 121, 183
Izzo, Renato 219, 223

Jennings, Tom 169, 228
Jesse & Lester: Two Brothers in a Place Called Trinity 238
Jim il Primo xvii
Job, Enrico 198
Joe Kidd 202
Johnny Guitar 243
Johnny Hamlet 26, 220
Johnny Oro 58, 60, 69, 75, 83, 195, 198, 207
Jordon, Nick 218, 220, 226
Journey Beneath the Desert 6
Juliet of the Spirits 91

Kanaly, Steve 245
Karloff, Boris 195
Kelly's Heroes 116, 126
Keoma 216, 253
Kill Baby Kill xi, 60, 127, 133
Kill Bill 166
The Killing 224
Kill Them All and Come Back Alone 121, 196, 209
King, David 237–238
King of Kings xi, 20
Kinski, Klaus xiv, 44, 87, 92, 203–204, 253
  and *The Big Silence* 196, 199–201, **199**, **203**
  and *A Bullet for the General* 96, **103**
  and *For a Few Dollars More* 44, **53**, 219
Kiss Kiss – Bang Bang 38
Knives of the Avenger xii, 224
Knox, Mickey 107, 216
Koch, Marianne 6
Krup, Mara 54
Kurosawa, Akira 3, 15

Lacerenza, Michele 12, 27, 36
Ladd, Alan xvi
La Dolce Vita 91, 125, 161
The Lady from Beirut 38
Lancaster, Burt 20, 42–43, 46, 88, 206, 215, 219
The Last Days of Pompeii 2, 58, 218
The Last Days of Sodom and Gomorrah xi, 3, 161
Last of the Mohicans xiii
Last of the Renegades xiv–xv, 231
The Last Sunset 138, 160
The Last Wagon viii, 83
Laurel, Stan 234
Law, John Phillip 160, 165, **167**, **168**
Lawrence of Arabia xi, 20
Left-handed Johnny West 6, 127, 218, 224
The Legend of Frenchie King 241
Le Mepris 208, 220
Leone, Francesca 47
Leone, Sergio 2–3, 20, 24, 31, 58, 78, 84, 87, 95, 101, 147–149, 152, 154, 160, 166, 174, 175, 179, 185–186, 195, 200, 203, 206–207, 216, 218, 225, 254
  and *Duck You Sucker* 114, 215, 244
  and *A Fistful of Dollars* vii, 2–15, 18–19, 30, 42–43, 127, 183

and *For a Few Dollars More* vii, 9, 41–48, 50–51, 53–54, 56, 118, 121, 159, 172, 183, 199, 239, 242
and *The Good, the Bad and the Ugly* vii, 56, 96, 107–118, 120–123, 162, 191, 242
and *My Name is Nobody* 241–242, 244–249, 251, 253–254
and *Once Upon a Time in the West* 123, 222, 242, 244
The Leopard xi, 19, 231
Levine, Joseph E. xi, 104, 145, 238
Lewis, Geoffrey 245
Liberatore, Ugo 137
The Life and Legend of Wyatt Earp (TV series) 46
The Life and Times of Judge Roy Bean 245
Lights of Variety 208
Light the Fuse…Sartana's Coming 226
The Lion of Thebes 84, 174
Lizzani, Carlo vii, 71–72, 74–76, 78–80, 96, 201
Loddi, Loris 75, 198
The Long Days of Vengeance 32, 38, 184
The Longest Day 5, 58
Long Live Your Death 216
Long Ride from Hell 68
Lopert, Tanya 85, 86
Lorenzon, Livio 108
Los Tarantos 6
Lovelock, Raymond 126
Lozano, Margherita 6
Lucio Vazquez 102
Lucky Luke 253
Lukschy, Wolfgang 5
Lulli, Piero xviii, 127
Luotto, Gene 235, 238

Macchi, Valentino 84, 97
Machiavelli, Nicoletta 73, 78, 84–85, 88, 92
Machine Gun McCain 167
Maciste in Hell xii, 71
Maesso, Jose Guittierez 58, 137
Magalotti, Paolo 73, 76, 236
The Magnificent Seven viii, xii, 4, 8, 30, 71, 74, 92, 101, 162, 220, 223, 225, 230–231, 235
The Magnificent Seven Ride 105, 162
Major Dundee 245
Malle, Louis 104, 207, 220
A Man Alone 43
A Man and a Woman 196
A Man called Sledge xviii, 201, 222, 250
The Man from Laramie viii, 72, 78
Man of the East 190, 252
The Man Who Killed Billy the Kid xx
Man With the Gun 150, 244
Mannaja 202, 253
Mancori, Alessandro 228
Mancori, Alvaro xvii
Mann, Anthony 72, 75–76, 78
Margheriti, Antonio 58, 60, 160, 218
Marseilles Connection 216
Martin, Daniel 6, 12
Martin, Dean 32, 65
Martin, Jean 244–245, 253
Martin, Jorge 22, 31, 35, 38
Martin, Jose Manuel xii, 20, 97, 105
Martin, Maria 138
Marvin, Lee 43, 215, 234

Mary Poppins 14
Massacre at Fort Holman 121, 189, 209, 242, 244
Master Stroke 185
Matchless 78
Mateos, Julian 138, 141, 145
Mattei, Giuseppe 220
May, Karl xiii, 12
Mazza, Mark 245
McGee, Vonetta 196
McLintock 45
McQueen, Steve 8, 74
Mendez, Guillermo 60
Merli, Maurizio 258
Merlini, Marisa 196
Micalizzi, Franco 237–238
Micheli, Elio 74
Michel Strogoff (TV series) vii
Mifune, Toshiro 3, 5, 150
Milian, Tomas 168, 174, 214, 216, 241
and *The Big Gundown* 148, 150, 154, **156**, 157
and *Django Kill* 66, 126–127, **129**, 130, **133**, 154
and *Face to Face* 172, **173**, 175, **177**, 179, 180
Millard, Joe 123
Mill of the Stone Women viii, 60
Minnesota Clay 6, 20, 22, 58, 59, 87, 97, 138, 195
The Mission 179
Mitchell, Cameron xvii, 58
Mitchell, Gordon 190
Modio, Jolanda 174
Modugno, Lucia 85
Mondo Cane xi, 188
The Mongols 208
Monte Carlo or Bust 85, 105, 231
Montenegro, Hugo vii, 123
Morandi, Fernando 147
Morricone, Ennio vii, viii, ix, 13, 96, 160, 168, 208, 211, 241, **245**, 254
and *The Big Gundown* 152–154, 179
and *The Big Silence* 200–201
and *A Bullet for the General* 102–103
and *Death Rides a Horse* 162, 166
and *Face to Face* 179, 200
and *A Fistful of Dollars* 9, 11–13, 27, 52, 144, 166, 252
and *For a Few Dollars More* 50–53, 245, 252
and *The Good,, the Bad and the Ugly* 36, 112, 118–121, 122–123, 153, 252
and *The Hellbenders* 36, 142, 144
and *The Hills Run Red* 76–78
and *My Name is Nobody* 252
and *Navajo Joe* 88, 90–93
and *Once Upon a Time in the West* 243, 252
and *A Pistol for Ringo* 25–27, 36, 77–78
and *A Professional Gun* 211, 213–214
and *The Return of Ringo* 36
Morsella, Fulvio 42, 242, 253
Mulock, Al 118, 138, 144, 185
The Murder Clinic 220
Murphy, Audie 38–39, 148, 196
Musante, Tony 208, **211**, 216
Il Musichiere (TV series) 20
My Darling Clementine 244
My Fair Lady 14, 23
My Name is Nobody vii, xxi, 187, 239, 240–254, **245**, **249**

abridgements 253
cast and credits 240–241
influence 252–253
inspiration 241–242, 247, 250
leading players 244–246
music 252
plot resume 242
release 252–253
shooting locations 246
My Name is Pecos 38, 54, 85, 198

The Naked Spur 72, 78
Nannuzzi, Armando 246
Navajo Joe vii, xxii, 78, 81–93, **85**, **89**, **92**, 137, 197, 207
cast and credits 81–82
influence 92–93
inspiration 82–83
leading players 83–86
music 91–92
plot resume 82
release 92–93
shooting locations 86–87
Navarro, Nieves 31, 38, 148, 151, **155**
Nero, Franco 60, 67, 105, 137, 202, 216, 231–232, 253
and *Django* 60, **63**, 65–66
and *A Professional Gun* 208–210, **211**, 214, **215**
Nicol, Alex xii, xvi, 72
Nicolai, Bruno ix, 103, 213, 226
Niento, Jose xii, 138
Nightmare Castle 140
Night of the Serpent 168
Night Star – Goddess of Electra xii
Nobody's the Greatest 105, 239, 252
Nosferatu the Vampyre 204
Novi, Angelo 108
Nusciak, Loredana 64, 66

Once Upon a Time in America 254
Once Upon a Time in the West viii, xviii, xxi–xxii, 43, 51, 108, 123, 176, 185, 196, 220, 222, 242–244, 246, 250, 252, 253
One Eyed Jacks 8
100 Rifles 93, 215
$100,000 for Ringo 27, 36, 75
One Million Years BC 97
One Silver Dollar 19, 36, 89, 174, 220
Operation Kid Brother 78
Ortolani, Riz 188–189, 244
Our Man Flint 73
The Ox-Bow Incident 244

Pacheco, Raphael 175
Pajarito 22, 31, 38
Palacios, Riccardo 44, 185
Palance, Jack 199, 208–209, **211**, 214–216, 241
Paleface 234
Pale Rider 202
Palmera, Mimmo 218
Pancho Villa 215
Panhandle Calibre .38 233
Parolini, Gianfranco vii, 180, 218–226, 228, 244
Pasolini, Pier Paolo 54, 64, 79, 108
Passport to Hell 147

Pat Garrett and Billy the Kid 245
Pavone, Rita 68
Pazzafini, Nello 154, 173–174
Peckinpah, Sam 61, 132, 215, 245, 247, 250–251, 253
Peña, Julio 138
Pernice, Gino 60, 138, 141
Pesce, Franco 22, 219
Petrilli, Vittoriano 194
Petroni, Giulio vii, 159, 161–165, 168, 183, 190, 244
Pevarello, Osiride 76, 236
Pigozzi, Luciano 220
The Pink Panther 65
Pinocchio 9
Pirro, Ugo 82
Pistilli, Luigi 44, 108, 160–161, 167–168, 196
A Pistol For Ringo vii, 17–28, **21**, **25**, 32–33, 35, 39, 97, 127
abridgements 27–28
cast and credits 17–18
influence 27
inspiration 14, 18–19, 30
leading players 19–22
music 26–27, 36, 77–78
plot resume 19
release 27–28
shooting locations 22, 26, 31
Pistols Don't Argue 11, 13–14, 138
Pizzuti, Riccardo 236
A Place in Hell xii
Planet of the Vampires xii, 138
Polesello, Franca 85–86
Pontecorvo, Gillo 95–96, 147, 206
Poor But Handsome 22
Posse from Hell 148
Pregadio, Roberto 237
The Price of Power 144, 191, 242, 244, 247
Prieto, Antonio 6
A Professional Gun vii, xxi–xxii, 66, 205–216, **211**, **215**
abridgements 214
cast and credits 205–206
historical references 207, 212
influence 214–216
inspiration 207–208
leading players 208–209
music **211**, 213
plot resume 206–207
release 213
shooting locations 209
The Professionals 215
The Proud Ones 58
Psycho 132
Puppo, Romano 108, 148, **155**, 162, 185–186, 220

Queen of the Pirates xi, 20
Quesada, Milo 127
Questi, Giulio vii, 125–130, 132–135
Que Viva Mexico! 96
A Quiet Place in the Country 208
Quinn, Anthony 216
Quo Vadis? 231

Rails into Laramie 43, 72
Ralli, Giovanna 208

Ramon the Mexican 14
Rampage at Apache Wells xv–xvi
Raoul 166
Rassimov, Rada 67, 108
Rawhide (TV series) xii, 4–5, 7, 10, 43, 55, 72
Red Lips 95
Red Pastures 58, 137, 140, 185
Red Sun 216
Reed, Oliver 181, 253
Reeves, Steve xi
Regnoli, Piero 71, 79, 82, 84
Reinl, Harald xiii, xvi
Requiescant xxi, 79, 189, 198
Ressel, Franco 210, 220
The Restless Breed 244
The Return of Ringo vii, 24, 29–39, **33**, **37**
  abridgements 38–39
  cast and credits 29
  influence 38–39
  inspiration 14, 30–31
  leading players 31
  music 35–36
  plot resume 30
  release 36
  shooting locations 31–32
Return of Sabata 224, 226–228
Return of the Seven 71, 145
Return of White Fang 202
Revenge of the Praetorians 19
Revolver 181
Rey, Fernando xii, 84
Reynolds, Burt xvi, 82–84, **85**, 86–89, **92**, 93, 215
Ride and Kill 22, 174
Ride Lonesome 43, 56
Ride the High Country 6, 245
Righi, Massimo 148
Rilla, Walter 185
Ringo and Gringo against Everyone 27
Ringo's Big Night 220
Rio Bravo viii, 12, 30–32, 45, 148, 160, 231,
  235–236
Rita of the West viii, 68, 231, 232
Riverboat (TV series) 83
Rizzo, Gianni 147, 174, 176, 219, 223
Robards, Jason 243
Robin Hood and the Pirates xii
Robledo, Lorenzo xix, 6, **9**, 10, 108, 148, 174
Rojo, Antonio Molino xix, 6, **9**, 10, 18, 39, 44, **53**,
  79, 108, 112, 148, 246
Roman, Maria Del Carmen Martinez 125
Romeo and Juliet 185
Romulus and Remus xi, 18, 58, 83, 185
Rope 232
Rosato, Lucio 68
Rosi, Francesco 95–96, 105, 167
Rossetti, Franco 58, 67
Rossi, Luciano 60
Ruiz, Antonio 100
Run Man Run 157, 181, 220
Rupp, Sieghardt xvi, 5
The Ruthless Four 161, 203
Ruzzolini, Giuseppe 246

Sabata vii, xxii, 168–169, 180, 192, 217–228, **221**,
  225, **227**

  abridgements 225
  cast and credits 217–218
  influence 225–228
  inspiration 46, 54, 164, 218–220
  leading players 220
  music 224
  plot resume 219
  release 224–225
  shooting locations 220–222, **227**
Sabata the Killer 224
Sabato, Antonio 79, 190
Salvatore Giuliano 96, 196
Sambrell, Aldo 12, 39, 79, 84, 93, 105, 215
  and *A Bullet for the General* 97
  and *Face to Face* 174
  and *A Fistful of Dollars* 6
  and *For a Few Dollars More* 44, 148
  and *The Good, the Bad and the Ugly* 108
  and *The Hellbenders* 138, 142
  and *Navajo Joe* 84, **89**, 90
Samson 218
Sanchez, Pedro 220, 225, 226
Sancho, Fernando 20, 36, 38, 59, 148, 156, 219
  and *The Big Gundown* 148
  and *A Pistol for Ringo* 20, 23, **25**
  and *The Return of Ringo* 148
Sandokan 157
Sandokan the Great xi
Sansone, Alfonso 159
Santi, Giancarlo 162, 183
Sanz, Paco 22, 127, 174, 176
Sartana viii, 54, 180, 218, 223
Sartana the Gravedigger xxii, 226
Sasso, Ugo xviii, 236
Satyricon 54, 86
Savage, Archie 161
The Savage Guns viii, xii
Savalas, Telly 215, 241, 244, 253
Saxson, Glenn 234
The Scalphunters 88
Scott, Gordon xviii, 18, 137
Scott, Randolph 72
Scratuglia, Ivan 60
The Searchers viii, 30, 62, 243
Secchi, Antonio 97
Senso 232
Serra, Gianna 73, 78
Seven for Pancho Villa 207
Seven Guns for the MacGregors 6, 18, 20, 24, 30, 34,
  84, 86, 234, 241
Seven Hills of Rome 108
Seven Hours of Gunfire xviii–xx, 84
Seven Samurai 4, 150
Seven Seas to Calais xi, 161
79AD 218
Seven Ways from Sundown 148
Seven Winchesters for a Massacre 68, 121
Seven Women for the MacGregors 234
Shalako 145
Shane viii, 208, 231, 236, 243, 248
Shatner, William xvi, 145
The Sheriff of Fractured Jaw xii, xvii, 45, 138
She Wore a Yellow Ribbon 30, 34
The Shortest Day 58
Sign of the Gladiator xi, 20

Silva, Henry 72, 74–75, **77**, 80
Silver Lode 43, 72
Silver Saddle 192
Simi, Carlo 7, 44, 47, 60–61, 86, 149, 183, 209, 223
The Singer Not the Song xii, 74
Ski Troop Attack 196
Slave Girls 97
The Slowest Gun in the West 43
Smith, Paul 238
Solinas, Franco 95–96, 100, 147, 206, 207, 209
Sollima, Sergio 2, 161, 168, 218, 254
   and *The Big Gundown* vii, 147–150, 152, 157, 241
   and *Face to Face* vii, 75, 171–176, 178–181, 220
Sonny & Jed 216
Son of El Cid xi
Son of Paleface 234
Son of Spartacus 58, 90, 138, 185, 195
Son of the Leopard 58
Sons of Thunder xi, 18–20, 22, 35, 184, 231
South Pacific 161
Southwest to Sonora 7
Spagnolo, Gianna 76, 91
The Spanish Affair 97
Spartacus and the Ten Gladiators xi, 147
The Spartan Gladiators 127
The Specialists 60, 202–203
Spencer, Bud 189, 191, 224, 230–231, 252
   and *They Call Me Trinity* 231–233, **233**, 236, 238–239
Sperli, Alessandro 235
The Sphinx Smiles before Death 18
Spina, Sergio 206
Spolettini, Guglielmo 76
Stagecoach 19, 45
Stefanelli, Benito 185, 253
   and *The Big Gundown* 148, 152
   and *Day of Anger* 185–186
   and *A Fistful of Dollars* 6
   and *For a Few Dollars More* 44
   and *The Good, the Bad and the Ugly* 108
   and *The Hellbenders* 138
   and *My Name is Nobody* 246
Steiger, Rod 114, 215
Steffen, Anthony 66, 121
Stewart, James 24, 72, 75, 234, 251
Stott, Lally 238
The Stranger in Japan 15
A Stranger in Town viii, 14, 174
The Stranger Returns 14–15
Strangers on a Train 232
Strangler of Vienna 86
Sturges, John 30
Sturkie, Dan 232
Il Successo 26
Sugranes, Monica 35
Summers, Neil 245, 253
Susani, Angelo 116
The Swindle 20

Taberno, Julio Perez 10
Take a Hard Ride 185
The Tall T 72
Tarantino, Quentin 166
Tarantula 4
Taste of Death 202

10 Gladiators 218
Tension at Table Rock 250
The Tenth Victim 108
$10,000 Blood Money 54, 66
Tepepa 168, 207
The Terrible Sheriff 9
The Terror of Dr Hitchcock xi, 71, 242
Tessari, Duccio xi, 2, 36, 38, 42, 58, 105, 151, 184, 192, 216, 220, 254
   and *A Fistful of Dollars* 3, 14, 18–19, 30, 32, 34
   and *A Pistol for Ringo* vii, 14, 18–20, 22–28, 30–31, 35
   and *The Return of Ringo* vii, 14, 24, 30–36
Tevis, Peter 11, 13
Tex and the Lords of the Deep 192
Texas Adios xvii, 67, 161, 232
The Texican 38–39
They Call Me Hallelujah 239
They Call Me Providence 168, 239
They Call Me Trinity vii, xxii, 60, 229–239, **233**, **237**
   cast and credits 229–230
   influence 238–239, 253
   inspiration 230–231, 234
   leading players 231–232
   music 237–238
   plot resume 230–231
   release 238
   shooting locations 232–233
They Call Me Veritas 239
30 Winchesters for El Diablo 174
Thompkins, Bill 6
Three Golden Boys 79–80, 126, 224
Thunder at the Border xv
Thunderball 96, 160
Time of Vultures 190
The Tin Star 244
Toby Dammit 174
Today it's Me…Tomorrow You 68, 202, 231
Tolo, Marilu 105, 127
Torres, Jose 154, 157, 161, 173, 174
Torres, Juan 22, 39
Toto 58
Toto a Colori 108
Toto of Arabia 20
A Town called Bastard 253
A Train for Durango 38, 105
The Tramplers 137–138, 141
The Treasure of Silver Lake xiii–xiv
Trinity is Still My Name 230, 239, 241, 244, 247, 252
Trintignant, Jean-Louis 194, 196, **197**, **203**, 210
Tristana 216
The Trojan War xi, 185
The Twilight Zone (TV series) 43
Two Mules for Sister Sara 15, 168
Two R-R-Ringos from Texas 27
Two Sons of Trinity 238

Ubaldi, Giorgio 236
The Ugly Ones 127, 133, 174
Ukmar, Bruno 220
Ukmar, Franco 220
Ulloa, Alejandro 209
Unforgiven 202

Unger, Goffredo 174
The Unholy Four 68, 232
Ursus and the Tartar Princess xi

The Valachi Papers 189
Valerii, Tonino 144, 191, 242, 244, 254
　and *Day of Anger* vii, 183–184, 186–188, 220, 244, 247
　and *A Fistful of Dollars* 3, 6
　and *For a Few Dollars More* 185
　and *My Name is Nobody* vii, 241–242, 245–246, 248, 250–251, 253
Valturri, Patrizia 126
Van Cleef, Lee xvi, 38, 43, 54, 72, 105, 172, 190, 226–228, 243–244
　and *The Big Gundown* 148, **149**, 150, 152, 154, 156–157, **156**, 175
　and *Day of Anger* 166, 183–186, **187**, 189, **191**, 191–192
　and *Death Rides a Horse* 159–162, **163**, 164–169, **167**, **168**
　and *For a Few Dollars More* 43, 45–48, **45**, 51, 53, 55–56, 219, 222
　and *The Good, the Bad and the Ugly* 108, **111**, 116–117, **117**, 122, 148–149, 184
　and *Sabata* 169, 180, 192, 220, **221**, 222, 224–225, **227**, 228
Vandor, Ivan 129, 132–134
Vengeance 54
Vera Cruz 42–43, 46, 161
Veras, Linda 174, 220, 223, 225
Vertigo 23
Village of the Damned 185
Villa Rides 214–215
Vincenzoni, Luciano 42, 46–47, 50, 107, 159–161, 165, 206–207, 212, 254
Violent City 181, 241
The Violent Four 180
The Virgin and the Gypsy 216
Viridiana 6
Viva Maria! 104, 207–208, 220
Vivarelli, Piero 58
Viva Zapata 102
Volonte, Gian Maria 6, 54, 95, 180–181
　and *A Bullet for the General* 96, 99, **103**

　and *Face to Face* 172, 175, **177**
　and *A Fistful of Dollars* 6, 9, 99
　and *For a Few Dollars More* 44, 99

Wake Up and Kill 96, 108, 210
Wallach, Eli 108, **109**, 110, **111**, 112, 114, **115**, 121, 122, 216, 232
Warlock 244
War of the Planets 60
Warriors Five xii, 208
The Wasp Woman 196
Watch Out, We're Mad! 252, 289
Wayne, John 5, 62, 200, 216, 236, 243, 251
Way Out West 234
Welles, Orson xvi, 39, 168
Westbound 148
We Still Kill the Old Way 167
What am I doing in the Middle of a Revolution? 214
What Did you do in the War, Daddy? 208
When Women Had Tails 191
Where No Vultures Fly xiv
The Whip and the Flesh 242
White Comanche 145
White Yellow Black 216
Widmark, Richard 83
The Wild and the Innocent 196
The Wild Bunch viii, 125, 214–215, 250–251
Wild Wild Planet 60
Winchester '73 72
Winnetou and Shatterhand in the Valley of Death xvi
Winnetou the Warrior viii, **xiii**, xiv, 148, 243
The Witch 95
The Witches 108
Wolff, Frank xvi, 14, 190, 196, 230, 242
A Woman for Ringo 27
Woods, Robert 24, 38

Yankee 127
Yojimbo viii, 3–4, 7, 18, 42, 58, 61, 148, 166

Zacharias, Steffen 232, 235, 238
Zamperla, Nazzareno 22
Zingarelli, Italo 230–231
Zorro the Avenger viii, 7, 220
Zuanelli, Marco 220